Unleashing WOW!

The Creative Leader's Guide to Breakthrough Innovation

"Each time that you open this book, you will be opening much more than a book. You will be opening a door to **infinite** possibilities, infinite pathways, infinite solutions. The more you use the tools inside, the more you will find out just how much our minds are able to **create** something that is **amazing**, out of nothing. Just how much we are all full of **magic**. All we really need is the right tools and a system to turn simple thoughts into real, **beautiful**, big, original, and **actionable** ideas. To join the thoughts of many and the huge power a group of minds and their **ideas** can generate. This is how we can **make a difference**. This is how we can make improvements. This is how we can **solve** big problems. This is how we **invent** entirely new things we didn't even know we could think of. This is how we can make others say **WOW!** So, go ahead and open this book. It's going to be **fun**."

Dr. Detlef Reis

WOW![1] (interjection)
- An exclamation of amiration, amazement, etc.

WOW![2] (noun)
- A person or thing that is amazingly successful, attractive, etc.

WOW![3] (transition verb)
- To arouse great enthusiasm in (wowed, wow-ing, wows).

BE WARNED!
This book is **NOT** for everybody

I wrote Unleashing WOW! for the creative change agents who will disrupt old, established industries and antiquated business paradigms with breakthrough ideas and game-changing innovations in the coming two decades. Who are these creative movers and shakers who drive innovation and progress? They are entrepreneurs and inventors, business angels and venture capital investors, tech geeks and influencers, creative professionals and intrapreneurs, scientists and engineers, creative managers and knowledge workers.

My company, Thinkergy, and I are on a mission to empower these creative leaders and their teams to spark more creative breakthroughs that we believe are vital to solving humanity's biggest challenges and igniting a 21st-century Innonaissance (a new Innovation Renaissance).

Ask yourself: Who would you bet on coming up with the breakthrough solutions needed to address humanity's fundamental challenges? The top managers in settled corporations in old industries responsible for many of these problems? Politicians, governments, and established international institutions? Or a critical number of creative leaders (and their creative teams) operating on higher levels of consciousness and creativity?

Interestingly, according to Roger's Diffusion of Innovation theory, only three in every twenty people belong to this progressive group. Another seven in twenty perhaps will sympathize with some ideas and concepts discussed in this book but initially rest too firmly in their comfort zone to take action before eventually catching fire. Yet, I expect half of you reading these lines to put this book down again quickly as its content doesn't resonate with you. And that's fine.

For those of you who keep reading, this book provides a blueprint for unleashing the WOW in you and your business. But first, let me ask you a few questions: When was the last time you were wowed by someone or something? When did you last do something extraordinary that made another person say, *"Wow!"*? And what's the WOW all about, anyway?

Let's talk more about the WOW!

Imagine sparking a *"Wow!"* from everyone who encounters your work—that moment of awe and admiration for something truly fresh, original, and meaningful. Picture the power of transforming an audience into a chorus of amazement when listening to you pitching a brilliant idea or introducing your latest innovation with the plentiful benefits it brings. Clearly, the wow factor isn't just gratifying—it's the hallmark of innovation success.

Every *"Wow!"* is a celebration of the unexpected, a salute to the breakthrough creativity that dares to be different and extraordinary. In a world where being *"okay"* or *"good"* is the norm, why not shoot for *"WOW"*? Why not dare to stand out as a genuine creative leader, a true innovator known not just for busily doing things but for finding unusual ways to make the impossible possible?

Why unleashing the WOW is more needed than ever

We're in the era of the innovation economy. We are also at the beginning of a new long cycle of technological change, the Sixth Wave of Technology Innovation (driven by digital, clean, and human-centered technologies). Innovation can no longer be considered a 'nice-to-have'; it's vital for companies to survive and thrive. What once sounded like a cliché has become true today: Innovate or Die!

In a rapidly evolving business landscape, where speed, complexity, and exponential change are the only constants, true creative leaders thrive. They understand that mastering and delivering The Wow is not just a buzzword but a necessity for sustained growth. Steve Jobs said it best: *"Innovation distinguishes between a leader and a follower."*

Yet, many business executives and seasoned managers in established corporations find themselves at a standstill, unable to spark that game-changing innovation. So, what are the missing pieces? Innovative ideas, a culture that celebrates creativity, and, most crucially, the creative leaders who can navigate this complex landscape. That's where Thinkergy comes in. Our four innovation methods don't just fill in the gaps—they open the doors to The Wow, equipping you to lead innovation in your industry.

But there's another reason many companies fail to innovate: many businesspeople lack the necessary know-how to wow. Fortunately, I do. In this book, I share with you all the building blocks and concepts of innovation you need to understand and master to unleash The WOW!

Why do I do what I do? And why did I write this book?

I was WOWed twice in my life. The first time happened when I was a Ph.D. student desperate to gain an idea for a tough conceptual operationalization problem that I had already struggled to solve for two years within a one-week deadline. I got the breakthrough idea in a Eureka moment in the late afternoon of day four after

committing to an abnormal approach that normal people would consider counterproductive at best or even literally *"suicidal"*.

My second WOW happened on the first day of the Chinese New Year 2003 in Bangkok. I suddenly realized who I really was and what I should do with my life. The moment when the energy and light of that second Eureka washed over me, I was not the same person anymore. I was transformed. I was elevated to a higher level of consciousness. (Interestingly, that day was the beginning of the Year of the Black Sheep, and I felt at ease with the realization that I had been a black sheep all along).

One and a half years later, I quit a well-paying international career in corporate banking to boldly go on a journey and live my true calling: Empowering creative leaders and their teams to achieve creative breakthroughs and drive meaningful innovation. For more than two decades, I have traveled on this less-trodden path to follow my passion and be true to my purpose.

I founded Thinkergy and invented and fine-tuned four innovation methods that I am going to introduce to you as part of this book. These four methods integrate into an innovation product system that forms a Gestalt, meaning that the whole is greater than the sum of its parts. At Thinkergy, we think of this as our WOW-know-how.

In parallel to being an entrepreneur and inventor, I have been a faculty member at various Asian universities, lecturing about and conducting research in the domains I am passionate about: business creativity, creative leadership, and innovation management. Practicing these dual roles as an entrepreneur and academic over two decades has enabled me to acquire a broad theoretical understanding of these domains and lots of deep practical experiences working in the field with

companies on real-life innovation challenges. That's why the tagline of the company I founded reads: Thinkergy—know how to wow.

How is this book structured?

In this book, I am going to share with you the theoretical knowledge and practical know-how on how to Unleash the WOW! in your business, regardless of whether you're a startup, a scale-up venture, or an established company. You get the opportunity to collect all the theoretical and practical dots you need to connect for innovation success. We do this by looking at the key concepts of creativity and innovation through different frames of reference.

Let me introduce you to how you can learn about the domains by scaling up and down between the grand, the big, and the small pictures of creativity and innovation. Learn how to scan the environment, understand the key concepts, and finally familiarize yourself with the specific applications of creativity and innovation in business

Now, let's explore the structure and chapters of this book together.

Start with the grand picture: The environment

Suppose you were a neophyte in innovation (many busy executives and managers are). What would be the first thing I wanted you to understand? The modern business environment, or in other words, the context in which innovation unfolds nowadays. When investigating this grand stage on which the innovation play takes place, we address the question: *"What meta-factors drive and influence creativity and innovation at a grand scale?"*

In *Chapter 1* of this book, you learn about the advent of the innovation economy, the drivers and cycles of change, and why the world hates change, among other things. These environmental factors set the opening scene before we scale one level down.

The big picture: The key concepts

Next, let's take a big-picture view of creativity and innovation and investigate the essential concepts and key rules of the innovation game:

Chapter 2 answers an important question that many domain beginners have in mind: *"What are key concepts related to creativity and innovation that I need to grasp to get into the game?"* Here, you learn how we define creativity and innovation in simple yet powerful terms. We also discuss the importance of making meaning to move from an invention to innovation, look at the wide spectrum of modern innovation types, and talk about the financial premium that innovation leaders in an industry can enjoy.

Chances are that some of you wonder: *"Why do only a few companies succeed in the innovation game and lead innovation in their industry? And why do so many others not?"* To answer these questions in *Chapter 3*, I share with you the secret rules of how to play on the full spectrum of innovation types. You also learn how to distinguish innovations based on their impact and understand the dilemma of innovation management and the paradoxes in innovation.

Appreciating the big picture of innovation first gives you a sound foundational knowledge platform that allows you to scale down to the lowest level of abstraction.

The small pictures: The applications

The small pictures of innovation capture four concrete application areas you need to understand when you want to succeed in innovation as a creative leader, team, and company. If you ask me how to sustainably innovate successfully, I'd say it all comes down to mastering four areas of innovation — creative process, people, culture, and leadership:

- The first small-picture application that every innovation novice should know more about is how to better undertake an innovation project with a team. Correspondingly, *Chapter 4* introduces you to the realm of creative process methods and thinking tools: *"What's it all about? How do they work? Why can a well-structured innovation method like X-IDEA reliably help wanna-be innovators produce standout ideas and innovation outputs?"*

- The second small frame captures another critical dimension of successfully doing innovation: people. Here, the key question that *Chapter 5* answers is: *"Who can best contribute to a firm's innovation efforts, and in what ways?"* The good news is that everyone can play a role in innovation. But depending on your preferred cognitive style, you might enjoy creating —or even leading— innovation from the front end or organizing or managing it from the back end. Innovation-centered personality profiling tools like TIPS can help you align and use your innovation troops according to their preferred cognitive styles and innate talents.

- Another people-related small-picture aspect of innovation features an important stopper or enabler of innovation: organizational culture. *Chapter 6* gives insights into how you can evolve your organization's culture to support creativity, innovation, and change, thereby touching on issues such as how organizations respond to failure or motivate their staff, among other things.

- Creative leadership is the last small picture frame I'd like you to understand. Just talking the innovation talk like many executives without walking their talk doesn't cut it. Again, allow me to quote Steve Jobs here: *"Innovation distinguishes between leader and follower."* Companies that lead innovation in their industry have one genuine creative leader driving innovation at the top and many creative leaders who authentically lead their teams at lower levels. *Chapter 7* outlines how organizations can develop creative leaders to spearhead innovation with the help of creative leadership development methods, which need to be both effective and creative, such as *Genius Journey*.

Scaling back up to the grand picture: The future of innovation

In this book's final *Chapter 8*, I'd like to take you back to the environmental level to take an outlook on the future of innovation. In what directions might the discipline of innovation evolve in the future? What might and might not change in how we practice innovation, and why? Arguably, predicting the future means making informed guesses, but I expect certain trends, like the shift to an entrepreneurial society, digital transformation, and generational shifts, to influence the direction of innovation. I also predict the importance of other practices, like open innovation, to decline over time.

I hope you will enjoy scaling up and down through the frames and selected snapshots of creativity and innovation together with me. Are you ready to start the journey to learn about how you can unleash the WOW? Then, let's go.

Unleashing WOW!

The Creative Leader's Guide to Breakthrough Innovation

Dr. Detlef Reis

Copyright 2024 © by Dr. Detlef Reis

Manufactured in the United States of America.

This book is copyright under the Berne Convention.
All Rights Reserved

No part of this book may be reproduced or transmitted in any form by any means: graphic, electronic, or mechanical, including photocopying, recording, taping or by any information storage or retrieval system without permission, in writing, from the authors, except for the inclusion of brief quotations in a review, article, book, or academic paper.
The authors and publisher of this book and the associated materials have used their best efforts in preparing this material. The authors and publisher make no representations or warranties with respect to accuracy, applicability, fitness or completeness of the contents of this material. They disclaim any warranties expressed or implied, merchantability, or fitness for any particular purpose. The authors and publisher shall in no event be held liable for any loss or other damages, including but not limited to special, incidental, consequential, or other damages. If you have any questions or concerns, the advice of a competent professional should be sought.

PUBLISHED by WildeSpark, Coronado, CA

WRITTEN & DESIGNED by Dr. Detlef Reis

EDITED by Kevin Ehlinger (Editor), William A. Tucker & Dr. Brian Hunt (Co-editors)

ILLUSTRATIONS by Nuttapong Tonhirunmas, Dr. Triyuth Promsiri, Adam-Cabourne-Jones, Amadeus Norén & Dr. Detlef Reis

ALL LOGO & VISUAL IDENTITY DESIGNS by Adam Cabourne-Jones

All images copyright by the author (with signed model release forms) or have been licensed by the author unless otherwise noted.

® Thinkergy, X-IDEA, Genius Journey, TIPS Innovation Profiling, and CooL-Creativity UnLimited are registered trademarks of Dr Detlef Reis / Thinkergy Limited 2009-2024.

While every precaution has been taken in the preparation of this book, the author assumes no responsibility for errors and omissions, or for damages resulting from the use of the information contained herein.

When WOW turns to OW!
The story behind the original cover design of this book

Sometimes, I come up with what I think is a WOW idea, but somehow, other people don't get it. Who's to blame? Regardless of how clever I believe the idea is, if other people don't see its value or get its clue, I have two options: Either do a better job selling the idea or discard it as, "It's probably not as wow as I initially thought". Here is one such idea and its backstory related to the original design of this book's back and front cover.

Apart from running Thinkergy, I have been lecturing to graduate and Ph.D. students at various universities in Hong Kong and Thailand during the past two decades. For many years, I co-lectured a *Principles of Management* course next to my own, *Business Creativity*. The longer I taught these two courses in parallel, the more I realized that one was about the past and the other about the future of doing business. Let me explain:

- The 20th century was the time of management. True to the managerial functions, managers planned, directed, organized, and controlled the efforts of their subordinates, who were expected to do as they were told and not think independently. This approach was relevant and effective at that time because the business environment was rather static, with many market parameters being less volatile or even fixed, and thus, the overall complexity of doing business was reduced.

- In contrast, modern business in the 21st century unfolds in a highly dynamic market environment, with high volatility and uncertainty, mounting complexities, regular surprises, and fast, exponential change. It's a world where agile creative leaders thrive by coaching their teams to play, create, design, experiment, prototype, pitch, act, and innovate.

I believe business success in the 21st century will be all about creative leadership, not management. So, when I thought about showcasing these insights on the cover of this book, a metaphor popped into my mind: *"Comparing the evolution of business in recent decades is like touring different sections in an art museum."*

If you visit an art museum, paintings from a particular style period are all collected in the same section. When you walk through an open doorframe from one room to the next, you might suddenly step into a whole new art epoch where the style and technique of the paintings have evolved and are remarkably different from how art was painted before. Just think of the striking difference between viewing a classical Baroque period painting by Rembrandt and then moving to the next room and encountering a modern Cubist painting by Picasso.

Original cover design spread illustrating the transition from the 20th Century to modern business.

I used this metaphor in this book's original front and back cover designs to visualize the striking difference between business in the 20th and 21st centuries. The scene on the left (originally thought of as the back cover) depicts a museum room with *"classical paintings"* depicting the bygone days of managing a business in the 20th century. Now, step through the door to the room on the right side to enter the modern business world of the early 21st century. This scene (supposed to be the original front cover of the book) shows how creative leaders and their teams play to get breakthrough ideas and then collaborate to innovate. It's the way of *Unleashing WOW!*

If you picked up the prototype of our book and looked at the front and back covers, you would see two rooms in a museum and could walk through the door (the spine of the book) from one room to the other. Unfortunately, most people didn't get the clue without further explanation. So, we decided to abandon the original cover design but wanted to present it to you in the following, together with this little story.

TABLE OF CONTENTS

Chapter 1: The Innovation Environment
The Grand Picture (I) 15

1. Mastering the Drivers of Future Change — 16
2. Welcome to the Innovation Economy — 19
3. The Shift to an Entrepreneurial Society — 22
4. Tracking the Dimensions of Change Over Time — 25
5. Cyclicality: Riding the Cycles of Change — 28
6. The World Hates Innovation. Here is Why — 32
7. The More Things Change, the More They Stay the Same — 35
8. Invite the World to a Party — 37
* Executive Summary — 40

Chapter 2: The Core Principles of Innovation
The Big Picture (I) 41

1. Creativity Defined — 42
2. Creativity Is… — 45
3. The Innovation Formula — 50
4. True Innovation Is About Making Meaning — 53
5. Climb Up the Value Pyramid to Higher Profitability — 55
6. Modern Innovation Types — 58
7. How Innovation Affects Financial Performance — 63
8. Why and How to Protect Your Intellectual Property — 67
* Executive Summary — 70

Chapter 3: The Innovation Rules
The Big Picture (II) 71

1. The Ten Rules of the Innovation Types Game — 72
2. Innovation Impact Types: How Much Innovation Do You Want to Have? — 77
3. Innovation Adoption: How Fast Do You Embrace Innovation? — 80
4. Ten Ideas About Ideas — 83
5. Open Innovation: The Good, the Bad, and the Ugly — 85
6. Dealing With the Paradoxes of Innovation Management — 89
7. Resolving the Dilemma of Innovation Management — 92
8. In-NO-vation Explained — 97
* Executive Summary — 98

Chapter 4: The Innovation Process & Tools
Small Picture (I) 99

1. Innovation: It's All About Mastering Process and Projects — 100
2. Innovation Process Methods: What? Why? How? — 103
3. Understanding the Inner Workings of Thinking Tools and Creativity Tools — 109
4. Brainstorming; The Good, the Bad and the Ugly — 112
5. It's Not Only What Tools You Use But How You Use Them — 115
6. X-IDEA: Introducing the Know-How of Wow — 119
7. Why Using Only One Creative Process Stage Leads to Dull Ideas — 124
8. Dos and Don'ts for a Successful Innovation Project — 127
* Executive Summary — 130

Chapter 5: Innovative People
Small Picture (II) 131

1. Cognitive Profiling Methods: What? Why? How? — 132
2. Scrutinizing Popular Cognitive Profiling Methods — 137
3. Introducing the TIPS Innovation Profiling Method — 141
4. Flow Along the Company Life Cycle with TIPS — 146
5. How TIPS Helps Resolving Main Corporate Innovation Challenges — 149
6. What's Your Style to Innovate? — 155
7. Understanding Who Really Makes Innovation Happen — 158
8. Creative Leaders vs Innovation Managers: Same or Different? — 160
* *Executive Summary* — 164

Chapter 6: Innovative Culture
Small Picture (III) 165

1. Me Too Limited: Would You Want to Work Here? — 166
2. Innovative Companies vs. In-NO-vative Companies: Who's Who? — 168
3. Boring Meetings? Play In-NO-vation Bingo! — 172
4. Finding the Factors That Matter for Organizational Innovation — 174
5. Are You Ready to Commit Time for Innovation? — 179
6. Want to Succeed? Plan to Fail — 183
7. The Creative Transformation Marathon — 187
8. What Gets Measured Gets Innovated — 191
* *Executive Summary* — 194

Chapter 7: Creative Leaders
Small Picture (IV) 195

1. The Rise of Creative Leadership — 196
2. Creative Leadership: Hot or Not? — 198
3. Why Creative Leadership Matters Now — 201
4. Creative Leaders: Who? What? Why? — 204
5. Incubation: A Walk on the Mysterious Side of Creativity — 207
6. How to Creatively and Effectively Develop Creative Leaders? — 210
7. Introducing the Design Features of the Genius Journey Method — 215
8. Rediscover Your Creative Self — 220
* *Executive Summary* — 228

Chapter 8: What Else? An Innovation Outlook
The Grand Picture (II) 229

1. Is the Pendulum Swinging Back? — 230
2. Why So Afraid of the Future? Human Up! — 234
3. How the Generational Shift Will Impact Business and Innovation — 238
4. These Creative Laws Govern Innovation — 245
5. Innovative Spaces: From Cubeville to Idea City — 248
6. Innovation: Are You Just Talking the Talk or Walking Your Talk? — 254
7. What's Your Innovation Mastery Level? — 260
8. Success Ingredients of Top Achievers in Innovation and Beyond — 263
* *Executive Summary* — 266

Supplement: How to Write a Good Creative Brief — 267
References & Resources — 269
About the Author: Dr. Detlef Reis — 276

PAST — PRESENT — FUTURE

THE GRAND PICTURE OF INNOVATION

Chapter 1: The Innovation Environment
Grand Picture (I)

What factors drive and influence innovation and change nowadays?

Chapter 8: What else? An Innovation Outlook
Grand Picture (II)

In what ways may innovation (not) change in future? Why (not)?

THE BIG PICTURE OF INNOVATION

Chapter 2: Core Innovation Principles
Big Picture (I)

What are key concepts to grasp to get into the game?

Chapter 3: The Innovation Rules
Big Picture (II)

Why do a few succeed in the game? And why many others do not?

Chapter 4: Innovation Process & Tools
Small Picture (I)

How to better undertake an innovation project as a team?

Chapter 5: Innovative People
Small Picture (II)

Who can contribute in what ways to our innovation efforts?

THE SMALL PICTURES OF INNOVATION

Chapter 6: Innovation Culture
Small Picture (III)

How can we evolve our culture to support innovation and change?

Chapter 7: Creative Leadership
Small Picture (IV)

How to develop authentic creative leaders to spearhead innovation?

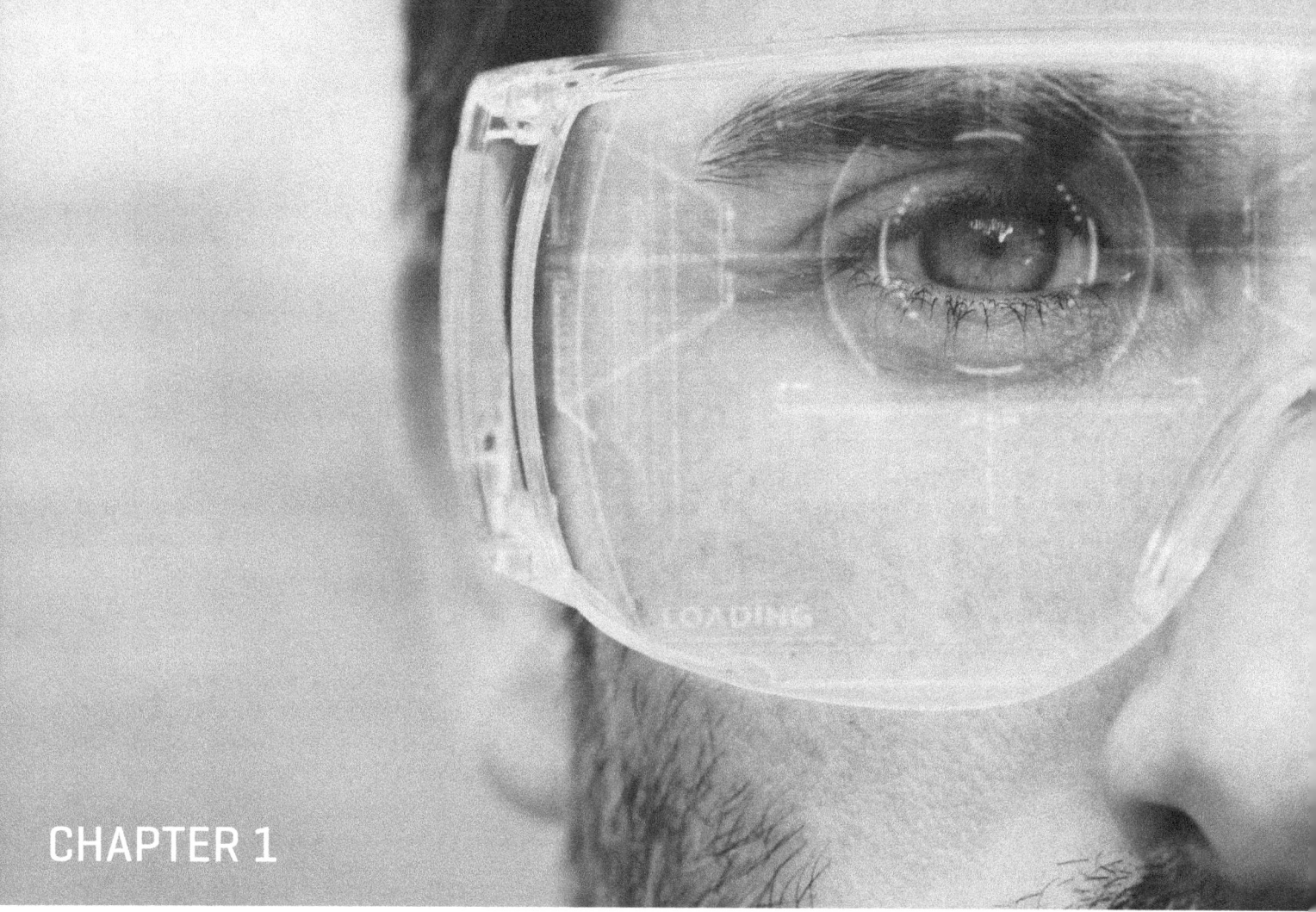

CHAPTER 1

THE INNOVATION ENVIRONMENT
GRAND PICTURE (I)

Understand more about the modern business environment wherein the games of business and innovation are played.

1. Mastering the Drivers of Future Change
2. Welcome to the Innovation Economy
3. The Shift to an Entrepreneurial Society
4. Tracking the Dimensions of Change Over Time
5. Cyclicality: Riding the Cycles of Change
6. The World Hates Innovation. Here is Why
7. The More Things Change, the More They Stay the Same
8. Invite the World to a Party
* *Executive Summary*

1.1. MASTERING THE DRIVERS OF FUTURE CHANGE

Do you know which parameters drive the trends of the future? James Canton, a leading US futurist, identified five major drivers of what he calls *"The Extreme Future"* in his likewise-titled book. What are these drivers of change in the early 21st century?

1. SPEED: Faster, faster, faster.

The speed of business and life has noticeably accelerated in the past 2-3 decades. Where mail used to be delivered to your desk or home once a day, it now arrives largely digitally, instantly, and round-the-clock in your computer or smart device's email inbox.

When it once took firms decades to build up a business, they now can reach billion-dollar market valuations within 1-2 years. Google acquired YouTube for USD 1.65 billion only 20 months after its video-sharing website went live; only one year after making its social networking site open to the general public, Facebook founder Mark Zuckerberg sold 1.6% shares of his company to Microsoft for a sum of USD 246 million (equaling a market valuation of 15.6 billion). The automobile needed 62 years and the telephone 50 years to reach 50 million users; YouTube did it in only four, Facebook in three, and Twitter in just two years.

As media mogul Rupert Murdoch noted: *"The world is changing very fast. Big will not beat small anymore. It will be the fast beating the slow."*

2. We are living in times of exponential CHANGE.

Take a minute to reflect on what has changed in the last twenty years: What new products and services have emerged? What new companies have surfaced, and which former corporate giants have lost their importance — or even disappeared completely? How have your own work and lifestyle changed?

If you invest some time pondering these questions, you will notice that there has been huge change, massive change in the last two decades. Many changes were driven by advances in IT coupled with the advent of the Internet (both powered by Moore's Law, which states that key performance features of microchips double every 2 years) and globalization. Thanks to these meta-driving forces and our first driver (speed), many changes unfold following an exponential growth pattern rather than a linear one.

One truism seems to be really true: *"The only thing that will never change is change."* So, take note of a key insight from Charles Darwin's theory of evolution: *"It is not the strongest of the species that survives, nor the most intelligent, but the one most responsive to change."*

3. COMPLEXITY: More, more, more.

A third major driver of change is mounting complexity. Everything seems to get more intricate and complicated, with ever more parameters and variables to consider and maneuver in an increasingly hazy, ambiguous world.

Think about the number of TV channels, newspapers, magazines, books, mobile phones, fashion malls, or airlines that you can choose from as today's consumer. How do you keep track? How to make the right choices? One consequence of the previous two drivers is that our lives have become much more complex — and complexity has a tendency to become overwhelming. So how can you best deal with this? Unfortunately, complexity can hardly be rationally managed, as Albert Einstein noted: *"When the number of factors coming into play in a phenomenological complex is too large, scientific method in most cases fails."*

4. RISKS: More, higher and new risks.

In the new millennium, the risk landscape for both individuals and businesses has changed dramatically: We face more risks (driven by technology, globalization, increasing complexity), new risks (just think of terrorism, new diseases, new competitors, etc.), and higher risks (significantly higher volatility in global markets, such as the ones for stocks, bonds, foreign exchange, commodities). As the global financial crisis in 2008 vividly illustrated, in an increasingly complex world, traditional risk management analyses tend to fail in their attempt to proactively deal with imminent risks.

5. SURPRISES: Get ready for more.

Surprises can be positive and negative:

- At the end of 1989, the fall of the Berlin Wall and the subsequent collapse of the Iron Curtain and communism in Eastern Europe was a sudden, extremely nice surprise that dramatically altered the world map and offered massive new business opportunities overnight.

- In late 2008, the collapse of Lehman Brothers in the aftermath of the subprime crises came as a negative surprise, nearly leading to the collapse of the global financial system.

While Canton might slightly exaggerate by suggesting that surprises will become a feature of daily life, expect them to amaze or shock you regularly and more often.

COLD WAR ERA <> EAST-WEST DIVIDE <> WESTERN CAPITALISM VS. EASTERN COMMUNISM <> FIXED ECONOMIC BLOGS (VS. COMECON) <> FIXED MILITARY BLOCKS (NATO VS. WARSAW PACT) <> LARGELY REGIONAL OR NATIONAL CONFLICTS <> GLOBAL TRADE WITH MOSTLY LOCAL OR REGIONAL PRODUCTION <> FIXED (BRETTON WOODS SYSTEM) OR CONTROLLED FOREIGN EXCHANGE RATE MECHANISMS <> CONTROLLED OR LARGELY LOCALIZED CAPITAL MARKETS <> INNOVATION=R&D-DRIVEN NEW PRODUCT DEVELOPMENT <> EIGHT TO FIVE, FIVE DAYS A WEEK <> ONCE A DAY (MAIL, NEWSPAPERS) <> STATIC COMMUNICATION (LANDLINES, CABLES) <> TOP-DOWN ANALOG MEDIA / INFO-SHARING

THE **STATIC ENVIRONMENT** IN THE 2ND HALF OF THE 20TH CENTURY

1950s	1960s	1970s	1980s	1990s

Conclusion: Thrive in the extreme future by driving it proactively and creatively.

The second half of the last century was largely static, with two opposing political and economic blocs, largely oligopolistic or closed markets and controlled flows of capital and information. Such a stable environment makes it easy for managers to plan, organize, staff, coordinate and control all activities inside a company and outside toward predictable markets.

We live in a highly dynamic environment in the first half of the 21st century. How can you master and succeed in a fast-changing and ever-more complex, risky, and surprising world? Think creatively and act fast to seize opening opportunities and capitalize on complexity. As Albert Einstein noted, *"We cannot solve our problems with the same thinking we used when we created them."* So, get creative and innovative!

> "It's tough when markets change and your people within the company don't."
> —HARVARD BUSINESS REVIEW

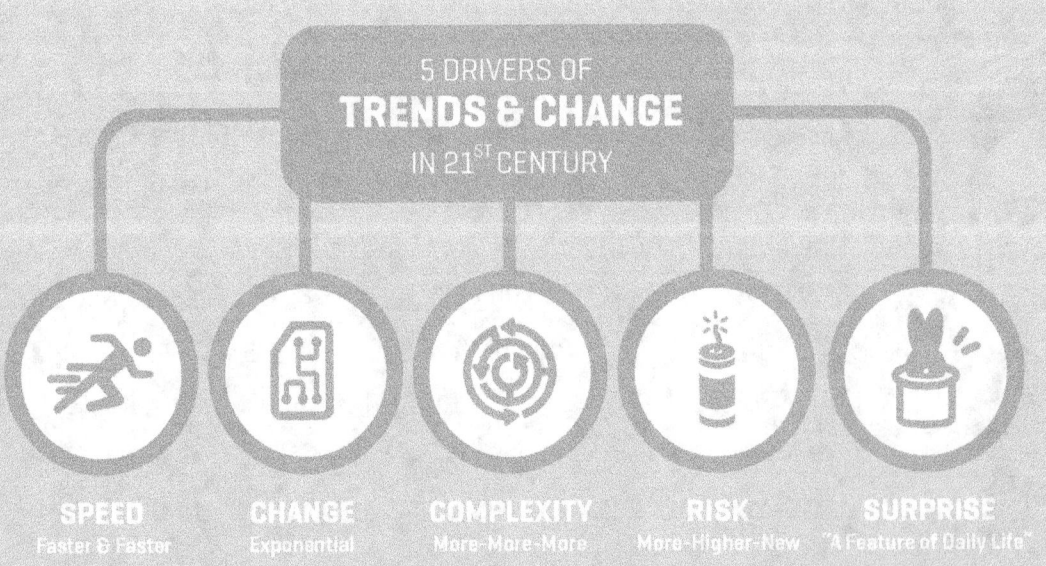

1.2. WELCOME TO THE INNOVATION ECONOMY

Which mobile phone were you using when the new millennium began? You might not remember the exact model, but you probably remember which company made it. Was it a Nokia or a Motorola? Chances are it was one of those. At that time, those two companies dominated the mobile phone industry with what were then state-of-the-art products.

Do you still use a Nokia or Motorola today? Probably not. Both companies still make phones, but they are niche players in a market driven by the smart devices from Apple and Samsung. Motorola's mobile phone division was acquired by Google in 2012 — who has since sold it to Lenovo — and Nokia's by Microsoft in 2013. Ten years ago, would you have predicted those changes? What does it mean that market leaders can become bit players in a few years' time?

The rise of the innovation economy

In the last 15 years, we've witnessed the advent of the innovation economy. We live in the age of creation. Leading business thinkers and futurists agree that innovation is now key to economic success. *"Innovation is the central issue in economic prosperity,"* said the US professor of management Michael Porter. Similarly, the Austrian-born American management guru Peter F. Drucker said, *"An established company which in an age demanding innovation, is not capable of innovation, is doomed to decline and extinction."*

Whether they call it the Creative Economy, Innovation Economy, Age of Creation Intensification, New Value Creation Economy, or Age of Value Creation, these and other prominent business thinkers agree that we have entered a new age of economic development. How did we get here? And what does it mean for all of us to compete in the innovation economy?

Economic evolution: From hunters and gatherers to the innovation economy

As human culture has evolved, so has our economy:

- We started as hunters and gatherers who hunted prey and picked leaves, fruit, nuts and other plants to sustain ourselves, relying on simple tools and weapons as our means of production.

- Agriculture began about 12,000 years ago. We learned to grow crops and herd livestock, and we settled into stable villages.

- The industrial age began 250 years ago, and we learned to use energy-powered machines to mass-produce goods. Economies of scale were the key to economic success and achieving low unit costs required standardization of processes and outputs.

- The information age started roughly 40-50 years ago. We learned to build computerized systems to process, store, and use data faster and more effectively. Economic success relied on achieving a high economy of scope—the efficient differentiation of products—through computerization of economic activities.

- Now, we find ourselves in the age of creation. The new means of production that we need to succeed are ideas, know-how, and theories. The key competitive advantage of successful economic players is the ability to create or creatively transform know-how into meaningful value propositions.

HUMANITY'S ECONOMIC EVOLUTION

INNOVATION ECONOMY
New Value Creation Economy
Age of Value Creation
CREATIVITY ECONOMY
Age of Creation Intensification
Era of Ideanomics

	CA. 2000	AGE OF CREATION	IDEAS, CONCEPTS, KNOW-HOW, THEORIES	CREATION	NETWORK
	CA. 1970	INFORMATION AGE	DATA & SYSTEMS	SCOPE	COMPUTERIZATION
	CA. 1760	INDUSTRIAL AGE	ENERGY & MACHINES	SCALE	STANDARDIZATION
	CA. 10,000 B.C.	AGRICULTURAL AGE	IMPLEMENTS & LAND	COOPERATION	COOPERATION
	Before 10,000 B.C.	HUNTERS & GATHERERS	TOOLS	COOPERATION	COOPERATION
	START TIME	ECONOMIC SOCIETY	MEANS OF PRODUCTION	COMPETITIVE ADVANTAGE	MANAGEMENT

This value creation no longer happens in rigid organizational hierarchies but often in networks that flexibly form to work on creative projects. Once a project is complete, the network disbands to start a new project with a new configuration of creators and contributors.

So welcome to the Innovation Economy! *"The Innovation Economy represents the largest future threat or opportunity for your career or business — depending on whether or not you prepare for it,"* said the US futurist and advisor to several US presidents James Canton — and added: *"Twenty-first-century economies will survive and prosper only if they embrace innovation."* Harvard's Michael Porter similarly pointed out that: *"Innovation is the central issue in economic prosperity."*

Creativity and innovation rule in the innovation economy

Why have creativity and innovation become so important? Because of the changes in the business environment powered by the five drivers of change we discussed in the previous section. Modern business happens in a highly dynamic and global environment powered by the exponential advances in information technology made possible by Moore's law and amplified by the Internet. As the pace of modern business continues to increase, we have to deal with accelerating change, ever-higher complexity, higher risks, and frequent surprises.

Agile, creative, dynamic companies can quickly capitalize on the new opportunities that emerge by innovating and creating meaningful new value. On the other hand, giant corporate behemoths may face their demise faster than seems possible. Again, let's recall Charles Darwin here, *"It is not the strongest of the species that survives, nor the most intelligent, but the one most responsive to change."*

What does the innovation economy mean for you and your business?

Think about these questions:

- How fast-moving and fast-changing is your industry?
- What new technologies or trends may change the dominant paradigm in your industry?
- Who lurks on the borders of your industry, looking for their chance to invade?
- The American social philosopher Eric Hoffer said, *"In a time of drastic change, it is the learners who inherit the future. The learned usually find themselves equipped to live in a world that no longer exists."* Are you learning what you need to inherit the future?
- How creative are you? Are you able to create new value? What can you do today to improve your ability to create the future tomorrow?

> *"An established company which in an age demanding innovation, is not capable of innovation, is doomed to decline and extinction."*
> —PETER DRUCKER

1.3. THE SHIFT TO AN ENTREPRENEURIAL SOCIETY

Picture the careers of your parent's generation. Chances are—especially when you come from countries in Europe or Asia—that most of the Silent Generation and early-to-mid Baby Boomers started to work with one company and retired from the same company 3-4 decades later.

In section 1, we fleshed out the slow-paced, gradually changing, simple and well-predictable business environment that characterized the second half of the 20th century. In this static period, most companies were run by managers positioned on different levels in a top-down hierarchical command structure not unlike those of the military. The hierarchy was the organizational model of the Industrial Age and of most parts of the Information Age. Rank-and-file employees were willing to go along with the limited individual opportunities and the strict rules and controls of the industrial organization in exchange for safe jobs, stable and predictable incomes, and essentially a life-long employment guarantee.

Ten years ago, the futurist John Naisbitt predicted that *"We are shifting from a managerial society to an entrepreneurial society."* Why?

As we've learned in the first two sections of this chapter, business in the early 21st century is highly dynamic and full of speed, complexity, changes, risks, and surprises; these modern environmental conditions favor agility, flexibility, creativity, and risk tolerance. Moreover, humanity has climbed up to the next level of its economic evolution, the innovation economy, where the ability to transform theories, know-how and ideas into original, meaningful new value is the key competitive advantage for business players. Who do you think is better able to successfully maneuver and flourish in a highly dynamic environment? A manager? Or an entrepreneur?

A manager is someone who plans, organizes, directs, controls and coordinates (the managerial functions that the French management theorist and engineer Henri Fayol formulated roughly a hundred years ago). All of these managerial activities worked well in the hierarchical corporations of the static, stable and controlled business world of the 20th century.

In contrast, an entrepreneur is someone who's able to create something out of nothing and is willing to undertake a risk by founding a venture that brings this something to market. Entrepreneurs thrive in fast-changing, flexible, and risky environments. They see opportunity, whereas managers only see crises and risks. They say *"yes"* to seize these opportunities, whereas managers habitually say *"no"* to new initiatives that may fail. They make things happen and create change. They feel comfortable working in networks that use modern technology to coordinate the activities of a group of global and local (*"glocal"*) creative collaborators who deliver a project together and then may move on again to another project.

Entrepreneurs and *"Intrapreneurs"* (corporate employees with entrepreneurial mindsets) are destined to drive new business initiatives and growth in the 21st century. In contrast, managers continue to exploit former business successes and *"milk the cash cows"* of the past.

For mature corporations, this can provide continued revenue streams to fund the transition into the innovation economy. No wonder that at least in some countries, some of the brightest talents who enter the job market don't want to pursue a corporate career, but seek their chance and found or join an entrepreneurial venture.

There is another reason why the 21st century will be an entrepreneurial and not managerial one. Just as the first wave of automation killed many industrial blue-collar jobs, so will a new wave of automation powered by advances in artificial intelligence wash away a lot of bureaucratic and analytical *"white-collar"* jobs in the next two decades, affecting millions of white-collar workers and managers. Some of them may leave with a *"golden handshake"* big enough to last through their retirement, but many others may be forced to —or finally have the means and courage to want to— start a second career on their own or a joint entrepreneurial venture.

Conclusion: The number of entrepreneurs will drastically increase in the coming years, whether out of volition or necessity.

> "Entrepreneurship is neither a science nor an art. It is a practice."
> —PETER DRUCKER

LEARN TO APPRECIATE ENTREPRENEURS

When we celebrated the tenth anniversary of the foundation of my innovation company, Thinkergy, in August 2015, I wrote an article to reflect on my experiences of being an entrepreneur. Allow me to share with you some points to think about as we shift into an entrepreneurial society.

Entrepreneurs are undervalued. Just a few years ago, a survey in my home country of Germany found most people had a negative view of *Unternehmer* (*"entrepreneurs"*). Most German youngsters want to work for large, well-regarded corporations or as government officials when they grow up. Even though most Germans work for small or medium-sized businesses, entrepreneurs are still often seen as greedy, abusive oppressors. As a result, I never considered becoming an entrepreneur.

Entrepreneurs have a better reputation in many parts of North America and Asia, but still those in well-established organizations still look down on fledgling entrepreneurs and their ventures. This condescension irritates me because I believe entrepreneurs should be respected, even celebrated. After all, it's entrepreneurs who get things started and drive progress.

Who is an entrepreneur? The word comes from a French word meaning *"to undertake."* Entrepreneurs are willing to undertake the risks associated with a new business venture. In the US, only 30% of startups are still in business after 10 years. Given that, no rational person would start a new business. That's why we should admire those who are passionate—or crazy—enough to start a new venture and wish them luck.

Entrepreneurs rock. The American anthropologist Margaret Mead said: *"Never doubt that a small group of committed people can change the world. Indeed, it is the only thing that ever has."* Every great corporation owes its existence to a few people who had the courage to start something new and accept the risk. That's why when we train innovators, we teach the participants about the people who took risks and created the company that employs them. We do this to reconnect the employees to the company founders and help them appreciate and emulate their creativity, courage and drive.

One entrepreneur named Henri Nestlé started a company in 1866 that became the Nestlé we know today. His courage and hard work back then today provide for 281,000 employees and their families or a million people.

Who started the organization you work for? What do you know about them? You owe them gratitude because your job exists today because of their courage, hard work, and vision. Be sure to treat the entrepreneurs you meet with respect, as their work today may provide jobs for your great-grandchildren. Also, pay them a fair price and pay them promptly, lest they be forced out of business.

Celebrate entrepreneurial anniversaries. Many firms mark their date of incorporation as their anniversary. But a new business does not start with an entry in a government registry. If you ask an entrepreneur, the real birthday was when the entrepreneur had the idea for the venture.

"Everything begins with an idea," said Earl Nightingale, an American motivational speaker. The power of an idea gives an entrepreneur the courage to break from the past, begin something new, and invest the hard work necessary for success.

We celebrate Thinkergy's official foundation on August 5, 2005, but its real birthday is February 1. On that day in 2003, I was somehow called on a mission to create more creative leaders and innovators. I had this Eureka moment while watching the sunset on the first day of the 4,700th Chinese year, the year of the Black Sheep. What more auspicious moment could there be for an innovation company full of black sheep whose role is to be different and think differently?

Conclusion: A healthy entrepreneurial ecosystem is a vital driver of innovation, economic growth and employment. Take a moment today to appreciate the importance of entrepreneurs to the economy and to give thanks to them.

1.4. TRACKING THE DIMENSIONS OF CHANGE OVER TIME

Innovation means change. Tracking and mapping political, economic, social and technological change is one of the activities you need to undertake at the beginning of a strategy innovation project. Naturally, the changes of the emerging future are grounded in the changes that take place at present and the changes that took place in the past.

What if you had a tool to track down identifiable time patterns of past and present changes in business and society to better forecast the probable changes in future?

To discern patterns of change over time in your industry and the wider business environment, track and map out three dimensions of change: velocity, direction and impact of observable change over time.

Change velocity: How fast do things change here?

The first dimension captures how fast things change in a category or industry. Every industry moves forward at a certain velocity, albeit at very different speeds:

- Information Technology- (IT-) and Internet-driven industries, as well as fashion-related industries, change the fastest, with novelties introduced in a semi-annual rhythm.

- On the opposite end are utilities and infrastructure construction; here, new projects take years to complete and then are operated for decades without much change.

- Between these two extremes, things vary by industry, starting from the still speedy, fast-moving consumer goods and electronics industries to the medium-paced automobile industry to slow-paced, asset-driven industries such as finance or oil and gas.

Note three interesting phenomena while considering the velocity of change in an industry:

1. Over the past 2-3 decades, change velocity has accelerated in most industries. Here, consider how the key performance indicator *"time to market"* has shortened in your industry.

2. Second, the boundaries between industries have become more porous due to technological and IT-driven changes.

3. Third, agile innovation leaders of modern, speedy industries have started to cross over into older, slower industries. Think of efforts by Google and Tesla to reinvent the good old internal combustion engine (ICE) car or new frictionless and safe payment solutions from Amazon, Google, and Apple that threaten banks with losing market share of parts of the lucrative cash management business.

Change direction: What's the path that a change moves along here?

The second dimension of change is direction. Here, we can discern four patterns of how change unfolds over time:

- *Linear timing* asserts that change moves forward in a linear, typically progressive way. This is seen in humanity's economic evolution from a hunter-gatherer society in the agrarian age to the industrial age, into the IT age, and now into the innovation age.

- *Cyclical timing* chronicles change as a wave with four clear cycle phases (trough, rise, peak, and decline). Well-known examples are the macroeconomic cycle, the product life cycle, and the industry cycle.

CHANGE VELOCITY

INDUSTRIES

		MOVIE	ENTERTAINMENT	REAL ESTATE	EDUCATION	UTILITIES
FASHION		AGRICULTURE	GASTRONOMY	CONSTRUCTION	CHEMICAL	OIL & GAS
ADVERTISING		TELECOM	FMCG	HOUSEHOLD GOODS	INSURANCE	ENERGY
RETAIL	CONSULTING	COMPUTER	FOOD & BEVERAGE	AUTOMOTIVE	BANKING	ACCOUNTING

TIME → CURRENT | SHORT-TERM | MEDIUM-TERM | LONG-TERM
0 | 6 MTHS | 1 YR | 2-3 YRS | 3-4 YRS | 5-8 YRS | >8 YRS

CHANGE DIRECTION

CHANGE IMPACT

LINEAR TIMING

CYCLICAL TIMING (THE WAVE)

REVOLUTIONARY "WOW!!!"

THE PENDULUM

THE SPIRAL

EVOLUTIONARY "GREAT!"

INCREMENTAL "GOOD"

Checking our present position in these cycles points you to the direction of possible strategic actions in the future.

- A *pendulum* is a third way to describe change over time. Starting from a neutral, integrated position, a pendulum swings back and forth between two extreme poles. For example, political developments often swing back and forth between a regressive, traditional, religious, materialistic and nationalistic pole and a progressive, modern, secular, idealistic and cosmopolitan pole. The pendulum is also at work in most large and multinational corporations, where organizational structures swing back and forth between the poles of centralization versus decentralization.

- Finally, the *spiral* describes how social and economic change flows in a circular motion before spiraling up again to a higher level, where a new cycle starts that eventually leads to a new leap. This model suggests that a business, industry or society develops, grows, matures and gradually declines until a new wave of innovation spearheaded by a small group of innovators spurs activity to a higher level, where a fresh industry cycle starts.

Such a leap is often triggered by the rise of a new lead technology, which happens every two to four decades. Think of how IT in the 1970s to mid-1990s drove business until the Internet emerged as new lead technology and spiraled us up to the next level.

Change impact: What's the impact of change?

The third dimension tracks the impact of an innovation or change initiative, such as a new technology. Probably the easiest way to categorize impact is by using the labels *"incremental change"*, *"evolutionary change"*, and *"revolutionary change"*. Once you have quantitative data available (such as change in revenue growth or change in market capitalization), however, you may also use a more objective metric system to map out the scope of change.

Conclusion: Once we understand the historic and current speed, direction, and impact of change in your industry, we can map these phenomena out to project possible future directions of change that may guide the strategic actions of the business. Unfortunately, this is easier said than done, as it requires you to collect objective data for all change phenomena and then map them in a three-dimensional map.

> "They always say time changes things, but you actually have to change them yourself."
> —ANDY WARHOL

1.5. CYCLICALITY: RIDING THE WAVES OF CHANGE

What do the state of the economy, a product, a corporate venture, a leading technology, the four seasons, and living things such as human beings have in common? They all evolve and revolve in cycles, in *"waves of change."* Innovation, which means meaningful change, often kicks off a new cycle. In the following, let's understand how cyclicality influences the flow of business and innovation.

What is cyclicality?

Cyclicality can be defined as the property or characteristic of being cyclical or revolving in cycles. Cycles are series of events that are regularly repeated in the same order. Many business and economic developments unfold in a cycle comprising several distinct stages over a certain period of time. Just as a wave flows up and down, a particular economic development moves upwards until it reaches a peak, then falls and ebbs out in a trough.

When tracking a particular cyclical flow in business, we can distinguish between three factors — the type of cycle, its stages and its duration:

- The cycle type captures what kind of business parameters a cycle describes and how it is measured. Think of a product or company life cycle, a business or economic cycle, and long cycles that capture pace-setting technologies.

- A cycle typically unfolds in distinct stages. Many business cycles unfold in four stages, and some economists likened these to the four seasons: spring (growth), summer (peak), autumn (decline), and winter (trough).

- Finally, the cycle duration captures how long it takes to complete a full cycle. Some business cycles are short-lived and complete after a couple of quarters, many take years, and some are long-term and unfold over decades.

What are the types of cycles in business?

Let's look at the four most important cycles in business that leaders and innovators should be aware of:

- The **product life cycle** captures how a product evolves in the market by tracking its sales and profits over time. Typical stages that the product lifecycle concept distinguishes are development and introduction (spring), growth (summer), maturity (autumn), and decline (winter). The duration varies in different industries: fashion companies think in months, tech ventures in quarters, fast-moving consumer goods companies in years, and energy companies in decades.

- The **company life cycle** often maps the stages of the product life cycle. A startup creates and launches an innovative product (spring). Then, it evolves into a growth- and sales-focused small- and medium-sized enterprise (summer), which later matures into an established large corporation (autumn) that eventually begins its long, steady decline (winter) before it is closed down. A recent World Economic Forum study put the average life span of today's multinational, Fortune 500-size corporation at 40 to 50 years; interestingly, corporate life spans have shortened in recent years.

- The **business cycle** (or economic cycle) captures upward and downward movements of a country's economy as measured by the gross domestic product. These GDP fluctuations involve shifts between periods of dynamic economic growth (expansions and booms) and periods of decline and stagnation (recessions and depressions). For example, the US economy passed through 11 business cycles from 1945 to 2009, with the average cycle lasting about 69 months, or slightly less than six years. Expansions tend to last longer than contractions (58 months vs. 11 months for the US).

- **Long cycles** describe major technological shifts that happen in long waves of four to six decades, known as Kondratiev waves for the Russian economist who uncovered these tech-driven long cycles. In the last 235 years, we have passed through five such long cycles, each of which was driven by distinct lead technologies: Water power, textiles and iron led the first wave (1785-1845), followed by steam, railway and steel (1845-1900), electricity, chemicals and automobiles (1900-1950) and petrochemicals, aviation, and electronics (1950-1990). The Fifth Wave (1990-2020) was driven by information and communication technologies and the Internet. The Sixth Wave (2020-2045) is expected to be driven by digital, clean, and human-centered technologies, thereby jointly promoting greater resource efficiency and the notion of *"less but better."* Interestingly, the duration of the long waves shortens with each new one—and so does the average life span of corporations.

These four major cycle types not only connect to each other but also influence many other phenomena in business. For example, the stock market tends to move with the business cycle. Industries (and the technologies that get them started) move into a new season with each new long wave. Moreover, each long wave comprises five or more business cycles. Some analysts even suggest that peace and war cycles can be explained with the help of long waves.

Other cycles that may be relevant for a business are seasonal cycles, fashion cycles or generational cycles, among others.

Why is it important to track cyclicality in business?

Depending on the season (or cycle phase), a business needs to have a different focus, embrace a different leadership type, and shoot for a different type of creativity:

- In spring, focus on creating new value (a product or technology) and launching it in the market. This phase requires upfront investment and an agile creative leader who drives fast, meaningful change. Creativity is often technology-driven and pushes for bold, revolutionary ideas.
- In summer, the focus shifts to customers and sales. Here, a people-oriented leader is the best choice to entice customers and motivate the team to reach ambitious growth targets. Creativity is marketing- and customer-driven and targets more evolutionary ideas.
- In autumn, revenue growth flattens but profitability is still high. Now, a business needs to consolidate its growth with stable operations. The ideal leader here is a person focused on operational excellence and getting things done. Creativity focuses on practical improvements and customer service.
- In winter, the emphasis shifts to setting up efficient, well-structured processes and systems that allow for scaling the business. As revenues and profits start to decline, the best leader is someone who enjoys tracking performance and enforcing organizational efficiency and financial discipline. Creativity targets incremental improvements of products and processes following an adaptive approach.

SEASONAL CYCLE
(12 months duration, equal stages of 3 months)

PRODUCT LIFE CYCLE
(years; upfront stages shorter than later stages)

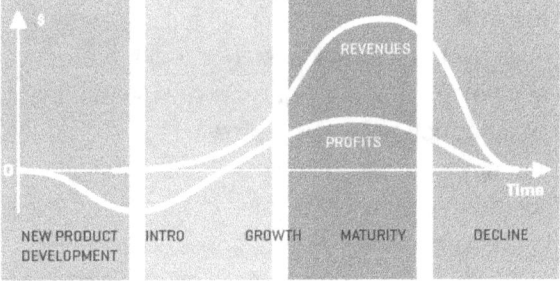

COMPANY LIFE CYCLE
(decades, upfront much stages shorter than later ones)

BUSINESS CYCLE
(ca. 6 years; later stages shorter than early stages)

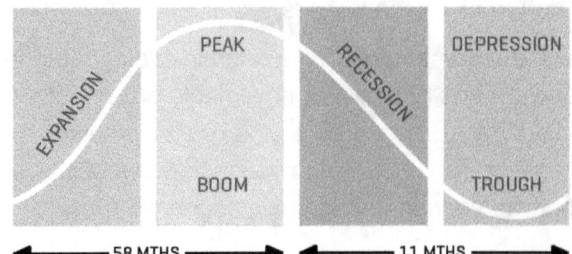

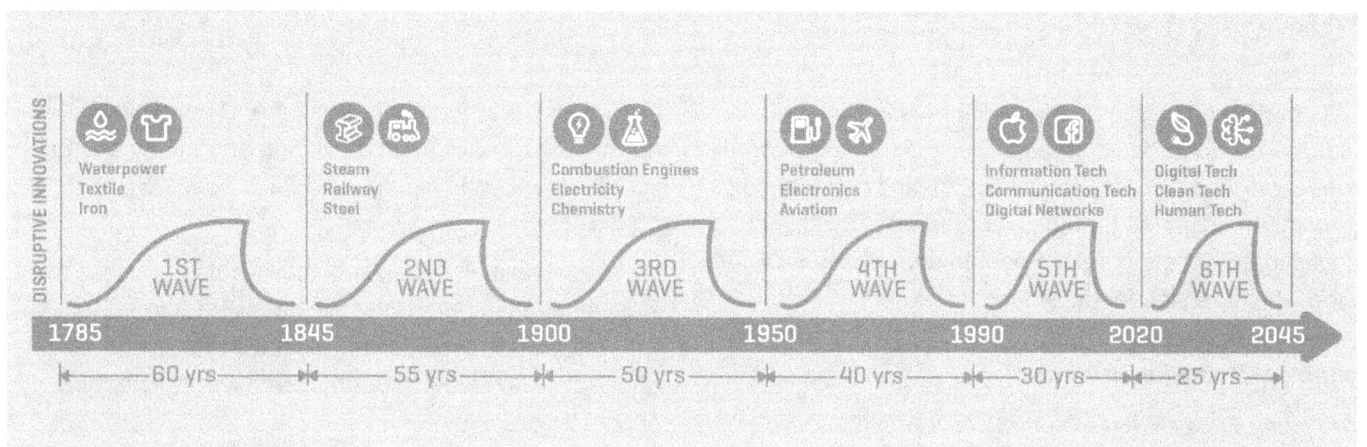

What does cyclicality mean for you and your business?

Ponder your answers to the following questions:

1. At what stage of the product life cycle is your most important product?

2. What stage and season is your company in? Are you creating, growing, solidifying, or consolidating? If you're in winter, how can you avoid death and achieve rebirth by starting a new cycle?

3. What technology drives the success of your company and industry? Where in the cycle is this technology? Has it newly emerged? Is it a leading one right now? Is it a maturing one, or even declining? If so, what new technologies may emerge on the horizon to eventually replace it?

4. Where in the business cycle is the economy right now? What does it mean for your business and industry?

5. How do you want to ride the sixth long wave, which is about to begin in the coming decade and will drive the next economic meta-cycle?

6. How does your personality type fit your role in business when considering cyclicality? Are you in the right industry at the right place at the right point of time?

> "There are two concepts we can hold to with confidence:
> # Rule No. 1: Most things will prove to be cyclical.
> # Rule No. 2: Some of the greatest opportunities for gain and loss come when other people forget Rule No. 1."
> —HOWARD MARKS

1.6. THE WORLD HATES INNOVATION. THIS IS WHY

The prolific American innovator Charles F. Kettering once said: *"The world hates change. Yet it is the only thing that has brought progress."* Innovation means change, so one might conclude that the world hates innovation. Let's investigate Kettering's statement to understand why — and what it means for us as innovators.

Innovation means progress

Let's first examine the second part of Kettering's message. Change means innovation, and as you will learn later in Chapter 2, innovation means meaningful new changes that improve our lives and make the world a better place. So, innovation means progress.

What has brought humanity out of caves into comfortable homes full of appliances and modern technology? The accumulation of many innovations that unfolded in several waves over thousands of years. Would you go back to living in a cold, damp, smoky cave? Maybe that's too radical, so let's make it easier: Would you give me your mobile phone and go back to having only landlines at home and at work and pay phones on the street? Or if this proposition is still too extreme, would you swap your smartphone for a dumb phone? You're likely to decline these offers.

Clearly, Charles Kettering was right in saying that innovation or change is the only thing that has brought us progress. But what about the first part of the sentence?

Does the world really hate innovation or change?

In 2005, Alan Deutschman wrote a fascinating article for *Fast Company*, titled *"Change or Die,"* on an interesting real-life decision scenario: What if you were given a choice by a well-informed, trusted and benevolent authority: You have to radically and enduringly change your life — or you have to die. Which option would you choose?

Clearly, almost all people say they would choose to make significant changes in their lives to avoid death. But when we contrast this proclaimed intent with the actual number of people who follow through, nine out of ten people choose to die. Why?

The scenario relates to patients who had undergone heart bypass surgery and were told by their cardiologist to shift to a healthy lifestyle to avoid a relapse. Yet very few did. Statistics show that two years after surgery, 90% of the patients have not changed their lifestyle — and within a few years, they died after a new heart attack.

Why is it so difficult for most people to change?

People differ in their response to change because of their personality and their preferred cognitive styles. Few people have what *Good to Great* author Jim Collins calls *"psycho-dynamic"* minds, which relish or even drive change. However, many people have *"psycho-static"* minds that make them distaste change.

Why do most people hate change?

First, humans are creatures of habit. Many behaviors are ingrained into our brains, and because they served us well in the past (or did no noticeable harm), we are reluctant to do something radically new. People with psycho-static minds, in particular, relish their habits and cherish rules and traditions.

Second, most people are afraid of the unknown, and every change is a departure from the status quo.

Third, when people try something new, they run the risk of failure and—especially in some cultures—the related risk of losing face. Sticking with what's familiar is a safer option.

Lastly, many people feel comfortable in their established ways, and some are really lazy. Every change means more work, new challenges, new learnings, and temporary discomforts. Why bother?

Change needs an impetus and a positive frame

Every change initiative needs a powerful motivation to succeed permanently. As the American life coach Anthony Robbins noted, people are motivated to make changes either by moving away from pain or moving toward pleasure. But isn't the fear of death one of the most powerful motivators there is? Why, then, do nine out of ten people still choose death?

Alan Deutschman suggested that a powerful impetus to change alone might not be good enough, but the odds of success increase when we use a positive frame of reference. More bypass patients stick with healthier lifestyles when their doctors reframe the challenge from a negative (*"change to avoid death"*) to a positive frame (*"change to enjoy life"*). Moving towards pleasure seems to motivate more people to make lasting changes than moving away from pain.

In addition, humans need support groups and mechanisms as well as fast visible successes (*"quick wins"*) to stick with new behaviors long enough to embed new habits.

From *"change or die"* to *"innovate or die"*

To recap: when confronted with the threat of early death, ten out of ten bypass patients say they're ready to make healthy lifestyle changes, but only one in ten follows through. Isn't this just like many executives in mature corporations with declining revenues and margins approach innovation? Everyone is talking the innovation talk, but few are walking their talk in earnest (we will discuss this below in a separate section, see 3.2).

When innovation started to become a hot topic in business about a decade ago, some consultants and self-proclaimed innovation experts promoted their services by using the dramatic *"innovate or die"* slogan. (Some still do nowadays.)

Of course, they do have a point: If the world around us is changing rapidly (or even exponentially), and we don't move along, we rather sooner than later fall so much behind that we become irrelevant — and become forgotten and eventually die, be it as a person, a company, a country, a civilization, a product, or a technology. As Charles Darwin put it in his theory of evolution: *"Favorable variations have a tendency to be preserved, unfavorable to be destroyed."*

But we all die eventually whether we are living organisms or organizations. Just like in the medical *"change or die"* example earlier, we should really say *"Innovate or die sooner."*

But why are more struggling corporations not motivated to avoid *"sudden death"* by making serious innovation efforts? Perhaps, just like the bypass patients, *"innovate or die"* doesn't motivate enough people in an organization to make the necessary sacrifices for a creative change succeed.

So, use a positive frame (*"Let's change to lead innovation in our industry"*) and move towards pleasure. Then, link this positive frame with a compelling vision of a bright future. Finally, carefully design the stages of creative change to give the people the support structures and wins needed to hang in and see it through to success.

Steve Jobs did this when he returned to Apple in 1997 and saved the company with a focused series of new computers (including the colorful iMacs) and his *"Think Different"* campaigns. More recently, Jeffrey Immelt renewed General Electric by stimulating new creative growth with a focus on clean and green technology through the *"Ecomagination"* initiative. (We'll discuss creative cultural change below in Chapter 6.)

Conclusion: Charles Kettering was right: although it brought so much progress everyone enjoys and doesn't want to live without, *"the world hates change"*, the world hates innovation. We can even quantify this surprising truth. How many percent of people hate innovation or change?

84 percent. How do I arrive at this number? We will discuss this in section 3.6, when we will explore how an innovation is typically adopted by the overall population.

"The over-all point is that new technology will not necessarily replace old technology, but it will date it. By definition. Eventually, it will replace it. But it's like people who had black-and-white TVs when color came out. They eventually decided whether or not the new technology was worth the investment.
—STEVE JOBS"

**HUMAN ESSENCE:
CORE NEEDS & ACTIONS,
CORE VALUES**
What we do
Why we do it

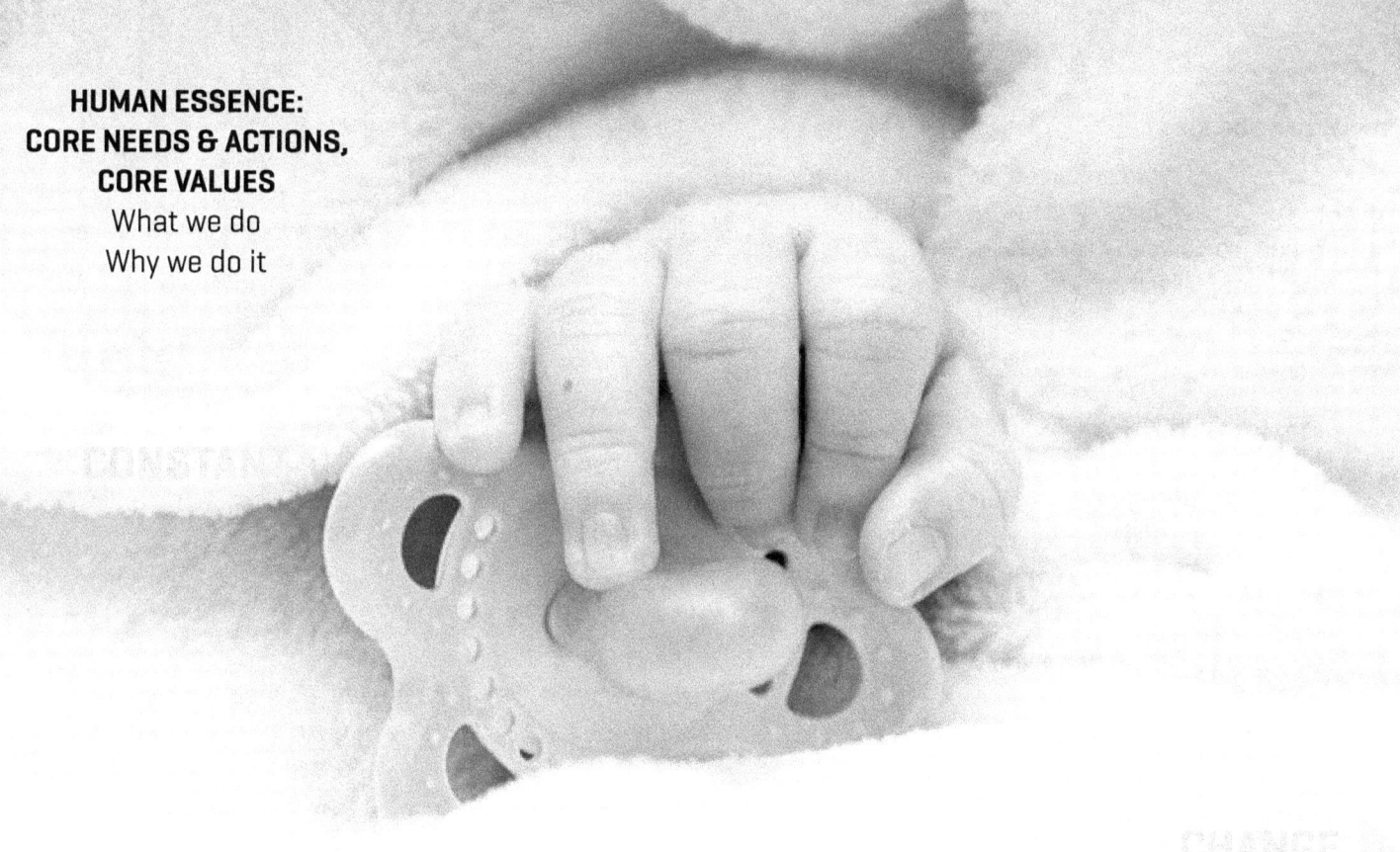

DETAILS: How we do it

1.7. THE MORE THINGS CHANGE, THE MORE THEY STAY THE SAME

"The only constant in the world is change," some people say. Is that really true, or is it just hype? After all, management gurus, business consultants, futurists, innovation consultants, change management experts, and the media use the idea of a constantly changing world to sell their services. Let's take a closer look at change to understand what really changes and what doesn't so that we can become better business thinkers.

What has changed?

Take two minutes and think about what has changed over the past thirty years. Write down all the aspects of these changes you can think of. When you review your list, most items will fall into these categories:

- Economic changes, such as the global integration of economies and businesses,
- Political changes, such as the fall of the Iron Curtain and the rise of China,
- Technological changes, such as the increased reach of IT and the constant stream of new gadgets,
- Transportation, such as the emergence of low-cost airlines, high-speed trains, and inner-city transportation upgrades in the big cities in developing countries,
- Communication and media changes, such as the rise of the World Wide Web, e-mail, SMS, and social media,
- Health, leisure, and lifestyle-related changes, such as spas, fitness and yoga studios, and cosmetic surgery.

Clearly, during the past 30 years, we have witnessed great changes or, as futurist James Canton put it, exponential change. So it seems that the only constant is indeed change. But is this really true?

What stays the same?

In his book *Mind Set!*, futurist John Naisbitt explains that while some things change, most things remain constant.

While the way we live changes, the cycle of life remains constant. We are born, we live, and we die. We learn and play, move and act, sleep, communicate, work, eat, and love.

Our basic values and motivations remain constant. We share universal, fundamental human values. We strive for accomplishment, happiness, community, health, love, security, and validation. We try to avoid pain. Whatever changes in the environment, these basic emotions and desires remain constant.

The French novelist Jean-Baptiste Alphonse Karr rightly pointed out that *"the more things change, the more they stay the same."* John Naisbitt helps us understand why: what changes are the details of how we do things. What remains the same is the essence of what we do and why we do it.

Look for spirals

The Greek philosopher Heraclitus noted, *"You cannot step twice into the same stream."* In their book *Future Think*, the futurists Edie Weiner and Arnold Brown adopt this idea and suggest thinking about change as a spiral rather than a pendulum. Much of life — waking and sleeping, or the seasons — follows cyclical patterns. Business and economic activities are no exception.

For example, one economic sector — online businesses, say — heats up until a speculative bubble bursts and sends the economy into a recession. After some time, another sector, like real estate, does the same. Although these cycles are likened to the swing of a pendulum, the pendulum does not simply swing back to the old position, as other things in the environment have changed.

A better metaphor is a spiral where, after circling around, you're in a similar, but slightly different, place. The spiral encompasses both change and cyclical constancy. When you think of change, think of a spiral and ask yourself what's the same as before and what has changed.

> "Nothing is stronger than habit."
> —OVID

Consider this metaphor: Understanding the dynamics of the world's population is like hosting a party for the world. Based on United Nations (UN; www.unpopulation.org) data and projections, let's invite the world to a party to learn more about its population today and in the decades to come.

Throughout this exercise, keep in mind these two questions: *"What does this mean for my business? What does it mean for me?"*

Hosting a party for the world

Imagine that you've been given a budget to host a party for 100 guests in the five rooms of your house. Your sponsor has imposed one condition: the number of guests from each country must roughly match their share of the world's population (8.0 billion people as of mid-2023).

What would such a party look like?

- Eighteen of your guests each—almost one out of five—will either come from China or India (which recently overtook the former as the most populous country). You give each one an entire room to host their private Chinese and Indian parties. However, as a party room can accommodate 20 guests, you split the four Pakistanis into two groups to fill the space in each of the first two party rooms.

- Before you invite more partygoers, you notice with surprise that the guests from these three Asian countries alone fill two of your five party rooms. Moreover, should you believe in reincarnation, you realize that the odds of being born as either Chinese or Indian in your next life is 35%.

- The third-party room includes people from seven nations: four US Americans, four Indonesians, three Brazilians and Nigerians, and two guests each from Bangladesh, Russia, and Ethiopia.

- A sliding glass door divides the fourth room into two halves. The ten guests on the left side of the room include a Mexican couple, two Japanese, a Filipino, a Vietnamese, a German, an Egyptian, an Iranian, and a Congolese,. Things get more challenging to distinguish among the ten people on the right-hand side of the room. However, you can still single out one person each from Turkey, France, the United Kingdom, Thailand, Tanzania, Italy, South Africa, and Korea (a descendent from mixed Southern and Northern parents).

- Finally, in the last room, you'll find twenty people, each with ancestors from several countries, who collectively represent the remaining countries.

It's worth noting that the world population distribution follows the Pareto Principle (or 80/20-Thinking): 80% of the world's population lives in just 15% of the 234 countries the United Nations considers.

Fast-forward to 2050

Guess what? Your world party in 2023 was a huge success. To celebrate the 27th anniversary of your party, your sponsor asks you to host another world party in the same venue. This time, though, there are new conditions. In addition to making sure that the mix of nationalities matches each country's share of the world population again, you must also account for the overall increase in world population and the portion of the population over

60 years old. Here are some of the challenges you will face:

- Due to the 20% increase in the overall world population to almost 9.7 billion people, your house will now have to accommodate 120 guests for the party, which means that you will have to shoehorn an additional four guests into each room.

- You give one room to the 21 guests from India. To avoid the first party's unpleasantness (a brawl between some Indian and the two Pakistani guests), you ask the three guests from Bangladesh to join their Indian neighbors this time.

- The second room contains 16 Chinese, five guests from Pakistan, two Russians, and one Iranian. These countries cooperate closely with each other to form an economic counterweight to rising India and the affluent Indo-Pacific Economic Bloc.

- The third room is occupied by guests from economically well-off nations, mainly from the Indo-Pacific Economic Bloc. Five US Americans enjoy hanging out mostly with the three Brazilians and two Mexicans at one end of the room, joined by one guest each from old European powers (Germany, United Kingdom, France, and Turkey). Guests from Asian nations that benefited from the last long cycle that just ended (the Sixth Wave of technology innovation) flock together at the other end of the room: four Indonesians and two Filipinos are joined by one guest each from Vietnam, Thailand, Japan, and the recently unified Korea.

- The lively fourth room is almost entirely filled by guests from the world economy's new growth engine, Africa. Picture five Nigerians dancing with three Congolese, three Ethiopians, two Egyptians,

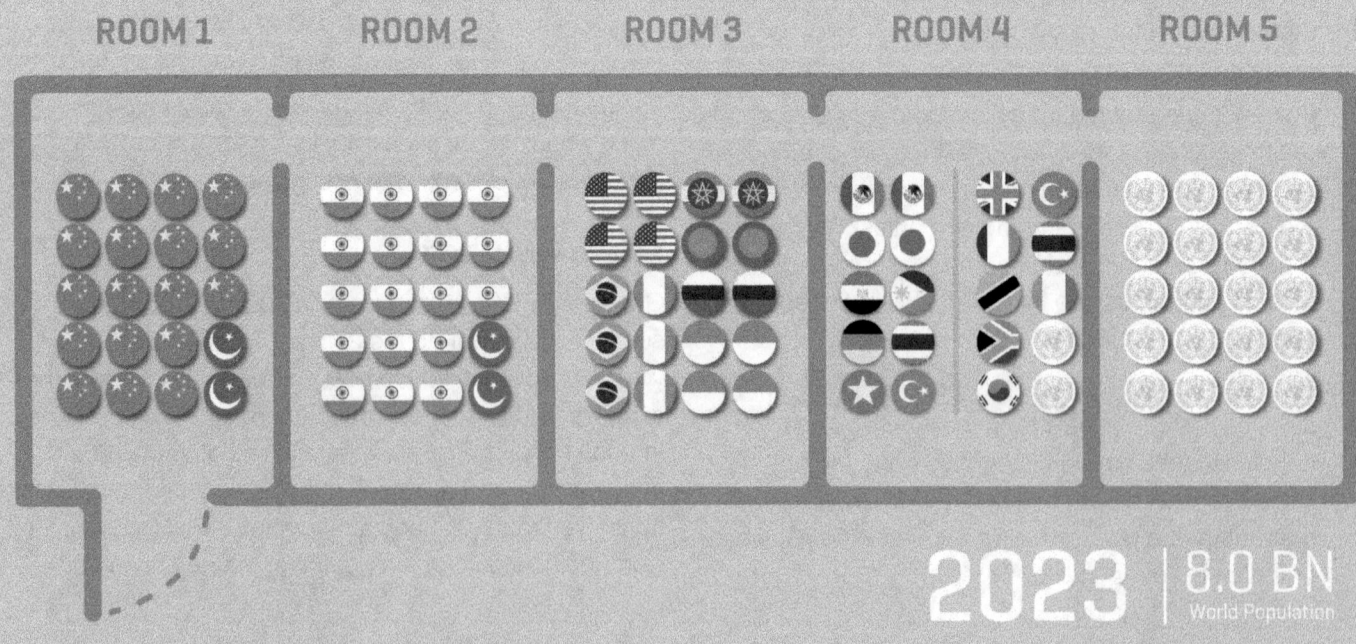

2023 | 8.0 BN
World Population

two Tanzanians, and one guest each from Uganda, Kenya, Sudan, South Africa, Angola, Niger, and Mozambique. For some peculiar reasons, an Iraqi and an Afghan observe the wild celebrations stoically from the back of this room.

- The fifth and final room is filled with 24 guests with a multicultural background representing the 201 other nations that were not populous enough to send one national delegate themselves. You decided to let the United Nations nominate these delegates, as you're busy trying to comply with your last condition: age distribution.

- To match their overall share in the world population of 16.5%, twenty guests at the party must be aged 65 or above. Surprised by this number, you look more closely at the demographics. You notice that four of the sixteen Chinese are over 65, as should be one guest from North Asia. This is because Japan has the highest proportion of elderly citizens in the world (38.5% of citizens aged 65 or above), beating South Korea by just 1 percent. Other wealthy Asian neighbors from Singapore, Hong Kong, and Macao are around or well above 30%. In Europe, Italy has the largest portion of elderly citizens of 65 or above, with almost 35%, followed by Finland, Greece, and Germany. In contrast, populations are noticeably younger in the United States (23.5%) and India (14.5%), meaning that only one American and three Indians will be aged 65 or above. By the way, if you're reading this book, and all goes well, you will be part of this elderly population.

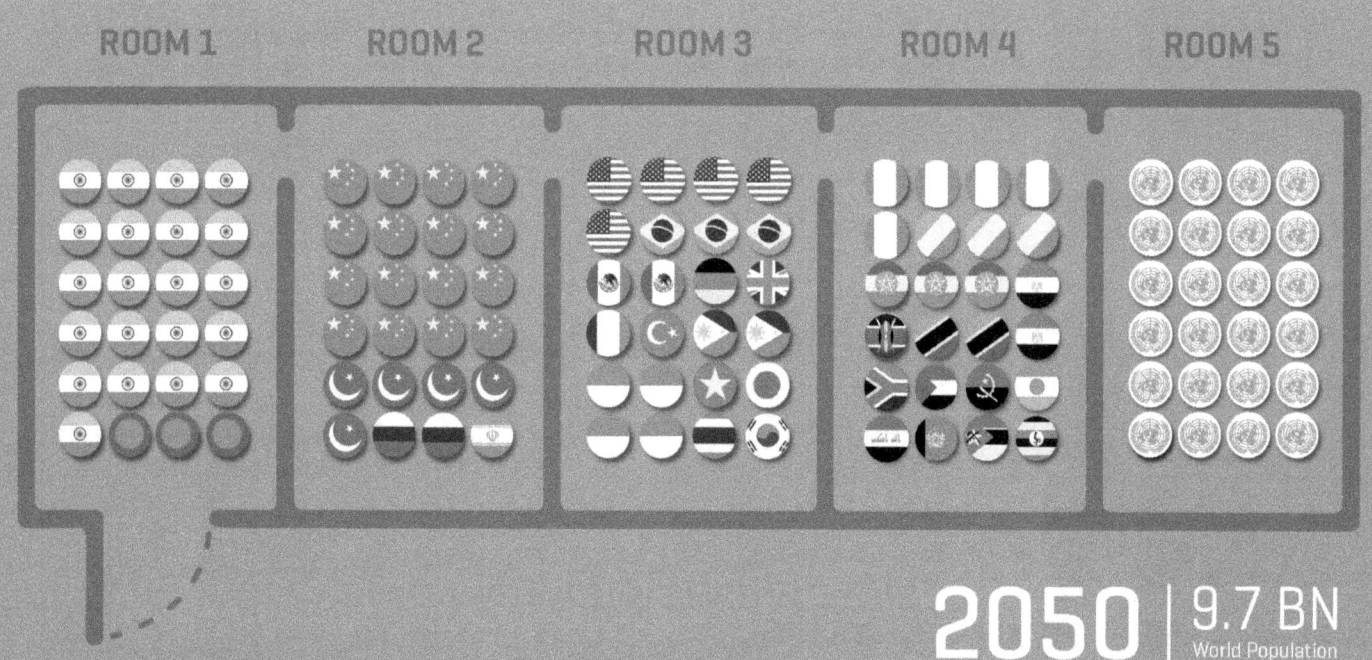

2050 | 9.7 BN World Population

> "Some people don't like change, but you need to embrace change if the alternative is disaster."
> – ELON MUST

CHAPTER 1 — EXECUTIVE SUMMARY: THE MODERN INNOVATION ENVIRONMENT

❖ Five meta-factors drive the modern business environment of the early 21st century: accelerating speed leading to shorter cycle times; exponential changes; mounting complexity; new, more and higher risks; and regular surprises that can turn out positive or negative. This highly dynamic environment is strikingly different from the static, predictable business world in the second half of the last century.

❖ Humanity has progressed in its economic evolution from the hunter and gatherer societies over the agricultural age, industrial age, and information age into a new era: the age of creation. In the innovation economy, ideas and know-how are the central means of production, and the core competitive advantage of a business is the ability to create value.

❖ The five drivers of the change in the innovation economy give more economic opportunities to agile, flexible and creative entrepreneurs who create and compete in global networks. As such, business is shifting from a managerial (20th century) to an entrepreneurial (21st century) society.

❖ To discern different patterns of how changes unfold over time, we can track three parameters of change: velocity (how fast things change), direction (linear, cyclical, pendulum, spiral), and impact (incremental, evolutionary, revolutionary).

❖ Many economic parameters unfold in cyclical waves of change on different time scales. The most relevant waves to track for businesspeople are product life cycle, company life cycle, business cycles, and long cycles.

❖ Innovation means change. Unfortunately, eight to nine out of ten people respond negatively to change. Successful innovators need to develop strategies to overcome people's inertia or resistance to change.

❖ While many things change, others stay the same: While the details of how humans do things change, the essential activities and core motivations of humans remain constant.

❖ By 2050, the world population will rise to over 9.5 billion. The growth dynamic impacting business will vary between countries and regions with rising and shrinking populations.

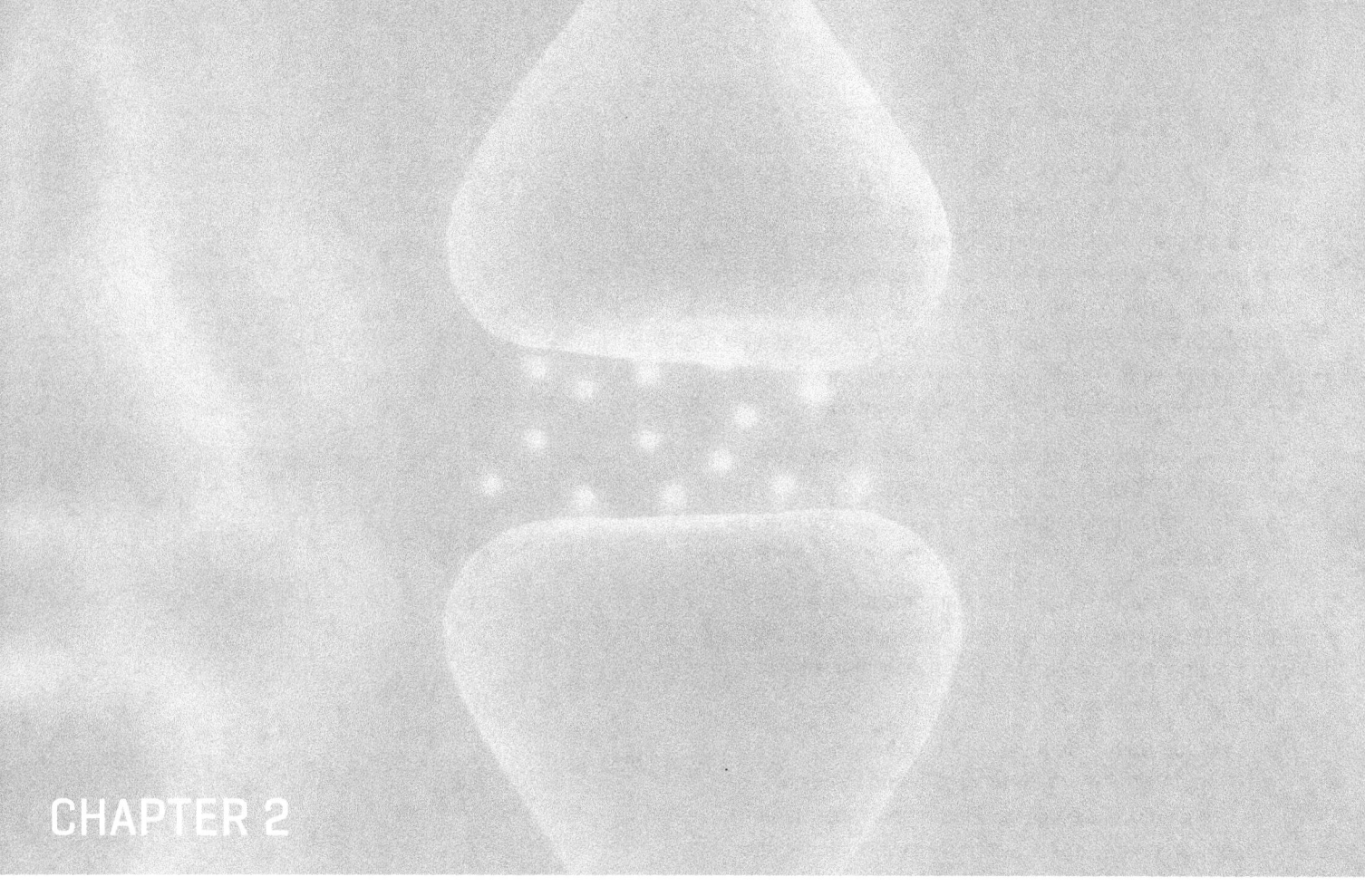

CHAPTER 2

CORE INNOVATION PRINCIPLES
BIG PICTURE (I)

Learn about the essential facets of creativity and innovation.

1. Creativity Defined
2. Creativity is...
3. The Innovation Formula
4. True Innovation Is About Making Meaning
5. Climb Up the Value Pyramid to Higher Profitability
6. Modern Innovation Types
7. How Innovation Affects Financial Performance
8. Why and How to Protect Your Intellectual Property
* *Executive Summary*

2.1. CREATIVITY DEFINED

Definitions are boring, you may think. But they are important. A definition is an exact statement or description of the nature, scope, or meaning of something. In Chapter 2, we first invest time to define the term creativity (and later innovation) to provide clarity and a common understanding of these key concepts in this book. Let's start with defining what creativity means.

If you look through the literature, you can nowadays find hundreds of definitions of creativity (and the same holds true for innovation). All have their point, and it's up to personal taste to settle on a definition that works for you.

However, when we look for commonalities between different approaches to defining the term creativity, we can notice that they tend to focus on either a person, a product or a process:

- *Person*-based definitions of creativity center on people who are seen as creative to the extent they demonstrate certain abilities, achievements and/or personality traits. Such personal traits found in creative people are high individuality, non-conformity to rules and the status quo, striving for originality and novelty, flexibility, persistence and passion, among others. (We will take a more in-depth look at personality traits of creative people in Chapter 7, when we discuss individual creativity and creative leadership.)
- *Process*-oriented definitions of creativity emphasize cognitive processes that lead to solutions, ideas, conceptualizations, artistic forms, theories, or products that are unique, novel, and meaningful. For example, the psychologist Robert Sternberg defines creative thinking as *"the process of producing*

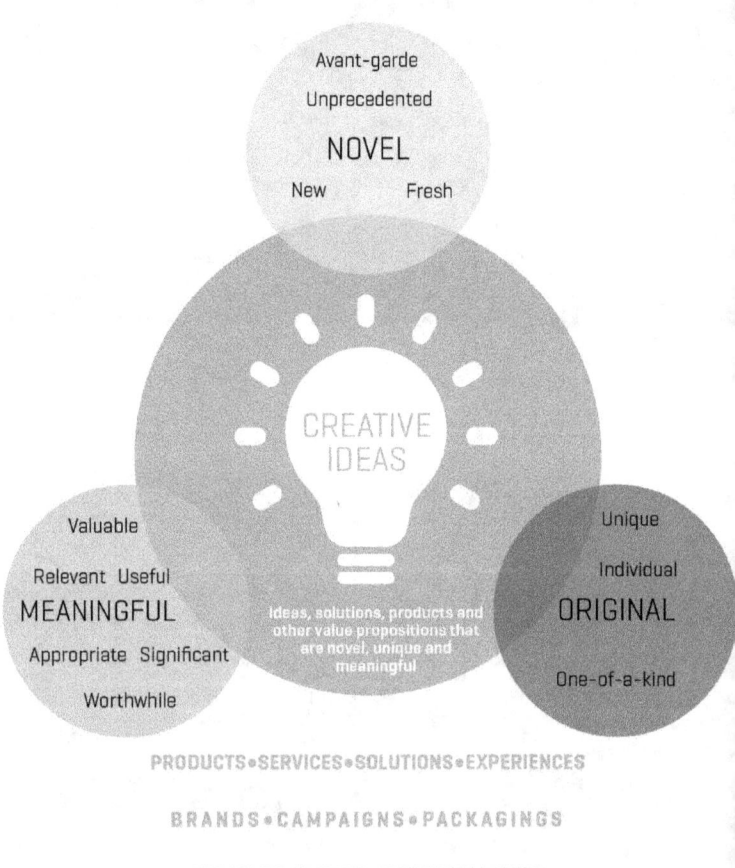

something that is both original and worthwhile utilizing given resources more efficiently and effectively than others combining the existing knowledge to create or constructing more unique, diverse, and appropriate solutions to the problem." (We will discuss such creative process methods in Chapter 4.)

- *Product*-oriented definitions of creativity focus on essential features of a creative product or outcome, among them novelty, appropriateness, relevance, worth or value, uniqueness and originality. An example of such a product-based attempt to define creativity comes from Harvard Business School's professor Teresa Amabile: *"A product or response will be judged as creative to the extent that it is both a novel and appropriate, useful correct or valuable response to the task at hand, and the task is heuristic rather than algorithmic."*

What do all these definitions of creativity have in common? To be judged creative, a person, process or product must meet three essential criteria: *novelty* (the person or thing has to be fresh, new, avant-garde, unprecedented), *meaningful* (valuable, worthwhile, useful, relevant) and *unique* (original, one-of-a-kind, individual). As such, let's simply define creativity as follows:

CREATIVITY = [NOVEL ∩ MEANINGFUL ∩ ORIGINAL] IDEAS

Putting other concepts related to creativity into context

Many synonyms (and buzzwords) of creative thinking float around in books and articles: Right-brain thinking. Lateral thinking. Out-of-the-box thinking. In the following, let's also clarify some of these concepts related to thinking in general and creative thinking in particular:

- Creative thinking is often contrasted with analytical thinking. Analytical thinking means examining or thinking about the different parts or details of something to better understand or explain it or to work logically and systematically to resolve an issue or case. In contrast, as we've just learned, creative thinking describes cognitive processes that lead to ideas, solutions, conceptualizations, artistic forms, theories, or products that are unique, novel, and meaningful.

- Roger Sperry's split-brain theory suggested that analytical thinking and creative thinking take place in different parts of the neocortex (the sophisticated *"outer shell"* of the human brain that evolved last): The left hemisphere is said to be more analytic, rational and logical in nature, while the right hemisphere is more creative, holistic and intuitive. While more recent brain research revealed this distinction is not strictly true, Daniel Pink suggested in his book *A Whole New Mind* we can still say that analytical thinking is *predominantly* left brain-*directed*, while creative thinking is *largely* right brain-*directed*, and that most geniuses are integrated whole-brain thinkers.

- Another distinction often made relates to the thinking direction: When we narrow down our thinking towards one point, which is often the case when thinking analytically, we engage in convergent thinking. In contrast, when we broaden our thinking from one starting point (such as generating many ideas for a creative challenge), we engage in divergent thinking. As we will discuss later in Chapter 4, most creative thinking processes (or innovation methods) unfold in a harmonious rhythm of alternating phases of divergent thinking followed by convergent thinking.

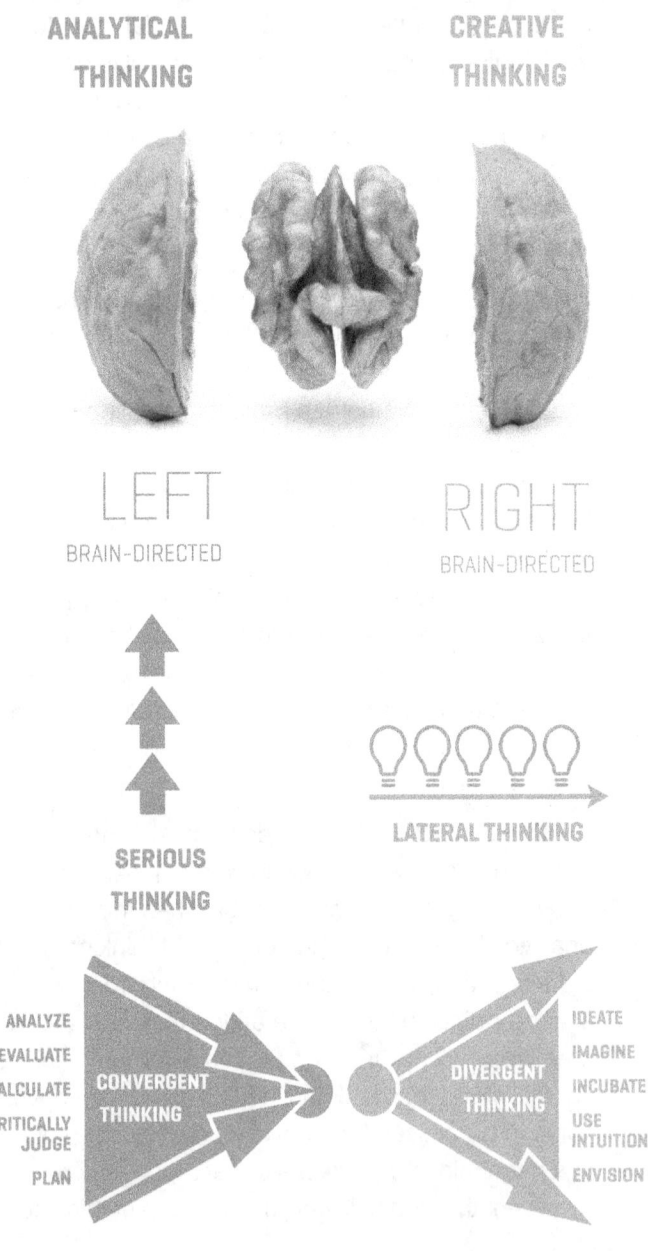

- Edward de Bono popularized the term lateral thinking as a synonym for creative thinking. When we create ideas, we make an effort to generate many ideas without judgment that stand laterally next to each other. In contrast, when we engage in serious thinking, we typically think analytically and progress sequentially.

And how about *"thinking out-of-the-box"*? This synonym for creativity and creative thinking turned buzzword and business jargon originates from a creative puzzle that is more than a hundred years old: The famous Nine Dots Puzzle. This puzzle challenges you to connect nine dots squarely arranged as three points, each in three lines with a pen by not more than four straight lines without lifting the pen. If you haven't seen this well-known puzzle so far, then google and try to solve it.

Enough with definitions for the moment. So, all of you who dislike definitions, let's have some fun by taking a more light-hearted look at what creativity is...

"Creativity is just connecting things."
—STEVE JOBS

2.2. CREATIVITY IS...

"Love is...", a comic strip by Kim Casali that was popular in the 1970s, portrayed different aspects of loving and being loved, using simple messages shared between two lovers. But this is a creative leader's guide to creativity and innovation, not love. So, let's talk about the different aspects of creativity. What is creativity? What does it mean and encompass? How do we know if something is creative? What are the key aspects of creativity?

1. Creativity is... useful.

"The value of an idea lies in the using of it," said the American inventor and entrepreneur Thomas Edison. A great creative idea must be useful; it must be meaningful and make the world a better place; it must address a worthwhile issue in a relevant, appropriate, functional way. How do you know if your idea is useful? Here's Edison again: *"Anything that won't sell, I don't want to invent. Its sale is proof of utility, and utility is success."* And *"The Father of Advertising,"* David Ogilvy, echoed this when he said, *"If it doesn't sell, it isn't creative."*

45

2. Creativity is… fresh and new.

"Creativity is seeing something that doesn't exist already. You need to find out how you can bring it into being and that way be a playmate with God," said Michele Shea. All truly creative ideas are really new. While they usually build on existing concepts, creative ideas are fresh and unprecedented. And like fresh milk, ideas should be dated so you can act on them before they go sour.

3. Creativity is… original and unique.

If it's not original, it's not creative. Albert Einstein was joking when he said, *"The secret to creativity is knowing how to hide your sources."* Truly creative ideas are one-of-a-kind. They are unique. And like those ideas, the geniuses who produce them are themselves one-of-a-kind, and they celebrate what makes them unique — even when it means being deemed misfits or *"black sheep"* who do not belong in the flock.

4. Creativity is… beautiful.

Richard Buckminster Fuller said, *"When I'm working on a problem, I never think about beauty. I think only how to solve the problem. But when I have finished, if the solution is not beautiful, I know it is wrong."* Aside from being fresh, original, useful and functional, the best creative solutions are beautiful.

5. Creativity is… simple.

Leonardo da Vinci said, *"Simplicity is the ultimate sophistication."* Simplicity is another hallmark of creativity. But why?

"Any intelligent fool can make things bigger, more complex, and more violent. It takes a touch of genius — and a lot of courage — to move in the opposite direction," said Albert Einstein.

Some of the most creative products or solutions are notable for their simplicity. As jazz musician Charles Mingus said, *"Making the simple complicated is commonplace; making the complicated simple, awesomely simple, that's creativity."*

6. Creativity is… playful, funny, and fun.

"The creation of something new is not accomplished by the intellect but by the play instinct acting from inner necessity. The creative mind plays with the objects it loves," said the Swiss psychologist Carl Jung.

Having a surprising insight or conceiving a new, original idea is often a by-product of creative play. As fellow creativity coach Mitch Ditkoff said, *"It's no accident that AHA and HAHA are spelled almost the same way."* Because creativity and play go hand in hand, outstanding creative concepts contain elements of fun, wit and playfulness, and most creative geniuses are witty, playful people, too.

For example, Pablo Picasso said, *"God is really another artist. He invented the giraffe, the elephant and the cat. He has no real style. He just goes on trying other things."*

7. Creativity is… pleasurable, addictive, hedonistic, and sexy.

"Creativity is a drug I cannot live without," said the Hollywood movie producer Cecil B. DeMille. Living a creative life is addictive and pleasurable, which is why anyone who has the courage to live life creatively cannot go back to working in what Scott Adams calls *"Cubicleville."*

The pleasure that creativity gives those who create is often reflected in outputs that are pleasurable to watch, use, and interact with, and may even have sex appeal. Deepak Chopra said, *"Creativity is ultimately sexual — I'm sorry — but it is!"*

8. Creativity is… infectious.

Here is another interesting insight from Albert Einstein: *"Creativity is contagious. Pass it on."* If you enjoyed reading this book, please pass it on to your friends and colleagues.

9. Creativity is… the courage to fail.

"An essential aspect of creativity is not being afraid to fail," noted the American inventor and founder of Polaroid Edwin H. Land.

Other famous inventors like James Dyson (*"The key to success is failure… Success is made of 99 percent failure"*), Charles F. Kettering (*"It is not a disgrace to fail. Failing is one of the greatest arts in the world"*) and Thomas Edison (*"I have not failed. I've just found 10000 ways that won't work."*) likewise emphasized the importance of temporary setbacks and failure as essential part of a rapid prototyping approach and of the creative (learning) process on how to eventually create new value and make things work.

Hence, let's conclude in the words of Joseph Chilton Pierce: *"To live a creative life, we must lose our fear of being wrong."*

10. Creativity is… the interplay of creation and destruction.

"The difficulty lies not so much in developing new ideas as in escaping from old ones," noticed the famous British economist John Maynard Keyes.

Everyone knows that great creativity creates something new and useful, but few are aware that great creativity often starts with destroying the old to make space for the new. Thus, *"the old"* or *"traditional"* may be a rule, policy, or guideline that is nonsensical or a sacred cow (a once cherished, highly successful idea that is outdated and whose time has come to be retired).

So adopt the mindset of the American composer John Cage: *"I can't understand why people are frightened of new ideas. I'm frightened of the old ones,"* and when you create, be ready to also destroy in line with Pablo Picasso's advice: *"Every act of creation is first an act of destruction."*

11. Creativity is… perfect imperfection.

"Perfectionism is the enemy of creation," believed the writer John Updike. And he is not alone. *"Artists who seek perfection in everything are those who cannot attain it in anything,"* commented the French artist Eugene Delacroix. Likewise, the Spanish artist Salvador Dali advised: *"Have no fear of perfection—you'll never reach it."*

Truly excellent creative concepts often border perfection yet resemble more a state that I call *"perfect imperfection,"* which is in line with Vince Lombardi's insight that *"Perfection is not attainable, but if we chase perfection we can catch excellence."*

12. Creativity is … pure passion.

"Creativity is the quality that you bring to the activity that you are doing. It is an attitude, an inner approach—how you look at things . . . Whatsoever you do, if you do it joyfully, if you do it lovingly, if your act of doing is not purely economical, then it is creative," observed the spiritual teacher Osho.

Clearly, creatives are driven by passion for their chosen creative work and the joy of successfully resolving a creative challenge, not money.

US psychologist Teresa Amabile summarized her research findings on the motivational side of creativity as follows: *"People will be most creative when they feel motivated primarily by the interest, satisfaction, and challenge of the work itself—and not by external pressures."*

13. Creativity is… sensitivity to problems and opportunities.

"Creativity is… seeing something that doesn't exist already. You need to find out how you can bring it into being and that way be a playmate with God," noted Michele Shea. A central aspect of a creative mind is problem or opportunity sensitivity, the ability to turn a problem into an opportunity or to spot an opportunity to create something new and valuable out of nothing.

"Anyone can look for fashion in a boutique or history in a museum. The creative explorer looks for history in a hardware store and fashion in an airport," suggests Robert Wieder.

But note that finding a problem or opportunity alone is only a starting point to creation, as the American poet James Russel Lowell reminds us: *"Creativity is not the finding of a thing, but the making something out of it after it is found."*

14. Creativity is … playing with constraints.

"Creativity arises out of the tension between spontaneity and limitations, the latter (like the river banks) forcing the spontaneity into the various forms which are essential to the work of art or poem," noted Rollo May. Playing with this seemingly paradoxical balance between freedom and constraints is a key creative strategy.

For example, when we ask *"What if"* questions such as *"What if you had to double your revenues within a year? Or within a month?"*, we impose a time constraint, while with the question *"What if senior management tripled the budgets for your division?"*, we remove a monetary constraint.

In both cases, this play between imposing and removing limiting constraints is a surefire way to set your imagination on fire.

15. Creativity is… freedom.

The Russian expressionist Wassily Kandinsky noted: *"There is no must in art because art is free."*

Imagine an institution or society that limits and restricts open access to certain types of information and monitors what information people view and share; that dislikes when its people ask a lot of questions (and particularly impermissible ones). Do you expect the people who live and work inside such a tightly controlled box to really

think outside the box? To come up with outstanding creativity?

"Creativity is the greatest expression of liberty," believes the American author Bryant H. McGill rightly. Clearly, creativity is all about freedom and flourishes in free environments and societies. To put it in the words of the US economist Brian S. Wesbury: *"When freedom prevails, the ingenuity and inventiveness of people creates incredible wealth. This is the source of the natural improvement of the human condition."*

16. Creativity is… you.

"There is a genius in all of us," noted Albert Einstein. I agree. Although you may not agree with Einstein and me, there is also a creative genius in you. At least, you were a highly creative beginner when you were a young child, as we all were.

Conclusion:

"Creativity is inventing, experimenting, growing, taking risks, breaking rules, making mistakes, and having fun," as the American author Mary Lou Cook summarizes it in one sentence. When would now be a good time to indulge in some creative activity? And what other key dimensions of creativity have you noticed?

Please note that this list of sixteen principles of great creativity is by no means conclusive — so feel invited to add to your own views on what *"Creativity is…"* for you.

> *"Creativity is a type of learning where the teacher and the pupil are located in the same individual."*
> —ARTHUR KOESTLER

2.3. THE INNOVATION FORMULA

What is innovation?

You've just learned how we can define creativity in a simple way that captures the gist of most other definitions of the term:

(NOVEL + MEANINGFUL + ORIGINAL) IDEAS = CREATIVITY

When you review the literature on innovation, you can find hundreds of definitions of the term, too, most or all of them making a good point. So, where do we start when we want to define innovation?

When looking for a suitable definition more than a decade ago, I thought: *"Why not listen to a company that has delivered innovation for decades instead of just talking or writing about it academically?"* A fine definition that I greatly liked comes from a long-term innovation leader, the company 3M. They define innovation as *"new ideas—plus action and implementation—which leads to an improvement, a gain or a profit."* At this point, I recalled Albert Einstein's advice: *"Everything should be made as simple as possible, but not simpler."* So, I simplified this definition even further by expressing the relations between all concepts involved as a simple equation:

CREATIVITY + ACTION = INNOVATION

We call this equation the Thinkergy innovation formula. It is a simple yet powerful blueprint to highlight three important interrelationships between the concepts. I am going to share these 3 corollaries of the innovation formula with you in the following.

1. After we moved from the knowledge economy into the innovation economy, many top executives of big corporations realized: *"We need to quickly get innovative to successfully compete in the innovation economy. So, let's hire an innovation manager and charge him with setting up an innovation management system."* They do this and 1-2 years later, they ask the innovation manager in the annual performance review: *"So how much innovation have we produced?"* And the awkward answer is: *"None—or only a few incremental innovations."* Why is that? They wrongly started at the *right* side of the innovation formula.

   Many efficiency- and systems-driven corporate executives fail to realize that innovation always begins with ideas—ideas that come out of individual brains. So, if we want to produce innovation, let's start on the left side of the innovation formula. Creatively empower employees to come up with more creative ideas, for example, by exposing them to structured training programs teaching them creative thinking and how to use a structured innovation method (see Chapter 4). Moreover, also create a climate that encourages creative people to put their ideas out there and take initiative on them (we will discuss this later in Chapter 6). So, here is

   COROLLARY 1 OF THE INNOVATION FORMULA:
   Innovation begins with great creative ideas.

2. But creativity alone is also not enough. Many people come up with great ideas every other day, but never do anything about those ideas. Sometimes, they're too lazy to act, but more often, they don't take action on their ideas because they lack the guts. They're afraid to fail, afraid to lose face, afraid that people will laugh at them. We call these creative people who never dare to take action on their ideas, dreamers. As American computer science professor Robert M. Hayes once said, *"Held in the palms of thousands of disgruntled people over the centuries have been ideas worth millions—if they only had taken the first step and then followed through."*

   We probably all know at least one dreamer in our immediate network, someone who lacked the courage to pursue a great idea. Chances are that at some point in your life, you were one of these dreamers, too.

   What's the difference between a creative dreamer and an innovator? Taking action. Here is

   COROLLARY 2 OF THE INNOVATION FORMULA:
   You must take action on your ideas to arrive at innovation.

3. There is a third and final aspect we need to discuss: Before taking action on an idea, make sure that it is truly creative, or in other words, novel, original, and meaningful. (The most important aspect here is the last one. Creative ideas need to make meaning. For that reason, we will discuss in the next section what the concept of making meaning means, and how we can check if an idea is meaningful.) This leads us to

   COROLLARY 3 OF THE INNOVATION FORMULA:
   Act only on truly creative ideas that are really new, original, and meaningful.

Conclusion: Companies that seek innovation need to focus first on the left side of the innovation formula (creativity and action) to arrive at innovation on the right side of the equation.

While it's OK to have an innovation manager and a well-designed innovation management system with clear innovation performance measures, these *"hard"* factors alone are insufficient to become more innovative. It's equally or even more important to invest time and money in the *"soft factors"*—in training employees to think more creatively, then have them apply their creative know-how and skills in real-life innovation project workshops, and finally in building a creative culture.

Now that you understand the innovation formula and its interdependencies, it's easy to get creative and get innovative:

- First, creatively empower yourself and your people to create novel, original and meaningful ideas.
- Then, take action on your top creative ideas—and
- Eventually, you will arrive at innovation.

In short, follow the innovation formula: CREATIVITY + ACTION = INNOVATION. It's as easy as this, and many companies that we've trained in business creativity and innovation have adopted the Thinkergy innovation formula.

> ""Innovation is the ability to convert ideas into invoices."
> —LEWIS DUNCAN

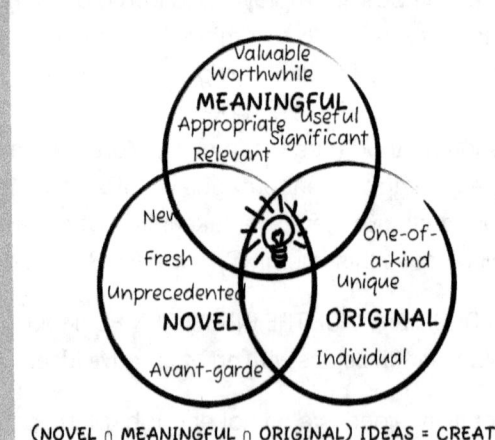

Innovation is: production or adoption, assimilation, and exploitation of a value-added novelty in economic and social spheres; renewal and enlargement of products, services, and markets; development of new methods of production; and establishment of new management systems. It is both a process and an outcome.
—OECD MANUAL

Innovation is the specific function of entrepreneurship, whether in an existing business, a public service institution, or a new venture started by a lone individual in the family kitchen. It is the means by which the entrepreneur either creates new wealth-producing resources or endows existing resources with enhanced potential for creating wealth.
—PETER DRUCKER

Creativity is thinking up new things. Innovation is doing new things.
—THEODORE LEVITT

Innovation: New IDEAS – plus ACTION or IMPLEMENTATION – which results in an improvement, a gain or a profit.
—3M

(NOVEL ∩ MEANINGFUL ∩ ORIGINAL) IDEAS = CREATIVITY

CREATIVITY + ACTION = INNOVATION

2.4. TRUE INNOVATION IS ABOUT MAKING MEANING

One aspect of our innovation formula is so important that we want to discuss it in a separate section. Before we take action on an idea, we need to check if it is truly novel, original and —in particular— meaningful. Creativity and innovation are no ends in themselves. Their ultimate objective is to create meaningful new value. So, let's get a better understanding of the concepts of value creation and making meaning.

Guy Kawasaki, a Silicon Valley-based Venture Capitalist, former Apple fellow and author of the book *The Art of the Start,* relates the following advice to wanna-be entrepreneurs: *"The core of entrepreneurship is about making meaning. Many people start companies to make money — the quick flip, the dot.com phenomena. I have noticed that those companies that are fundamentally founded to change the world, to make this world a better place, to make meaning, are the companies that make a difference. They are the ones to succeed. My naïve and romantic belief is that if you make meaning, you probably make money. But if you set out to make money, you will probably not make meaning and you won't make money. So you need to make meaning — that should be the core of why you start a company."* Similarly, making meaning —and not making money— is at the core of creativity and innovation.

Now what exactly does it mean: Making meaning? And how can we do it?

Making meaning implies adding significance or value to something; doing something that is novel, relevant, appropriate, worthwhile, and highly useful. For example, suppose you wanted to start a new business in Bangkok (where I reside). Then, you probably would not consider opening yet another spa or coffee shop, while coming up with business solutions to make buildings greener, cooler, and able to better deal with heavy rainfall would represent a significant value proposition. As Guy Kawasaki points out, making meaning is all about making our world a better place. We can achieve this noble objective by following one of three paths towards meaningful value creation:

1. **Look for ways to increase the quality of life.**
   Many truly great innovations in the history of humanity greatly increased the quality of people's lives. Can you imagine what our daily lives look like in a world without computers? Without mobile phones or the Internet? Without air-conditioning or electric lighting? Without the airplane, car, other means of transportation, or even roads? Clearly, we need to bear this path in mind as we embark on a new innovation project. Insofar, ask: How can we increase the quality of life of our customers with what we're doing? For example, an estimated 450 million products sold testify to the significance of how the iPod has increased the quality of lives of music lovers around the world during its lifetime.

2. **Right a wrong.**
   The second path towards meaning is to identify a wrong that you can right. Take notice of problems that you encounter as you go through life, note down these problems in a *"Bug List"*, and look for ways to turn these bugs into business or innovation

> *"First focus on making meaning, then you will make money."*
> —GUY KAWASAKI

opportunities. What are bugs that annoy you and need to be fixed? What does not work as well as it should? What is poorly designed and needs improvement? What wider unmet—and often unarticulated—need has not yet been addressed by the market? What really sucks — and could be influenced and changed for the better by you? The emergence of online music is a good example here: First, at the beginning of the new millennium, the emergence of P2P-sharing services (to freely exchange music) addressed a wider need to easily find one's favorite songs online. In October 2003, Apple righted another wrong by offering a legal way to acquire songs online with the opening of the iTunes Music Store.

3. **Prevent the end of something good.**
   These days, the world is changing very fast. People vary greatly in their perception of which of these changes are good, and which ones are bad. This points to a third way to make meaning: preventing the end of something good. Is there something good, beautiful, and wonderful that is about to come to an end due to changes in the environment? That is being eroded, being changed, being discontinued, or being ruined to your great dissatisfaction or even anger? If you just cannot stand the fact that something good is about to end — once again, turn the problem around into an opportunity to start a business, an innovation project or a social movement. For example, in Africa, national parks with premium safari lodges help preserve the beauty of the African wilderness while creating job opportunities for the locals and tourism income for the country and its entrepreneurs.

Conclusion: If we want to sum up the three ways to make meaning, we can do it as follows:

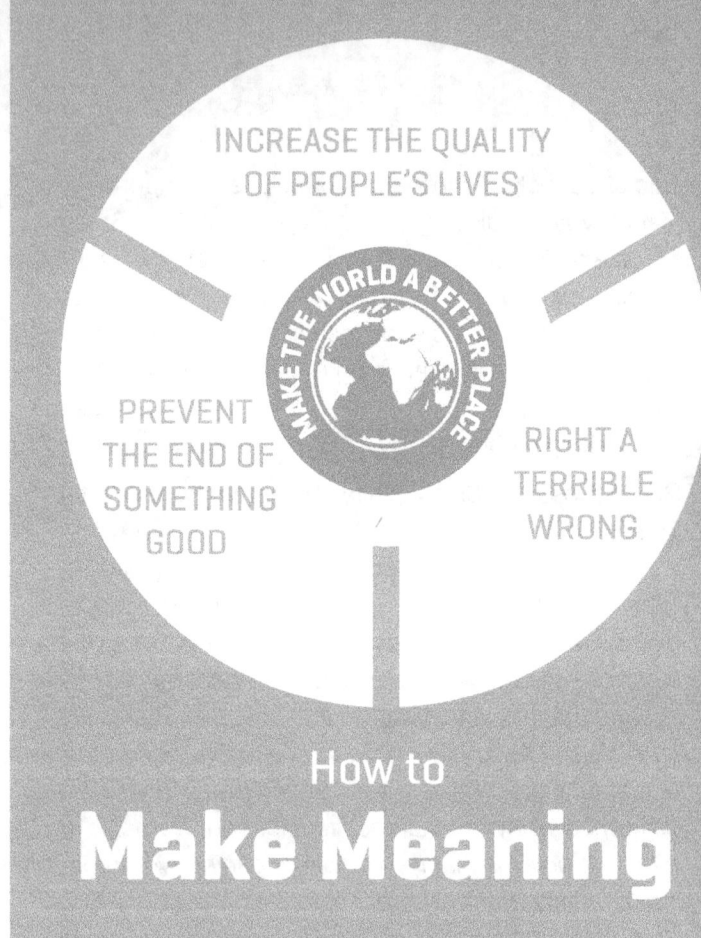

Making meaning is all about making the world a better place.

"Anything that won't sell, I don't want to invent. Its sale is proof of utility, and utility is success," said Thomas Edison. Like Guy Kawasaki, the world's greatest inventor knew: To make money, first focus your innovation efforts on making meaning. Make it your prime motivation to engage in creativity and your main judgment criteria to decide if an activated idea is an innovation success or not. When will you start making meaning and creating value propositions that truly make this world a better place?

2.5. CLIMB UP THE VALUE PYRAMID TO HIGHER PROFITABILITY

In the age of meaningful value creation, the magic word to open a customer's wallet is not *"Abracadabra"* but rather "Innovation" through the creation of meaningful, novel customer value. So how can we create more value for our customers?

Let's have a look at what I call the Value Pyramid Model. This model can be applied to many industries and expands our traditional understanding of economic offerings to include modern forms of market offerings that have emerged in recent years.

The Value Pyramid Concept

Imagine a pyramid that consists of 6 layers of economic offerings that rise from the bottom of the pyramid to the top as follows: commodities, goods, services, solutions, experiences and dreams. Together, we will ascend the value pyramid level by level, and you will notice by comparing the illustrative examples how both the value of an economic offering (as perceived by the buyer) and the profit margin rise and how, at the same time, the number of competitors declines.

The Base Level: Commodities

Commodities (such as oil, rice, precious metals, etc.) and raw materials are at the base of the value pyramid. On this lowest level, prices are often set in global commodity markets, and the profit margins for a producer are very thin as the commodity can easily be sourced from other suppliers. Two examples:

On the commodity level, the price for the quantity of coffee beans needed per cup of coffee is less than 1-2 US cents.

Looking back at my former career as a Corporate banker at Deutsche Bank, simple foreign exchange transactions with corporate customers have a commodity character; price is the sole decisive factor in determining which bank wins a deal.

Level 2: Goods

Let's move up to the second level of the value pyramid, goods. In most product categories, we notice various well-established producers who all compete on similar product characteristics and increasingly come under attack by new low-cost market entrants from emerging markets like China and India. Hence, a low price is still a major buying factor here, and there is an ever-increasing pressure on the profit margins. At the goods level for coffee, pre-packaged coffee sells for about 2-5¢ per serving of coffee.

Looking at a typical corporate banking product, the competition for a term loan is mainly price-driven, although it may also involve some qualitative variations regarding the scope of documentation and the basic loan structure.

Level 3: Services

Services are on the third level of our value pyramid. They offer more variety for differentiation and thus allow companies to realize a wider profit margin. Services can either be offered on a stand-alone basis (such as a cleaning service, a security service, a spa, or a hospital) or as a complementing value-added to goods (e.g., training courses for a particular computer software).

Once a simple coffee service such as selling brewed

coffee in a bakery or small coffee shop is added to the equation, the coffee price rises up further to roughly 75¢-1.50 USD.

Simple cash management transactions or trade services are examples of corporate banking services. Here, additional factors other than price (such as speed, reliability, network size) become important considerations when a corporate client selects its partner banks.

Level 4: Solutions

On the solutions level, a company can create further differentiation by providing tailor-made solutions to clients.

In the past, tailor-made solutions were mostly limited to the B2B world (business-to-business). In corporate banking, sophisticated individualized client solutions such as tailor-made collection services in cash management (which can add immense value in geographically widespread areas that are prevalent in most Asian countries) are a way for a bank to achieve a very close relationship with an attractive corporate client; typically, this results in a significant revenue increase and a higher share of the client's wallet for the bank.

Over the last decade, we have witnessed the emergence of a flood of individualized, meaningful business-to-consumer internet-based solutions such as YouTube, Facebook, and all the Google solutions that help individuals to express and share their individual creations with a global audience via new B2C-internet solutions (business-to-consumer).

Level 5: Experiences

Experiences can be found one level below the top of the value pyramid. Experiences distinctly differ from services and solutions as they offer unique, memorable sensations to buyers that are personally cared for like guests in a family-like community.

Harley Davidson does not simply sell a product, as one of its executives emphasized: *"What we sell is the ability for a 43-year-old accountant to dress in black leather, ride through small towns and have people be afraid of him."* The company has multiplied this unique experience with the creation of HOG (Harley Owner Group) communities that allow Harley owners to regularly ride out together in an impressive group.

Back to our coffee example: Starbucks charges customers $2-$5 for a cup of coffee (depending on the size and the type you order). Now, we may rightly ask: Why anybody in their right mind would pay up to 5 USD for a cup of coffee that has a commodity price value of a couple of cents? The answer is simple: Starbucks customers don't pay for the coffee but for the experience of being in the "third place" between your home (where you live) and your office (where you work). And at this third place, well-trained Starbucks baristas who have learned your name and remember your favorite drink soon become like good old friends, and here you can chill and relax over a cup of coffee together with other like-minded sophisticated members of the Starbucks family who also don't mind paying up to five bucks for their coffee.

In our corporate banking context, a bank may create an elite club system where meaningful incentives (such as VIP tickets to prestigious sports, cultural or business events; workshops or speaker series on interesting business topics; privileged economic or industry-specific research reports) are provided for free to its invitation-only members. The criteria for this meaningful club membership for the executives would depend on the amount of revenues and business volume that the bank generates with the client.

Level 6: Dreams

Finally, Dreams or *"Experiences Plus" as management guru Tom Peters calls them) are the ultimate value-adding strategy to win customers' hearts. "A dream is a complete moment in the life of a client. Important experiences that tempt the client to commit substantial resources. The essence of the desires of the consumer. The opportunity to help clients become what they want to be,"* notes Gian Luigi Longinotti-Buitoni, one of the proponents of the Dream Economy.

Given the additional increase in value associated with making dreams come true and helping clients become who they want to be, dreams command the pinnacle of the pyramid.

One company that has already been in the Dream Business for many decades is Disney with its Disney World theme parks, where Walt Disney realized his vision to make the dreams of children (and their happy parents) come true.

What is the essential value delivered by the cosmetic surgery dream industry to its customers? The desire to look more sexy, the dream of finally transforming into the *"right"* gender, and the illusion of being young again. The founder of Revlon cosmetics, Charles Revson, noted that his company *"sells hope in a bottle."*

The emergence of the space tourism industry, which offers trips into the stratosphere, may serve as a last example of a *"dreams business."* Richard Branson's Virgin Galactic, Jeff Bezos' Blue Origin, and Elon Musk's SpaceX all offer flights into space for wealthy individuals, thus allowing more people to realize their dreams of being astronauts.

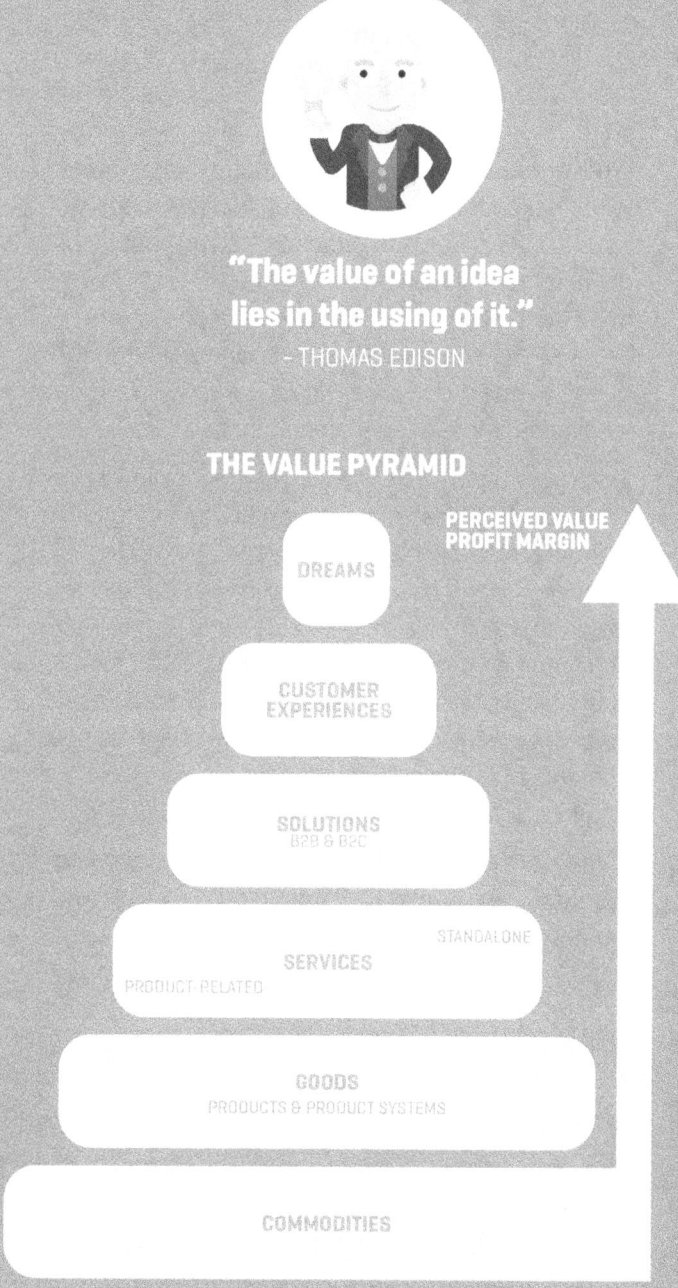

"The value of an idea lies in the using of it."
– THOMAS EDISON

THE VALUE PYRAMID

PERCEIVED VALUE
PROFIT MARGIN

- DREAMS
- CUSTOMER EXPERIENCES
- SOLUTIONS B2B & B2C
- SERVICES (PRODUCT-RELATED / STANDALONE)
- GOODS PRODUCTS & PRODUCT SYSTEMS
- COMMODITIES

2.6. MODERN INNOVATION TYPES

What are areas where your company can innovate? When asked this question, many businesspeople typically think first, and often exclusively, about the development of new products. In addition, a few managers may recall some business process re-engineering exercises their company went through during the past decades, which is known as Process Innovation. More often than not, that's about it.

This *"black-and-white"* view of the innovation world is outdated. It ignores many new potential opportunities to innovate. In the last two decades, the modern innovation world has evolved dramatically. Similarly, we don't watch television anymore in a big wooden box featuring a black-and-white screen and two channels, but instead use flat-screen color TVs fed by cable or satellite with hundreds of channels and contents-on-demand, we nowadays have many more and new areas to innovate.

If you want to find innovation opportunities for your company, you can play on four different levels and a variety of related modern innovation types: You may optimize, create, leverage and rebuild. Let's look at each of these four levels and discuss the related innovation types.

Innovation level 1: OPTIMIZE internal operations

The entry-level of innovation aims to OPTIMIZE existing operations by increasing operational efficiencies and reducing costs. You can do this in two ways:

- **Process Innovation** focuses on streamlining and simplifying specific work processes. Do you want

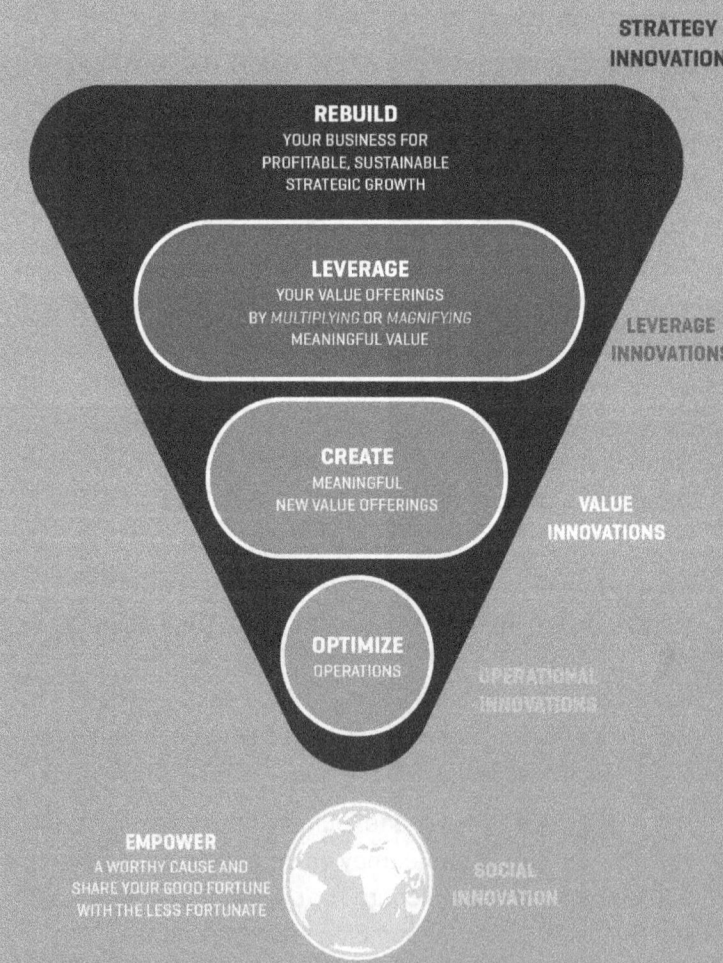

LEVELS TO POSITION MODERN INNOVATIONS

to fix a bugged, bloated process that causes errors, delays and money? Do you want to set up a new process from scratch? Then, do a process innovation project to (re-)design lean, fast, and effective processes for your business.

- **Structure Innovation** looks for ways to restructure your overall operational set-up to become leaner, fitter and faster.

Innovation level 2: CREATE meaningful new value

On the very important second level of innovation, you work hard to CREATE meaningful new value propositions for your existing and target customers that go beyond the value that is already out there in the market. Value innovation can be done by focusing on any of the following areas:

- **Product Innovation:** Designing meaningful innovative products—or significantly improving on features of existing products—is what great Product Innovation (also known as New Product Development) is all about. Sometimes, related products may also become more valuable if you bundle and sell them in an integrated product system (such as Microsoft Office, which offers different work productivity software programs bundled in one integrated suite). X-IDEA is designed to cater to all types of products—fast-moving consumer goods, high-tech goods, food & beverages, or industrial products, just to name a few.
- **Service Innovation:** Many 21st-century economies are driven by businesses in the service sector. Service innovation focuses on improving the services offered by a firm, be it by creating brand-new services or taking the quality of existing services to a whole new level. Moreover, value-adding services may also complement an existing product (e.g., think of repair and check-up services for cars offered by automobile companies) or come as a new stand-alone service (like Virgin Atlantic's airline service innovations).
- **Solution Designs:** Whenever you recognize a wider, unsatisfied customer need or notice a major problem that one of your premium clients faces, you've uncovered an opportunity to surprise them with an innovative solution. Solution Design projects focus on how to turn the problems of your customers into profitable growth opportunities for your business. Examples of tailor-made business solutions were the individualized IT consulting solutions that IBM began offering to companies as the Fifth Wave unfolded, while YouTube (sharing your videos online) and Facebook (connecting to old and new friends) exemplify consumer-focused Internet solutions.
- **Customer Experience Design:** How can you stage memorable, personal, sensory-appealing experiences for your priority customers? How can you create special moments that live on in consumers' minds and make them want to come back to you? Design ideas to boost the experience of those who enjoy your value offerings. You may even go one level higher to the *"experience plus"* level and think about how to make your customers' dreams come true or help them become who they dream to be.

Note that when a company evolves its value propositions and moves from products over services to solutions and, finally, customer experiences, its profit margin typically increases. This is because the number of competitors who can deliver more advanced value offerings decreases, while the value perceptions in the eyes of the customers increase. Having fewer competitors means less pressure to cut prices, and offering more value means customers are willing to pay more. Both lead to a rise in profit margins for the value-providing company. As such, one promising direction for a company to create more value for its customers is to move up to higher levels of the Value Pyramid.

Innovation level 3: LEVERAGE by MULTIPLYING or MAGNIFYING meaningful value

After you have created a meaningful novel value—and only after having done this—you are then able to look for ways to leverage it. Leverage is a neutral servant that works both positively and negatively. It can boost your profits if you have created meaningful new value that improves people's lives and makes the world a better place. On the other hand, it may cause huge damage to your firm's reputation and profits if your value proposition is substandard or poor. Hence, first create meaningful value, then boost your firm's revenues and profitability by leveraging value through value multiplication or value magnification.

LEVERAGE by MULTIPLYING meaningful value

When you multiply meaningful new value propositions, you want to multiply your revenues. In other words, you want to make more money by selling something not only one time but "x"-times or by finding new ways to sell or make money out of a value offering. What modern innovation types allow you to leverage through multiplication?

- **Channel Innovation:** What alternative new channels can we use to bring our products and other value offerings to the market? Channel Innovation projects focus on amplifying your sales by creating new ways to connect your products and services with existing and new buyers.

- **Network, Partner & Platform Innovation:** Multiply your sales by creating new networks, partnerships and delivery pathways that allow you to reach more customers and lock them into a platform. Many consumer-focused and web-based solutions use platforms and the worldwide network of the Internet to multiply meaningful solutions. For example, we may frame an innovation challenge here as follows: How to use virtual and real networks and partners to leverage the value deliverables that we offer to the market (and multiply our revenues and profits)?

- **Business Model Innovation:** *"How else might we get paid for the value deliverables we offer?"* Resolve this challenge in a Business Model Innovation project and journey stage by stage through X-IDEA (or another creative process method you fancy) to generate ideas on how to more creatively monetize your value offerings and thus multiply your revenues.

LEVERAGE by MAGNIFYING meaningful value

When you leverage value through magnification, you want to make more money out of a meaningful new value offering by making it look even more valuable. You magnify value by making a product, service, solution or experience shine even brighter using one of these innovation types:

- **Packaging Design:** A great product becomes even more valuable if it is wrapped in appealing packaging. Packaging Design explores new ways to create unique, sleek, aesthetically beautiful, and sensory-pleasant packaging that enhances the appearance of value of a meaningful product.

- **Promotion & Campaign Design:** A surprising, witty or clever promotion or advertising campaign can add more glamour or intrigue to a great product, service or brand. A promotion & campaign design project aims to create new ideas to amplify buying desire or to inspire people to support a cause or follow through on a desired course of action.
- **Brand & Image Design:** Strong brands enjoy higher margins and *"brand equity"* (as part of their intangible assets). This is because customers are willing to pay a premium for well-branded goods and services. Just think of your favorite luxury brands and the higher prices they can charge for their products. In a brand or image design project, look for ways to enhance the emotional appeal and story of your brand or corporate image to magnify your firm and its products or services.

Innovation level 4: REBUILD your business for profitable, sustainable growth

Thanks to globalization and information technology-driven changes, many businesses are trapped in declining industries and market segments with declining revenues and profits. How can you rebuild your business from scratch? How can you uncover new uncontested market space that allows for sustainable, profitable growth? How to create differentiating value proposition and be able to offer them at lower costs to become a dominant player in this new market field? Through strategy innovation.

- **Strategy Innovation:** In a strategy innovation project, you rebuild a flailing business for sustainable profitable growth in promising new business fields. Thereby, you want to play strong in offense *and* defense:
  - On the one hand, you explore uncontested future market space based on foresight, proactivity, and individualization and then create meaningful and new value propositions (plus new ways to multiply and magnify those).
  - On the other hand, you also aim to use modern technology, network structures, and leaner processes to offer your customers differentiating value at a much lower cost.

As a result, you create new and more profitable revenue streams and, at the same time, lower your cost base to achieve superior profit margins. At the end of a Strategy Innovation Project, you have a strategic road map filled with meaningful strategic actions that will set your business up for sustainable, profitable growth.

Add-on Innovation level: EMPOWER a worthy cause and share good fortune with the less fortunate

Last but not least, you may focus your innovation efforts on worthy social causes that improve the lives of the less fortunate or those who need help.

- **Social Innovation** projects focus on creating new solutions to right a wrong or to prevent the end of something good, or on helping a non-governmental organization (NGO) to resolve a worthy social challenge.

> "If you are not willing to risk the unusual, you will have to settle for the ordinary."
> —JIM ROHN

MODERN INNOVATION TYPOLOGY
How you can innovate today (and what to expect tomorrow)

DO GOOD
- Reduce poverty & livelihood threats
- Raise education levels
- Promote healthy, sustainable growth
- Save the planet

Create solutions to empower the less fortunate, and make the world a better place

SOCIAL INNOVATION

STRATEGY INNOVATION
- New Profitable Revenue Growth & Profit Margin Growth
- Lower Costs Base

Create meaningful strategic actions for prolonged, sustainable growth

LEVERAGE
Make more money from existing value offerings

LEVERAGE INNOVATIONS

Multiply revenues — Channel Innovation | Network Innovation | Business Model Innovation

Raise profit margins — Packaging Design | Promotion & Campaign Design | Brand & Image Design

VALUE INNOVATIONS
Product Innovation | Service Innovation | Solution Design | Customer Experience Design

CREATE
Create meaningful, new value offerings
- Generate new revenue streams and revenue & profit growth
- Increase profit margins

OPERATIONS INNOVATIONS
Process Innovation | Structure Innovation

OPTIMIZE
Enhance & optimize processes
- Increase efficiency
- Reduce costs

2.7. HOW INNOVATION AFFECTS FINANCIAL PERFORMANCE

Does innovation really deliver tangible financial results to the bottom line? Do investments in innovation yield a positive return? Does innovation pay? And if yes, how much?

Tracking the innovation premium

In 2006, Business Week (BW) and Boston Consulting Group (BCG) jointly determined a ranking of the world's 25 most innovative companies. The list was led by Apple, Google, and 3M, and also included Toyota, Microsoft, General Electric, Procter & Gamble, Nokia, Starbucks, IBM, Virgin and Samsung, among others. Then, BW and BCG compared the profit margins and stock prices of these Top 25 innovators to those of the median Standard & Poor's Global 1200 company over a ten-year time horizon.

The Top 25 innovators delivered median profit margin growth of 3.4% a year over the period 1995-2005, compared with 0.4% for the median S&P's Global 1200 company. This striking difference, which BW attributed "in large parts to innovation", also showed when comparing the median annual stock returns of both groups: The Top 25 innovators yielded 14.3% on average over the ten-year time horizon, a full 3% better than the S&P 1200 median. No wonder that BW titled the article *"Creativity Pays. Here's How Much"*.

In a follow-up study in 2009, BCG found a similar result: Innovative companies achieved significantly higher total shareholder return premiums than their less innovative industry peers (with a 4.3% higher 3-year premium and a 2.6% higher ten-year premium). Interestingly, Asia-Pacific innovators enjoyed even higher total shareholder return premiums (17.7% over 3 years and 5.5% over 10 years) than their peers, suggesting that it pays even more to lead innovation in traditionally less innovative environments.

The superior stock performance of top innovators becomes even more evident if we look at one standout example: When Steve Jobs returned to Apple on July 9, 1997, the firm was on the verge of bankruptcy and its stock closed at 0.49 USD (in today's prices after various share splits in between). Ten years later, the share price had soared to 18.62 USD, a multiple of 38 compared to July 1997.

Twenty years later, the price had skyrocketed to 145.06 USD, a multiple of nearly 300. In other words: Had you purchased two Apple shares for one buck on the day of Steve Jobs' return, they would have risen nearly 300 dollars.

So, twenty years of fanatic focus on innovation under Steve Jobs' leadership and legacy have led to tremendous value not only for the end consumers who benefited from a multitude of groundbreaking innovations (such as the iPod, the iPhone and the iPad, among many others), but also led to massive wealth gains for Apple's shareholders.

Investing in design pays, too

Several studies also confirmed it pays for companies to invest in design (see section 2.6, leverage through magnification):

- A 2007 study by the British Design Council found that design-focused firms didn't need to compete on price as much as their peers, that every £100 they invested in design increased turnover by £225, and that their shares outperformed key stock market indices by 200%.
- In a 2014 Harvard Business Review article, Jeneanne Rae introduced the Design Value Index, a new tool to track the financial results of design-centric companies against those that are not. When comparing the stock performance of 15 design-focused companies with the performance at the S&P over a 10-year period, the design-centric firms beat the index by 228%. Unsurprisingly, many top innovators that had already featured in the BCG studies on top innovators also featured on the list of design-centric firms, among them Apple, IBM, Procter & Gamble, Starbucks, Target, Walt Disney, and Nike.

To wrap up, all these study findings suggest that investing in innovation and design pays huge dividends for companies and their shareholders alike.

Why do innovative firms perform better financially?

BCG found out that innovative companies tend to grow faster, have richer product mixes than their peers, expand their offerings into adjacent or new categories (especially if these promise to yield higher margins), and produce more patents than less innovative companies.

Innovative companies also enjoy higher profit margins than their peers because customers are willing to pay higher prices for more innovative products that they perceive to offer more value than vanilla products (as we discussed before in the value pyramid concept).

Innovative companies can charge even higher prices for their more innovative value offering (products, services, solutions and experiences) if they also invest in standout design, which further magnifies the perceived value in the eyes of their customers. Ergo, they enjoy considerably higher operating profit margins — and the best innovators even amplify those further through operational innovations (optimized processes and innovative structures) that allow them to produce superior value at a lower cost base than their peers.

Moreover, innovative products sell faster and more frequently than normal ones, thus boosting revenues even further, especially if the top innovators also multiply revenues through the leverage of innovation types.

Conclusion: Mapping out the financial dynamics and implications of innovation investments

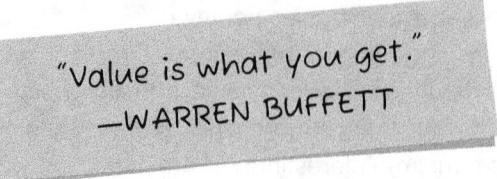

"Value is what you get."
—WARREN BUFFETT

We can sum up the financial implication of investing in innovations as follows (see also chart):

1. Innovative value offerings sell at higher prices and in higher volumes, both of which increase revenues. The higher the value differential, the higher the revenue growth driven by both price and volumes.

2. Firms that magnify the perception of value of their products (and other value offerings) through design can achieve higher prices, which again boosts revenues and increases (operating) profit margins.

3. Likewise, companies who make operational innovations typically can produce their value offerings at lower costs, which also increases profit margins (albeit to a much lower degree).

4. Companies that market a value proposition through innovative channels, networks, platforms, partnerships and business models can multiply their revenues even further.

5. Strong revenue and profit margin growth increase the demand for the stock and its share price and may trigger a positively reinforcing loop. If the innovative company shares part of its superior profits with its investors in the form of dividends, the share price and demand for the stock rise even further. Rising share prices increase the market capitalization of firms and, over time, shift the dynamic from being a potential acquisition target to being a dominant player with ample opportunities for strategic acquisitions.

Let me end with a suggestion to all the conservative laggards and people who hate change: Embrace innovation and invest in innovative firms. It seems to be a safe bet to increase your wealth in the long run.

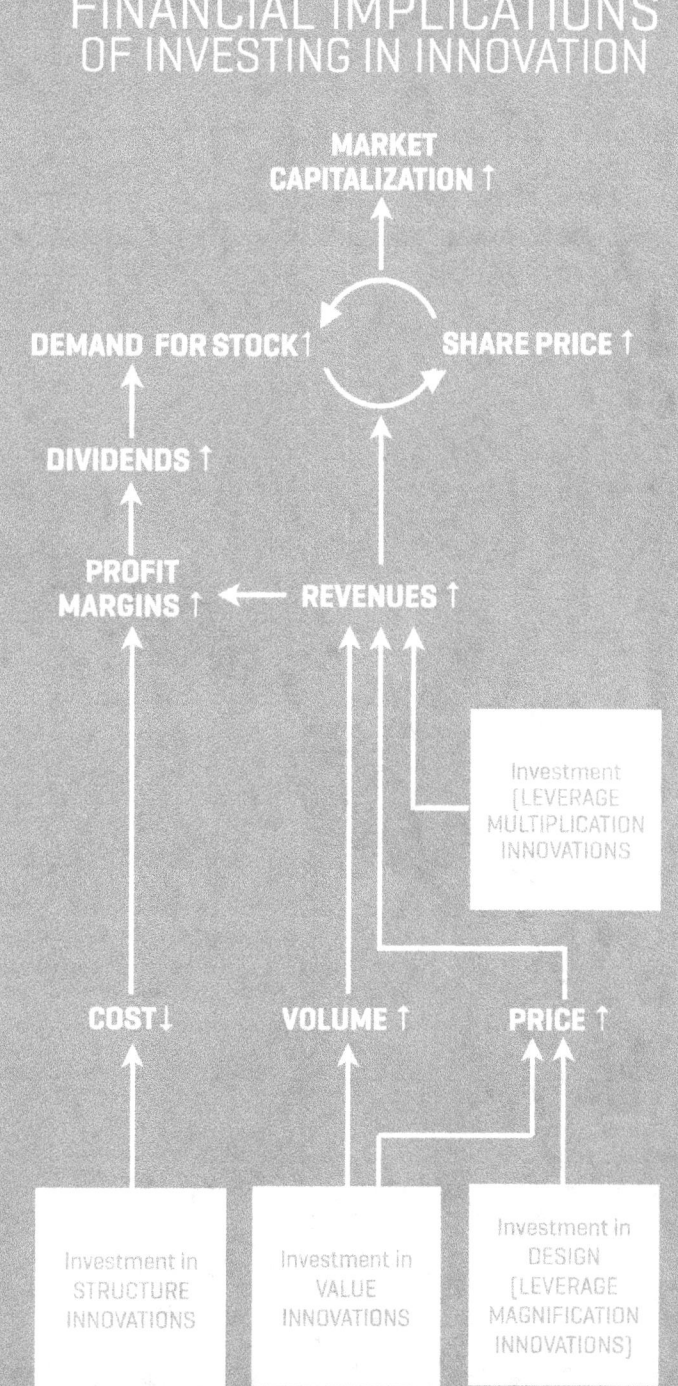

2.8. WHY AND HOW TO PROTECT YOUR INTELLECTUAL PROPERTY

In the previous section, we've just learned that innovation pays, and how much of a premium innovators can enjoy over their less innovative peers. That is, provided they also secure the intellectual property rights of their innovations.

What is Intellectual property?

Intellectual property (IP) was formally recognized in two important treaties at the end of the 19th century: the Paris Convention for the Protection of Industrial Property (1883) and the Berne Convention for the Protection of Literary and Artistic Works (1886).

According to the World Intellectual Property Organization (WIPO, which administers both treaties), Intellectual property alludes to creations of the mind or intellect. Creators can file an application to be assigned exclusive ownership for their creations, which can be inventions or discoveries; artistic works including literature and music; and symbols, names, phrases, designs and images used commercially.

What are the most important types of IP rights?

Like any other property right for tangible goods and assets, IP rights allow creators (IP owners), to benefit from their own creative work and the related upfront investment in time, money and other resources. IP rights include patents, industrial design rights, trademarks (all considered to be forms of *industrial* property) and copyright:

- **Patents** ensure that inventions cannot be commercially made, used, distributed or sold without the patent owner's consent. A patent application can be filed for a product or a process (that provides a new way of doing something or that offers a new technical solution to a problem). In order to be granted the patent, the applicant must demonstrate that the invention is novel, original and useful (= truly creative; see Section 2.1) and that it has an *"inventive step"* that a person with average knowledge of the technical domain cannot deduce.
- **Industrial design rights** protect new and original (but non-functional) ornamental or aesthetic aspects (shapes, patterns, lines, colors) of an industrial product or handicraft from infringements. They are applied to a wide range of products, including technical and medical instruments, watches, jewelry and other luxury items, housewares, electrical appliances, vehicles, architectural structures, textiles and leisure goods, among others.
- **Trademarks** are distinctive signs that signal to customers that certain products or services are produced or provided by a trusted company or individual and not by a counterfeiter. Trademarks may include words, letters and numerals, drawings, symbols and three-dimensional signs, such as the shape and packaging of goods (think of the shape of a Coca-Cola bottle, the logo and the ribbon).
- **Copyright** protects the literary and artistic *"works"* of authors, artists and other creators. Works covered by copyright include novels, poems, plays, reference works, newspapers, advertisements, software, databases, films, musical compositions, choreography, paintings, drawings, photographs, sculpture, architecture, maps, technical drawings, web content, TV and sound recordings, among others.

Other IP rights are geographical indications (such as *"Swiss"* or *"Made in Germany"*) including appellations of origin (e.g., *"Bordeaux"* wine, *"Champagne"*, *"Prosciutto di Parma"*, *"Habana"* cigars) as well as trade secrets (in some jurisdictions only).

Why should innovators secure their IP?

Innovators should secure their intellectual property through appropriate IP rights to have a chance to gain financial compensation for their often substantial upfront investments of time, money and other resources for the creation of novel, original and meaningful IP, and a financial and reputational reward for their outstanding creativity during the creation process. They can monetize their IP either by marketing it directly or by licensing or selling it to others.

IP rights also protect consumers and society at large from criminal counterfeiters and *"cheap"* copycats eager to free-ride on an innovation without investing their own time, money and brain cells.

Moreover, patents in particular expand the total body of technical knowledge and stimulate further creativity and innovation in the world, as patent owners need to publicly disclose information on their inventions in exchange for patent protection.

But how about those creators who want to create intellectual property and then share it openly or make it available to others for free? While it's a noble deed, they run the risk that others will monetize their inventions and creations (and maybe secure the IP rights for themselves) and will not be able to monetize their creativity. If you ask me, the more you can monetize your creations, the more money you have to invest in new creative initiatives, and the more you will be taken seriously by other business players.

The Dark Side of IP

Does investing in securing IP rights mean that you're always protected? Sadly, you may not be able to enforce it for various reasons. Smaller players such as individual creators, entrepreneurs or small- and medium-sized enterprises (SME) may lack the deep pockets and shrewd IP lawyers to fight a lengthy IP infringement lawsuit in court against a big player. Moreover, in developing countries with a corrupt or nationalistic judiciary, even famous multinational corporations (MNC) lost lawsuits against a local counter-party who blatantly violated IP rights. In short, even if you're right and have done everything right, you may not be able to protect an IP right against unfair practices.

How do the different IP rights relate to the innovation typology?

Copyrights and patents typically relate to products or other value offerings (value innovation). In contrast, trademarks and industrial design rights are mostly linked to innovation types that leverage value offerings through magnification, such as brand design and packaging design (leverage innovation). Finally, copyrighted works may either relate to a value innovation (products, solutions) or leverage innovations (e.g., ad campaign designs).

INTELLECTUAL PROPERTY (IP)

Types of IP	Examples	Registration of IP — Unregistered	Registration of IP — Registered	Protection of IP — Duration
Patent	Inventions and products, e.g. machines and machine parts, tools, medicines	Not possible	Registered Patent	Generally 20 years
Industrial design right	Appearance of a product including, shape, packaging, patterns, colors, decoration	Design right	Registered design	Typically 10 or 15 years
Trademark	Product names, logos, jingles	Unregistered Trademark ™	Registered Trademark ®	Ca. 10 years (renewable)
Copyright	Writing and literary works, art, photography, films, TV, music, web content, sound recordings	Unregistered Copyright ©	Registered Copyright ©	50 years after death of creator

"Creative things have to sell to get acknowledged as such."
— STEVE WOZNIAK

CHAPTER 2 — EXECUTIVE SUMMARY: BASIC PRINCIPLES OF INNOVATION

- While definitions of creativity typically emphasize either a person-, process- or product-based perspective, they all tend to emphasize that creativity means novelty, originality and meaning. Here, we define creativity from a product-based view in a simple equation inspired by set theory: CREATIVITY = (NOVEL ∩ MEANINGFUL ∩ ORIGINAL) IDEAS

- "Creativity is..." captures many other facets of creativity beyond its definition.

- The innovation formula encapsulates the dynamic interdependency between creativity and innovation in a simple equation: CREATIVITY + ACTION = INNOVATION. Many companies wrongly focus in their efforts to become more innovative on the right side of the equation, because they fail to notice that innovation always begins with creative ideas.

- Before we act on an idea, we need to ensure that is not only novel and original, but also meaningful. Making meaning means the idea makes the world a better place by improving people's lives, righting a wrong, or preventing the end of something good.

- The value pyramid is a model to position older and newer forms of economic offerings as a hierarchy. The shape and levels of the pyramid show that as value in the perception of customers (and profit margins of companies) increases level by level, the number of players able to create and deliver these value offerings decreases.

- Innovation goes beyond the two classic innovation types of product and process innovation. A myriad of modern innovation types has emerged that allows companies to innovate their operations, value offerings, routes to market, designs, and strategies.

- Studies confirm that investments in innovation and design pay. Companies with innovative products and value propositions can command higher prices, achieve higher revenues and profit margins, and stronger growth, all of which lead to higher stock returns for their shareholders.

- Intellectual Property (IP) rights such as patents, trademarks and copyrights protect the investments of innovators against copycats, thus positively impacting financial returns.

CHAPTER 3

THE INNOVATION RULES
BIG PICTURE (II)

What are the rules to play by —and break— in innovation?

1. The Ten Rules of the Innovation Types Game
2. Innovation Impact Types
3. Innovation Adoption: How Fast Do You embrace Innovation?
4. Ten Ideas About Ideas
5. Open Innovation: The Good, the Bad, and the Ugly
6. Dealing With the Paradoxes of Innovation Management
7. Resolving the Dilemma of Innovation Management
8. In-NO-vation Explained
* Executive Summary

3.1. THE TEN RULES OF THE INNOVATION GAME

When companies pursued innovation in the past, they typically worked on one of two innovation types: product innovation (also called new product development) and process innovation. Over the last two decades, however, a compendium of modern innovation types has emerged that allows companies to play the innovation game in many new ways. But as with any other game, you need to follow a set of rules when playing with innovation types. Below, we'll review the spectrum of modern innovation types, and then learn more about the 10 rules that you need to understand and follow.

> "Learn the rules of the game, then play better than everyone else."
> – ALBERT EINSTEIN

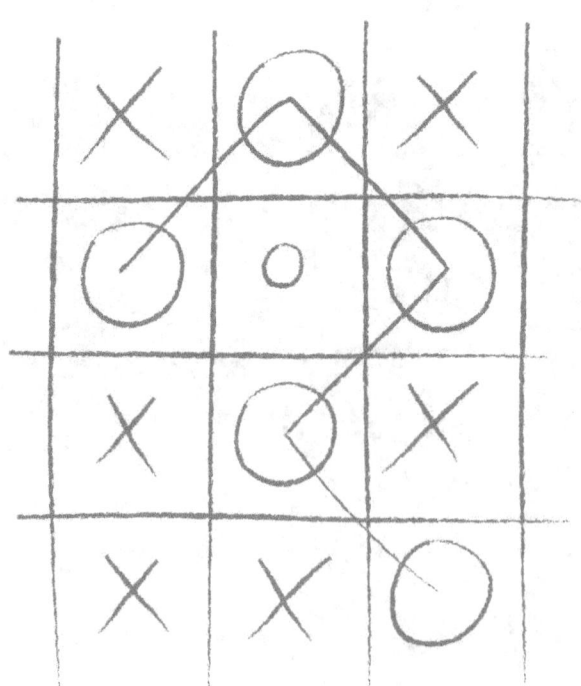

The spectrum of modern innovation types

At Thinkergy, we position modern innovation types on three levels related to operations, value creation, and the leverage of a created value offering:

- **Operation innovations** are located at the entry level. Companies pursue them to enhance and optimize the operations needed to create value propositions. Here we can see two innovation types: process innovation (redesigning operational processes in leaner, more efficient and cheaper ways) and structure innovation (restructuring the units and related assets needed for creating value).

- **Value innovations** aim to create meaningful, novel and original value propositions. The related innovation types encompass product innovation (developing new products in an established or new category), service innovation (new services offered stand-alone or in conjunction with a product), solution design (new solutions that address specific problems of business clients or end-consumers), and customer experience design (crafting an impactful customer journey full of emotional, sensory-pleasing and *"sticky"* moments).

- Finally, **leverage innovations** aim to allow organizations to multiply revenues or magnify profits from their value propositions. Innovation types include channel innovation (delivering value through new channel concepts), network innovation (mushrooming analog and digital networks through delivery partnerships and digital platforms), business model innovation (creating new ways to get paid for a given value), brand design (creating an impactful, emotive brand that attracts a tribe of loyal customers), campaign design (crafting moving, clever and effective campaigns) and packaging design (presenting a value offering in elegant, sensory-pleasing and aesthetics coverings).

Now you have a good overview of modern innovation types, with the exception of strategy innovation and social innovation, which we will cover later. But what about the rules for playing the innovation types game? Read on.

Rule #1: Play to stay in the game.

In the innovation economy, you need to play the innovation game on the pitch to avoid falling behind. Watching the moves of other innovators as a spectator in the stands won't suffice if all major players invest in efforts to innovate. What happens to a company that only settles for milking the cash cows of a once glorious past? Gradual decline and eventual extinction.

Nowadays, depending on the industry you're in, you may fall behind faster than you think possible. Who dominated the photographic film business before the turn of the millennium? Kodak, which missed the transition from analog to digital imaging. Who led the mobile phone market in the mid-nineties to early-noughties? Motorola and Nokia, which were slow to embrace the shift from dumb to smartphones. As Rupert Murdoch said: *"The world is changing very fast. Big will not beat small anymore. It will be the fast beating the slow."* So, get on the pitch and start playing. And if you're already on the pitch, keep playing and enjoy the innovation game.

Rule #2: You won't win with a strong defense only.

The easiest way to innovate is through operation innovations, which is why most corporations do it. Successful process and structure innovation initiatives help save costs, increase efficiencies and improve the bottom line. They add a few pennies to your corporate piggy bank but won't bring you industry-leading profits. Having a strong defense is keeping you in the game longer, but it won't bring you a major trophy.

Rule #3: Create meaningful new value first.

Value innovations such as product and service innovation, as well as solutions and customer experience design, are on the next level. Focus your efforts on creating a novel, original, and meaningful value proposition first. In particular, ensure that a new product, service, solution, or experience truly makes meaning to customers; when it does, it will make you money, too. But when it does not, you end up with a wacky invention such as the Dynasphere (a monowheel electric vehicle from 1932) that may be new and original but fails to impress buyers. As Thomas Edison said: *"Anything that won't sell, I don't want to invent. Its sale is proof of utility, and utility is success."*

Rule #4: Shift the value differential in your favor.

While pursuing value innovation, aim to boost your profit margins by raising the value perception in the eyes of your customers. You can do this through one of two strategies:

- Aim to add significantly more value to an existing value proposition. For example, Dyson has concentrated on product innovation in traditional household goods such as vacuum cleaners, cooling fans and hair dryers. While staying in established product categories, Dyson has pushed the value differential to new levels of usability, aesthetics and performance, enabling the company to command higher prices and enjoy higher margins. Inventor James Dyson puts it simply: *"People buy products if they're better."*

- Climb up the value pyramid to higher levels of value perception by moving from products or services to solutions and customer experiences. For example, car makers are promoting car-sharing solutions to urban consumers who don't want to own a vehicle. Likewise, Starbucks is not just a coffee shop; it has designed an experience that allows guests to hang out in a *"third place"* between home and work where they can relax and connect with like-minded, sophisticated people.

Rule #5: Leverage MEANINGFUL value only

Once you have created a meaningful new value proposition (a new product, service, solution, or experience), you can move to the top level of innovation types and leverage. Why do you need to wait until you know your value differential is good? Leverage is a neutral agent. It boosts your reputation and profits if your value wows your customers, and it can sink your firm if your new value proposition sucks.

In order to leverage a value offering, you can use two different strategies (and related innovation types):

- Leverage through multiplication helps you to sell a meaningful value creation not only a few times but multiple times. This multiple can be dozens, hundreds, thousands, and nowadays, thanks to the Internet, even millions of times. Innovation types that leverage through multiplication are channel innovation (using various physical and virtual distribution channels to deliver your value to the market), network innovation (multiplying through strategic partnerships, physical and virtual networks, and —in recent years— digital platforms), and business model innovation (multiplying revenues through new ways to get paid for your value).

- The second way to leverage a meaningful value proposition that you created is through magnification. Thereby, you make your product appear more valuable in the eyes of your customers through designing a strong brand, cool campaigns, or sensual packaging. If you successfully magnify the value perception, you entice customers to pay more for your product and thus increase your profit margin.

Rule #6: Strategy innovation: Redraw the business on all levels

Proactive corporations —or those with their backs up against the wall— may chose to pursue a strategy innovation project at least once every decade. Strategy innovation aims to both create and leverage meaningful new value propositions that are also produced in more cost-effective ways. Ideally done in an uncontested and/or newly emerging market space, strategy innovation can lead to sustainable revenue growth and profit margin growth at a lower cost base because it runs through all three innovation type levels (operations, value creation, value leverage).

For example, Cirque du Soleil reinvented the circus by dropping all those elements that were perceived as antiquated (animals, clowns, etc.) and keeping and amplifying the artistic and aesthetic elements to deliver artistic, sensational show experiences under a circus tent. Compared to a traditional circus, Cirque du Soleil has enjoyed higher profit margins because it created a memorable customer experience magnified through a globally acknowledged brand and delivered at reduced cost.

Rule #7: Top innovation leaders play on the full spectrum of innovation types

Many companies that lead innovation in their industry have gradually built their dominance by starting with one innovation type and then adding more and more over time until they virtually play on the full spectrum on all levels.

For example, after Steve Jobs returned as CEO in 1997, Apple created not only super strong products including some game-changing new devices (iPhone, iPad) that launched new categories (smartphones and tablets), but also established repair and training services, opened experiential flagship stores, and hosted cult-like product launch events and developer conferences. Apple also

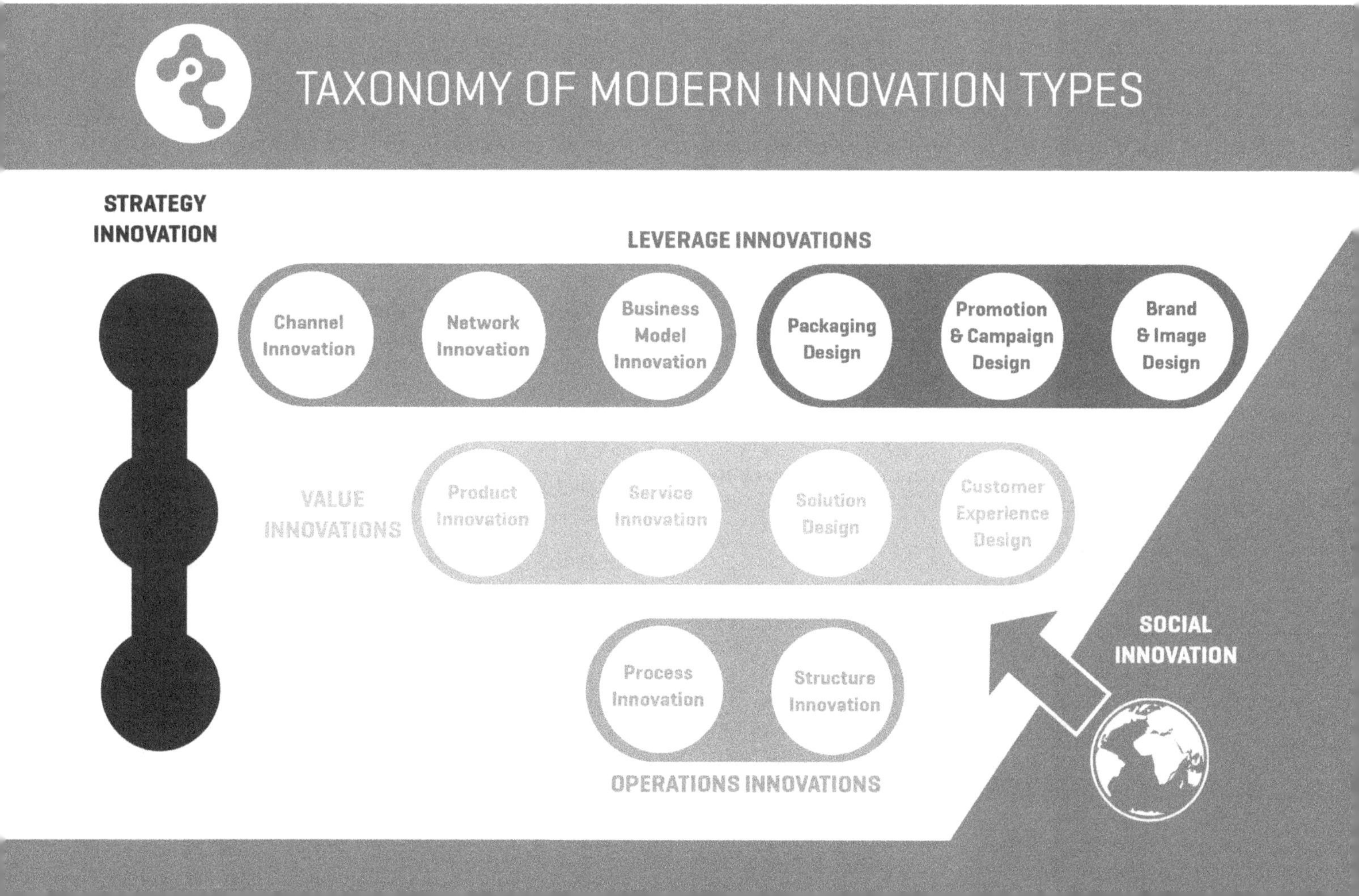

TAXONOMY OF MODERN INNOVATION TYPES

STRATEGY INNOVATION

LEVERAGE INNOVATIONS

- Channel Innovation
- Network Innovation
- Business Model Innovation
- Packaging Design
- Promotion & Campaign Design
- Brand & Image Design

VALUE INNOVATIONS

- Product Innovation
- Service Innovation
- Solution Design
- Customer Experience Design

OPERATIONS INNOVATIONS

- Process Innovation
- Structure Innovation

SOCIAL INNOVATION

created new channels and platforms (iTunes, App Store) to multiply its revenues, and is also a design-driven company with eclectic brands, sleek packaging and trendy campaigns and events.

Rule #8: Focus on innovation types that are largely ignored by your industry

Most players in an industry focus their innovation efforts on the same range of *"traditional"* innovation types. One easy way to stand out is to identify what types are deemphasized or completely ignored by an industry and then think about how to innovate using those orphaned innovation types.

For example, Nestlé started to sell its Nespresso coffee machines and capsules in luxury shopping malls, which was a channel innovation in an industry used to selling coffee in supermarkets or coffee shops. Likewise, Tesla Motors and Space X achieved prominent positions in electric cars and space transportation because of Elon Musk's insistence on developing all required components in-house (a structure innovation that allows them to be significantly faster and much cheaper than their peers in the respective industries who have outsourced the production of major components to external suppliers).

Rule #9: Connect the dots between a few innovation types on different levels

Newcomers to an industry can create new value for customers —and shell-shock the incumbents— by combining a focused selection of innovation types on all three levels (operations, value creation, leverage).

For example, Airbnb has created a digital solution to connect people in need of affordable accommodation with people who can supply affordable lodging. This new solution may even allow guests to experience a city or place like a local and make a personal connection with the hosts.

Likewise, Uber created a meaningful new solution to connect consumers who need car transportation with drivers eager to earn income with their personal car. Uber has also brought transportation services to users living in remote areas with no or low taxi penetration.

Both Airbnb and Uber facilitate the match between the demand and supply side via their mobile apps and their website. These digital platforms are network innovations that allow firms to easily leverage their matching solutions and quickly multiply them in different cities and countries. Best of all, unlike their competitors, neither Airbnb nor Uber need to commit any physical assets themselves. Nowadays, Airbnb is considered the largest accommodation company in the world without owning any hotel rooms, while Uber is the biggest taxi company without owning any cars. Both companies have integrated this structure innovation into their business set-up.

Rule #10: Innovate for the less fortunate or needy through social innovation

Last but not least, social innovation aims to empower the less fortunate and make the world a better place. But how can you actually innovate here? First, consider a particular social issue and then pick the innovation type that best suits your challenge.

For example, micro-financing is a social service innovation of Grameen Bank to reduce poverty in Bangladesh by providing micro-loans to poor mothers only. In contrast, Greenpeace rights environmental wrongs by creating whopping action campaigns with local, regional or even global impact (social campaign design).

3.2. INNOVATION IMPACT TYPES

What innovation types do you know? When confronted with this question, most businesspeople think of product innovation, process innovation, service innovation, customer experience design, strategy innovation, and so on. Thereby, we use the kind of value offering that an innovation targets as criteria to classify different categories of innovation types.

So far, so good. But are you aware that there is another way to think about innovation types? Another viewpoint that focuses more on the ends than on the means? Here, let me introduce this *impact*-related view on innovation types to you — and more importantly, explain what this more recent perspective on innovation types means for your businesses.

Draw the Innovation Type-Impact Matrix

In his book *Change by Design*, Tim Brown suggests classifying innovations using a 2x2 matrix based on their impact and the degree of change that they cause. The horizontal axis of the matrix focuses on users (or customers), with *"Existing users"* on the left and *"New users"* on the right, while the vertical axis looks at the degree of new value offered, with *"New value"* adjacent to the upper cell and *"Improvement of an already existing value"* next to the lower cell. The result is the following matrix with four quadrants:

- The bottom left quadrant contains innovations that target existing users with variations or feature changes of existing value offerings. An example of such incremental improvements is a new vanilla-flavored coffee drink offered in the Ready To Drink-coffee category.

- The bottom right quadrant captures evolutionary innovations that allow a firm to extend existing value propositions by adapting them to the needs of a new user group. For example, a few years ago, when an FMCG firm in the hair care category wanted to reach out to the less affluent consumers in Southeast Asia, it started to offer its shampoo in small sachets (rather than plastic bottles) that sold at a low price and neatly fitted into the cramped space of the archetypical Asian mom-and-pop store.

- Evolutionary innovations can also be found in the top left. In this case, however, the evolutionary innovation enables a firm to extend its relationship with existing users by offering them a new value proposition that often ties into another value offering that the customer already uses. For example, Google's Gmail extended its lead in search engines by offering e-mail services for small businesses with personalized address options.

- Finally, the top right quadrant will contain innovations that offer a new value proposition to new users. These revolutionary innovations are game-changers that create new categories or radically new value propositions. Amazon.com offered radically new solutions to conveniently buy books that revolutionized the traditional book sales channel; and Apple's iPad is a wonderful example of a game-changing product — it created a new category of devices and enabled senior citizens (such as my Mom) to finally appreciate the computer age.

Linking the Innovation Type-Impact Matrix to your Innovation Pipeline

Approaching innovation types by considering their impact and the degree of change that they cause is an important perspective for every firm when looking at their historic innovation achievements, and more importantly, at their current and desired future innovation pipeline:

- When you take a close-up look at the innovation track record of many firms, then the vast majority of examples cited as innovation success represent incremental improvements of already existing value propositions that are marketed to the firm's existing user or customer base. While it is normal to have a healthy base of incremental improvements in your innovation pipeline, realize that they don't drastically alter the value differential in either the customer's or your favor and tend to cannibalize the revenues of your existing value offerings.

- In contrast, adding a significant number of evolutionary innovations to your innovation pipeline allows you to markedly boost your revenues—but only in the short- to medium-run, as these innovations are often relatively easy for your competitors to copy.

- There's no doubt about it: It's really the revolutionary innovations that change the game in your favor, set you apart from your peers, and enable you to achieve significant volume and margin growth in the medium- to long-run, as it will take competitors significant time, costs, and effort to catch up with your big idea.

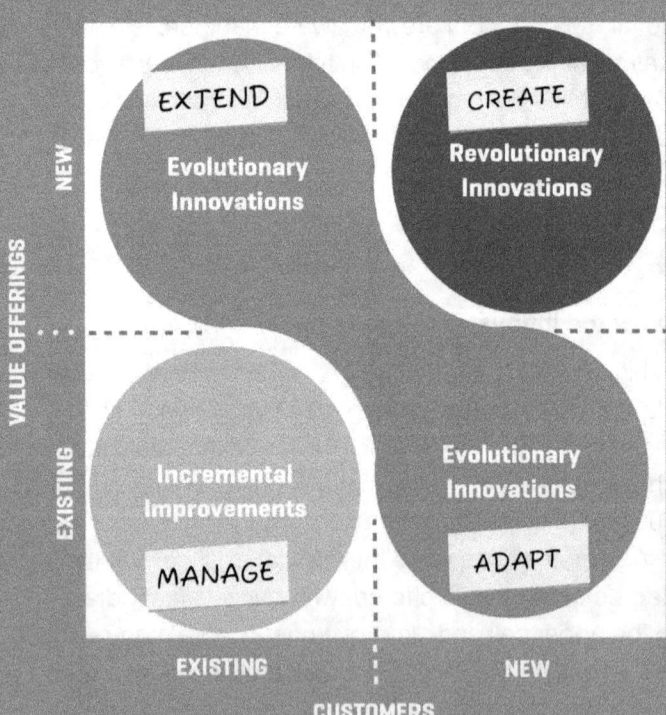

Source: Adapted from Brown, T. (2009). Change by Design. New York, HarperCollins, 6.

What do these insights mean for you and the innovation direction of your organization?

Contemplate these questions:

1. Look at your firm's historic innovation achievements over the past 3-5 years and the degree of change each of these caused. What quadrant does each of your past innovation results fall into? What is the proportional mix for each of the four quadrants? In percentage terms, how many of your innovations are incremental improvements, evolutionary innovations, and revolutionary innovations?

2. What do you want the proportional mix of your innovation pipeline to look like in 2-3 years from now? Why?

3. What do you plan to do differently to get where you want to be in the future? What can you do today to get started?

Acting on the Innovation Type-Impact Matrix

When a prospective client is interested in booking an X-IDEA Innovation Project with Thinkergy, we usually expose them to the Innovation Type-Impact Matrix and query: *"How much innovation do you want to produce with your project? What degree of change do you target?"*

We ask these questions to make the project sponsor realize an important aspect: In innovation, as in many other areas of life, there is a close connection between what you put into a project and what you get from it. As a rule of thumb, we observed the following relationships between input and output to be true for innovation projects:

- The more important an innovation project and the more evolutionary or even revolutionary the desired innovation results, the more generous the overall resource commitment to the project should be.

- First of all, it takes time to move beyond incremental improvements of the existing offerings and to produce evolutionary and particularly revolutionary innovation results.

- Secondly, you need to have the right number (at least 16-20) and composition of people (ideally a diverse mix of business functions or divisions across different hierarchy levels).

- Finally, you need to have a sufficient monetary budget for renting a spacious venue and hiring a quality innovation firm to guide you through the project towards evolutionary and revolutionary results.

A popular truism in the world of IT is: *"Garbage In, Garbage Out."* (GIGO) Realize that this maxim applies to your next innovation project, too: What you put in is what you get.

> *"Genius is in the idea. Impact, however, comes from action."*
> —SIMON SINEK

3.3. INNOVATION ADOPTION: HOW FAST DO YOU EMBRACE AN INNOVATION?

In Chapter 1, I discussed why the world hates change and shared with you how many people dislike change: 84 percent. How do I arrive at this number? It relates to findings on how fast different segments of an overall population adopt an innovation over time.

Diffusion of innovations theory

The American communication studies professor Everett Rogers synthesized the findings of more than 500 studies on how new idea spreads through a population in his famous diffusion of innovation theory. The word diffuse means *"spread or cause to spread over a wide area or a large number of people,"* and the diffusion of innovation theory explains how, why, and at what rate new ideas and technology spread.

Innovation adoption curve

The innovation adoption curve (see chart on next page) describes how different population segments adopt a new innovation over time. The orange line (bell curve) shows how successive groups of users or customers adopt the innovation over time, while the S-shaped blue curve illustrates its market share over time.

How do different adopter segments respond to change?

In a famous research study that led to the theory on the diffusion of innovation, Everett Rogers investigated the degree and speed of adoption of an innovation by the overall population. Rogers' findings can be visualized as a bell-shaped curve with the vertical axis showing how many new people adopt a new innovation as time, on the horizontal axis, progresses. Rogers distinguished the following five groups of people:

- Innovators are at the forefront of change. They are comfortable taking risks and are often the first to adopt emerging technologies and then develop them into new products, services, and solutions. All innovation depends on this 2.5% of the overall population who create change.

- New innovations are then picked up by the so-called early adopters. Representing 13.5% of the overall population, they are the next to understand a superior value proposition of a meaningful innovation or new technology. Consequently, they play a pivotal role in convincing other people to try new things. Early adopters are either technology enthusiasts who approve of and endorse the technological features of the innovation or enchanting, well-connected evangelists who spread the word about the idea. In his book *The Tipping Point*, Malcolm Gladwell calls these two sub-groups mavens and super-connectors, respectively.

In his book of the same title, marketer Geoffrey A. Moore asserts that only once a disruptive innovation is able to build enough momentum to *Crossing the Chasm* between early adopters and the pragmatic early majority will it become a major success, leading to an initially exponential rise in sales and boost in profits.

- The first large adoption segment comes next: The early majority (34% of people) are those who try out a new innovation based on the positive experiences and recommendations of the early adopters.

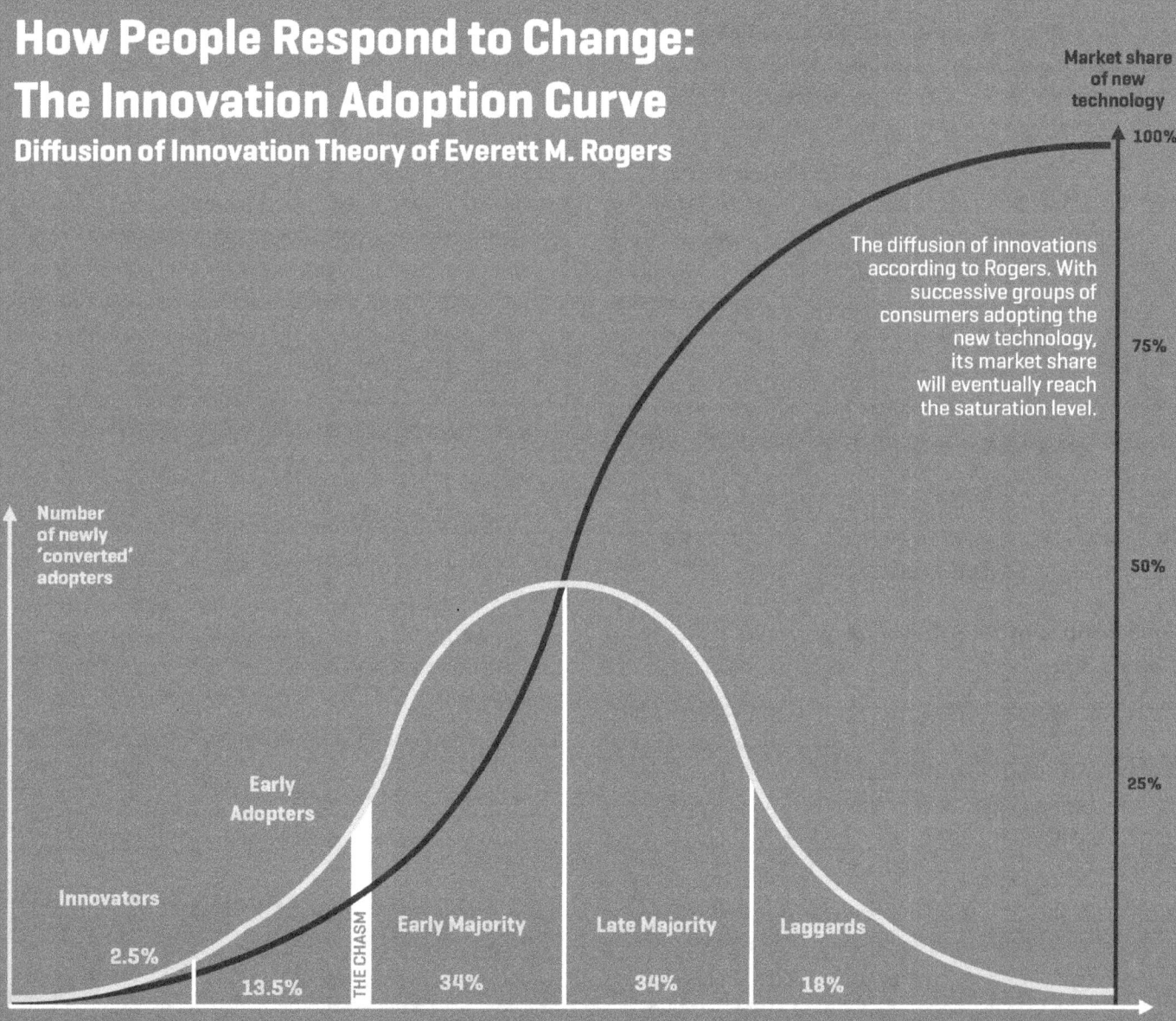

- The positive experiences of the early majority motivate the more skeptical and change-resistant late majority (likewise making up 34% of the overall population) to also adopt the innovation.
- At last, the laggards account for the remaining 16%. Many months or even years after the initial launch of a disruptive innovation, the naysayers and skeptics are finally convinced to join the bandwagon. However, by then, the innovators and early adopters have already moved on and created and propagated the next big thing.

If we sum up the different segments, we can conclude that 16% of people drive change (innovators and early adopters), while 84% of people (early and late majority, laggards) oppose change with varying intensities of resistance. So, what does this mean for us if we want to participate in the innovation game?

Implications of the diffusion of innovations theory for innovators

- If you're an innovator —or support innovation as an early adopter—, you need to be courageous. Do you have the guts to take it up with 84% of other people to push an innovation into the early majority and make it a success?
- As an innovator eager to diffuse an innovation into the majority, make an effort to first identify who are the mavens and super-connectors for this particular innovation that typically form the early adopters. In his book *The Tipping Point*, Malcolm Gladwell classified such early adopters who carry a new innovation into the early majority into three sub-groups: *"connectors,"* representing hubs in a social network, information brokers (*"mavens"*), and *"salesmen"* who are masters at spreading the word. (In Chapter 5, when we discuss the people side of innovation, you will get to know two cognitive profiles that fulfill a similar function as Gladwell's early adopter sub-groups).
- As an innovator, also consider strategies to incentivize and motivate the early adopters to help you carry your innovation over the chasm into the early majority. How? For example, you may provide early adopters (especially the mavens) with free versions that allow them to test your product; you could pay some of the super-connectors to be your evangelist in some form; or you could give early adopters special pricing as they take more risks than the subsequently following adopter groups, and also do the work of endorsing and promoting the innovation to others.

Once you succeed in carrying an innovation into the early majority, get ready for explosive growth. One possible danger here is that sales grow so fast that the organization cannot keep up with fulfilling orders in a timely way or encounters quality issues regarding both products (ensuring consistent quality as volumes increase) and/or operations.

> *"Diffusion is essentially a social process through which people talking to people spread an innovation."*
> —EVERETT ROGERS

3.4. TEN IDEAS ABOUT IDEAS

"We are entering the era of Ideanomics," said former Chairman of the US Federal Reserve Alan Greenspan at the beginning of the new Millennium, indicating the central importance of ideas in the innovation economy. So, what do you know about ideas? Here are ten ideas about ideas to help expand your knowledge on *"the currency of the 21st century."*

1. Ideas are the starting point of innovation.

Ideas are the driving force behind the development of mankind. They kick-start innovation. This finds its reflection in the definition of the term innovation by long-term innovation leader 3M as *"new ideas —plus action or implementation— which results in an improvement, a gain or a profit."* As such, you may have the best innovation management system in place in your firm, but if you and your team think you're not creative and cannot generate interesting ideas, you will not have tangible innovation results. So, remember the words of the French cleric Ernest Dimnet: *"Ideas are the root of creation."*

2. Ideas are intangible.

The Irish dramatist George Bernard Shaw helps us to understand another important aspect of ideas: *"If you have an apple and I have an apple and we exchange apples then you and I will still each have one apple. But if you have an idea and I have an idea and we exchange these ideas, then each of us will have two ideas."* While apples are tangible, ideas are intangible. Because of their intangible nature, more than one person can use an idea. For a creator, this is both good news and bad news.

The good news is that it allows us to collaborate with others during ideation and brainstorming exercises; one person might have an idea, and others can build on it or refine and improve on it. The bad news is that the intangible and exchangeable character of an idea makes it easy for people to steal a good idea and use it for their own benefit without compensating the creator. As an innovator or an innovative company, make sure to protect your idea by registering your Intellectual Property. Then, trust or hope that you can legally enforce your ownership rights in court in case of IP violations (as we discussed earlier in section 2.8).

3. Ideas are transient.

Here is a question for you: If you order a pizza from a delivery service, do you immediately start eating the pizza when it arrives? Or do you wait for minutes, hours, or days until the pizza is cold, rancid, and stale? Learn a lesson from this metaphor on how to treat your ideas: Eat the pizza while it's hot. Write down a good idea the moment you think of it.

Ideas vanish from our minds if we don't write them down immediately. Thus, make it a habit to jot down ideas right away in a notebook, on a napkin or any piece of paper. Or, if you are geekier, speak your idea out loud while recording it on your mobile phone. Remember that you can deal with an idea at a later stage, but you must note it down as soon as possible.

4. Ideas need to have an action element.

An idea can be defined as *"a thought or suggestion about a possible course of action."* Do you still remember 3M's definition of innovation from the beginning of this section? In short, it's novel, original and meaningful ideas

+ action = innovation (our innovation formula from section 2.3). Here, note that an idea sentence must have an action element to enable you to take action and arrive at innovation. So linguistically speaking, if you write down an idea, your idea sentence needs to contain a verb. An idea sentence consists of at least one verb and one noun (or adjective). For example, *"Advertise in the New York Times"* is an idea, but *"New York Times"* is not.

5. Ideas come to us as visuals.

Think of the moment when you receive or hear an idea. Does the idea come to your mind in the form of a written sentence that you cognitively see in front of your mind and then read out? Or is it more that you see the idea as an image or activated short movie in front of your eyes? Or even both? Chances are that ideas come to you as visuals, particularly if you are naturally more of a visual thinker. In addition to verbally expressing your idea in an idea sentence as described above, consider adding visual explanations and context to your idea with a simple sketch or a quick-and-dirty drawing. If you communicate your idea both verbally and visually, it is easier for others to understand your idea and its value, and you will notice that people are more attracted to an idea that contains a visual element.

6. Ideas need both soloists and team players to succeed.

An idea always comes out of an individual brain. However, nowadays it typically takes more than an individual creator to turn a great new idea into a breakthrough innovation that will shake the world. Having the original idea is only the beginning of the story. Then, many brains and hands need to put in a lot of effort and time to develop, enhance, pitch, and activate the original idea to make it an innovation success.

While innovation starts with an individual moment of ingenuity, it is followed by many hours of intense collaborative work. In innovation, as in sports, you both need an ingenious individualist and strong, hard-working team players to win the big trophies.

7. Powerful ideas cannot be unthought and stopped.

The moment a big idea has been thought, expressed and publicly shared with others it cannot be unthought again. Once a big idea is out in the public domain and people understand its value, no one will be able permanently to suppress it even with great force or violence. *"You cannot put a rope around the neck of an idea: you cannot put an idea up against a barracks-square wall and riddle it with bullets: you cannot confine it in the strongest prison cell that your slaves could ever build,"* noted the Irish playwright Sean O'Casey in this context.

Throughout history, many dictators or reigning institutions have learned the lesson that all their intense efforts to suppress and kill a *"dangerous"* big idea ultimately failed, whether the idea was *"The Earth is not in the center of the universe"* or titled *"Democracy."* As the French writer Victor Hugo rightly remarked: *"There is nothing more powerful than an idea whose time has come."*

8. The bigger the idea, the harsher the response by the establishment.

"A person with a new idea is a crank until the idea succeeds," remarked Mark Twain. Every bold, big idea has never been done before, and because of this, the establishment welcomes it with sharp criticism and ridicule. *"Every really new idea looks crazy at first,"* noted the British mathematician Alfred North Whitehead, and Oracle Co-Founder Larry Ellison similarly noted: *"When people start telling you that you're crazy, you just might*

be on to the most important innovation in your life." As Nelson Mandela reminds us: *"It always seems impossible until it's done."*

So, avoid labeling prematurely new ideas as crazy, impossible or total nonsense, and instead approach them with curiosity and an open beginner's mind. *"Big ideas are so hard to recognize, so fragile, so easy to kill. Don't forget that, all of you who don't have them,"* cautions John Elliot, Jr., the former Chairman of the ad agency Ogilvy and Mather.

9. Have many ideas to have a good one.

The US American psychologist P. Guilford crystallized years of research into individual creativity into the following insight: *"The person who is capable of producing a large number of ideas per unit of time, other things being equal, has a greater chance of having significant ideas."*

What's true for playing the lottery holds equally true for ideation — statistically, the odds of hitting the jackpot rise with the number of tickets you hold in your hand.

10. Ideas follow a life cycle.

Have you ever noticed that just like human beings, ideas have a life cycle? Let's go through the life phases of an idea. Somebody thinks *"Bingo!"* and a new idea is born. In its first moments, the idea needs to be acknowledged (e.g., by writing it down and giving it a name), nurtured and well protected from the attacks of critics by its creator. Once the idea has survived its critical *"baby days,"* it develops. Over time, more and more people understand and appreciate the great value that the idea adds and fall in love with it. The idea matures further until the point where it reaches the peak of its fame and appreciation. Then, slowly but steadily, the idea starts to decline in importance and appreciation until the day when it finally dies—and a fresh idea takes its place.

Let's look at an example. Twenty years ago, the Sony Walkman was a fantastic product that symbolized a whole product category and significantly improved the quality of leisure life of many people.

Back to today. Do you see many people walking around with their Sony Walkman these days? The Sony Walkman died a few years ago, and a new, much better product has taken its place. The Sony Walkman's successor was Apple's iPod, which had a market share of roughly 70% of digital music players before it became part of the iPhone.

What are the chances that 20 years from now, you will still listen to music on the iPhone? That's how the life cycle of ideas works in practice—not only for products but also for industries, lead technologies, or scientific models and theories.

What can we learn from this story? For one, don't get overly attached to a great idea — it makes it easier to fall out of love with it again once a better fresh idea arrives. For two, innovation never stops. Once you have brought up one idea to the stage that it is loved, immediately start working on your next big idea to stay ahead in the innovation game.

> *"Daring ideas are like chessmen moved forward; they may be beaten, but they may start a winning game."*
> —JOHANN WOLFGANG VONG GOETHE

3.5. OPEN INNOVATION: THE GOOD, THE BAD, AND THE UGLY

While attending the International Society of Professional Innovation Management (ISPIM) Innovation Conference in Budapest in 2015, I noticed that open innovation was the hottest topic that was repeatedly featured in panel talks and academic papers. While listening to the various presentations and debates, it suddenly dawned upon me why I have always felt lukewarm about this innovation approach: Open innovation has a good, a bad and a truly ugly side that is a well-kept secret.

What is open innovation?

In a nutshell, open innovation is a collaborative approach to innovation where internal ideas are supported by external ideas from outside innovation partners: scientists and research labs, consultants and think tanks, students and academics, or anyone else who takes a liking to a particular innovation challenge.

Henry Chesbrough, a professor who popularized open innovation roughly a decade ago in a best-selling book of the same name, summarizes the concept as follows: *"Open innovation means that valuable ideas can come from inside or outside the company and can go to market from inside or outside the company as well."*

How does open innovation work?

One of the more common and popular ways to practice open innovation works as follows: An organization poses an open innovation challenge via the Internet to the general public. Quite often, this is done in the form of an open innovation contest or competition. Moreover, the organization hosting the innovation challenge may engage the services of an open innovation service or platform provider to facilitate the process (e.g., by appropriately framing an open innovation challenge or administering the online idea submission system) and to connect the organization to external innovation resources (thanks to possessing a *"way of right"* to a network of open innovation partners).

Then, the external collaborators work out and submit their solutions to the innovation challenge to the organization either directly or indirectly via the open innovation intermediary. Finally, the organization reviews all idea submissions and selects and rewards the winning entries before implementing these top ideas.

What's good about open innovation?

Nowadays, more and more large corporations rely on open innovation as an important pillar of their overall innovation strategy for a good reason: It is a comparatively cheap way to reach out to external collaborators and to widen their overall idea pool. In particular, open innovation offers organizations a promising way to break out of the narrow tunnel of expertise and conventional thinking in which most internal ideas typically reside, and to tap into a wider external idea pool that tends to include more unusual, interesting and even *"wild"* ideas that uninhibited outsiders are more prone to come up with.

What's bad about open innovation?

FFor one, open innovation lacks intimate human interaction, fun, and energy because it largely relies on a technology-driven and technocratically managed process. While this approach may well suit the more introverted and geeky thinkers (such as scientists, engineers, technicians, and inventors), open innovation tends to quickly lose its appeal to all those creative types (think of designers, entrepreneurs, marketers, influencers, or architects) whose personality is more outgoing, interpersonal and human-centered.

Second, the technocratic (i.e., theory- and systems-driven) nature of open innovation works well for scientific and technological innovation challenges. However, it seems to be less of a fit when an organization wants to pursue human-centered and consumer-focused innovation projects, where it's important to empathize with consumers and uncover unmet—and maybe even unnoticed—consumer wants and needs.

Third, internal innovation resources typically have to implement a winning solution of an external open innovation partner — and they may not always wholeheartedly believe in and support the idea. Idea implementation is hard work. It is often a long, arduous journey full of obstacles and tough tests and trials to master. Who is more likely to work harder to realize the full potential of a meaningful idea — an internal activation team that is deeply passionate about an idea that its members helped to create? Or an internal team that is mandated by management to implement an idea from an external contributor?

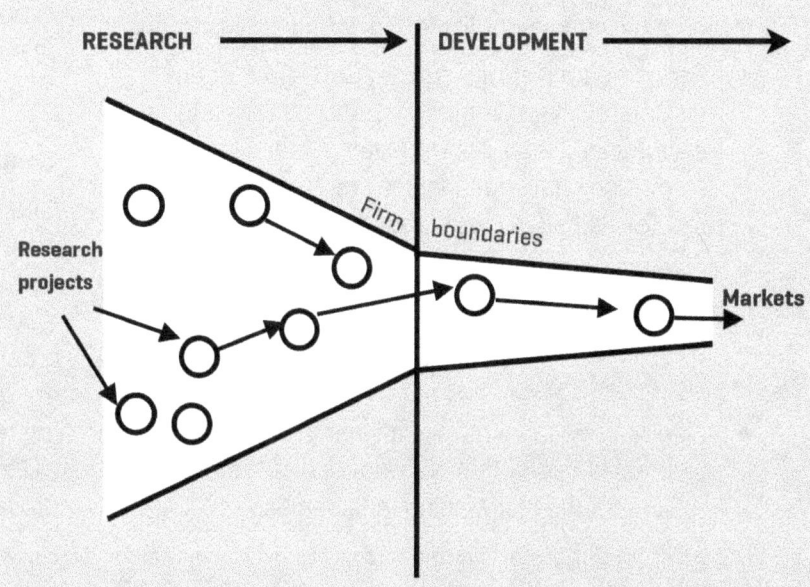

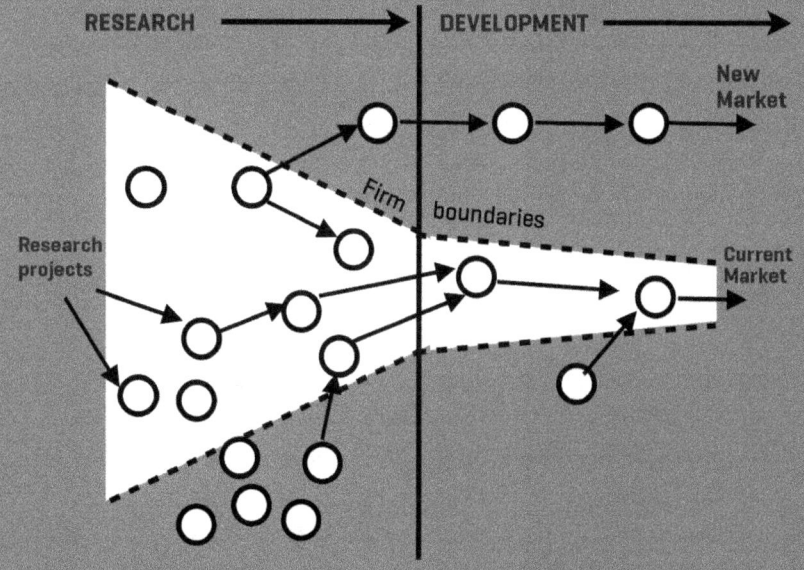

Source: Chesbrough (2003)

What's the ugly, well-kept secret of open innovation?

Open innovation seems like a win-win-win proposition:

- For comparatively little money and effort, open innovation allows large corporations to win big by insourcing a large pool of external ideas for an innovation challenge that they have put forth, and to then exploit all of these ideas for their profit.
- Open innovation intermediaries (service or platform providers) also benefit from the practice by generating profitable fee income that increases their firm's valuation.
- Finally, open innovation is a small win for one or a few external idea contributors who receive a monetary reward for the few winning idea entries.

So, given that there are winners abound, who are the losers? All those many, many, many contributors who submit non-winning entries for an open innovation challenge and never get fairly compensated for their solution development efforts. Open innovation seems to knowingly play on a survivorship bias: i.e., concentrating on those people who *"survived"* the process while keeping silent on those who did not because of their lack of visibility. For example, in the case of an open innovation contest with 50 idea submissions, there are typically one to three winning *"survivors"* and 47 to 49 idea contributors who worked on and submitted ideas for the innovation challenge without getting compensated for their efforts.

Ask yourself: Would you want to spend 1-2 days of your precious time to work on an innovation challenge when your odds of winning were somewhere in the range of 1 in 50? Would you accept this gamble if you have a family to feed, a mortgage to pay, and other alternatives to earn money with much better odds of winning? And if you had accepted the open innovation gamble several times without winning, how long would you continue spending time on open innovation challenges before you eventually quit?

Conclusion

Open innovation is a viable channel for corporations to source external ideas for their innovation challenges and seems to be particularly suited for resolving tough technical or scientific challenges. Idea-seeking organizations can cheaply insource meaningful, profit-margin-boosting solutions while sharing only a tiny fraction of the upside of a winning idea entry with one or a few *"survivors"* of the open innovation selection process.

However, unless its ugly side is addressed and collaborators with "non-winning" idea entries also get adequate compensation for their work efforts, open innovation is likely to run out of steam as a popular management fad that busied managers and made a few consultants and service providers rich.

Well, this is my take on the topic of open innovation. As this is probably an extreme view, I suggest you read Henry Chesbrough's book or articles (see reference list) to form your own opinion on open innovation and evaluate whether it may be a promising road to innovation for your organization.

> *"Open innovation is a paradigm that assumes that firms can and should use external ideas as well as internal ideas, and internal and external paths to market, as the firms look to advance their technology."*
> —HENRY CHESBROUGH

3.6. DEALING WITH THE PARADOXES OF INNOVATION MANAGEMENT

"Actions are always more complex and nuanced than they seem. We have to be willing to wrestle with paradox in pursuing understanding," said the British journalist Harold Evans. If you are a creative business leader or a wanna-be innovator, you better get ready to wrestle.

What is a paradox?

A paradox can be defined as a statement or proposition that seems self-contradictory or absurd but in reality expresses a possible truth (e.g., *"Only one thing is certain—that is, nothing is certain"*) or as a counterintuitive conclusion or outcome (e.g., *"It is an interesting paradox that wherever you are and whatever you do, you think of being somewhere else doing something else"*). The second definition is particularly relevant for creativity and innovation, where we find many counterintuitive situations and phenomena.

Many people strongly dislike paradoxes. This holds particularly true for managers, who love clear recipes and a structured process for every business situation they can possibly encounter. Unfortunately, the business landscape of the early 21st century as well as the world of innovation is not framed in the simple 1-or-0-binary code of the Information Age.

In the Innovation Economy, we are confronted with a myriad of paradoxes, which are difficult to deal with if one prefers clear yes-or-no answers like most managers do. Here are twelve examples of paradoxes in business creativity and innovation that you have to be aware of as a creative leader.

1. The paradox of incubation.

To get a breakthrough idea for a tough problem, you need to first deeply immerse yourself in the case and then dare to completely let go of the problem. This counterintuitive practice increases the chances of activating the process of incubation; when you least expect it, the breakthrough solution suddenly pops up.

2. The paradox of failure.

Plan to fail to succeed sooner in an innovation project. Evolution is based on trial and error and the principle of negative feedback, as is creation. Find a way to encourage your employees to show initiative and plan to fail while at the same time making sure that they rock but don't sink the boat.

3. The paradox of knowledge.

In an innovation project, it is more important to find out what you do not yet know about your challenge instead of what you know about the situation; too much knowledge often locks you inside a perceptual tunnel (*"expert syndrome"*) that prevents you from gaining novel insights in your challenge. So get ready to unlearn what you have learned and re-learn to gain true understanding.

4. The paradox of business success.

To bring a radical innovation to the market, you need to now invest in its development, which may guarantee your long-term success but reduces your short-term success.

5. The paradox of strategic directions.

In a Strategy Innovation project, aim to stretch the boundaries of your market offerings by finding uncontested new market space while at the same time considering the core competencies of your firm.

6. The paradox of culture.

Creativity and innovation require employees who break the rules and challenge conventional organizational wisdom while at the same time being expected to respect the company culture (*"The way we do things around here"*).

7. The paradox of rewarding innovation.

An innovative company needs to find a way to fairly reward the crucial contributions of both the team involved in successfully bringing an innovation to market and the individual idea creator without demotivating either side.

8. The paradox of efficiency.

Many companies that have undergone Total Quality Management (TQM) and Six Sigma initiatives during the past two decades need to find a way to keep their improved efficiency while at the same time becoming more creative.

9. The paradox of ideation.

The paradox of ideation is based on the interesting phenomenon that in order to design a truly great solution, you need to either create a lot of ideas (i.e., a wide range of raw ideas produced through conscious ideation efforts) or just one (i.e., a breakthrough idea that emerges from your subconscious mind after incubating on the challenge for a prolonged period of time).

10. The paradox of originality.

"It seems to be one of the paradoxes of creativity that in order to think originally, we must familiarize ourselves with the ideas of others," noted George Kneller. Indeed, it is a paradoxical phenomenon that one's own original ideas often only emerge after one has studied and responded to the original ideas of earlier creators.

11. The paradox of innovation speed.

Radical ideas (such as Charles Darwin's theory of evolution) require substantial, time-consuming efforts to prove their value. But the more time you invest to substantiate a truly bold idea, the more likely it is that someone else will propose it first (as nearly happened in Darwin's case). Here, take note of the counterintuitive advice of the British inventor James Dyson: *"I learned that the moment you want to slow down is the moment you should accelerate."*

12. The paradox of creative destruction.

"Artistic temperament sometimes seems a battleground, a dark angel of destruction and a bright angel of creativity wrestling," stated the American writer Madeline L'Engle.

It is often necessary to first destroy something existing (such as a *"sacred cow,"* a previously hugely successful idea whose time has come to be phased out) to create space for creativity and innovation to emerge and fill the space with something more meaningful.

Schumpeter called this process of ending an old business cycle and starting a new one *"creative destruction."* Here, also remember Salvador Dali's advice: *"You have to systematically create confusion, it sets creativity free. Everything that is contradictory creates life."*

Conclusion: Innovators feel at ease juggling with paradoxes.

Once you have developed an awareness of paradoxes, you notice that the worlds of innovation and business are full of them, and so is life. So as a creative business leader, better adopt the mindset of Danish physicist Niels Bohr and see the positive side of paradoxes: *"How wonderful that we have met with a paradox. Now we have some hope of making progress."*

Appreciate every paradox as a great intellectual challenge in line with the Danish philosopher Soren Kierkegaard: *"The paradox is really the pathos of intellectual life and just as only great souls are exposed to passions it is only the great thinker who is exposed to what I call paradoxes, which are nothing else than grandiose thoughts in embryo."*

See them as a unique opportunity to differentiate yourself from the herd by doing your own thinking and finding your own way to deal with them. Then, move forward and be flexible to make adjustments if your chosen approach to master a paradoxical challenge does not work out as envisaged. In any case, US author Wayne Dyer rightly notes: *"You are doomed to make choices. This is life's greatest paradox."*

> "A hen is only an egg's way of making another egg."
> —SAMUEL BUTLER

3.7. RESOLVING THE DILEMMA OF INNOVATION MANAGEMENT

Embracing the paradoxical nature of creativity and innovation is just one of the puzzling challenges sensible managers need to get used to in the innovation economy. Another baffling challenge lies in understanding —and resolving— the dilemma of innovation management.

Introducing the dilemma of innovation management

The *"dilemma of innovation management"* captures the fact companies cannot organize their activities in ways that simultaneously promote both high organizational efficiency and high organizational creativity:

- Organizing for efficiency means arranging operations to minimize variance in business processes, products, people, etc. The method is to standardize everything by means of clear guidelines, optimized and controlled processes, a uniform workforce with similar educational background, etc. Organizations that focus on exploiting old ways typically organize for routine work.

- Organizing for creativity and innovation means doing the opposite. It means promoting a flexible, loose environment that encourages diversity in people and thought to produce good ideas and meaningful innovation. Organizations that prefer exploring new ways tend to organize for innovative work.

In times of the innovation economy, companies must find a way to support innovation while retaining efficiency. While efficiency-centered companies are also able to contribute to innovation, these efforts typically lead to continuous improvements or incremental innovations only. If a company wants to produce evolutionary or even revolutionary innovations, however, it needs to find organizational solutions that promote higher levels of creativity and a risk-tolerant environment.

How to best resolve the dilemma of innovation management? Allow me to introduce three possible solution paths: choosing between different transactional models to organize your activities, the functional approach, and the cognitive approach.

Solution 1: The transaction model approach

High organizational efficiency and high organizational creativity are extremes on a continuum, and different companies will fall at different places on that scale according to how they organize their economic activities. I prefer to use the following metaphor to describe the difficult choice related to the Dilemma of Innovation Management: Simultaneously organizing a company for both high efficiency and high creativity is like trying to be at the North Pole and South Pole at the same time:

- Organizing for high efficiency (the "North Pole") means minimizing variances in your business processes, people, product and service offerings, and so on. In other words, you aim to make everything as standardized and similar as possible through rigid, clear guidelines, optimized processes, a uniform workforce with similar educational backgrounds, etc. Most manufacturing operations and companies in conservative or asset-driven industries are organized for high efficiency, and they are not known for producing a lot of innovation.

- On the other side of the globe at the South Pole, the situation is completely reversed. Innovation is the result of taking action on meaningful ideas—and ideas thrive in an unrestricted, flexible and loose environment that encourages diversity, variances and

THE DILEMMA OF INNOVATION MANAGEMENT
MANAGING THE TENSION BETWEEN THE NEED FOR CREATIVITY AND EFFICIENCY

EXPLORING the new:
Organize for INNOVATIVE Work
- Enhance variance
- Many possible ways of doing things — and many possible solutions
- See old things in new ways — and spotting new opportunities
- Break from the past to create novelty
- Goal: Make money later

High Organizational EFFICIENCY

Serious, stable and controlled environments foster stable routines, which are required for achieving a **high efficiency** of the daily operations

EXPLOITING the old:
Organize for ROUTINE Work
- Drive out variance
- Only one way of doing things (focus on the one right solution)
- See old things in old ways
- Replicate the past
- Goal: Make money now

differences. Companies like Apple or Nike are global innovation leaders in their product and marketing strategies and are exclusively organized for high creativity. These extreme *"South Pole companies"* have outsourced efficiency as all their production is done by original equipment manufacturers (OEMs) that are mostly located in Asia.

Of course, there are some organizational models in between the extreme poles, and each approach tries to solve the dilemma of innovation management in a different way:

- Right below the North Pole is the traditional model of organizing for innovation: the old-fashioned R&D department is isolated from the efficiency-geared rest of the operation and could thus develop an innovation-friendly culture within its R&D ivory tower.

- Probably a more modern extension of the traditional organizational innovation model is the new trend for open innovation. While companies may largely be set up to high organizational efficiency, they complement their internal R&D and innovation efforts with ideas and scientific solutions provided by external partners or individuals using open innovation platforms and approaches. For example, Eli Lilly has set up the website *InnoCentive* to *"crowd-source"* solutions to specified scientific problems over the Internet from a global virtual scientist community. IBM and other pharmaceutical companies have set up similar platforms. Another interesting open innovation initiative is Procter & Gamble's *"Connect & Develop"* program which aims for a 50-50% split between ideas that are developed within the organization and those that are provided by outside partners and virtual networks.

- Further down South but still well above the equator, we have companies that have set up innovation teams within each division or—even better—cross-divisional project teams that work on an innovation project relatively independent from the rest of the organization. While the normal business units still lean towards an efficiency-centered organization, the innovation project teams are set free and work in flexible, stimulus-rich, and playful environments that inspire creativity.

- A few companies apply an organization model based on the anthropological small village theory, which suggests that traditional human communities split up when getting bigger than 150 people. Gore-Tex is the most prominent company that aims to balance the need for innovation and efficiency by having many *"small village"* companies within the group, where the small size allows both flexibility and control. As such, they are located on the equator of our creativity-efficiency globe.

- Moving into the Southern hemisphere, a popular approach in the pharmaceutical and biotechnology industries is to spin off a promising internal R&D initiative from the core company by setting up a creativity-friendly new venture and retaining control in these entrepreneurial start-ups by holding the majority of shares.

Where on the transactional "Innovation Globe" is your company located? And what might be a more effective position going forward? Before making changes, however, note that most of these transactional approaches have a significant drawback in that they require companies to adjust or even change their organizational structure, which costs time and money and causes organizational friction.

Solution 2: The functional approach

Is there an easier alternative to the transaction models discussed above that can resolve the dilemma of innovation management? The answer is a functional approach. To use this, consider each business team or business unit and ask: *"What will best enable this function to make our company thrive in the innovation economy? High organizational efficiency? High organizational creativity? Or something in between?"*

When you do this, you will notice that functions generally fall into one of three categories:

- Efficiency-focused functions. Process-driven and back-office support functions require a focus on high organizational efficiency. These functional areas include manufacturing, logistics, supply chain management, operations, finance, accounting, compliance and legal. In these functions, creativity is not desired at all (think of *"creative accounting"*) or is only required at a modest level for resolving operational problems or discovering incremental process improvements. Efficiency-driven teams and business units should largely continue doing what they do and need not be actively involved in organizational change programs to promote more innovation.

- Creativity-focused functions. On the other hand, market- and value-driven corporate functions benefit from organizing for high organizational creativity.

Teams or business units related to new product development, design, content creation, concept creation, in-house consulting, marketing, and public relations, among others, thrive in flexible environments that promote diversity, spontaneity, and freedom of thought and action. In these functions, creativity clearly takes precedence over efficiency, although you should still measure outputs and use structured methodological approaches and tools. If you want to transform your company into a more innovation-friendly organization, focus your efforts on making these creativity-focused business teams and units more innovation-friendly.

- Combined efficiency- and creativity-focused functions. Some functional areas gain from both efficiency and creativity, albeit at lower levels than the extremes discussed above. For example, human resources (HR) requires efficient management processes, but creating tactical actions to attract talent to the company clearly requires a good dose of creativity. Other functions in the middle that rely on both structured processes and creative insights and problem-solving include IT, market research and sales. In an innovation-focused organizational transformation program, these hybrid business units and teams should be involved, but need to find the right balance between efficiency and creativity that best supports the organizational goals. To help with this, a team may look at their various tasks to identify if the team requires more efficiency or more creativity.

Solution 3: The cognitive approach

A final way to resolve the dilemma of innovation management relates to the cognitive people profiling method TIPS that you will read about later (see section 5.7). TIPS reveals that certain talent profiles are more prone to appear —and call the shots— in certain industries and ecosystems: While creative profile types tend to frequent start-ups and fast-moving as well as technology-driven industries, while efficiency-focused profiles tend to dominate in conservative and asset-driven industries and in mature large or even multinational corporations.

When linked to the four TIPS bases (theories, ideas, people, systems), we can say that companies in ideas-driven ecosystems should organize more for high organizational creativity, while systems-focused environments support organizing for high organizational efficiency. Finally, organizations that lean to the theories- or people-bases require a blend of creativity and efficiency (similar to the *"middle way"* in the functional approach).

Conclusion: If you are committed to making your organization more innovation-friendly, the easiest path is to take a functional look at it, even if it follows a divisional structure, to determine what business units and teams should participate in the exercise. This allows your organization to effectively deal with the dilemma of innovation management, maintaining efficiency while increasing creativity and innovation.

> "Organizations, by their very nature are designed to promote order and routine. They are inhospitable environments for innovation."
> —THEODORE LEVITT

RESOLVING THE DILEMMA OF INNOVATION MANAGEMENT

TRANSACTIONAL ORGANIZATIONAL APPROACH

Pure Manufacturing Companies, Me Too-Companies, companies in conservative or asset-driven industries

Traditional R&D Department Model (i.e., creative R&D team separated from efficiency-oriented rest of the organization)

Open Innovation Initiatives complementing in-house innovation initiatives (P&G, IBM, Eli Lilly)

Intra- or cross-divisional Innovation Teams with a work focus on a particular innovation project

"Small Village Theory"- Companies (e.g., Gore-Tex)

Promising R&D initiatives spun-off from main company into new venture (share control retained); popular in pharmaceutical and biotech industry

Innovative companies such as Apple, Nike, Disney, Pixar, Ad Agencies, Design Companies, Innovation Companies

Organizing for High EFFICIENCY

Organizing for High CREATIVITY

FUNCTIONAL APPROACH

Mainly EFFICIENCY-driven Business Units / Functions
- Finance
- Accounting
- Compliance
- Legal
- Manufacturing
- Operations

Both EFFICIENCY- & CREATIVITY-driven Business Units / Functions
- (Market) Research
- Human Resources
- Sales
- Customer Service
- IT

Mainly CREATIVITY-driven Business Units / Functions
- Business Development
- New Product Development
- Content Creation
- Design
- Marketing
- (Market) Communication
- Public Relations

COGNITIVE APPROACH

EFFICIENCY-driven

Both EFFICIENCY- & CREATIVITY-driven

CREATIVITY-driven

3.8. IN-NO-VATION EXPLAINED

Do you know that most companies misspell the word innovation? Nowadays, innovation has become a buzzword. Everybody talks about innovation, and most companies list innovation as an important corporate value and a core enabler to live up to their mission statements.

Unfortunately, most companies write innovation in the wrong way — at least, if we judge them by their everyday actions. They don't go for innovation but for in-NO-vation:

- in-NO-vation is NOT having enough IDEAS in general, and NO WOW ideas especially. Or in having NO tenacity to seize upon a WOW idea and effectively activate and launch it.
- in-NO-vation means NOT using a creative PROCESS to systematically produce tangible innovation results.
- in-NO-vation is having NO creative PEOPLE, or NOT knowing who the creatives in your workforce are.
- in-NO-vation means having NO innovation-friendly CULTURE. And having NO desire to depart from what made you successful in the past but won't do so in the future.
- in-NO-vation like in having NO authentic creative LEADERS. And having NO clue about how to identify potential creative leaders and—once you've found them—how to effectively develop the candidates into true creative leaders.

So what?

Becoming a truly innovative company requires that you stop talking about innovation and start doing innovation:

- Start using a creative process method to systematically produce Wow ideas and turn them into tangible innovations.
- Start finding the creative people in your workforce and creatively empowering them.
- Start building an innovation-friendly company culture.
- Last but not least, start developing authentic creative leaders to lead innovation.

These are the successful ways to effectively move from in-NO-vation to innovation. So, stop being a spectator in the innovation game. Get on the pitch and start playing. In the following four chapters, you will learn more about how you can play the innovation game.

> "I have enjoyed life a lot more by saying 'Yes' than by saying 'No'."
> —RICHARD BRANSON

> "Marketing is what you do when your product is no good."
> – EDWIN H. LAND

CHAPTER 3 — EXECUTIVE SUMMARY
THE RULES OF THE INNOVATION GAME

- Follow ten rules when you play with modern innovation types to ensure that you can maximize the return on investment on your innovation investments, such as first create value, then leverage it, or connect the dots on all three innovation levels, among others.

- Innovations can be classified based on their impact (or the scope of change that they trigger) into incremental improvements, evolutionary and revolutionary innovations. The Innovation Type-Impact Matrix captures four cases of how these changes can be delivered to existing and new users.

- The diffusion of innovation follows a predictable pattern: the adoption curve describes how a new technology or innovation is first embraced by the innovators, who need the support of the early adopters to cross the chasm into the early majority and make the new thing take off, so that the late majority and laggards will eventually also embrace it. The theory suggest that 16% of people drive change, while 84% dislike it and buy into it only gradually.

- Ideas have many special interesting properties that innovators need to understand to harness their full power in the age of "ideanomics."

- Open innovation aims to expand the organizational boundaries of innovation by sourcing in external ideas from outside collaborators and offering internal ideas to other market players. It needs to be a win-win for all players for the approach to succeed in the long run.

- Unlike many other aspects in business, innovation isn't black and white but comes in many shades and colors. One of the reasons why many companies struggle with creativity and innovation is that they are confronted with many paradoxes that cannot be rationally managed but require creative responses and tolerance for uncertainty and ambiguity.

- The dilemma of innovation management captures the inability of a company to organize at the same time for high organizational efficiency and high organizational creativity.

- Many company spell innovation wrongly by emphasizing the NO in in-NO-vation: No ideas, no creative process, no creative culture, no creative leaders. In the following four chapters, we will address each of these barriers to help firms moving from in-NO-vation:to innovation, positively impacting financial returns.

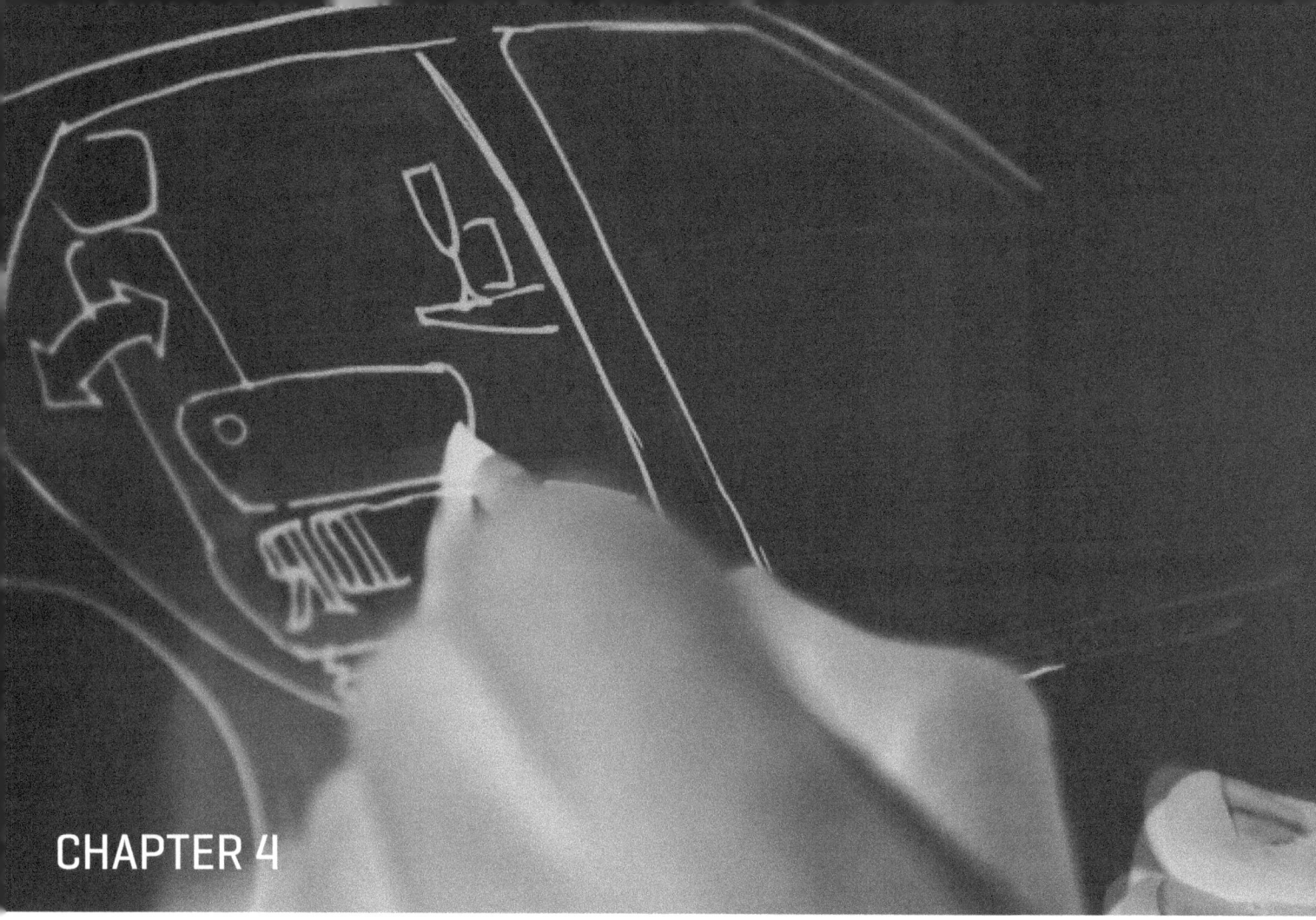

CHAPTER 4

THE INNOVATION PROCESS & TOOLS
SMALL PICTURE (I)

How to produce wow results in an innovation project.

1. Innovation: It's All About Mastering Process and Projects
2. Innovation Process Methods: What? Why? How?
3. Understanding the Inner Workings of Thinking Tools and Creativity Tools
4. Brainstorming; The Good, the Bad and the Ugly
5. It's Not Only What Tools You Use But How You Use Them
6. X-IDEA: Introducing the Know-How of Wow
7. Why Using Only One Creative Process Stage Leads to Dull Ideas
8. Dos and Don'ts for a Successful Innovation Project
* *Executive Summary*

4.1. INNOVATION: IT'S ALL ABOUT MASTERING PROCESS AND PROJECTS

Have you ever noticed that business in general and innovation in special is essentially about two things? It's all about mastering process and project:

- PROJECT addresses the WHAT and WHY: What do we want to do that adds value to our customers and our business? Why do we believe this is valuable?

- In contrast, PROCESS addresses the HOW: How can we undergo a certain activity in the most effective way? Why do we believe this is the best way of doing it?

How does this relate to what we have already discussed earlier in this book — and what we are going to discuss in this chapter?

The *PROJECT* side of iinnovation relates to the innovation types featured in Chapters 2 and 3. For example, you may do an innovation project to create a new, healthy snack for 6- to 10-year-old kids (product innovation), design a better experience for a guest stay at a luxury hotel (customer experience design), or clean up and simplify a production planning process of a toy manufacturing plant that has become bloated over time (process innovation). All these project cases pursue a concrete target output (product, experience, process) linked to one of the modern innovation types.

Once we have specified a worthy project case, a different question arises: How can we best pursue this challenge? How do we move through the innovation project to create the desired target outputs? These questions lead to the *PROCESS* side of innovation.

One way to go through an innovation project is to just follow our intuition on what to do when to produce the desired results — or to follow the trusted old ways of how we've always done things around here.

Another —and probably better— way to proceed is to employ the help of a sophisticated and effective creative process method and related thinking tools. Chapter 4 will introduce you to innovation methods and thinking tools — what they do for you, what are prominent examples, why they are useful, and how they work in a nutshell.

Now we have a worthy innovation project that we are working on using an effective innovation process method and thinking tools to produce a desired innovation target output. But there is a final aspect that we need to consider: People.

Innovation projects are typically identified by a project owner (e.g., a brand manager or marketing communication executive) and funded by a project sponsor (typically a business division or business unit that benefits from the project).

The project owner usually invites people to join one or more innovation team to pursue the project. Ideally, the project owner has an eye on composing diverse innovation teams by making sure a team has a mix of different functional roles and business units, educational backgrounds, genders and cultures, and age spans, among other factors.

Moreover, an innovation project team should have people with a well-rounded mix of preferred cognitive styles so

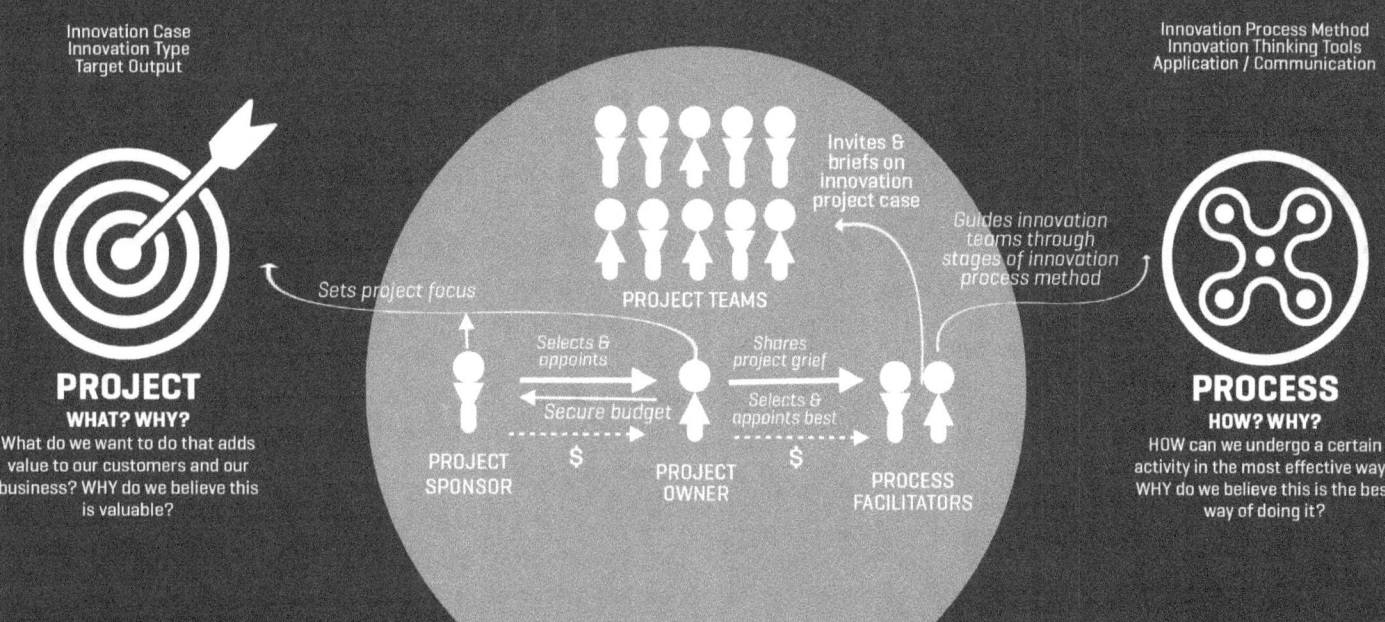

that the team members can complement each other and different team members drive the activities and thinking at different stages in the process. (Chapter 5 will discuss these cognitive aspects).

Finally, you need to nominate an internal innovation process facilitator with previous project experience. Even better, recruit the services of an external innovation facilitator or a professional innovation company to guide your team through the innovation project journey.

Why do such external innovation process experts add value to your innovation project? They take care of the innovation *process* and all its intricate details, thus allowing the members of your innovation teams to focus on the innovation *project*. Sadly, after their first experience in an innovation project run by outside innovation professionals, many businesspeople get overconfident and think: *"This was easy. The next time around, we can do this ourselves and save money."* They're prone to fail — and burn more money than they save in fees. Why?

Top innovation experts are worth their money because they've acquired both the expertise and experience needed to make you succeed. They've learned from mishaps in previous projects so that you can avoid wasting everyone's time in a poorly run internal innovation workshop. Innovation projects are not as easy as they seem; you need to master many process variables — innovation types and a fitting innovation method, thinking tools and how to best apply them, and people dynamics, among others. Mastering the innovation process is both science and art, as you will learn.

> There is nothing so useless as doing efficiently that which should not be done at all.
> —PETER DRUCKER

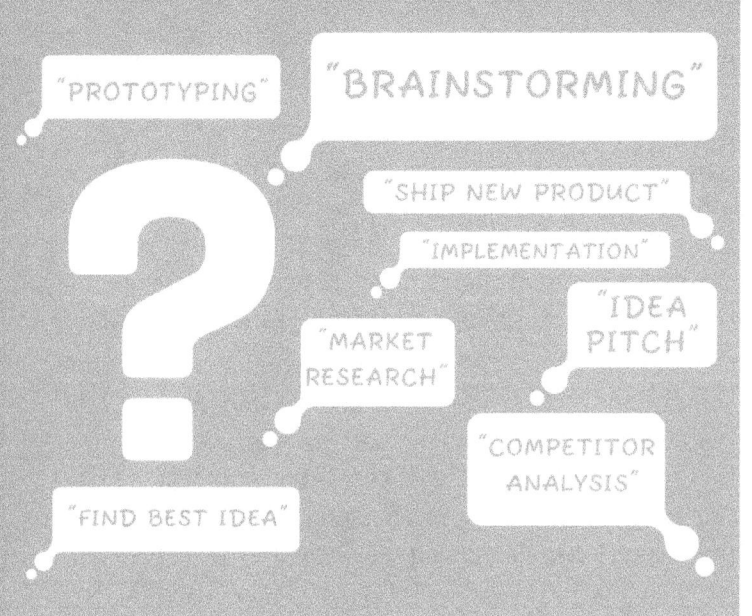
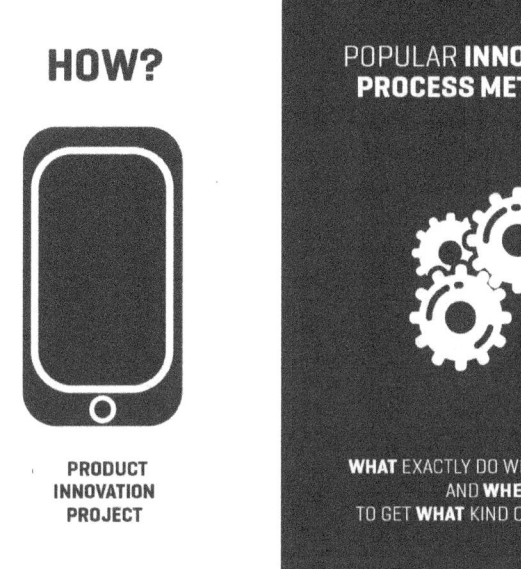

4.2. INNOVATION PROCESS METHODS: WHAT? WHY? HOW?

Take a moment to think about the following question: What activities do you need to do while working on an innovation project, say, aiming to develop a new product?

So what innovation project-related activities have you come up with? When I ask this question to graduate students and delegates in innovation courses, typical answers that emerge include:

"Brainstorm for ideas" ... "Implement the idea" ... "Do market research"... "Create a prototype"... "Analyze our competitors and their products" ... "Pitch our idea." ... "Look at trends" ... "Ship the product" ... "Select the best ideas" ... "Empathize with the users" ... "Frame the innovation challenge" ... "Calculate the expected ROI from an idea" ... "Check on project-related facts and evidence" ... "Evaluate ideas" ... and so on.

If you have thought of some of these activities or similar ones, then congratulations and well done. You're generally on track to eventually becoming an innovator if you do such things. But here is another question:

WHAT EXACTLY DO WE NEED TO DO AND WHEN TO GET WHAT KIND OF RESULTS?

In other words, what activities do we need to perform in an innovation project to produce what kind of outputs? This is an interesting question indeed. To answer it, some creativity aficionados (including myself) who enjoy thinking about these questions have created different kinds of innovation methods.

What are innovation methods? And what are prominent examples?

Innovation methods (sometimes also called creative problem-solving methods or creative processes) are systematic process flows that outline the steps and cognitive activities that an individual or a team needs to follow while thinking through an innovation challenge or solving a problem creatively.

The classic Creative Problem-Solving Model (CPS), which dates back to the work of creativity pioneers Alex Osborne and Sid Parnes, is probably the longest-serving and best-known process method. It is also a cornerstone of what students who pursue a Master in Business Creativity learn at Buffalo State University in Buffalo, NY, and has been featured in adapted versions in books of other creativity coaches such as Art VanGundy, Brian Clegg and Paul Birch, and Andrew and Mary Bragg.

In recent years, Design Thinking has gained tremendous popularity based on the work of the Silicon Valley innovation company IDEO and their academic offspring, the D-School at Stanford University.

A few other creativity experts and innovation practitioners have also shared suggestions for creative thinking processes in books, such as *"The Idea Machine"* by Nadja Schnetzler of the Swiss innovation company Brainstore, Systematic Inventive Thinking by the Israeli company of the same name, and Gijs van Wulfen's FORTH method.

Finally, X-IDEA is an up-and-coming new innovation method I created for Thinkergy. Later in this chapter, we will take a look at how X-IDEA is designed with the intent to improve on identified shortcomings of some of the other methods.

Why are innovation methods useful?

All innovation process methods are based on the idea that if you follow a systematic thinking process, you will get better ideas and results than if you think through a creative project in a largely unstructured way.

Innovation projects are messy and lengthy affairs. They may last from a few days to weeks, months or even years. They often involve a smaller core team and dozens of supporters who join in for certain activities (such as idea generation). They also lead to a large number of throughputs (for example, dozens of new insights or hundreds of raw ideas) to arrive at a few target outputs (new innovation deliverables).

An elegant, well-designed and effective innovation process method can cut through the messiness and safely guide individuals and —more typically— teams working on an innovation project case towards meaningful results and outputs. It gives focus to the innovation efforts by specifying what to do next to produce what kind of target outputs, which are then further processed in the following steps.

How do innovation methods work?

When nalyzing the design logic and inner workings of an innovation method or a creative process, we need to consider several factors: the number of steps (and related work and thinking activities), the sequence of steps, circularity, and the aggregation of steps into stages, among others. Let's briefly review each of these aspects.

An innovation method provides a systematic order of working or thinking **steps**: First, do this, then do that, then do a third thing, followed by another task, until you eventually arrive at a final step that concludes the process.

As such, most innovation processes propose a linear **sequence** of steps and associated cognitive activities or tasks that the wanna-be innovators or creative problem-solvers need to perform while working on a case.

Some innovation methods are more detailed and

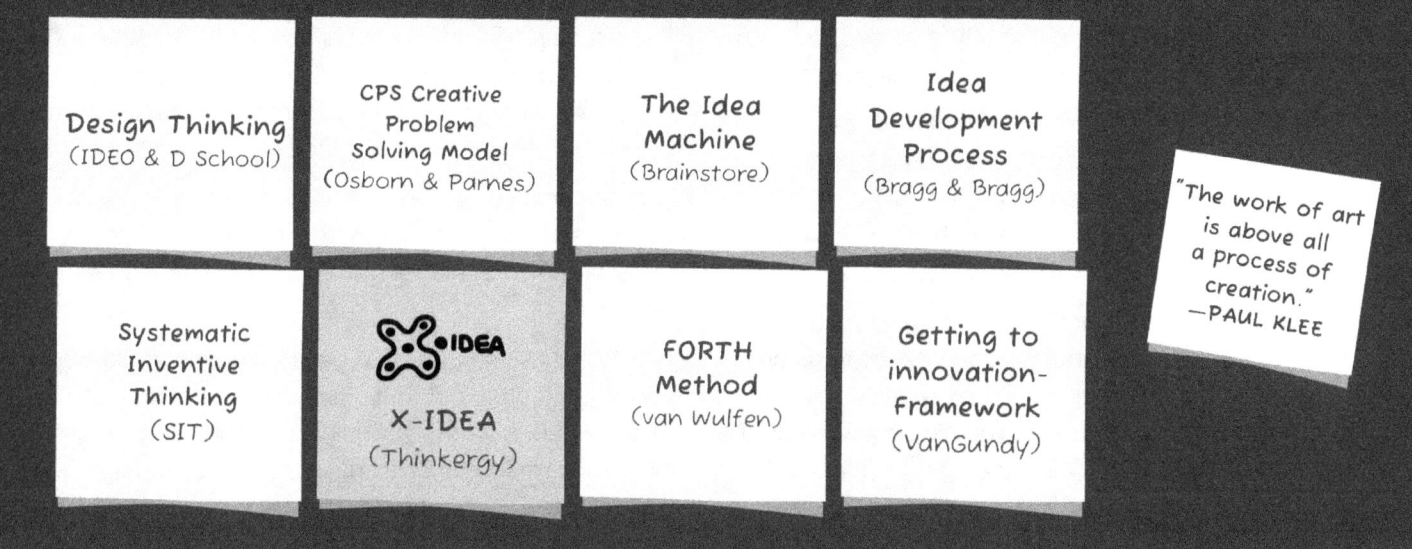

comprehensive than others. Typically, this means that they have a larger number of steps and detailed activities to go through. That's good news inasmuch as it allows creative problem-solvers and innovators to work more thoroughly. And it's bad because the more steps and details a method has, the more difficult it is to learn for innovation neophytes — and to remember all steps in the correct order for innovation facilitators and thinkers. To resolve this dilemma between seeking high accuracy and simplicity alike, such sophisticated innovation methods often aggregate three or more process steps on a higher level of abstraction in a process **stage**.

For example, looking at the activities listed at the beginning of our *"warm-up exercise"* of this section, we may integrate *"Evaluate ideas," "Prototype ideas"* and *"Select the best ideas"* in a stage that we call *"Evaluation."*

As a result, more thorough innovation process methods such as Design Thinking or X-IDEA consist of typically 3-5 process stages, whereby each stage typically comes with a number of subordinated work steps.

However, the different methods vary in the number of stages or thinking steps that they suggest a thinker to pass through:

- For example, the classic CPS Model suggests thinkers follow a six-stage process of objective finding, fact finding, problem finding, idea finding, solution finding, and acceptance finding.

- Thinkergy's X-IDEA method invites you to pass through the five stages Xploration, Ideation, Development, Evaluation, and Action. Each of the 5 stages proposes 3 subordinated steps with related cognitive work activities. Gijs van Wulfen also favors a five-stage approach in his FORTH method.

- In their *"Idea Machine"* method, the Swiss IdeaFactory BrainStore AG suggests a four-stage process (amassing, extraction, selection, preparation) with a number of subordinated steps. Likewise, many other books on creativity advocate following a four-stage approach (e.g., see the books of von Oech, Clegg & Birch, and Bragg & Bragg).

- Finally, the industrial design company IDEO (and the related D School of Stanford University) propagate a 3-stage process (inspiration, ideation, implementation); they divide each of these stages further into 4 to 8 subordinated steps.

While analyzing the methods cited above, I used as much as possible what I perceived to be the original version of a method. Having said this, please note that many innovation methods are dynamic and evolve further by their original creators. Also, they get modified by practitioners who license a particular innovation method or use with or without permission of the original creators. As such, you may come across modified versions of the above-cited methods where the details may vary, but the overall design logic and integrity should still be intact.

Circularity is another important aspect to mention here. Most innovation process methods imply circularity on two levels:

- At the micro level, you may have to circle back to the previous step and repeat the work. This is necessary if you work on an activity and notice that the inputs from the previous step are insufficient in quality or quality to produce the desired outputs.
- At the macro level, circularity means that once you've successfully completed an innovation project, start a new one. In other words, once you've completed the last step of the innovation process, go back to the start: Enter a new project into your innovation process method and take step one in stage one. The more innovation projects you've done using a particular innovation method, the more learning cycles you've completed, and the better your innovation outputs are likely to be. So, whenever you've completed the last step and stage of your innovation method and reached the end of an innovation project, harness your learnings and new experiences. Then, over time, you will become a savvy innovation practitioner.

Now that you've got a better understanding of the inner workings of innovation methods, you surely have one question on your mind: Which innovation method should I follow?

Well, don't ask me. I have a clear recommendation for you, and I am biased. But after putting on a neutral thinking cap, my advice would be as follows: Select an innovation method that promises to fit your situation with regard to how often you do innovation projects, how sophisticated or straightforward you want the method to be, and what innovation types you typically pursue. Then, experiment with different creative processes and innovation methods to find out which one suits your needs and your people.

One final point: In my list of popular or sound innovation methods, you may have missed some *"methods"* that have been in fashion in recent years (such as *"Business Model Innovation"*) or are widely known (such as *"Brainstorming"* or *"Six Thinking Hats"*). Why haven't I included them here?

First of all, due to space limitations in this book, my list cannot be all-inclusive, so pardon me for any viable innovation methods I haven't listed here. Second, from my point of view, some "methods" like the ones mentioned before aren't full-fledged innovation methods but rather qualify as thinking tools or creativity techniques. In the following section, we're going to talk about both thinking tools in general and creativity techniques like Brainstorming in particular.

UNDERSTANDING THE INNER WORKINGS OF INNOVATION METHODS

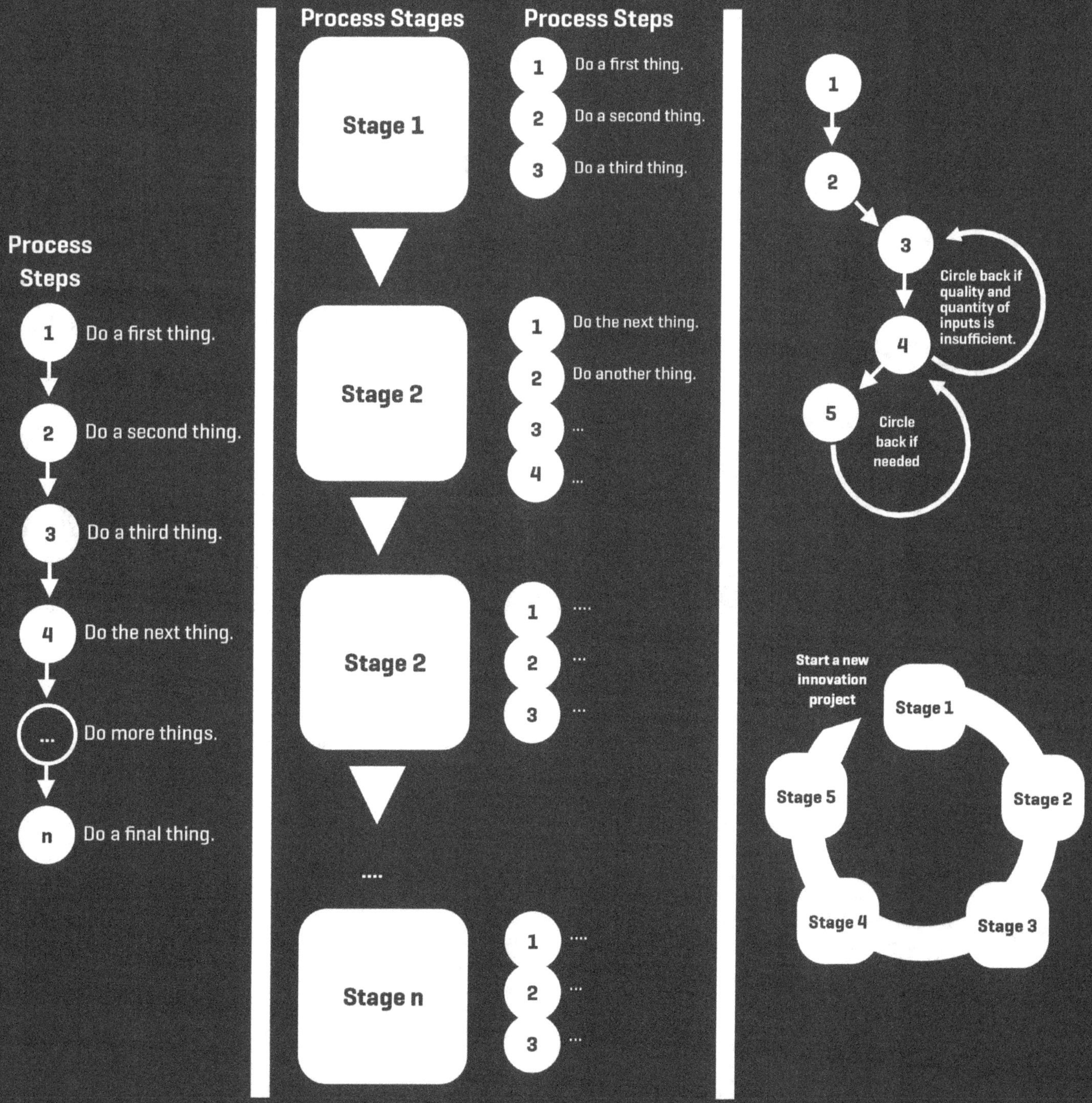

Process Steps

1. Do a first thing.
2. Do a second thing.
3. Do a third thing.
4. Do the next thing.
... Do more things.
n. Do a final thing.

Process Stages

- **Stage 1**
- **Stage 2**
- **Stage 2**
- ....
- **Stage n**

Process Steps

Stage 1:
1. Do a first thing.
2. Do a second thing.
3. Do a third thing.

Stage 2:
1. Do the next thing.
2. Do another thing.
3. ...
4. ...

Stage 2:
1. ....
2. ...
3. ...

Stage n:
1. ....
2. ...
3. ...

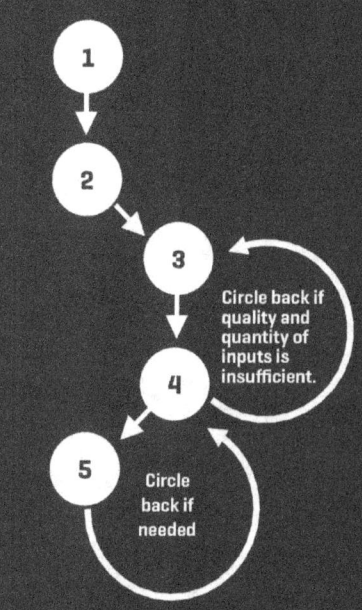

1 → 2 → 3 → 4 → 5

Circle back if quality and quantity of inputs is insufficient.

Circle back if needed

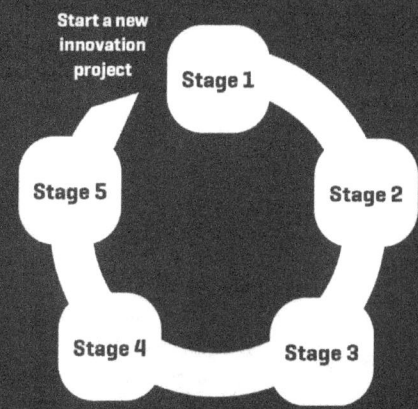

Start a new innovation project

Stage 1 → Stage 2 → Stage 3 → Stage 4 → Stage 5

The table below shows the process stages of a number of popular innovation methods. The creative stage is highlighted — and you'll see that most stages have only one. creative stage. We'll talk about this later.

Name of Innovation Process Method	Creative Problem-Solving (CPS) Model	X-IDEA	FORTH Method	Idea Development Process	Getting to innovation	Idea Machine	Design Thinking (IDEO Method)
Creator / Source	Osborn & Parnes	Thinkergy (Reis)	van Wulfen	Bragg & Bragg	VanGundy	Schnetzler (Brainstore)	IDEO (Stanford D-School)
No. of stages:	6	5	5	4	4	4	3
First process stage Second stage **Creative process stage highlighted in bold** Etc.	1. Objective finding 2. Fact Finding 3. Problem finding 4. **Idea finding** 5. Solution finding 6. Acceptance finding	1. Xploration 2. **Ideation** 3. Development 4. Evaluation 5. Action	1. Full Steam Ahead 2. Observe and Learn 3. **Raise Ideas** 4. Test Ideas 5. Homecoming	1. Seeking and shaping opportunities 2. **Generating new ideas** 3. Evaluating & selecting ideas 4. Planning for implementation	1. Innovation framing 2. **Idea generation** 3. Evaluation and selection 4. Implementation	1. **Amassing** 2. Extraction 3. Selection 4. Preparation	1. Inspiration 2. **Ideation** 3. Implementation

4.3. UNDERSTANDING THE INNER WORKINGS OF THINKING TOOLS AND CREATIVITY TOOLS

As a kid, did you ever take apart a toy to see what's inside? Or as an adult, have you ever taken apart an electronic gadget—or maybe even your car—to understand the inner workings of its different parts? In the following lines, we'll take a look below the surface of thinking tools in general and creativity tools in particular: why we need them, what they are, how they work and even how you can create your own.

What are thinking tools?

Thinking tools outline a structured flow of working steps a thinker needs to complete one by one to produce a desired target output (e.g., ideas).

Thinking tools can be distinguished into three subsets:

- *Serious thinking tools* for analytical thinking, critical thinking and decision making, such as Stakeholder Analysis, SWOT Analysis, PMI (Plus, Minus, Interesting), or Project Plan;
- *Creativity tools* for idea generation and idea concept design, such as Brainstorming, Morphological Matrix, What If, or SCAMPER;
- *Whole-brain tools* employ both analytical and creative thinking at different work steps, such as Concept Maps, Six Thinking Hats, Force Field Analysis, or Rapid Prototyping.

While running an innovation project case through the different process stages of a structured innovation method, a savvy innovation facilitator exposes a team to one to three dozen thinking tools (depending on the number of days of time available).

Why do we use many different thinking tools to work through an innovation challenge? *"If the only tool you have is a hammer, you tend to see every problem as a nail,"* noted the American psychologist Abraham Maslow. We need to use a variety of thinking tools to ensure that we frame the innovation challenge correctly, that we produce a diverse pool of ideas, that we appropriately evaluate the ideas to find the best ones, and that we can successfully implement a top idea. The cognitive focus of our work varies considerably in different stages of an innovation process method, which requires an innovation facilitator to have a good mix of thinking tools in our toolbox to bring into play at the appropriate point of time.

What are creativity tools?

When I train people in creative thinking, I invite participants early on to a brainstorming exercise for a given creative challenge. When we review the ideas of each team afterward, the same interesting pattern always emerges: many ideas appear in each of the different brainstorming teams. This is a clear indication that such an idea is not highly original but rather common and obvious. Why is this?

When people do simple brainstorming, they are likely to produce rather obvious ideas that are all within a very narrow range of thinking. They are stuck in what I call the *"tunnel of expertise and conventional thoughts."* So, how can you get out of the tunnel? Here is where creativity techniques come in.

Creativity techniques are mechanistic processes that — with the help of one or more triggers — can reliably push your individual thinking into a new direction and to a new starting point located outside the tunnel of your expertise and conventional ways of thinking. The new starting point allows you to take a fresh view on your innovation challenge (i.e., a problem you face or an opportunity you want to seize), and to come up with more original, unconventional and even wild ideas that are all outside the narrow tunnel of your usual ways of thinking.

How do creativity tools work?

A creativity tool works like a revolver. When you pull the trigger, you reliably set in motion a mechanistic process that propels a bullet out of the gun towards a target. Similarly, creativity tools reliably push your thinking to a new starting point that is outside of your *"tunnel of expertise and conventional thoughts."* From this fresh starting point, you are able to come up with new ideas that are more uncommon and original.

What kind of triggers do creativity tools use?

Like a good car mechanic strips an engine to understand how it works, let's similarly dissect creativity tools even further by trying to understand the underlying principles of their working. Here we come to the trigger that propels us to a new starting point. These *"motors of a creativity tool"* typically use one of the following schemes:

- First, a trigger can be a fresh perspective or novel point of view that allows you to look at the underlying problem in a completely different way, thus allowing you to come up with really different ideas. For example, in a strategy innovation case, imagine how a visiting Alien without any "emotional baggage" and historical attachment would reposition your company for the future.

- Secondly, a trigger may enable you to come up with many new associations — the mental images that pop up in your mind when you hear a certain word or concept. For example, when you hear *New York*, you may think of *9/11*, the *Empire State Building*, *Central Park, Wall Street,* and other concepts that you associate with the concept of *"New York"*.

- Thirdly, a trigger may be a formal framework or a sequence of thinking steps that you need to follow in a systematic order. For example, in the creativity tool Morphological Matrix, you first construct a table of inputs; then, you use the elements in the matrix as stimuli for generating fresh ideas.

- Fourthly and lastly, a trigger can be a question that fires up your imagination or that takes your thinking to unusual heights. This last type of trigger is exemplified by What If-questions like *"What if you were granted 3 wishes by a good fairy?"*

Triggers may introduce a stimulus that is either related or unrelated to your innovation case. Suppose an airline wanted to improve its inflight experience on long-haul flights for economy-class passengers; here, a related stimulus may invite you to consider the needs of a tourist or a kid, while unrelated ones may probe for those of a clown or a superhero.

Once you have understood the inner workings of the *"motor"* of creativity techniques and how to combine and pull the different triggers, you can easily compose your own.

Conclusion: Understand creativity techniques, then build your own

Creativity techniques help you to fight two enemies of creativity: They remove your tunnel vision caused by the *"expert syndrome"* and your habitual conventional ways of thinking. Moreover, they also overcome a lack of inspiration or complacency, as using creativity tool is usually great fun. When will you be ready to play for ideas?

> *"We change our tools and then our tools change us."*
> —JEFF BEZOS

A selection of well-known thinking tools — and how they align to different types of thinking

Serious Thinking Tools	"Whole-Brain" Thinking Tools	Creativity Tools
Challenge Framing Assumptions Check Stakeholder Analysis SWOT Analysis	Challenge Restatement Force Field Analysis Concept Map Business Model Canvas	Brainstorming Morphological Matrix Attribute Listing What If
PMI - Plus, Minus, Interesting Weighted Scoring Model Project Plan	Six Thinking Hats Force Field Analysis Rapid Prototyping	SCAMPER Pass The Buck Get Real

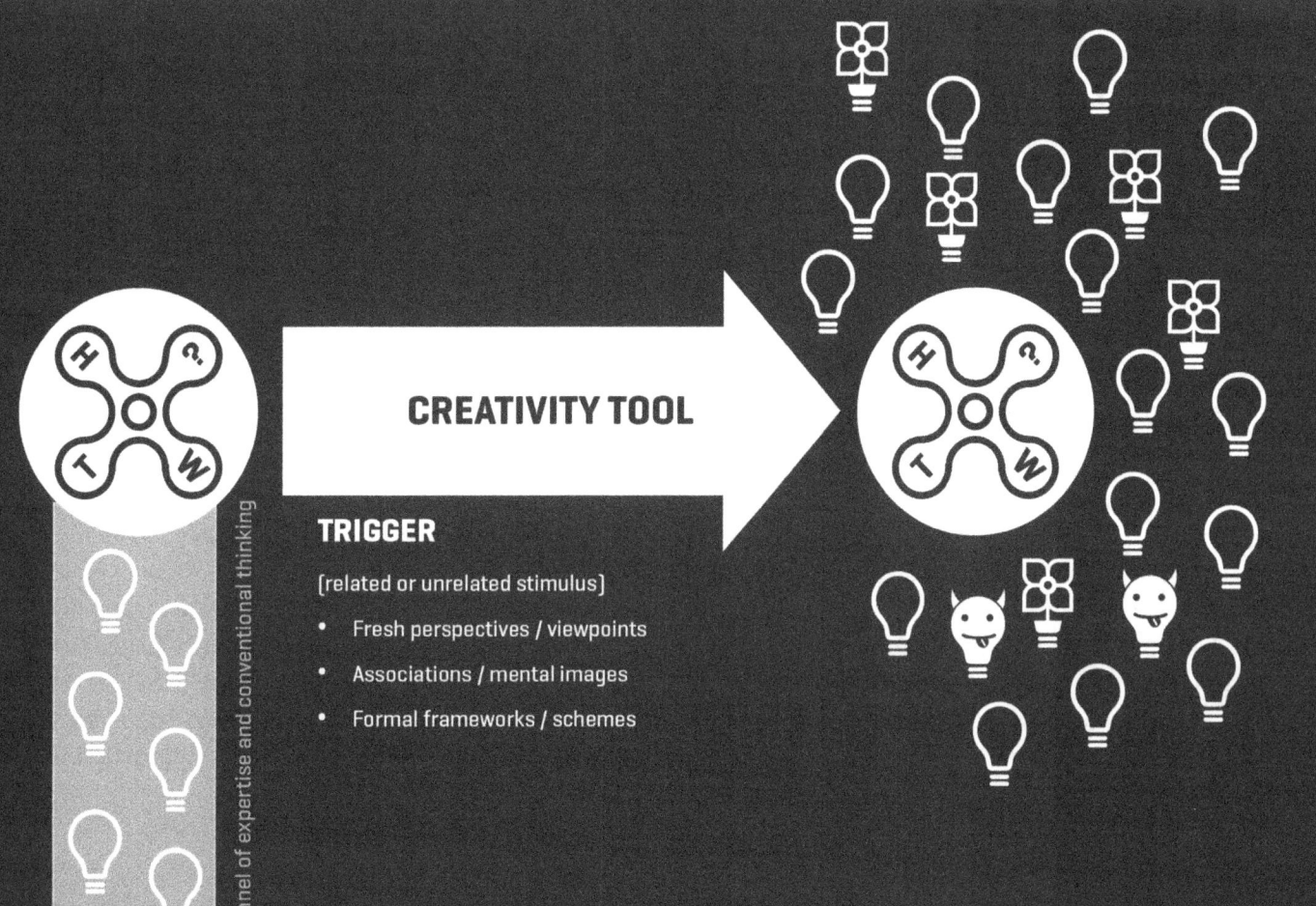

CREATIVITY TOOL

Tunnel of expertise and conventional thinking

TRIGGER

(related or unrelated stimulus)

- Fresh perspectives / viewpoints
- Associations / mental images
- Formal frameworks / schemes

4.4. BRAINSTORMING: THE GOOD, THE BAD AND THE UGLY

Whenever a business or a work team needs some ideas, someone in the group invariably suggests: *"Ok, let's brainstorm for ideas then."* Brainstorming is arguably the most widely used creativity technique ever since Alex Osborn introduced the tool in his classic 1953 book *Applied Imagination*. Need some evidence? Brainstorming has played a central role in every book on creativity techniques.

Some people even use the word brainstorming synonymously with creativity. A reent search on Google delivered about 11.8 million results for the word *"Brainstorming"* as compared to only 1.5 million hits for the term "creativity technique" – although from a set theory point of view, the subset Brainstorming is only a part of the whole set *"creativity technique."* Take the simple *"Google"*-popularity test as a warning sign: It suggests that Brainstorming is often used in a context different from its original scope of being an idea generation tool.

Here we arrive at some of the problems with Brainstorming. With reference to the title of the classic Western movie *"The Good, the Bad and the Ugly,"* you need to understand the good, bad and ugly sides of brainstorming in order to produce creative results for your company when using this tool. So, let's get started in gaining a greater understanding by looking at the ugly sides of brainstorming first.

The ugly side of Brainstorming:

My experience as a creativity coach has taught me that in most companies, brainstorming is done in an incorrect manner, thus delivering only comparatively few ideas that are rather unoriginal.

Most companies start on the correct path by assigning a facilitator to run the session and a recorder to jot down the ideas of the group in an appropriate size (eight plus/minus two is a good rule of thumb here). However, they fail when it comes to following through on the all-important four Ground Rules of Brainstorming:

1. Firstly, defer judgment until the end of the session – or in other words, no killing of ideas during brainstorming. Judgment is like driving with one foot on the gas and one foot on the brake – so take the foot off the brake to accelerate the idea output in a Brainstorming session.

2. Secondly, go for quantity – as quantity breeds quality. Here, remember that the chances that one great idea comes out of an ideation session will be higher if you get four hundred ideas as compared to only one hundred ideas - as Nobel Prize-winning chemist Linus Pauling noted: *"The best way to get a good idea is to get a lot of ideas."*

3. Thirdly, the wilder the better – shoot for crazy, wild, absurd ideas – in line with Albert Einstein's advice: *"If at first, the idea is not absurd, then there is no hope for it."*

4. Finally, combine ideas and improve on the ideas of others.

The bad side of Brainstorming:

Moving on to the bad sides of Brainstorming, Many research studies confirm that Brainstorming is an inferior technique for producing a high number of ideas. In a given time period, a group of *"brainwriters"* who individually write down their ideas will produce roughly four times more ideas than a same-size brainstorming group.

Researchers Diehl and Stroebe attribute this result to three effects that explain the deficiencies of Brainstorming:

- Firstly, some members of the group don't participate and let others do all the work (the *"free-rider phenomenon"*);

- Secondly, some group participants avoid expressing wild or original ideas out of fear how other group members might privately judge them (the problem of *"evaluation apprehension"*); and

- Thirdly and most importantly, the *"blocking effect"* that stems from the fact that only one person can speak at a time and then blocks the thinking of other members who listen to the suggested idea instead of thinking for themselves.

The good side of Brainstorming:

Finally, let's talk about the good side: Brainstorming has become such a popular technique because it is a highly enjoyable, energetic activity that people love to do—and having fun and being playful and childlike (as opposed to childish) are all very beneficial for unleashing creativity. Brainstorming is a key ingredient in the creative culture of the industrial design powerhouse IDEO, and the innovation results delivered by this company speak for the benefits of this technique if it is used appropriately.

Lesson: Use the good, cure the bad and avoid the ugly side of Brainstorming

So how can we cure the bad and ugly sides of brainstorming while continuing to enjoy the benefits of its good side? Here are five recommendations on how you can develop a correct Brainstorming culture in your company:

1. Start the process by sending your employees to a quality creativity training workshop to learn the basics of idea generation and condition the delegates to comply with the very sensible ground rules of Ideation.

2. Start with an individual Brainwriting exercise so you already have a few ideas before beginning the brainstorming exercise.

3. Review the brainstorming ground rules before the start of a session.

4. Set an idea quota for each session – say, at least 150 ideas in one hour that keeps the group focused on moving forward instead of falling into the judgment trap.

5. Finally, have an experienced facilitator run the session, who introduces other creativity techniques (such as *"Metaphors"* or *"What If"*) into the session once the group starts running dry on ideas.

> "Regular brainstorming is as critical to an organization as regular exercise is to your health. It creates a responsive, innovative culture."
> —TOM KELLEY

4.5. IT'S NOT ONLY WHAT TOOLS YOU USE, BUT HOW YOU USE THEM

When you work with a team on an innovation project case, what matters is not only what kind of thinking tool you use when in the innovation process. To do sound thinking and produce adequate outputs, it also matters how exactly you use the tool — or in other words, how you communicate and interact with other team members while applying a particular tool and how you capture outputs.

Background: The problem with *"brainstorming"*

When hearing the words *"creativity"* and *"innovation,"* many businesspeople automatically think of another word: brainstorming. Unsurprisingly, they also indiscriminately use this word while working on an innovation case, such as: *"We need to brainstorm for ideas,"* or *"Let's brainstorm what we know about our case."*

While applying a particular thinking tool, however, you may alternatively use a range of other —and often better— communication styles. Why shouldn't you always simply *"brainstorm" f*or outputs with your team?

Using a variety of communication styles has the following benefits: For one, it often can help teams to noticeably enhance the quantity and quality of their outputs. For two, going beyond *"brainstorming"* for ideas or outputs is also an effective way to circumvent intercultural issues like *"saving face"* or *"respecting seniority or authority."*

For three, varying communication styles can also enhance the levels of fun and enjoyment of an innovation session for the various team members, who often differ in their personalities and preferred cognitive styles.

For example, while the more social and extroverted types enjoy *"brainstorming,"* the more theoretical and private types tend to prefer less dynamic and more well-structured application styles, thus allowing them to contribute more and better outputs.

Apart from *"brainstorming"* for ideas or outputs in a group, you may also fall back on other interaction styles depending on the cognitive styles of the different team members and the nature of the thinking tools you intend to use. For example, we may do solo-brainwriting or pool-brainwriting, enjoy a round of buddy storming or brainstorming, among others.

Variables to decide on while applying thinking tools

Say you're an innovation facilitator who's guiding an innovation team through the application of one particular thinking tool. Apart from setting the time available for the exercise and ideally a target output quota, you also have to decide on the following variables with regard to the precise application of the tool by a team:

- *Team member split:* Do we apply this tool by working with the whole team, in pairs or individually?

- *Feedback:* Do we apply a thinking tool so that the output of other team members may stimulate a delegate while producing more outputs (feedback), or do we use it without feedback? e.g., when you exchange idea worksheets, you may read one idea that inspires a new one.

- *Rotation:* If a group of participants uses various tools in parallel, do we rotate the participants working on a specific tool after some time to provide additional input to the work of other participants on another tool? Or do we keep the workgroups static?

- *Output capturing:* How do you capture outputs? For example, do you write ideas on a flip chart, blank paper sheets, Post-it notes, or worksheets? Do you have one person writing down the outputs for the group, or is everyone writing and producing outputs in parallel?
- *Repetition:* Do we apply the tool in one go (which is the norm), or do we allow for multiple rounds?

What communication styles do we distinguish?

When an innovation team works on an innovation case, they have the following options to apply a thinking tool within a certain stage of an innovation process method:

- **Brainstorming:** This is the default way of how most teams typically apply a particular thinking tool, especially a creativity tool. The team works together as a whole group to produce the desired outputs (e.g., ideas). Thereby, each team member can freely —and without any formal order— suggest thoughts and ideas, which are recorded by at least one person on a paper sheet, a flip-chart or a whiteboard.
- **Round Robin Brainstorming:** Sitting at a table or in a circle with your team, you go around and share a thought or idea one by one. Once a round is completed, you start again with the first person and continue going around; when it's their turn, team members may say *"I pass"* if they need more time to think (or temporarily go blank). Just as with brainstorming, make sure to have one person to record the comments or ideas.
- **Bodystorming:** As a group, enact a role play where you use your bodies to check out or act out a value offering or subject under investigation, such as boarding an airplane or queuing options for immigration checks at airports. As s bodystormer, loudly communicate your experiences and feelings, which are recorded by one team member.
- **Buddystorming:** Pair up with your buddy (a newly befriended or already close team member), and work together on a tool to generate the desired outputs (which one of you may record on paper, worksheets or Post-it notes).
- **Think-Pair-Share:** This communication style blends solo, pair and teamwork. First think: Work alone silently and note down your thoughts and ideas. Then, pair: Exchange your thoughts and ideas with a buddy. Finally, share: one by one, work through all the thoughts and ideas from each team member, which gives the team the chance to add more content. Make sure to consolidate the individual and pair outputs, or capture the outputs of the sharing session at the end.
- **Solo Brainwriting:** Here, all team members silently work and think for themselves, and note down ideas and thoughts on paper sheets, worksheets or Post-it notes. As everyone works in parallel, the team typically produces a much higher output number in a given period of time compared to a team engaging in one of the *"brainstorming"* styles.
- **Pool Brainwriting:** Once again, all team members silently work and think in parallel as a group, but now they exchange the written ideas and thoughts (on worksheets or paper sheets) with their teammates, who then can piggyback on certain ideas or build on other's thoughts.

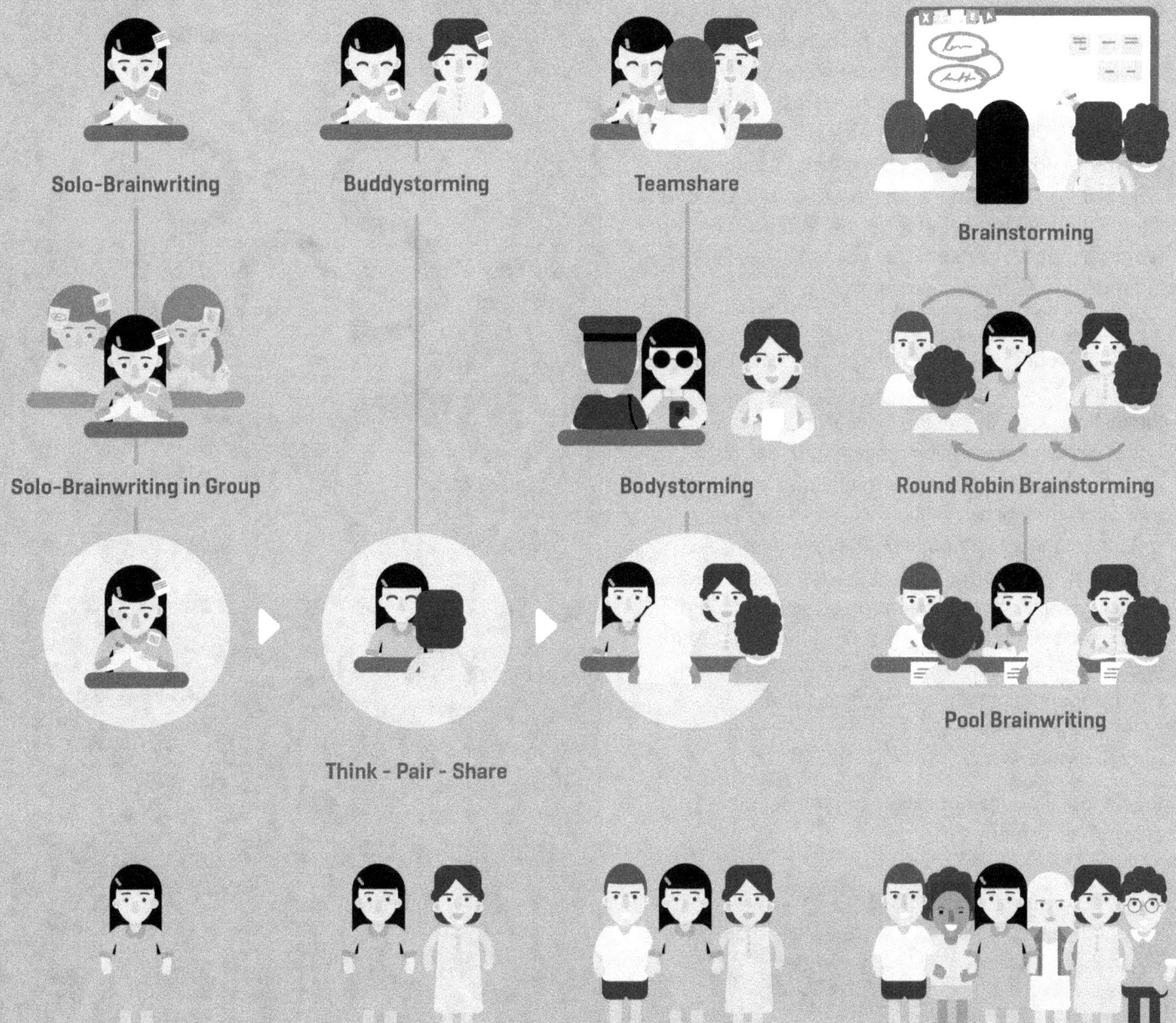

Conclusion: Producing outstanding results in innovation projects is largely a numbers game. An innovation team needs to produce a certain number of outputs, say raw ideas or idea concepts, while working through the different stages of an innovation method to arrive at novel, original and meaningful innovation deliverables by the end of an innovation project. Even if you reach the target output quota, you don't have a hundred percent certainty that you will always succeed in producing an innovation output that wows your target users.

However, your odds of success dramatically increase if you use an effective innovation process, select the thinking tools that fit the innovation type that you target with your innovation project, and then also have mastered the art of how to effectively use each tool within the context of the process method with regards to the key parameters (heads: team, solo, pair, small team, large team, or mixed?; feedback: with or without?; team dynamism: static or rotating? output recording: one for a group; several per group; or everyone individually?; interaction styles: brainstorming, round-robin brainstorming, buddystorming, bodystorming, think-pair-share, solo brainwriting, or pool brainwriting?).

In short, facilitating innovation projects is both a science and an art.

> "The best investment is in the tools of one's own trade."
> —BENJAMIN FRANKLIN

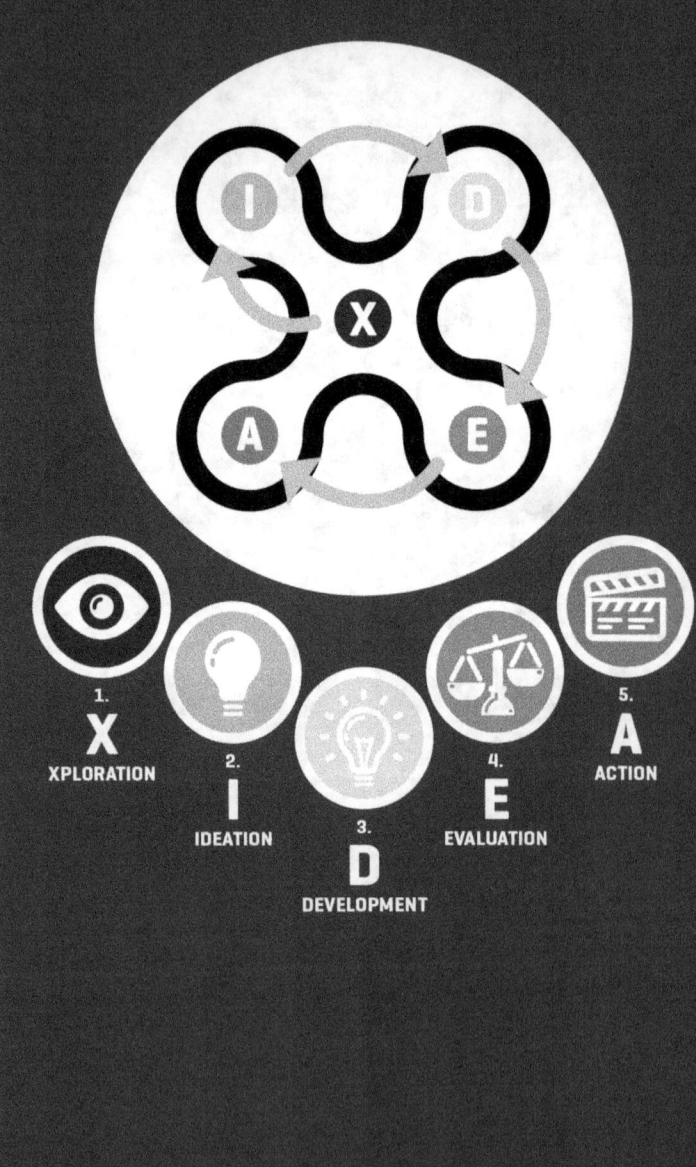

1. **X** XPLORATION
2. **I** IDEATION
3. **D** DEVELOPMENT
4. **E** EVALUATION
5. **A** ACTION

X·IDEA™
THE KNOW-HOW OF WOW

4.6. X-IDEA: INTRODUCING THE KNOW-HOW OF WOW

When I reviewed other creative process methods to identify a suitable one for use in innovation projects, I noticed that most innovation methods suffered from one or more of the following shortcomings:

- Many methods fail to systematically link thinking tools to their process steps and stages.
- They often lack a systematic IPO focus on inputs that are processed to produce specific target outputs.
- They tend to neglect cognitive biases and procedural traps that innovation teams encounter at specific moments while going through an innovation project.
- As most innovation methods were developed in the West, they tend to lack awareness of —and thus don't consider the negative influence of— intercultural issues that are common in many other cultures (such as the *"fear of losing face"* or the need to *"pay respect to seniority"*).
- Some methods cater to only one or a few innovation types.
- Last but not least, almost all innovation methods have only one creative process stage, which, as we will discuss in the next section, tends to make it difficult for innovation teams to produce extraordinary ideas.

In order to improve on these perceived short-comings of many other methods, I created my own innovation process method for my innovation company Thinkergy that we fine-tuned in over 200 innovation projects that we ran over more than a decade: X-IDEA

The X-IDEA Innovation Method comprises five process stages that innovation teams work through one by one with an innovation case. Each of the five main process stages of X-IDEA has different objectives, requires different thinking styles, and focuses on producing different yet specific target outputs.

Suppose you're a member of an innovation team working on an innovation challenge, say a campaign design case, and I am your innovation facilitator who guides you through the five stages of X-IDEA. What would our innovation journey through X-IDEA be like?

- **Stage X — XPLORATION:**
   In Stage X, we first invest time to deeply understand our innovation case, to find out what's really going on and to unveil our real challenge. We do this in three steps: First, we XPRESS our initial understanding of the challenge of our innovation case, and what we know and do not yet know about it. Then, we CALMly XPLORE our case by checking out four different pathways (Check-Ask-Look-Map) to learn more about trends, needs and wants of customers and different stakeholders, assumptions and rules, and other important nuances related to our case. Finally, we XTRACT novel and important insights that we got during Xploration, and encapsulate all our learnings in a succinct definition of our final challenge, a *"how to"* sentence that guides our work in the subsequent stages IDEA. Why do we not move straight into ideation? Experience from many projects suggests that after a thorough Xploration of the case, the initial perception of our innovation challenge changes in almost all cases. After we have uncovered our knowledge gaps (i.e., things we don't know well

enough to start ideation) and gained novel insights into the case, we're better able to determine our real challenge. That way, we ensure that later on, we work on and generate ideas for our real issue and avoid wasting time, effort, and money.

- **Stage I — IDEATION:**
  In Stage I, we generate hundreds of raw ideas using a selection of both classic creativity tools and our own in-house I-Tools. Thereby, we laterally IDEATE, IMAGINE and INCUBATE for ideas. Why do we target a raw idea quota of 500-1,000 (depending on the time at hand and the heads per team) here? Quantity breeds quality. The probability of having a few highly original, intriguing ideas increases the more ideas we have.

- **Stage D — DEVELOPMENT:**
  In Stage D, we turn idea quantity into quality and transform raw ideas into fully developed idea concepts. Thereby, we first DISCOVER intriguing raw ideas, then DESIGN those into relevant idea concepts through elaboration, combination and transmutation, and finally DEVELOP those concepts further by adding more meaning to them. In Stage D, each team targets to develop ca. two to three dozen idea concepts, mostly by falling back on our proprietary concept design tools (D-Tools). In the following section, 4.7, we will discuss why this second creative stage is crucially important to enable innovators to move towards more novel, original, and meaningful ideas.

- **Stage E — EVALUATION:**
  In Stage E, we first EVALUATE our portfolio of idea concepts to understand the pros, cons and interesting aspects of each concept. Then, we ENHANCE promising concepts by rapidly prototyping them and fixing identified bugs. Finally, we ELECT those vital few top concepts that we feel deserve to pitch for real-life activation. In Stage E, we separate the wheat from the chaff and identify those vital few top concepts that have a high-value potential and are feasible to implement. This ensures we focus our time, money, and effort on those few top concepts that promise to really stand a chance to succeed big in the market and can be activated.

- **Stage A — ACTION:**
  In the final Stage A, we take action and persist to overcome resistance and inertia to turn a top idea into a tangible innovation deliverable. Here, we first ASSESS the situation, then ALIGN our resources, and finally ACTIVATE our planned actions, whereby these work steps unfold in three phases (a pitch, a project, and a final review phase). Why do we need the Action-stage? Just recall our innovation formula from Chapter 2: CREATIVITY + ACTION = INNOVATION. We must take ACTION on a deserving novel, original, and meaningful top idea to transform it into a tangible innovation and to convert ourselves from a dreamer to an innovator.

The X-IDEA Thinking Toolbox

The X-IDEA Innovation Method doesn't come alone but is linked to a mighty thinking toolbox of more than 150 thinking tools, each of which has a logical default position within the X-IDEA method where we would apply the tool. These thinking tools include popular and well-known techniques such as Brainstorming, Rapid Prototyping, Observation or Concept Mapping that we adopted and adapted, as well as a range of our own X-IDEA Tools that we created and successfully tested in our innovation projects (like Human Touch, Speed D, Business Model Matrix, Yin And Yang, or Ding Dong). Why do we prefer to have so many tools?

- For one, recall Abraham Maslow's insight that we already mentioned earlier: *"If the only tool you have is a hammer, you tend to see every problem as a nail."*
- For two, the high number of tools allows us to cover the full spectrum of modern innovation types. The X-IDEA toolbox contains a set of ca. two dozen "base tools" that come into play in almost every project. From the remaining tools, our facilitators of an X-IDEA innovation project choose a mix that they deem most suited to help the teams produce the best outputs for the given innovation case and related innovation type. So, our "innovation guides" would pick different thinking tools depending on whether the teams would work on a strategy innovation project, a product innovation case, a process innovation challenge, or a customer experience design project.
- For three, if you always use the same tools, they tend to run stale after some time. Having many different tools allows for greater variety and ensures fresh ideas and thinking. After all, you also don't want to eat the same food each and every day, do you?.

Depending on the innovation type of your project case, we pull different thinking tools out of our X-IDEA Toolbox. Many X-IDEA tools come with accompanying worksheets (pre-structured templates to simplify the output recording) and stimulus cards (cards with images and accompanying explanations that inspire the creativity of delegates or are used by innovation guides to ask questions or give instructions).

Other conceptual features of X-IDEA

X-IDEA integrates a number of other conceptual features to address the identified delivery gaps of other innovation methods as follows:

An overview of selected thinking tools (rectangular) and related stimulus cards (round) from the X-IDEA Thinking Toolbox that complements the X-IDEA Innovation Method.

- Every X-IDEA thinking tool is linked to a logical default position with the process flow of stages and steps where it is typically used.
- X-IDEA includes a systematic IPO focus on three levels: the project, stage, and tool levels. In other words, before would-be innovators start working on an innovation project case, a process stage, or a particular thinking tool, they learn what specific inputs they need to have at hand to get started and what specific target outputs they are supposed to produce.
- X-IDEA Traps is a feature that warns innovation teams of certain cognitive biases (such as the overconfidence bias, confirmation or groupthink) and procedural traps (such as the ground rules of ideation and idea development that we will also review in the next section) that commonly wait for them at certain stages and work steps within the overall process flow. Once they are aware of the traps and learn how to avoid them, it's easy for the teams to stay safe and continue to think soundly.
- X-IDEA Roles helps to circumvent the negative influence of certain intercultural norms while working on an innovation case in non-Western cultures. The feature introduces a role for each stage that captures the spirit of thinking and cognitive mindset needed to succeed in each stage: the Xplorer (Xploration), the Child (Ideation), the Alchemist (Development), the Judge (Evaluation), and the Champion (Action). These five roles liberate would-be innovators from shackling cultural norms, as would-be innovators now feel safe to suggest wild ideas without fear of losing face because everyone is playing for ideas in the role of a Child, or feel encouraged by the role of a Judge to critique a flat idea concept of a senior team member.
- X-IDEA is designed to cater to the full spectrum of modern innovation types as featured in Chapters 2 and 3, from process to product to service innovation, from customer experience to brand and campaign design, from business model and strategy to social innovation.

Probably the most important design feature differentiating X-IDEA from most other innovation methods is that it uses two distinct creative process stages, Stage I-Ideation and Stage D-Development. In the next section, I will explain why process methods with only one creative stage don't allow innovation teams to move beyond ordinary, vanilla, and conventional ideas and why we need two creative stages to allow would-be innovators to produce extraordinary and meaningful ideas.

The table on the next page overviews the key conceptual design features of X-IDEA.

METHODOLOGICAL DESIGN FEATURES OF X-IDEA

Stage X-IDEA Feature	X Xploration	I Ideation	D Development	E Evaluation	A Action
Roles	Xplorer	Child	Alchemist	Judge	Champion
Stage Inputs	Challenge Evidence	Final Challenge	Raw Ideas Initial Ideas	Idea concepts Evaluation Criteria	Top Idea Concepts
Steps & Activities	1. Xpress 2. Xplore 3. Xtract	Ideate · Imagine · Incubate 1. Start 2. Play 3. End	1. Discover 2. Design 3. Develop	1. Evaluate 2. Enhance 3. Elect	1. Assess 2. Arrange 3. Activate
Tools (150) Worksheets (92) Stimulus Cards (473)	54 X Tools 32 X Worksheets 80 X Stimulus Cards	45 I Tools 8 I Worksheets 230 I Stimulus Cards	18 D Tools 25 D Worksheets 57 D Stimulus Cards	13 E Tools 12 E Worksheets 29 E Stimulus Cards	20 A Tools 15 A Worksheets 13 A Stimulus Cards
Traps	Cognitive biases such as overconfidence bias, confirmation bias, among others	Process traps (non-compliance to ground rules of ideation)	Process traps (non-compliance to ground rules of idea development)	Group-related biases such as the Abilene paradox or Groupthink, among others	Cognitive biases such as hindsight and non-rational escalation of commitment, etc.
Stage Outputs	Final Challenge Insights Initial Ideas Evaluation Criteria	Raw ideas	Idea Concepts	Top Concepts Early Prototypes	Tangible innovation deliverable Learnings

4.7. WHY USING ONLY ONE CREATIVE PROCESS STAGE LEADS TO DULL IDEAS

When you *"brainstorm"* for ideas with a team, do you typically deliver conventional ideas that —if you're honest— you could have got without dedicating extra time? Well, the reason you ended up with these ordinary low-hanging fruits doesn't mean that you and your teammates are not creative. Rather, it means that you used an ineffective creative process — if you used one at all.

Most innovation process methods don't allow you to move beyond the *"obvious"* ideas — the ones everyone else in your industry also thinks of first — because they use only one creative process stage. Today, let me explain how you can move from ordinary ideas to extraordinary ideas by adding a second creative stage to your innovation process.

The unspoken problem of most innovation processes:

Most innovation process methods have only one creative process stage. The classic Creative Problem-solving (CPS) model labels this creative stage *"idea finding"*; the models of Bragg & Bragg, Clegg & Birch or VanGundy call it *"idea generation"*; and Design Thinking names it *"ideation"*. In all these process methods, this sole creative process stage is directly followed by a stage used to critically evaluate the ideas and select the best ones for further implementation.

"That's precisely how we always do it, too," you may be saying. *"So what's wrong with that?"* Well, you're likely to end up with a small number of ideas that are all safe, sane, and set.

What causes the problem?

When generating ideas, innovation project team members are supposed to follow four ground rules of ideation suggested by Alex Osborn, the famous advertiser and inventor of Brainstorming and other creativity techniques:

- #1. No killing of any idea. Defer judgment.
- #2. Go for idea quantity as it breeds quality.
- #3. Shoot for wild, crazy, funny off-the-wall ideas.
- #4. Combine and improve on ideas.

Unfortunately, it's difficult to comply with these four ground rules if your innovation method has only one creative process stage. Why?

Why using one creative stage isn't enough

If idea generation is going to be followed directly by evaluation, are you likely to adhere to all ground rules of ideation? Quantity over quality? No idea being too wild or crazy?

Most probably not. It's highly likely that your inner voice of judgment dismisses any wild idea the very moment you think it — and you won't write it down. As such, you end up with fewer ideas overall — and most of them are ordinary or even boring.

There is another problem related to using only one creative process stage: Suppose that against all odds, you had really mustered up your courage to adhere to the ground rules of ideation. If there were only one

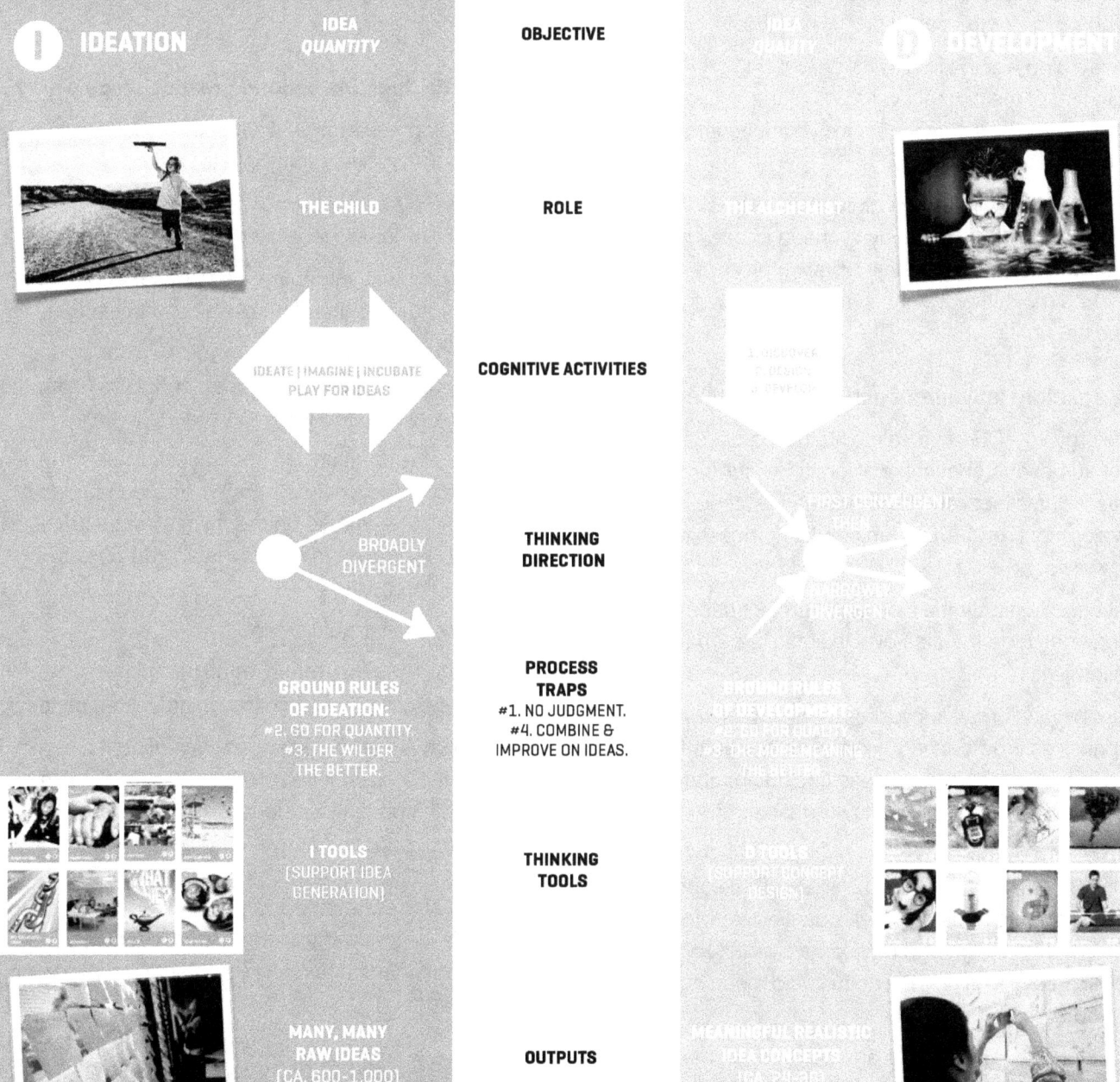

creative stage, would you be likely to select any wild idea for further in-depth evaluation?

No way! You would kill all wild ideas right at the beginning of the critical evaluation stage, as you regarded them as unfit to resolve your innovation challenge in meaningful ways.

Interestingly, a wild idea is often the seedling of a truly outstanding idea. That's why we need to have two creative stages to make an innovation process really work and move beyond the same set of conventional ideas.

The solution: Move from one to two creative stages

Thinkergy's X-IDEA innovation method is designed to move beyond conventional ideas by introducing a second, distinctively different creative stage, Development. In X-IDEA, the creative process flows as follows:

First we investigate the innovation project case in the Xploration stage to gain novel insights into what our real challenge is.

Then, the first creative process stage, Ideation, emphasizes idea *quantity*. Here we make an effort to produce hundreds of raw ideas (including many wild and uncommon ones) in a playful, fast and furious atmosphere.

In the second creative process stage, Development, we take our time to transform idea quantity into *quality*. Here, it's our job to design and develop a smaller portfolio of two to three dozen novel, original, and meaningful idea concepts.

Next, we evaluate the pros and cons of our idea concepts in a critical and realistic stage, Evaluation. Now we're finally allowed to judge our ideas, but not before.

Finally, we take Action on those ideas that we selected for real-life activation.

How exactly does the second creative stage work?

In the Development-stage, we discover, design and develop to turn idea quantity into idea quality:

First, we discover intriguing ideas within the large portfolio of raw ideas generated during Ideation.

Then, we use these intriguing ideas to design realistic idea concepts through refinement, combination and transmutation.

Finally, we develop these designed concepts further by looking for ways to add even more value to them.

Just like during Ideation, we also must follow four ground rules in the Development-stage. While ground rules #1 and #4 stay the same as before, two rules are changed compared to Ideation to reflect the altered objective of the Development stage:

- Rule #2: Go for quality, and take your time.
- Rule #3. The more meaningful, the better. Shoot for valuable, useful, realistic, meaningful idea concepts.

Conclusion: A creative process can unfold its magic only once it consists of two creative stages. If you are satisfied with conventional ideas, continue using a conventional, ordinary innovation process method with one creative stage. Or switch to an unconventional innovation process method with two creative stages (like X-IDEA) if you want to create unconventional, extraordinary ideas that make you stand out from your industry peers.

> "If at first the idea is not absurd, then there will be no hope for it."
> —ALBERT EINSTEIN

4.8. DOS AND DON'TS FOR A SUCCESSFUL INNOVATION PROJECT

Nowadays, many businesses consider doing innovation initiatives to refresh their products and services or the ways they promote and deliver them. Planning and successfully running an innovation project is both a science and an art. In the following, I share with you eight dos and don'ts of conducting a successful innovation project.

Beware of the don'ts to avoid project failure (mediocre, ordinary ideas and outputs), and heed as many of the dos as possible to enjoy project success (extraordinary ideas and innovation results).

1. **DON'T** aim for too much in just one innovation project. The German idiom *"egg-laying wool-milk-saw"* describes the ultimate farm animal or something that can do everything. Too often, companies likewise want it all in just one project: coming up with meaningful new products plus ancillary services, plus new ways to distribute those, plus cool promotion campaigns, plus new business models to make money in novel ways.

   DO focus on the most important issue you need to tackle. Run a product innovation project if you want to reinvigorate your product line. Do a campaign design project if you need new promotions. Conduct a business model innovation project to find novel ways to get paid for your products and services. You're more likely to produce outstanding results if you focus on one target.

2. **DON'T** attempt to do it all in one day — or even worse, in half a day.

   DO invest the time needed to give you the standout results you crave. How much time should you make available? Ask yourself: *"How important is success in this innovation project for our bottom line in the next 3 years?"* Answer using the scale below, which gives you the number of days you should invest: 5 – Vitally important; 4 – highly important: 3 – important; 2 – quite important; 1 – not so important; 0 – not important at all.

3. **DON'T** do innovation on the cheap. Invest in your future profitability.

   DO commit the required resources needed to produce ideas that go beyond what everyone else in the industry is thinking. Apart from an adequate amount of time, other resources to commit include a decent number of internal people and a budget. For innovation projects high up on the importance scale, consider inviting external collaborators (e.g., suppliers or distributors, lead customers and target consumers, creative agencies, and, of course, professional innovation experts).

4. **DON'T** head straight to idea generation (or Brainstorming) in your innovation project.

   DO take the time to first explore your innovation case thoroughly to gain fresh insights into what your challenge really is. In almost all cases, the final challenge differs from the perceived initial challenge.

5. **DON'T** use an ineffective innovation method with only one creative process stage.

"Pay peanuts and you get monkeys."
—DAVID OGILVY

DO ensure that the innovation method used in your innovation project has two separate creative process stages: First ideate to generate a large pool of raw ideas including wild ones. Then from the large pool of raw ideas, find those vital few ideas that really intrigue you, and design and develop those into full-fledged concepts that are well-elaborated, meaningful and realistic. In Thinkergy's awards-winning innovation method X-IDEA, we call the said two creative process stages Ideation and Development.

6. **DON'T** use only brainstorming as the sole or main creativity tool and interaction method. Brainstorming is popular but ineffective. Why's that? A total of 25 research studies on the efficacy of brainstorming vis-a-vis brainwriting and other creativity techniques concluded that brainstorming is an inferior technique and simply doesn't deliver on the main objective of ideation: to produce a large pool of raw ideas. Moreover, most brainstorming sessions led by inexperienced facilitators only lead to a small pool of *"safe, acceptable"* ideas. This is because typically, brainstormers fail to honor the four ground rules of Ideation (#1. No killing of ideas. #2. Go for quantity. #3. The wilder the better. Shoot for wild, crazy, funny, zany ideas. #4. Combine and improve on ideas.).

DO use other creativity and ideation tools (such as asking *"what if"*, employing metaphors or visiting *"other worlds"*) and ideation interaction methods (*such as brainwriting or pool brainwriting*).

7. **DON'T** run the innovation project all by yourself. You're an expert in your industry, not an expert in how to plan effectively, scope and successfully run an innovation project. That's why there is an entire niche industry of innovation companies such as Thinkergy that specialize in successfully guiding innovation teams towards meaningful innovation results.

DO engage the services of an experienced creativity coach or innovation company with a solid track record. Such professionals — back to Don't #5 — should use a well-rounded, effective systematic innovation method with a sufficient variety of related innovation tools and creativity techniques.

8. **DON'T** play it small and safe if you want to go beyond the normal, *"acceptable"* set of ordinary ideas that everyone else has, most of which would also emerge in a typical in-house brainstorming session.

DO dare to be bold and shoot for big ideas. After all, why would you want to innovate if you don't dare to be different and extraordinary?

"I begin with an idea…

…and then it becomes something else."

– Pablo Picasso

CHAPTER 4 - EXECUTIVE SUMMARY: INNOVATION METHOD AND TOOLS

Everything in business ultimately comes down to mastering specific projects with the help of effective processes. The same holds true when teams resolve an innovation project (that relates to a certain innovation type) with the help of an effective innovation process.

- Innovation methods are systematic process flows that outline the steps and cognitive activities that individual innovators or innovation teams need to follow while thinking their way through an innovation project. Popular methods include Design Thinking and the Creative Problem-Solving Model (CPS), among many others.

- Often used within the context of a specific innovation process stage, thinking tools specify work steps to direct thinking toward certain directions, perspectives, and desired outputs. We can categorize thinking tools into serious (or analytical) tools, whole-brain tools, or creativity tools. The latter use triggers to reliably push individual thinking to a new starting point from where it is easy to come up with more intriguing ideas outside the tunnel of expertise and conventional thinking.

- Most people know and have used the most popular creativity tool, Brainstorming, but few people know about its bad (low number of ideas) and ugly side (disregard of its ground rules).

- X-IDEA is an awards-winning innovation process method plus an integrated thinking toolbox designed to work for all modern innovation types. X-IDEA integrates a number of design features such as roles, traps, steps & related cognitive activities, inputs, and outputs that help cure certain shortcomings identified in some of the other innovation methods.

- X-IDEA differs from most other innovation methods because it uses two distinct creative stages that allow innovation teams to move beyond conventional ideas. These two creative stages, called Ideation and Development, use different roles, tools, process rules, and cognitive steps to produce different types of outputs (raw ideas vs. idea concepts).

- When you want to conduct a real-life innovation project with your company, there are certain things you need to do —and others you need to avoid doing— to ensure that your innovation project teams arrive at meaningful innovation deliverables by the end of the project.

CHAPTER 5

INNOVATIVE PEOPLE
SMALL PICTURE (II)

How to involve everyone in your innovation efforts in harmony with their talents and preferred cognitive styles.

1. Cognitive Profiling Methods: What? Why? How?
2. Scrutinizing Popular Cognitive Profiling Methods
3. Introducing the TIPS innovation Profiling Method
4. Flow Along the Company Life Cycle with TIPS
5. How TIPS Helps Resolve Main Corporate Innovation Challenges
6. What's Your Style to Innovate?
7. Understanding Who Really Makes Innovation Happen
8. Creative Leaders vs Innovation Managers: Same or Different?
* *Executive Summary*

5.1. COGNITIVE PROFILING METHODS: WHAT? WHY? HOW?

Imagine you were hired by a mature corporation as their new innovation manager. Suppose further that one of your tasks is to find all the creative talents within the organization. What will you do? Will you walk around and observe how people dress and behave at work to pinpoint the creative types? Or interview everyone?

Whatever you do, chances are that while you can surely expect to have some hits, you're likely to also have a lot of misses—and a lot of *"false positives."* So what else can you do? Here, cognitive profiling tools can come to your aid and rescue—provided you pick the right one.

What are cognitive profiling methods?

Cognitive profiling methods and—in a wider sense—personality-profiling instruments use well-structured questionnaires to determine people's preferred cognitive styles. Ideally, the questions asked in the survey relate to certain psychological dimensions or cognitive styles that form the theoretical underpinning of a particular method.

As such, these tests aim to capture differences in people's personal preferences in areas such as cognition, behavior at work, communication and creative problem-solving, and innovation.

Typically, respondents self-assess their preferred ways by answering a set of questions (known as personal assessment). In behavioral personality tests, however, other people report on the observed behavior of an evaluatee; in professional settings, this is often done as a *"360-degree evaluation"* involving a mix of superiors, subordinates, and professional peers.

Based on the chosen answers, the evaluatee is then assigned a profiling score and/or a personality profile that describes their psychological preferences or preferred cognitive styles.

Why are personality tests and cognitive profiling methods useful?

Critics belittle personal assessment tools by saying they are pseudo-scientific and no better than reading horoscopes. In contrast, proponents (and I am one of them) see value in using these methods to ensure a better alignment of people to environments that allow them to play on their natural talents.

Personality tests and cognitive profiling tools give the respondents greater self-awareness of their preferred ways and cognitive styles, natural talent, and likely strengths and weaknesses related to a particular profile or profiling result.

These tests also give people- and team-awareness to managers and colleagues who work together in a team so that they not only know what makes themselves tick but also what makes everyone else in a work team tick.

To harness such higher self- and people-awareness, some methods propose specific applications for improving business performance, such as more focused career planning, talent development, effective team building, and the like.

An overview of existing cognitive style profiling concepts

Nowadays, you can easily google the keywords *"personality test"* or *"cognitive profiling"* to find a myriad

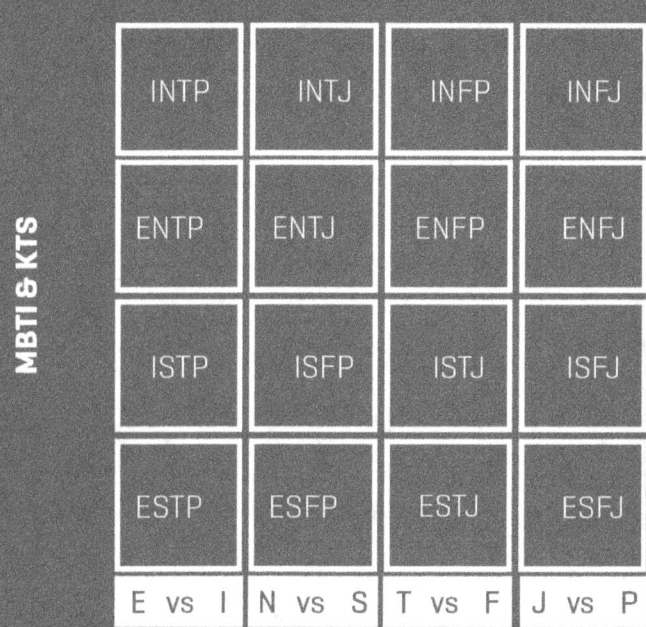
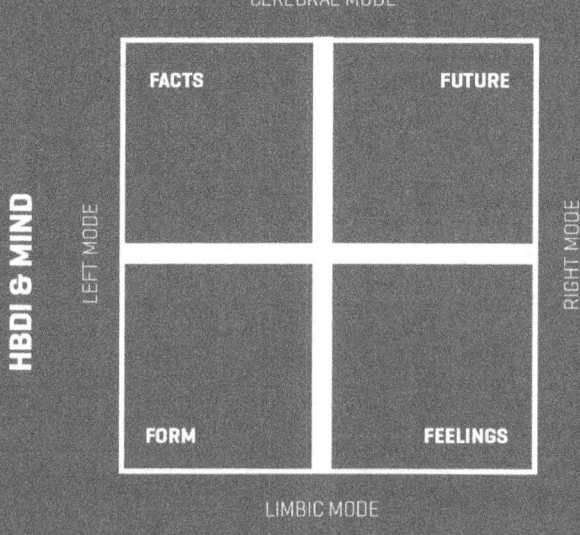

of different personality or cognitive profiling tools, each of which has its merit in one way or another. So, which cognitive profiling method may work for you?

Well, it all depends on what you want to find out and want to use the method for. So, to get started, let me introduce a few profiling concepts to you that are either highly popular or which caught my interest while I was investigating different methods for their suitability to explain and support the people-side of creativity and innovation:

- Arguably the most widely used psychometric instrument is the Myers-Briggs Type Indicator. MBTI goes back on the work of the Swiss psychoanalyst Carl Gustav Jung, who introduced three dimensions to capture differences in personal style: Extroversion (E) vs. Introversion (I); iNutuition (N) vs Sensing (S); and Thinking (T) vs. Feeling (F). Later on, Katharine Cook Briggs and her daughter Isabel Briggs Myers augmented the Jungian preferences by a fourth dimension (Judging (J) vs. Perceiving (P)) and developed the MBTI typology of sixteen personality types. After taking a questionnaire, test subjects are assigned their profile type based on the letter combination of the highest score for each preference (e.g., I usually come out as an ENTP).

- In his Keirsey Temperament Sorter (KTS), David Keirsey expanded the MBTI concept by introducing a new hierarchy of the MBTI dimensions and by grouping the types according to Plato's four classic temperaments (e.g., guardian, artisan, idealist, rational). In addition, Keirsey suggested useful descriptive names for each MBTI type (e.g., the inventor in the case of the ENTP).

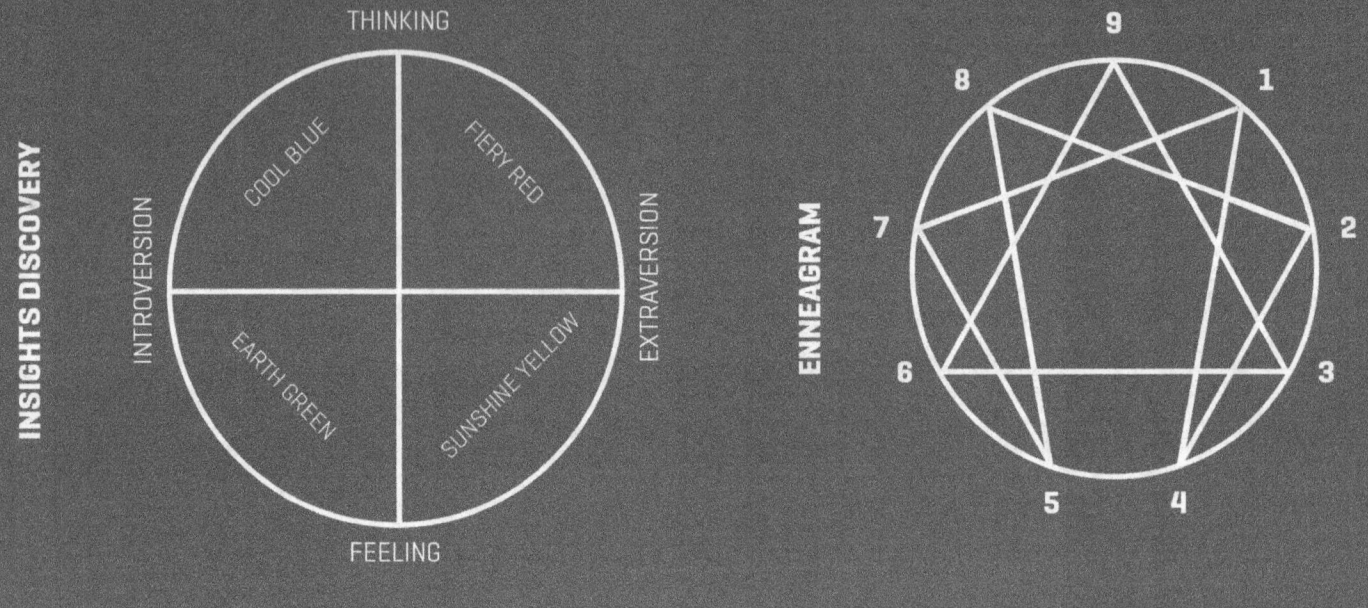

- Roger Hamilton's Wealth Dynamics (WD) concept also draws upon some constructs from Carl Jung's work on personality style but merges them with elements of the classic Chinese I Ching concept. WD uses four variables (dynamo, blaze, tempo, steel) to assign test subjects one of eight profiles (e.g., creator, star, supporter, deal maker). The WD concept is interesting insofar as it can explain how certain profile types are better suited to lead a company at different points of time as the venture evolves and moves through the company life cycle.

- One more profiling concept that works with only two Jungian dimensions (extroversion vs. introversion and thinking vs. feeling) is Insights Discovery. Created by a father-son team (Andi and Andy Lothian), the concept turns a 2x2-matrix into four color types (fiery red, sunshine yellow, earth green, cool blue) and then arrives at eight colored profile types with business-related names (e.g. director, motivator, inspirer).

- Another well-known profiling instrument is the DISC behavior assessment tool. Grounded in Marston's DISC theory, this tool measures the prevalence of four different behavioral traits (dominance, influence, steadiness, and compliance) in a person. In its original version, it assigns a person one of 15 profile patterns (named achiever, investigator, developer, among others) based on the test results.

- Developed by psychologist Ned Herrmann, the Herrmann Brain Dominance Instrument (HBDI) is yet another well-liked concept to measure and describe thinking preferences in people. HBDI is based on a two-dimensional model grounded in theories on the development of the human brain. It distinguishes four brain modes (a cerebral vs. limbic mode and a left vs. right mode) and measures four related cognitive

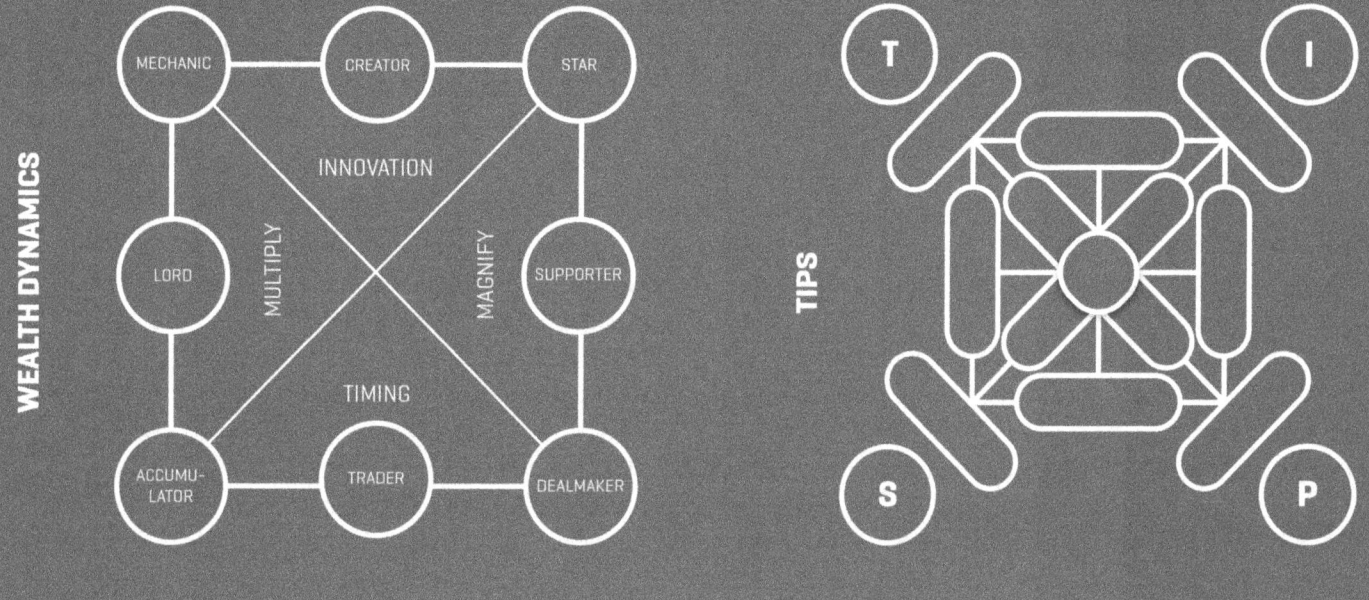

styles (A. analytical, B. practical, C. emotional, and D. experimental). The scores of an individual's test result are presented within the context of a profiling map that shows which of the four styles are predominantly used by a test subject.

- A related concept that leaning on Herrmann's model is the M.I.N.D. Design concept (MIND.) by Robert Alan Black. Like HBDI, Black distinguishes four styles that also christen the concept (M - Meditative; I - Intuitive; N - Negotiative; D - Directive) and uses the test results to indicate the extent to which a test subject draws upon each of the four styles. However, unlike the 120 profiling questions of HBDI, Black asks only nine questions to arrive at a largely accurate test result and descriptive report.
- Developed by Gerard Puccio, the FourSight Thinking Profile also tests for four thinking preferences, but here, it aligns them to the basic four-stage creative process blueprint used by many methods described in Chapter 4. After completing 40 questions related to activities that are performed in an innovation project or creative problem-solving case, FourSight assigns one of 15 possible thinking profiles: Four main *"1-peak"* profiles that directly link to a stage of the basic creative process (clarifier, ideator, developer, implementer), six *"two-peak"* profiles, four *"three-peak"* profiles, and an average *"four peak"* profile (integrator).
- An influential profiling tool to express style differences in creative problem-solving and innovation is Michael Kirton's Adaption-Innovation Inventory (KAI). KAI captures on a one-dimensional scale the degree to which someone prefers to think and work as an adapter (who likes improving on existing concepts) or an innovator (who enjoys coming up with new solutions).

135

- Other cognitive profiling tools you may come across include Miller's Innovation Styles concept, Lafferty's Life Styles Inventory (LSI), the Big Five personality traits (also known as the Five Factor Model), or the Enneagram.

Yet other popular profiling tests don't target personality or cognitive style but emphasize other aspects that may also give useful hints. For example, Don Clifton's Strengthsfinder test determines a person's top five strengths from an overall set of 34 talent themes (e.g., mine were *"intellection, ideation, input, learner, competition"* when I took the test in 2008).

So, which cognitive profiling tool should you use?

My advice is to test out every new profiling tool you come across and find appealing to possibly learn new nuances about yourself. You will notice that some tools really *"click"* with you and offer valuable new insights, while others may be well-reputed but don't resonate with you. Never mind, that's part of learning more about yourself.

In any case, the more tools you use, the more you notice that certain personality traits and cognitive styles seem to overlap across various tests, thus pointing to a particular direction where your unique personality and related cognitive styles and talents reside. And the more tests you do, the more you also come across some surprising new factors that make you one-of-a-kind. It's just like collecting more and more jigsaw pieces of nuances of your personality, and once you find the right missing piece, you suddenly see a wonderful wholesome picture of who you really are.

But coming back to our introductory scenario, what cognitive profiling tool can help you, as a supposedly newly appointed Innovation Manager, reliably identify those creative types in your organization who genuinely are drivers and agents of innovation and organizational change? And what tool can give you hints on how you can make everyone contribute to innovation in line with their preferred styles and natural talents?

For almost a decade, I hunted for such a cognitive profiling tool to lighten up the people side of innovation, testing method after method with always the same result: Most methods had certain aspects that I really liked and found valuable and accurate, but also had some "bugs" or delivery gaps that I perceived to be sub-optimal, missing or plain *"wrong"*. While thinking about how to improve on these perceived shortcomings, I suddenly conceived my own profiling concept: TIPS, Thinkergy's innovation people profiling system.

I created TIPS with the intent to give individuals and organizations clear insights into how everyone can contribute to corporate innovation by using the preferred styles of each profile type. The TIPS innovation people profiling method draws inspiration from theoretical constructs of a range of earlier personal assessment concepts listed above but also includes new concepts adapted from other disciplines (e.g., innovation theories, evolutionary economics, and social science).

In the following sections, we will first take a look at both commonalities and perceived shortcomings of popular personality and cognitive profiling methods before then introducing the design architecture and features of TIPS.

> *"Remember that people are built very differently and that different ways of seeing and thinking make people suitable for different jobs."*
> —RAY DALIO

5.2. SCRUTINIZING POPULAR COGNITIVE PROFILING METHODS

Since the early noughties, I've tested with a wide range of methods to profile personality and cognitive styles. Initially, I wanted to find out more about myself. Later on, I also was hunting for a suitable test to recommend to corporate clients eager to learn more about how to better handle the people side of innovation.

While experimenting with a great variety of different cognitive profiling tools and online personality tests, I've learned how to scrutinize the underlying conceptual constructs and design architecture of such methods. The various personal assessment tools have certain features that describe both commonalities and individual differences in the design of these methods. I also found that many methods had certain aspects that I liked, but also had a few perceptual blind spots or delivery gaps that from my personal perspective, I thought were wrong or missing.

What general design features do most cognitive profiling concepts share? How do these features differ across various methods?

Most cognitive profiling concepts share a set of common design features as follows:

- *Use of dimensions:* Most tools use between one and four dimensions to capture differences in personal styles. These theoretical constructs typically relate to particular cognitive or psychological theories. For example, the Myers-Briggs Type Indicator (MBTI) uses four *"preferences"* linked to Carl Jung's psychological theories to profile people; Herrman's Brain Dominance Instrument (HBDI) draws upon brain theories to profile people using two dimensions mapped out in a four-by-four matrix; and Kirton's Adaption-Innovation Inventory (KAI) falls back on his own theory to profile people using a one-dimensional construct.

- *Use of a questionnaire to measure differences:* All concepts capture individual differences by asking people to answer a profiling questionnaire. While the questionnaire design varies based on the overall architecture of each concept, a popular modus operandi is a four-box forced-choice questionnaire (e.g., DISC, M.I.N.D.).

- *Numerical scoring of profiling results:* After completing the questionnaire, most methods present the results in the form of numerical test scores (e.g., M Score of 0 + I Score of 11 + N Score of 0 + D Score of 1 = 12 is a sample result that I got after completing Black's M.I.N.D. Design test).

- *Use of a profiling map or table:* The numerical test scores are often visualized in a profiling map and/or profiling matrix (e.g., HBDI, Wealth Dynamics).

- *Assignment of profile types:* Some but not all concepts assign distinct profile types to a person based on the test results. At times, these profiles carry an abstract and technical label (e.g., ENTP is one of sixteen profile types of MBTI that I was mostly assigned as a test result), and at other times, they use descriptive names that relate to well-known professional roles (e.g., the supervisor and the architect are two of sixteen profile labels of Keirsey's KTS). The number of profile types of concepts I came across varies between two and forty-nine in those concepts I got myself tested in.

What are the common shortcomings of many cognitive profiling concepts?

By testing a wide variety of cognitive profiling tools over more than a decade, I encountered many aspects of other methods that I liked and deemed valuable. However, I also noticed certain shortcomings, perceptual blind spots, and application delivery gaps that got me thinking about how to fix these perceived suboptimal, missing, or even *"wrong"* elements. So, what are some of these suboptimal things I noticed?

1. *Varying and limited number of construct dimensions:* What is the best number of dimensions or theoretical constructs needed to adequately profile a person? While MBTI and KTS use four dimensions, many concepts suffice with only two-dimensional (WD, HBDI, MIND, Insights Discovery) or even one-dimensional constructs (KAI). Concepts with few dimensions emphasize certain aspects of personal style but tend to neglect other facets relevant to business and innovation. Interestingly, for a few profiling concepts (including some popular ones that I won't name), I was unable to understand their methodological design architecture and discern the underlying theoretical constructs.

2. *Binary design of constructs:* Many profiling tools interpret the test scores for a cognitive construct as an *"either-or"* result. For example, in MBTI, you ultimately come out as either an extrovert or an introvert. But could there be people who are both? Yes, I am one of them, and depending on the contextual situation and the required task at hand, I am as energized running a full-day innovation event in front of a large crowd as spending a day at my desk writing an article or a chapter of a book. Moreover, depending on the test version, I tend to come out more often as an Extrovert, but at other times get profiled as an introvert.

3. *Profile allocation even in cases of nearly identical scores:* In many profiling methods such as MBTI, you're assigned a profile even when there are only tiny score differences for one or more tested dimensions. Suppose your test results in MBTI would be Extroversion vs. Introversion 51-49, iNtuition vs. Sensing 51-49, Thinking vs. Feeling 51-49 and Judging vs. Perceiving 51-49. In this case, MBTI assigns you a personality type (ENTJ), and that's how everyone familiar with the method will look at you from now onwards. However, had 2-3 questions been formulated in a slightly different way, or had you not *"overthought"* your answers, you might have come out as an INFP instead. Of course, this problem is amplified if the expressions for two, three or even all four expressions are identical, making it difficult to classify such a balanced person within one of the 16 MBTI-profile *"boxes"* with confidence.

4. *Too many or too few profiling questions:* What is a fair number of questions to reliably measure the surveyed variables and to adequately profile a candidate? Here, the art is to strike the right balance between time effectiveness and accuracy of the result. While many candidates appreciate how quickly they can complete a short survey, some object that a short questionnaire is inadequate to capture sufficient aspects of their personal style — and vice versa in the case of a long questionnaire. Questions vary in number from as few as nine (M.I.N.D.) to sixteen (MBTI) or even more than a hundred (HBTI).

5. *Too many or too few profiles:* Suppose you're a team manager using a cognitive profiling concept to capture the different personalities of your

subordinates. Would you prefer to have no profiling types at all and have to recall the test scores only? Probably not. So, we agree that having profiles is useful. But what is the best number of profiles to provide sufficient distinctions in style differences without overwhelming users? Are two profile types (KAI) adequate to capture sufficient differences in style? Can you easily remember how fifteen (FourSight) or even sixteen profiles (MBTI, KTS) differ from each other? Here, eight to ten profiles seem to be a good number to strike a balance between offering diversity and avoiding over-complexity.

6. *No descriptive profile labels:* What do we call someone with a certain cognitive test score? Some profiling concepts (e.g., HBDI, MIND.) give candidates profile scores and detailed descriptions,

COMMON DESIGN FEATURES AND DIFFERENCES OF COGNITIVE PROFILING METHODS

ASSESSMENT TYPE	ASSESSMENT STYLE	# THEORETICAL CONSTRUCTS/DIMENSIONS	ADMISSION FORMS
✦ Preferred cognitive styles ✦ Observed behaviors ✦ Skills ✦ Mixed	✦ Personality (Self-Assessment) ✦ Behavioral (Peer- or 360° Assessment)	✦ None (Enneagram (?)) ✦ One (e.g., KAI) ✦ Two (e.g., HBDI) ✦ Four (e.g., MBTI) ✦ Five (TIPS) ✦ Multiple (Enneagram (?))	✦ Untimed ✦ Timed (time pressure)

TYPE OF QUESTIONS	NUMBER OF QUESTIONS	NUMBER OF PROFILES	PROFILE NAMES
✦ Forced choice ✦ Polar choices (most, least) ✦ Multiple choices ✦ Mixed	✦ 9 (MIND Design) ✦ 36 (Wealth Dynamics) ✦ 60 (TIPS) ✦ 120 (HBDI) ✦ 136 (MBTI)	✦ 0 (scores only; e.g. MIND) ✦ 2 (KAI) ✦ 4 (e.g. FourSight basic) ✦ 8 (WD, Insights Discovery) ✦ 10+1 (TIPS) ✦ 15 (FourSight expanded) ✦ 16 (MBTI, KTS) ✦ 49 (How To Fascinate)	✦ None ✦ Letter acronyms (e.g., ENTP, ISFJ) ✦ Role names (e.g., Healer, Teacher, Fieldmarshal) ✦ Business role names (e.g., Promoter, Organizer)

but don't use catchy names to describe a profile. Although the profile letters have become technical labels for trained insiders, MBTI suffers from this phenomenon, too. KTS resolved this problem by designating a more descriptive name related to well-known professional roles to each MBTI letter label. Laypeople shrug hearing about an *ENTP* but nod their heads when learning this is an *innovator*.

7. *No follow-up application suggestions:* While providing detailed descriptions of a resulting profile, several concepts don't offer enough concrete follow-up action recommendations to answer the questions: *"So what? How can I use a particular profiling result to make meaning? Specifically, how can I use this result to better perform in business in general and with innovation in particular?"*

8. *No consideration of the dynamic and cyclical nature of business:* In Chapter 1, I discussed that like many natural phenomena, most parameters in business (e.g., products, technologies, industries, and economies) pass through cyclical wave patterns. For example, Vernon's product life cycle concept suggests that successful products go through the phases of introduction, growth, maturity and decline. With the exception of Hamilton's Wealth Dynamics concept (and later on my own concept TIPS), I came across no other profiling method that entertained the idea that certain personality profiles are better suited to lead an organization through specific phases of the life cycle of a venture or a product.

For several years, I pondered how to best answer the conceptual design questions raised above and how to best solve some of those aspects that I perceived as suboptimal. I saw an opportunity to develop a more elegant, integrative, and innovation-focused profiling method to more effectively deal with the people side of innovation. Then, one day, my own cognitive profiling concept emerged in front of my eye: TIPS.

TIPS is the result of complementing selected theories (on human cognition and personal style, as well as innovation, social sciences, and evolutionary economics) with my practical experiences, in-the-field observations in real-life projects, and experimentations with innovators and business practitioners. In the following sections, I am going to introduce TIPS and selected application areas to you.

> "The secret to my success is that we've gone to exceptional lengths to hire the best people in the world."
> —STEVE JOBS

5.3. INTRODUCING THE TIPS INNOVATION PROFILING METHOD

Albert Einstein once said: *"If you judge a fish by its ability to climb a tree, it will live its whole life believing that it is stupid."* Clearly, a fish needs to swim in the water. A monkey to climb trees. A bird to fly in the sky. And we also need to do what comes naturally easy to us in an environment that supports our particular talents.

We all have a unique personal style that can show us our natural path to our talents and success. How can you find out more about your natural path to success? Simply use TIPS.

I have created a profiling method called TIPS that can help you to better understand how you tick and how others in your team tick.

Introducing the TIPS Innovation Profiling method

What is TIPS? TIPS is a new innovation people profiling method that I created for my innovation company Thinkergy.

TIPS helps individuals make better contributions to business success in general and innovation in particular by understanding their unique innovator profile and related personal styles to think, work, interact, live and innovate.

TIPS also enables companies to utilize their people in harmony with their natural talents and preferred personal styles and to compose more effective teams to work together in business units, projects and innovation.

TIPS is based on a key insight that I gained while working in the innovation field for over a decade: Everyone can contribute to innovation, albeit in very different ways and roles based on one's preferred personal styles.

How is TIPS designed?

TIPS combines six conceptual features into one elegant profiling concept. The design elements of TIPS are the TIPS bases, styles, questionnaire, profiling map, innovator profiles and style to innovate.

The TIPS bases ...

The **TIPS Bases** are four basic dimensions that can explain how major technological, social and political changes unfold over time. (I discussed the focus, speed, direction and impact of change in Chapter 1). These four bases that also make up the acronym *"TIPS"* are: **T** for **Theories**, **I** for **Ideas**, **P** for **People**, and **S** for **Systems**. Successful business leaders have chosen to do business in an industry and environment that matches their preferred energy. TIPS is based on the insight that we all are powered by one or more energies that drive our workplace behaviors.

For example, Walt Disney founded a creative venture that grew into a global entertainment empire by exclusively focusing on one base: Ideas. In contrast, Warren Buffet devised his systematic investment strategies using two bases: Theories and Systems.

... anchor the TIPS styles ...

The second feature of TIPS is the four cognitive styles. We all have preferred styles to think, work, interact and live that are linked to our dominating bases. What are these four **TIPS Styles**?

- *Figure vs. Fantasy* describes your preferred **thinking style**. Do you prefer engaging in analytical thinking (Figure) or creative thinking (Fantasy)? Or

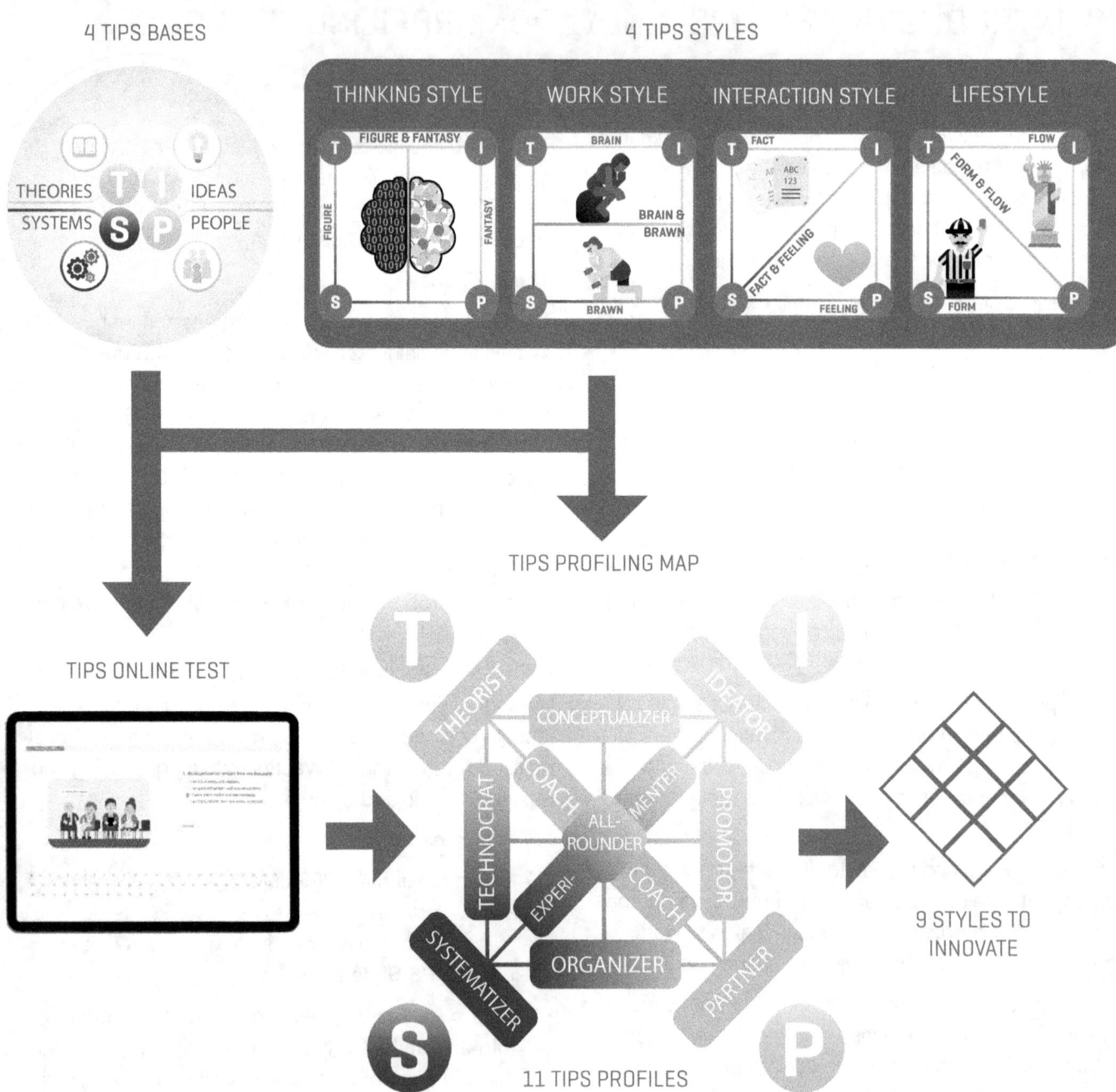

are you equally comfortable with both thinking styles (Figure and Fantasy)?

- **Brain vs. Brawn** illustrates your preferred **work style**. Do you love doing conceptual work (Brain) or concrete, practical work (Brawn)? Or do you feel equally at home working with both Brain and Brawn?
- **Fact vs. Feeling** explains your preferred **interaction style**. Do you enjoy communicating and making a case based on facts? Do you prefer interacting with others and making decisions using your emotions, intuition and feelings? Or do you employ both Facts and Feelings?
- Last but not least, **Form vs. Flow** describes your preferred **lifestyle**. Do you like to live in an orderly, well-organized, stable and rule-governed world (Form)? Do you enjoy living in a fluid and dynamic world (Flow)? Or do you like to live in a largely stable world with occasional changes (Form and Flow)?

Let's return to Walt Disney as one of our two case studies here. Disney was an outstanding creative thinker (Fantasy) and conceptual worker (Brain). He did business using both his head and heart (Fact and Feeling). He loved change and new, bold projects (Flow). All these styles are driven by Disney's dominant base: Ideas.

In contrast, Warren Buffet prefers an analytical and quantitative thinking style (Figure). He makes investment decisions based on Facts (interaction style) and after considering both the details and the big picture prospects of a possible investment (work style Brain and Brawn). He also prefers to follow a more regular, habitual, and traditional lifestyle (Form). All these styles are aligned with his two commanding bases, Theories and Systems.

... to profile people into 11 innovator profiles

We use the four TIPS bases and four TIPS styles to feed questions into the TIPS profiling questionnaire (feature 3) and to span the TIPS Profiling Map (feature 4). We use the four TIPS bases and the four TIPS styles to span the TIPS Profile Map, which gives room to position the eleven TIPS innovator profiles, our fifth feature. Thereby, we distinguish:

- 4 *pure* profiles that exclusively focus on one base: the Theorist, the Ideator, the Partner, and the Systematizer;
- 6 *dual* profiles that play on two bases: the Conceptualizer, the Promoter, the Organizer, the Technocrat, the Coach and the Experimenter; and
- 1 *multiple* profile that balances three or all four bases: the All-Rounder.

After learning more about your dominant energies and your preferred styles with the TIPS profiling test, we can tell you your personal innovator profile and related styles to think, work, interact with others and live.

Each of the 11 personas operates on a different life metaphor and succeeds in the business and innovation game by playing on a specific position in harmony with their natural talents and preferred cognitive styles.

For example, Walt Disney was a visionary Ideator located at the Ideas-base, who boldly operated at the forefront of change (dominant TIPS style: flow). Disney started a venture that grew into a multinational entertainment empire by creating new categories in a nascent industry (animated movies) and an established industry (family entertainment parks).

In contrast, Warren Buffet is a Technocrat who sits between the Theories and Systems base. Using his dominant TIPS style (Figure), he gradually and steadily grew a small investment firm in Omaha, Nebraska, into the multi-billion dollar, multinational conglomerate holding company Berkshire Hathaway, which is now one of the highest-valued companies in the S&P 500 Index.

The sixth and final feature of TIPS is the innovation style. Each profile has a preferred style to innovate which we will discuss in greater detail in the next section.

How does TIPS address the perceived shortcomings and delivery gaps of other methods?

TIPS uses a multi-layered design architecture employing five theoretical constructs (four styles and the bases). With 10+1 profile types (all labeled with business-related role names) and 60 profiling questions, TIPS aims for the middle ground between high accuracy and complexity on one hand and time-effectiveness and simplicity on the other. Finally, TIPS uses a trinary interpretation of the cognitive styles and assigns a neutral profile (All-Rounder) to balanced profiling results.

TIPS offers many applications in business and innovation

I created TIPS with a focus on innovation to help companies identify the agile, creative types and gain a better understanding of who can contribute in what ways to a firm's innovation efforts. It can help firms identify the creative types in their workforce who can drive or support creative change and who show the potential to become creative leaders. It can also give guidance on how to compose balanced teams when working on innovation projects and who will shine when while passing through the different stages of a systematic innovation process method such as X-IDEA. I will discuss some of the various innovation applications of TIPS in Section 5.6.

But TIPS also has many powerful business applications, covering all stages of the talent management lifecycle. For example, TIPS can guide individuals towards careers in ecosystems that allow them to play on their talent, in line with Einstein's "fish climbing a tree" metaphor quoted earlier. It can also teach executives and team leads how to better manage talents in harmony with their cognitive styles or how to better deal with conflicts at work. Finally, TIPS also explains how different TIPS profiles come to the fore as a new venture moves through the different phases of the corporate life cycle.

> Personalities are like impressionistic paintings. At a distance, each person is 'all of a piece'; up close, each is a bewildering complexity of moods, cognitions, and motives.
> —THEODORE MILLON

THE 11 TIPS INNOVATOR PROFILES

THE THEORIST
Life is all about... knowledge and truth.

THE COACH
Life is all about... development of human potential.

THE CONCEPTUALIZER
Life is all about... knowledge-based creation of concepts.

THE IDEATOR
Life is all about... ideas, innovation and change.

THE TECHNOCRAT
Life is all about... application of knowledge & numbers.

THE ALL-ROUNDER
Life is all about... juggling all responsibilities in balanced ways.

THE PROMOTER
Life is all about... communicating ideas to people.

THE SYSTEMATIZER
Life is all about... systems, structured order and control.

THE EXPERIMENTER
Life is all about... improving things by systematically testing ideas.

THE ORGANIZER
Life is all about... organized service & operational excellence.

THE PARTNER
Life is all about... people and relationships.

5.4. FLOW ALONG THE COMPANY LIFE CYCLE WITH TIPS

Like all living organisms, companies develop by passing through distinct phases in a life cycle (see Chapter 1.5). What's also true is that as a company develops from a startup to a multinational corporation, different basic innovator dimensions dominate at its different life stages. Let me explain.

How different dimensions drive and affect a company during its life cycle

Let's follow the life of a company to better understand how the need for the various innovator types — and their profiles — changes as this goes from a tiny new venture to a mighty behemoth:

Phase 1: Great companies start with great IDEAS

The idea on which a business is founded may be to fill an unmet need. An example of this is YouTube, whose founders Chad Hurley, Steve Chen, and Jawed Karim noticed the lack of an easy way to share videos on the web. The idea might also be to exploit a new technology or method, as in the case of Polaroid, founded by Edwin H. Land. The more radical, game-changing, and bold the idea, the more risky it is, the more reward it offers, and the more it can change the world. Ideators, those dynamic, bold idea creators, often create and lead start-ups through their initial phase.

Phase 2: Spread the word about the IDEAS to PEOPLE

The second phase of company growth calls on both the IDEAS and the PEOPLE dimensions. Once a new product has been developed, then it's time to build a brand and promote both the product and the brand. Among the 11 innovator types, the Promoter is most naturally suited to create convincing campaigns and to spread the word to the market.

Phase 3: Get PEOPLE for sales and customer growth

This third phase is all about PEOPLE. You need to find the right people to sell your product and brand to a growing base of happy customers. In short, you need people who care for customers. Partners are the innovator type most needed at this stage of a company's development.

Phase 4: PEOPLE use SYSTEMS to tame the chaos

If your sales team is successful, sooner or later you will have a new problem: your organization will have problems keeping up with growth and maintaining consistent quality in products, delivery and service. This phase involves mostly the PEOPLE and SYSTEMS dimensions, as management realizes the need for organization at the front end, as well as a need for a more sophisticated back-end organization to ensure consistent service quality and customer care. The Organizer is the talent and innovator type best suited to bring both order and a focus on service to a fast-growing company.

Phase 5: Build smooth-running SYSTEMS

As a company matures into a large corporation, the SYSTEMS dimension gains added importance. Senior management focuses on efficiency and productivity. The Systematizer is the ideal talent type to drive and direct the transformation of a company into an efficient,

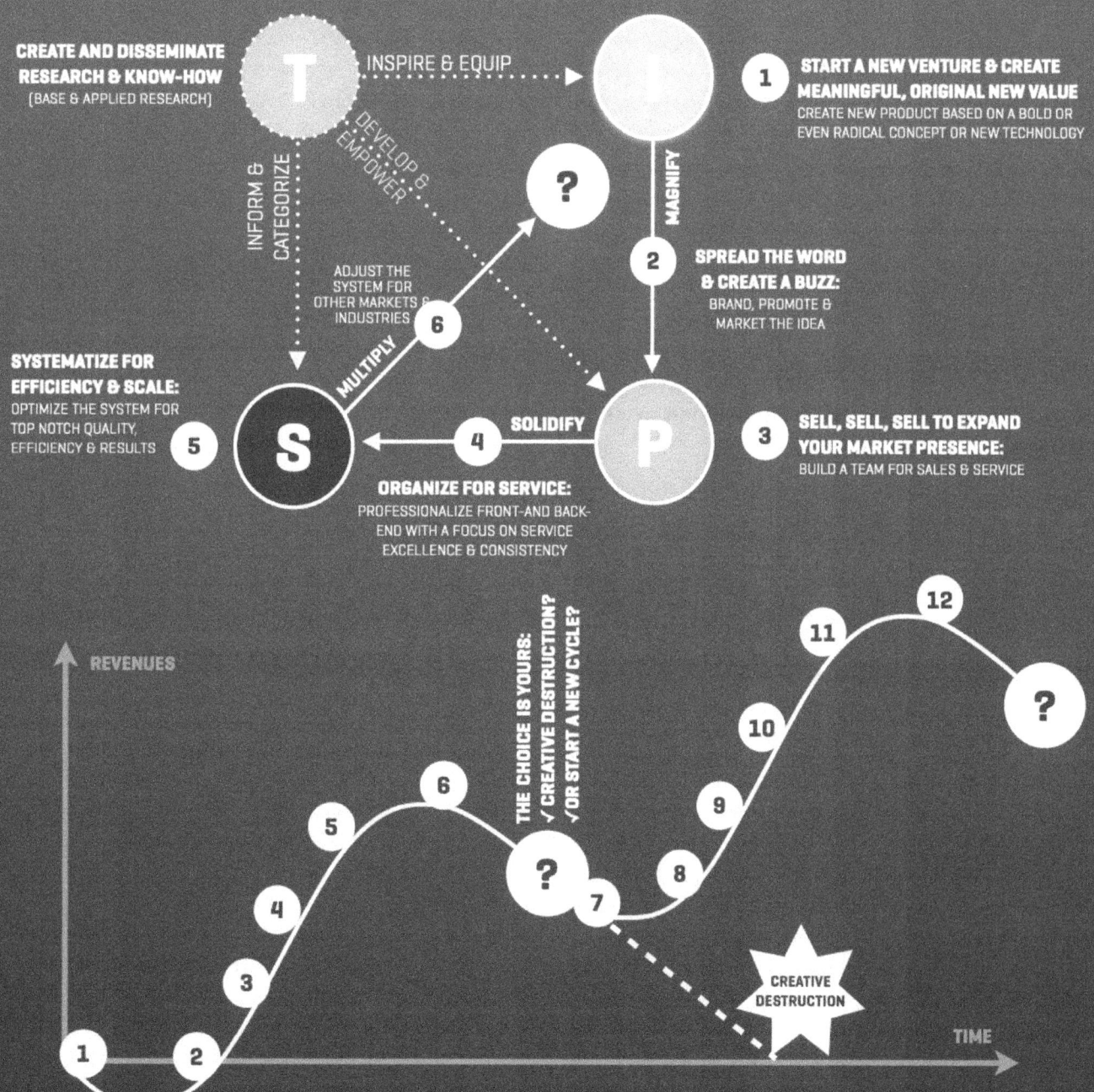

productive corporation that is self-sustaining and not dependent on any one individual.

Phase 6: IDEAS improve the SYSTEMS

Once well-oiled SYSTEMS have been put in place, they can be shaped to improve the company. In order to do this, fresh IDEAS are needed, along with the willingness to experiment and tinker with things to find improved business models, delivery channels, and partnerships to multiply the firm's value. The Experimenter is the innovator type best able to figure out how to extend a settled firm's value by leveraging it into different markets, countries, or even industries.

Phase ?: Reinvent yourself and start a new cycle — or decline and perish

By this time, your once-tiny startup has become a mature multinational corporation. However, natural systems have another phase in their life cycle: decline and, finally, death. Sooner or later, a new technology, business idea, or venture will emerge that challenges your company's existence. If your company cannot adapt, renovate or reinvent itself — often because everyone in the company ignores the world-changing events around them — your company will start to decline and may even perish.

So, the best way to avoid becoming a victim of Schumpeter's *"creative destruction"* is to start a new creative cycle: Bring in a fresh round of Ideators and related profiles at the Ideas-base — or set free those Ideas-people within your organization who have survived by moving backstage — and let them direct their creative energy on adapting your company's product range to emerging technologies that may ignite and drive a profitable cycle of fresh growth.

What about THEORIES?

If you've been paying attention, you may have noticed that so far, I've only mentioned the IDEAS, PEOPLE and SYSTEMS bases. Where do THEORIES come in? The answer is: all the time.

Theories and knowledge inform your actions at every phase of the cycle. However, the focus of the theories shifts as the other dimensions come to the fore:

- Scientific, conceptual or creativity-related theories (both basic research and applied research) lead to new technologies and concepts that the profiles surrounding the IDEAS-base pick up and turn into revolutionary new value propositions that they release into the market in new ventures.

- Once the new venture is growing and gaining momentum, it absorbs marketing and human capital-related knowledge, focusing on PEOPLE's needs, wants, and behaviors.

- Finally, building strong, durable yet pliable SYSTEMS requires a good theoretical grounding in operations, efficiency, and process, as well as in finance, accounting and law.

How about those talent and innovator types I haven't yet mentioned —Theorists, Conceptualizers, Coaches, and Technocrats? Their role is to create, disseminate, and apply theories and know-how throughout all phases of the corporate life cycle.

> *"Talent wins games, but teamwork and intelligence win championships."*
> —MICHAEL JORDAN

5.5. HOW TIPS HELPS RESOLVE MAIN CORPORATE INNOVATION CHALLENGES

TIPS is a new cognitive profiling tool created to help right the people side of innovation. It offers answers to questions such as: How do different people relate to the process, culture and leadership side of innovation? Who are the creative types that drive and may lead innovation? How do different people respond to innovation and change? How do the various profile types play a role when going through an innovation project using a well-structured innovation method? Let's discuss each of these and other aspects in the following.

Who are the creative profile types who have a naturally higher affinity to creativity?

Ideators, Promoters, Partners, as well as Imaginative Conceptualizers and Popular Coaches are the TIPS profiles whose thinking style is *"Fantasy"*, or in other words, who appreciate creativity and enjoy more engaging in cognitive activities associated with creative thinking, such as brainstorming and ideating, imagining and fantasizing, dreaming and daydreaming, crafting and telling stories, playing and making fun, empathizing with others and shifting perspectives to appreciate other points of view.

How and in what roles can we include and make everyone contribute to corporate innovation efforts?

Luckily, corporate innovation involves many activities that require different cognitive styles. As such, all eleven TIPS profiles can contribute to innovation success, albeit in specific roles and activities:

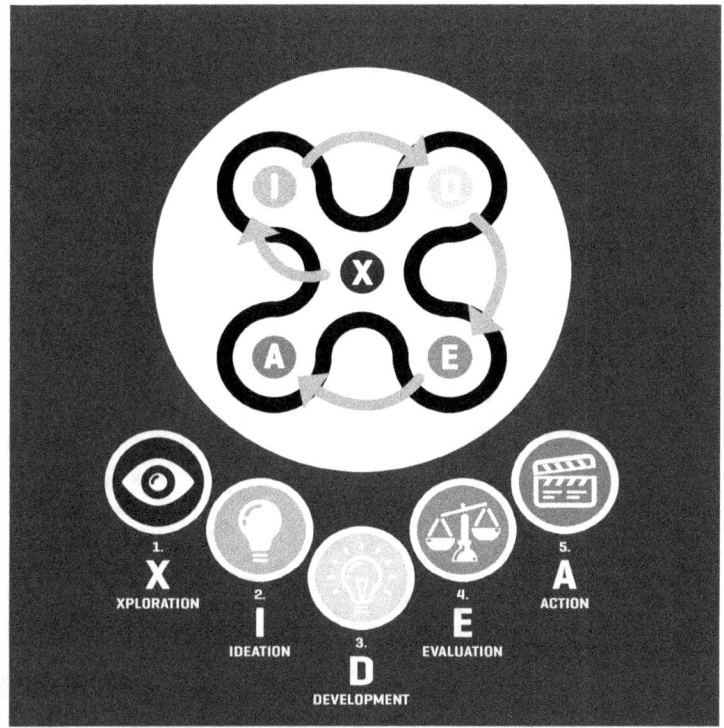

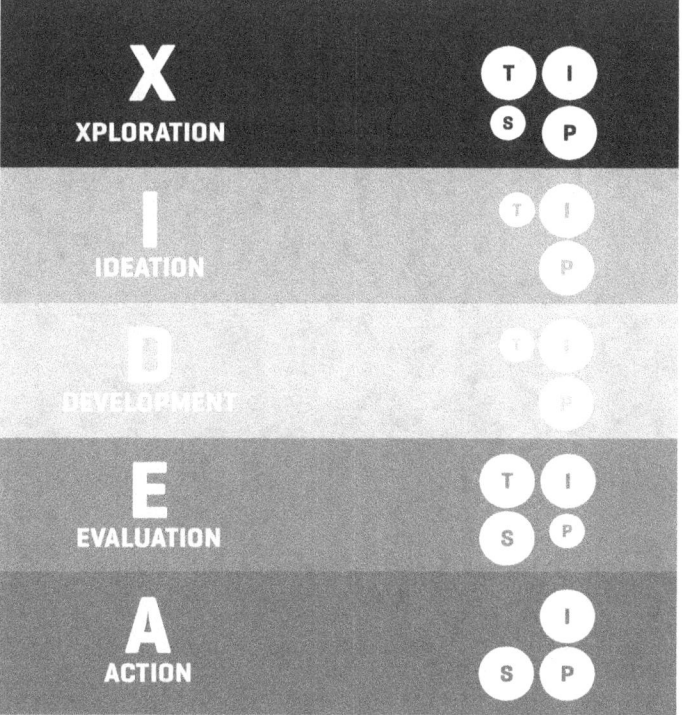

- *Theorists* can contribute know-how on the latest research and new technologies to innovation. They also alert you when you take intellectual shortcuts or shy away from an uncomfortable truth.

- The geeky, technology-savvy *Conceptualizers* easily spot trends and new technologies in the evolving wider market space. They also know lots of tools and methods that may be useful to solve tough innovation challenges.

- *Ideators* effortlessly come up with lots of ideas, including really bold ones. They fight for *"impossible"* ideas and have the drive and creativity to make them possible.

- Being born storytellers, *Promoters* can creatively and entertainingly pitch ideas and create a buzz for new products, ventures and brands. They convey the core value using simple, witty taglines and emotional stories.

- Being most intimate with customers, *Partners* contribute the human factor to innovation initiatives (supported by more anthropological, philosophical Coaches).

- *Organizers* are good at organizing innovation events and may manage or work in an implementation project team in charge of activating a funded top idea.

- *Systematizers* and *Technocrats* are suitable innovation managers to manage the entire corporate innovation management system (including an innovation pipeline, an online idea submission platform, innovation projects and events, and all other innovation-related activities). They may also keep track of an organization's innovation performance and effectiveness, thus checking how much we spend for different innovation activities, what each initiative achieves, as well as the overall results.

THE TIPS BASES AND THE MODERN INNOVATION TYPOLOGY

- *Experimenters* enjoy rapid prototyping and activating an idea, especially if this relates to a product or technology.
- Finally, *All-Rounders* can contribute their balanced talents to many different roles and innovation projects.

Of course, another way to involve all members of an organization in innovation efforts is to encourage them to contribute to an innovation project. We discuss this next.

How can everyone play a role in an innovation project, and when do they add the most value?

In Chapter 4, I discussed how innovation project teams can use effective innovation methods to think and work through different process stages and steps. How does this relate to TIPS? In short, at different stages, different profile types are prone to come to the fore and shine. Let's discuss this now using the example of the X-IDEA method:

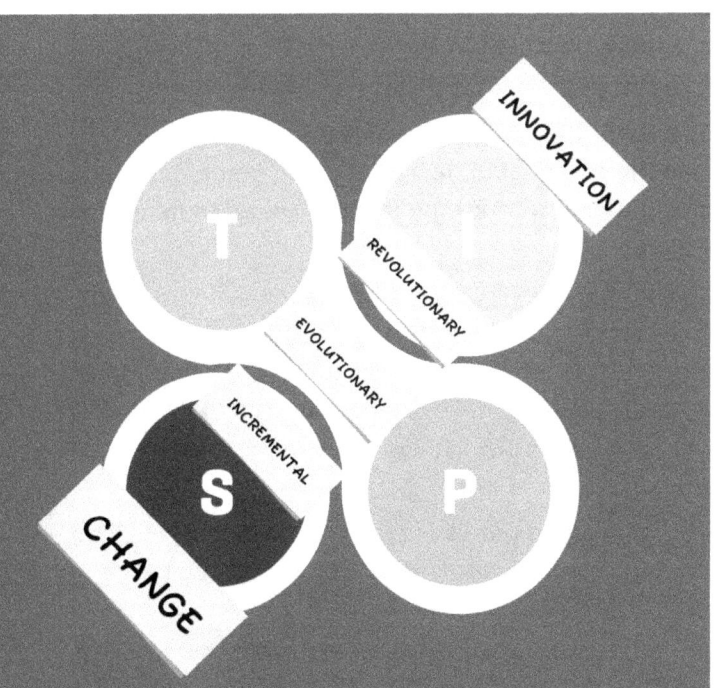

- Stage X-Xploration is rather conceptual in nature, meaning that the brainy TIPS profiles (Theorist, Conceptualizer, Ideator) tend to enjoy this stage most. In user-centric or customer-driven innovation projects, involve Promoters and Partners, too, to ensure capturing people-related perspectives and insights.
- Ideators, Promoters and Partners deeply enjoy the fast and furious Stage I-Ideation, where teams engage in creative play to develop hundreds of raw ideas, including really wild ones. But also involve Conceptualizers, Experimenters, Coaches and All-Rounders in this stage to ensure a large ground stock of raw ideas.
- In Stage D-Development, use the same innovation team members as in the previous stage to design the most intriguing raw ideas into realistic, meaningful idea concepts.
- The more serious, critical profile types (Systematizer, Organizer, Technocrat) join in Stage E-Evaluation to help the other profile types *"get real."* This stage requires a balanced mix of profiles and styles to weigh the pros and cons, prototype promising idea concepts, generate more ideas on how to fix identified bugs in an idea, and fight for and elect the most worthy top ideas.
- In the final Action-stage, Promoters are best suited to convincingly pitch an idea to investors or sponsors. Once an idea has been approved and funded, compose a well-balanced idea implementation team using a mix of more operational and creative profile types (Organizer, Partner, Promoter, Experimenter, and Ideator).

How the different innovation types relate to TIPS

Chapter 2 introduced the spectrum of modern innovation types. In general, we can say that depending on their dominant base, different profiles tend to enjoy working on different types of innovation projects:

- Operational innovations (targeting processes and operational structures) are largely Systems-driven (and may be supported by profiles at the People- and Theories-base).
- The profiles surrounding the Ideas-base excel at value innovations (focusing on new products, services, solutions, and customer experiences).
- Leverage innovations fall into two categories that are led by different bases: Innovation types that leverage through multiplication (channel, network, business model innovation) are often enjoyed by Theories-based profile types (supported to a lesser extent by those at the Systems-base). In contrast, Ideas- and People-based profiles enjoy working on innovation types that leverage through magnification (brand, campaign, promotion and packaging design).
- Strategy innovation projects are spearheaded by the conceptual profiles at the TIPS bases Theories and Ideas (Theorists, Ideators and in particular Conceptualizers).
- Finally, the profiles at the People-base love working on social innovation initiatives.

How do the TIPS bases relate to the impact of innovation or change?

As discussed in Chapters 1 and 3, we can distinguish innovations into three different intensity levels based on the impact that a change has: incremental, evolutionary and revolutionary innovations. How does this categorization relate to the four TIPS bases?

- The innovator profiles at the Systems-base prefer to focus more on continuous improvements or incremental innovations by practicing a more adaptive innovation style. They are satisfied with incremental change because, in general, they prefer preserving the status quo.
- In contrast, the profiles surrounding the TIPS base Ideas like to drive bold, radical change. They really enjoy pushing for creating revolutionary innovations, which they find way more exciting than working on evolutionary innovations.
- Finally, the profiles at the Theories- and People-bases can support either the incremental innovation efforts at the Systems-base or the more revolutionary innovation projects of the Ideas-base. However, they prefer working on evolutionary projects to create more and new value for existing users (more the profiles at the Theories-base) or to extend existing value to new users (more the profiles at the People-base).

Based on their cognitive style and profile, who has the potential to develop into an authentic creative leader, and who is more suited to managing efficiency?

Certain TIPS profiles have a greater natural affinity to evolve and be developed into authentic creative leaders to spearhead creativity-driven expansion and innovation efforts (while other profiles are more suited to lead efficiency-driven quality initiatives or consolidation phases).

TIPS profiles surrounding the Ideas base (such as the Ideator, Conceptualizer, Promoters, and Imaginative

CREATIVE LEADERSHIP POTENTIAL

PSYCHO-STATIC MINDSET — **PSYCHO-DYNAMIC MINDSET**

EFFICIENT MANAGERS — CREATIVE LEADERS

FOCUS ON HIGH ORGANIZATIONAL EFFICIENCY — **S** — **I** — FOCUS ON HIGH ORGANIZATIONAL CREATIVITY

Levels: NON | LOW | CAN | GOOD | HIGH

Roles:
- **T** — THEORIST
- TECHNOCRAT
- CONCEPTUALIZER
- SYSTEMATIZER
- COACH
- EXPERI-MENTER
- ALL-ROUNDER
- ORGANIZER
- COACH
- PROMOTER
- **P** — PARTNER

Response categories: PRESERVERS | LAGGARDS | SKEPTICS | CHANGE AGENTS | PIONEERS

CHANGE RESISTERS — CHANGE DRIVERS

RESPONSE TO CREATIVE ORGANIZATIONAL CHANGE

Experimenter) have a high potential to develop into creative leaders who can authentically lead innovation initiatives from the front. In addition, the Theories- and People-based profiles are possible creative leadership candidates, provided that they demonstrate an interest in evolving their creative potential.

In contrast, the Systems-driven TIPS profiles (such as the Systematizer, Technocrat, Organizer, and Systematic Experimenter) are less suited and have their strengths in other areas: They exhibit a more managerial focus on making operations, processes and systems more efficient.

Who responds how to creative organizational change?

In the coming years, many mature industries are likely to be confronted with disruptive changes due to digitization, new technologies and new competitors (both start-ups and cross-overs from the tech sector). To survive, many mature corporations need to transform their corporate culture into a more creativity- and innovation-friendly organization.

Most people tend to resist change, at least initially. Wouldn't it be great for organizations to understand who is responding in what ways to creative change initiatives? The TIPS profiles can hint at who are likely pioneers and change agents to help drive a creative cultural change into the organization and who will need to be convinced with arguments and persuasion to join the change efforts. Here, the same pattern applies as for the creative leadership potential:

- The psycho-dynamic profiles at the Ideas-base drive and thrive on creative organizational change as pioneers and change agents.
- Profiles at the Theories- and People-bases are initially skeptical or anxious about such a creative change initiative, but they will support it once they get plausible evidence and emotional reassurance that it is a route to future success and survival.
- The psycho-static TIPS profiles surrounding the Systems-base favor preserving the organizational status quo. Firms facing a *"change or die"*-situation need to support these profile types (e.g., through human capital development efforts) or use them in efficiency-driven roles that support change.

Conclusion: TIPS helps to right the people side of innovation by providing possible solutions to address key people-related questions related to process, culture, and leadership. In the following two sections, I will discuss two additional questions in greater detail:

- What are the preferred styles to innovate of different TIPS profiles?
- Who is responding how fast to technological change?

> "Many highly talented, brilliant, creative people think they're not - because the thing they were good at at school wasn't valued, or was actually stigmatized."
> —KEN ROBINSON

5.6. WHAT'S YOUR STYLE TO INNOVATE?

While facilitating over a hundred innovation projects over nearly a decade, I noticed that different people have very distinct innovation styles. While working out Thinkergy's innovation people profiling method TIPS, I developed a scheme to capture and systematize these personal innovation styles of different people.

Thereby, I blended the central aspects of a well-known innovation theory with my practical experiences and personal observations in real-life innovation projects. Let me share how understanding these two determinants can help you to identify your own innovation style.

The people side of innovation

The first factor of your personal innovation style is grounded in practice, and relates to what we may call *"the people side of innovation."*

While observing participants in an innovation project, I noticed that different people have a preferred way of working and —in particular— of generating ideas: Some people clearly prefer to brainstorm ideas in a team, while others would rather ideate alone.

Last but not least, there also seem to be some people who, at times, enjoy *"going solo"* but at other times crave the cross-fertilization of other team members.

How about you? Would you rather generate ideas alone or brainstorm together with others in a team? Or are you one of those people who can comfortably shift between going solo and working with your team members?

Kirton's adaption-innovation theory

The second factor of a person's innovation style is grounded in theory. In his well-known adaption-innovation theory, Michael Kirton suggests that people are either adaptors or innovators:

- *Adaptors* are people who like to adapt ideas. They are interested in resolving problems in tried and tested ways. Adaptors *"innovate"* by improving something that already exists in order to make it slightly better and more efficient. IAs a result, they incrementally improve or evolve the status quo.

- On the other hand, *innovators* prefer to shoot for ideas that are really novel, original and meaningful. They spot problems and wider unmet needs that they perceive as opportunities to create new solutions that are different and useful. Thereby, innovators enjoy pushing for distinct evolutionary innovations or even game-changing revolutionary innovations that radically challenge and change the status quo.

While I embrace Kirton's theory in general, I disagree with its binary view of people. Why? Can you imagine that there are people who, at times, like to adapt ideas and, at other times, enjoy pushing for bold new ideas? Well, according to my observations, these people do exist — and we capture them in a third classification that we call adaptor-innovators.

What about you? Do you prefer to improve on existing solutions (adaptor) or come up with unique, valuable and truly novel ideas (innovator)? Or do you see yourself as an adaptor-innovator who feels at home both at fixing and improving things that already exist and at creating the truly new?

Finding your innovation style

Now let's combine the two determinants (with their three classifications each) into a 3×3 matrix to arrive at 9 distinct innovation styles. In order to identify your personal innovation style, simply combine your answers to my two earlier questions, and locate your resulting innovation style (and related TIPS type) below:

- **Solo Adaptors** enjoy working alone in their office on incrementally improving documents that already exist. Think of a bureaucrat in a government agency formulating a policy or updating a handbook or manual. The corresponding TIPS profile is the **Technocrat**.
- **Solo-Team Adaptors** relish fine-tuning and optimizing the multitude of cogwheels that form a well-oiled organizational system. They continuously produce ideas for incremental improvements both alone and together with others in the team. These people who often make it to the corner offices of mature, asset-driven corporations identify as **Systematizer** within TIPS.
- **Team Adaptors** are called **Organizers** within the TIPS profile typology. They enjoy resolving operational problems (e.g., in manufacturing or a service organization) by working with other profiles in a team.
- **Solo Innovators** relish working out abstract concepts and new solutions alone in a coffee shop or quiet corner of their office. These people who often work in management consulting are labeled **Conceptualizers**.
- **Solo-Team Innovators** take great pleasure in shooting for really bold or even radical ideas by alternating between working and ideating alone and bouncing ideas off other team members. Such radical change agents are called **Ideators** in TIPS (and yes, I am one of them).
- **Team Innovators** are often found in advertising, marketing and public relations roles and are called **Promoters** in TIPS. They love to brainstorm for bold new slogans and promotional campaigns together with other team members.
- Imagine a career researcher or scientist sitting in an ivory tower resolving smaller abstract problems or contemplating a bolder intellectual challenge and you get a feeling for the style of a **Solo Adaptor-Innovator**. Within the TIPS profiling universe, we call these abstract logical thinkers **Theorists**.
- **Team Adaptor-Innovators** really don't care if they work on resolving an operational issue or brainstorm for a bold new service idea as long as they can do it together with others in a team. **Partner** is how we call this most social of the 11 TIPS profiles.
- Last but not least, **Solo-Team Adaptor-Innovators** are the most flexible types of all. Depending on the situational context, they feel at ease working alone or together with other team members on a challenge, and they enjoy both improving on an already existing solution and creating something really new. Fortunately, three TIPS Profiles exhibit this highly flexible innovation style: **Experimenters**, **Coaches** and **All-Rounders**.

For example, Walt Disney was an Ideator whose innovation style was that of a Solo-Team Innovator. This means that he preferred to pursue bold, radical ideas and felt comfortable doing creative work both alone and with the team.

In contrast, Warren Buffet is a Technocrat who operates in between Systems and Theories. His innovation style is that of a Solo Adaptor, which means he prefers to work alone in his private office and practices an adaptive approach where he incrementally improves on a set of investment guidelines, measures and strategies that have allowed him to gradually evolve his investment system.

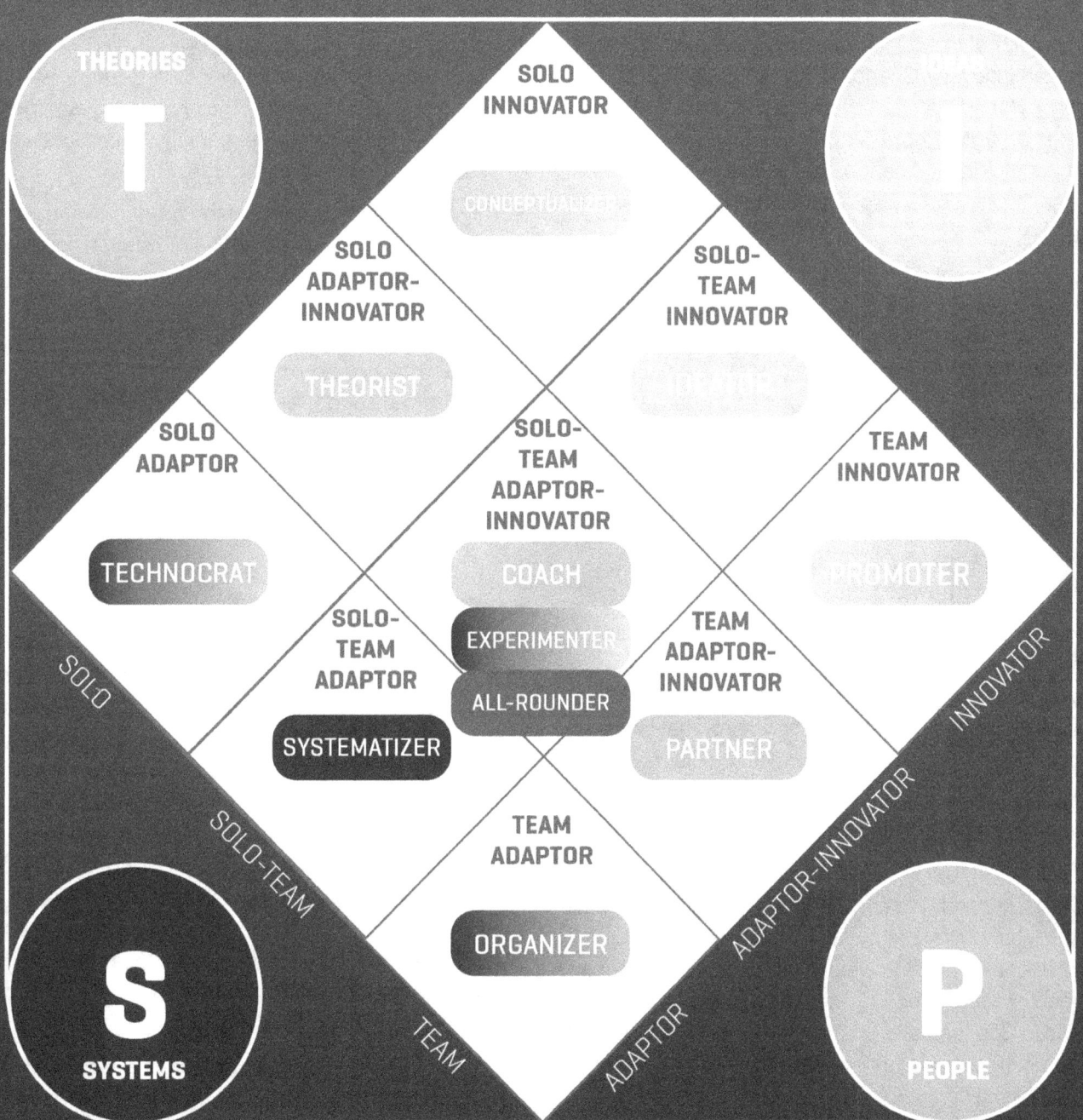

5.7. UNDERSTANDING WHO REALLY MAKES INNOVATION HAPPEN

In Chapter 1 of this book, we learned that the acclaimed American Innovator Charles F. Kettering was right in saying: *"The world hates change, yet it is the only thing that has brought progress."* Being habitual creatures, most people dislike change. As innovation always means change, most people also dislike innovation, at least initially.

In Chapter 3, we then quantified what percentage of the overall population hates change to a smaller or larger extent: 84 percent. That whopping number would be bad news for mankind if it were not for the remaining 16% who thrive on change and who drive innovation. But who are they? How can we find them? Here, enter TIPS, Thinkergy's innovation profiling method, which offers a route to identify those change drivers, change skeptics and change resisters.

Who responds how to innovation?

To understand the people side of innovation adoption better, let's go back to Everett Rogers' diffusion of innovation theory, which was featured in Chapter 3. How do the different population segments that Rogers identified relate to the TIPS bases and profiles?

At the forefront of change are the TIPS profiles closest to the Ideas-base — Ideators, Conceptualizers, Promoters, and Imaginative Experimenters:

- Ideators (and —to a lesser extent— also Imaginative Experimenters) are most likely to be one of those 2.5% of Rogers' innovators who create meaningful new products and the ventures that market them, while Conceptualizers and Promoters are more likely to be among the 2.5% of early adopters, where they perform different roles:

- Conceptualizers are technology-savvy, fast-learning geeks that Malcolm Gladwell called *"mavens"* in his book *The Tipping Point.* Their role is to test, approve of and endorse a new technology or product among the technological avant-garde.

- In contrast, Promoters are the alluring evangelists who spread the word about a new technology, product or brand that they find cool and hip; they can influence skeptical people in their network that a new technology, product, or brand is worth the money and won't disappoint. Promoters are Gladwell's *"salesmen"* and —especially as popular promoters close to the People-base— the *"connectors"* that connect ideas to the market.

- Together, Conceptualizers and Promoters can create the critical momentum and *"buzz"* needed to "cross the chasm" between the early adopters and the early majority and make an innovation take off.

The TIPS profiles at the bases Theories and People tend to belong to the early and late majority of people who are initially more skeptical towards an innovation that they hear about. This is because they either want more evidence that a new technology or product has what it takes to meet their functional needs (TIPS profiles close to the Theories-base) or because they need more emotional assurance that other people will approve of them supporting this novelty (TIPS profiles surrounding the People-base): So, Theorists, Coaches, Partners and All-Rounders are likely to be found in the majority when it comes to adopting an innovation.

The TIPS profiles close to the Systems base are likely to be among Rogers' laggards who are the last to adopt a new technology or innovative product. Organizers,

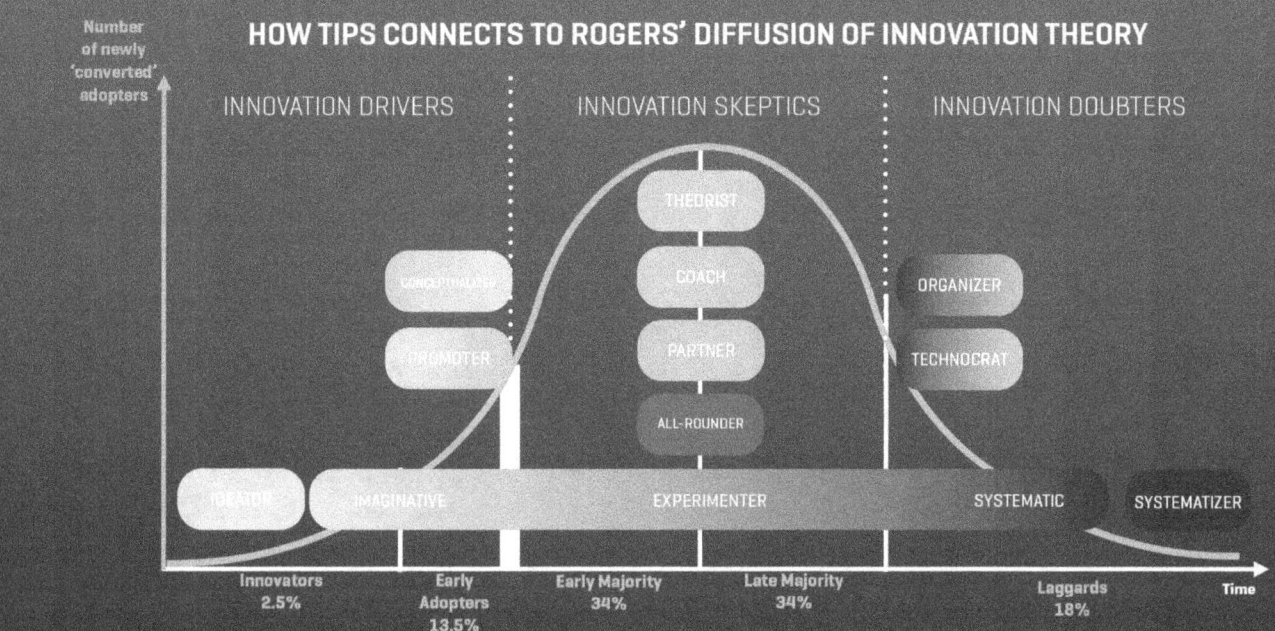

Technocrats, and—in particular—Systematizers are preservers of the status quo. These doubters tend to cherish the good old days and like to hang on to long-established technologies and products and those well-reputed heritage brands they trust.

Finally, one TIPS profile is positioned in between the polar opposites of preservation and change: Experimenters reside between the Systems- and Ideas-bases. They may be part of any of the three groups (innovation drivers, skeptics or doubters), depending on whether they lean more towards the Systems-base or Ideas-base:

- Systematic Experimenters like Henry Ford may hang on to a trusted systematic approach that has made them successful (*"Any customer can have a car painted any color that he wants so long as it is black."*), even if the market signals it embraces innovative change (such as colorful cars and a greater variety of models, which led to General Motors overtaking Ford in car sales).

- In contrast, Imaginative Experimenters are innovators who embrace the latest technologies to create revolutionary new products that define a new category and market standard.

What does adoption theory mean for innovation?

The cognitive implications of Rogers' diffusion of innovation theory of the related innovation adoption curve are profound for all companies who desire to become a player in innovation:

Only one in forty people is a born innovator. Who are those few Ideators in your firm who score high on the Ideas-base?

One in eight of your customers and employees are early adopters. These are likely to be Conceptualizers, Promoters and Experimenters who complement a high Ideas-score with one of the other bases (Theories, People or Systems). Do you know who they are? They are key to creating the momentum to turn a new innovation into a full-scale market success.

5.8. CREATIVE LEADERS VS INNOVATION MANAGERS: SAME OR DIFFERENT?

Do creative leaders and innovation managers perform the same innovation role? Some time ago, I had an interesting conversation related to this question with the global head of idea and innovation management of a tech multinational. When we talked about the responsibilities relating to his role, my counterpart revealed to my surprise that he sometimes has to key ideas into his organization's idea management system. Now know that this particular innovation executive is a strategic big-picture thinker who is ideally suited for creatively driving major innovation initiatives across his organization. Sweating the small stuff is a waste of his time and talent, if you ask me.

Many organizations seem to interpret the role of the executive spearheading the corporate innovation function as a *"Mr. Know-it-all-do-it-all."* I believe that's wrong, and we must make a distinction between the role of a creative leader and that of an innovation manager. Let me elaborate by discussing the responsibilities of each role and, with the help of the TIPS innovator profiling method, make a case for why these roles suit fundamentally different personality types..

Creative leaders: driving innovation from the front

Creative leaders run the *"innovation front office"* of their organization:

- They set or influence the innovation agenda by identifying new trends and technologies to focus on.

- They spearhead or participate in innovation initiatives of business units or dedicated innovation teams, such as new product development or product design teams.

- They participate in innovation events and conferences to promote innovation within and outside the organization.

Creative leaders inspire and drive innovation teams towards excellence to bring truly novel, original and meaningful ideas to life in the form of new products, new services, new solutions or new customer experiences. They look for new business models, strategic partnerships, networks and channel solutions to multiply revenue from innovation. Finally, they drive the campaign, packaging and branding initiatives that magnify the innovation in the eyes of customers.

Creative leaders ought to be at the very top of the executive structure, whether as CEO or chief innovation officer (CIO). This allows them to drive or at least influence the top management agenda and intervene and remove any internal barriers preventing innovation. Famous CEOs who exemplify the role of a creative leader are Thomas Edison, Walt Disney, Steve Jobs (Apple), Jeff Bezos (Amazon), Elon Musk, and Jeffrey Immelt (General Electrics), among others.

Innovation managers: driving innovation from the back

Innovation managers run the *"innovation back office"* of their organization. They take care of certain internal responsibilities related to innovation, such as:

- Organizing and administering the formal innovation management system (how innovation is organized and formalized within the organization);
- Managing the corporate innovation pipeline (top ideas earmarked for activation);
- Administering and maintaining an online idea submission and evaluation system;
- Organizing and coordinating innovation events and project initiatives;
- Developing and fine-tuning an innovation measurement system; and
- Measuring and controlling innovation performance and efficiency.

The innovation manager heads a dedicated administrative innovation team that supports and directly reports to the creative leader. A good example of an innovation manager's systematic, reliable mindset is Tim Cook, who took care of Apple's *"back office"* to support Steve Jobs before rising to CEO when the latter passed away.

Why does the innovation function benefit from two separate lead roles?

TIPS makes it easy to understand why it is beneficial to separate the two roles of a creative leader and an innovation manager: They draw upon diametrically opposite TIPS base energies and should be staffed by different profiles:

- Creative leaders are all about the TIPS base *"Ideas"*. Ideas people innately drive change, innovation and progress. They are strategic visionaries who enjoy focusing on boosting corporate performance, profitability and margins through innovations. TIPS profiles that naturally cater to this energy —and thus qualify to be a creative leader or be developed into a future one— are Ideators, Conceptualizers, Promoters and Imaginative Experimenters.

- In contrast, innovation managers draw on the TIPS base *"Systems"*. Systems people enjoy managing, organizing, directing, coordinating, and controlling internal activities. They take pleasure in setting up and administering an innovation management system, including defining measures that allow them to check on innovation performance and efficiency (How to increase our innovation outputs?

How to more efficiently employ internal and external resources for innovation?). TIPS profiles that innately operate on Systems energy —and thus make dependable innovation managers— are Systematizers, Organizers, Technocrats, and Systematic Experimenters.

But what if you insisted on keeping the two roles together? One compromise would be to staff the role of a *"creative innovation manager"* with a balanced Experimenter or an All-Rounder, both of whom can bridge the divide between the two polar energies *"Ideas"* and *"Systems."*. But, as with most compromises, you end up with a suboptimal result, because one person will be less effective than a real S-based innovation manager supporting a real I-based creative leader.

Conclusion: Not either or, but both

Both creative leaders and innovation managers care about driving innovation in an organization. But they do it by different means and by focusing on different ends. Both roles support and complement each other by letting each person play to their strengths while compensating for the weaknesses of each other's shadow side. So, separate the two functions of the creative leader and the innovation manager of your organization. And consider using TIPS to find out who is the right person for each role.

> *"Management is doing things right; leadership is doing the right things."*
> —PETER DRUCKER

By the way...Let me tell you a little secret about how I designed this book. *UNLEASHING WOW* uses an 8x8 grid (8 chapters with 8 sections each). To make the contents of this book relevant to a wide range of executives, managers, businesspeople and entrepreneurs, I used TIPS. I linked the nature of each section to the four TIPS Bases (Theories, Ideas, People, Systems).

In each chapter, I tried to have two sections catering to the favored style of each base. By design, you're likely to enjoy certain topics more than others, which is due to your TIPS base orientation and preferred cognitive styles. So, when you struggle with some content that is "too theoretical" or "too foolish" for your taste, rest assured that there are other readers who truly enjoy reading those sections you dislike.

LINK TO TIPS BASES		T — THEORIES		I — IDEAS		P — PEOPLE		S — SYSTEMS	
CHAPTER ↓	SECTIONS →	T1	T2	I1	I2	P1	P2	S1	S2
1. THE MODERN INNOVATION ENVIRONMENT		Welcome to the Innovation Economy	Mastering the Drivers of Future Change	Riding the Cycles of Change	Tracking the dimensions of change over time	The Entrepreneurial Society	Invite the world to a party	The more things change, the more they stay the same	The world hates Innovation. Here is why
2. THE CORE PRINCIPLES OF INNOVATION		Creativity defined	The Innovation Formula	Climb up the value pyramid to higher profitability	Modern Innovation Types	True innovation is about making meaning	Creativity Is…	How innovation affects financial performance	Why and how to protect your intellectual property
3. THE RULES OF THE INNOVATION GAME		Innovation Impact Types	Open innovation: The good, the bad, and the ugly	Ten ideas word about ideas	The 10 Rules of Playing with Innovation Types	in-NO-vation explained	Innovation Adoption: Where are you?	The Dilemma of Innovation Management	Dealing with the Paradoxes of Innovation
4. INNOVATION METHOD & THINKING TOOLS		Innovation process methods: What? Why? How?	Innovation: It's all about mastering process and projects	Why using only one creative process stage leads to dull ideas	Understanding the inner workings of thinking tools and creativity tools	Brainstorming; The Good, the Bad and the Ugly	It's not only what tools you use, but how you use them	X-IDEA: Introducing the Know-how of Wow	How to write a good creative brief
5. INNOVATIVE PEOPLE		Cognitive profiling methods: What? Why? How?	Scrutinizing popular cognitive profiling methods	Introducing the TIPS Innovation Profiling Method	Flow along the company life cycle with TIPS	What's your style to innovate?	Understanding who really makes innovation happen	How TIPS helps resolving main corporate innovation challenges	Creative leaders vs. innovation managers: Same or different
6. INNOVATION CULTURE		Finding the factors that matter for organizational innovation	The creative transformation marathon	Want to succeed faster? Plan to fail earlier	Boring meetings? Play In-no-vation Bingo!	Me Too Limited: Would you want to work here?	Innovative companies vs. in-NO-vative companies: Who's who?	Are you ready to commit time for innovation?	What gets measured gets innovated
7. INNOVATION LEADERSHIP		Why creative leadership matters now	Introducing the design features of the Genius Journey method	Incubation: A walk on the mysterious side of creativity	Rediscover your Creative Self	Creative Leaders: Who? What? Why?	Creative leadership: Are you hot or not?	The rise of creative leadership	How to creatively and effectively develop creative leaders?
8. THE FUTURE OF INNOVATION		How the generational shift will impact business and innovation	These creative laws govern innovation	What's your innovation mastery level?	Success ingredients of top achievers in innovation and beyond	Creative Spaces: From Cubeville to Idea City	Why so afraid of the future? Human up!	Innovation: Are you just talking the talk or walking your talk?	Is the pendulum swinging back?

"Great things in business are never done by one person. They're done by a team of people."
— STEVE JOBS

CHAPTER 5 — EXECUTIVE SUMMARY: INNOVATIVE PEOPLE & COGNITIVE PROFILING

❖ Personal assessment tools can help individuals become more self-aware and give companies more insights into their employees' preferred styles. Popular concepts include MBTI, HBTI, DISC, the Enneagram, and the Big Five.

❖ While most methods to profile personality and cognitive style share certain conceptual features, they differ in the details of the methodological design. Some methods have conceptual bugs that may lead to suboptimal profiling results or limit their applicability in business and innovation.

❖ The TIPS innovation profiling method uses four bases (Theories, Ideas, People, Systems) and four styles (to think, work, interact, and live) to profile people into ten plus one innovator profiles (Theorist, Ideator, Partner, Systematizer, Conceptualizer, Promoter, Organizer, Technocrat, Coach, Experimenter, and All-rounder).

❖ As new ventures move through the corporate life cycle and grow into mature corporations, different TIPS profiles drive the core activities until creative destruction ends the cycle—or, better, a new growth cycle starts.

❖ TIPS links to the "small picture" application areas of innovation by suggesting who shines when in the stages of an innovation method, who responds how to creative change, who has the potential to creatively lead innovation efforts (and who enjoys more to lead efficiency initiatives), and who enjoys working on what innovation types.

❖ TIPS also points to people's preferred style to innovate that is linked to their profile.

❖ In the first chapters of this book, we learned that 84% of the world more or less hates change and that 16% of people drive change. TIPS can explain which profiles will likely drive an innovation into the market, who's adopting it next, and who's lagging behind.

❖ While many companies use an innovation manager to oversee all corporate innovation activities, TIPS makes a case to separate the role of an innovation manager (who runs the innovation back office from the Systems-base with a focus on innovation performance) from that of a creative leader (who spearheads innovation projects from the front from the Ideas-base with a focus on corporate performance).

CHAPTER 6

INNOVATION CULTURE
SMALL PICTURE (III)

How to build an innovation-friendly culture in your organization.

1. Me Too Limited: Would You Want to Work Here?
2. Innovative vs. In-NO-vative Companies: Who's Who?
3. Boring Meetings? Play In-NO-vation Bingo!
4. Finding the Factors That Matter for Organizational Innovation
5. Are You Ready to Commit Time to Innovation?
6. Want to Succeed? Plan to Fail
7. The Creative Transformation Marathon
8. What Gets Measured Gets Innovated

* *Executive Summary*

6.1. ME TOO LIMITED: WOULD YOU WANT TO WORK HERE?

Reversal is a powerful creative thinking strategy where you switch your thinking around and look at the diametrically opposite situation of what you really want to achieve. In this section, allow me to invite you to visit Me Too Ltd., a traditional copycat company that exhibits all the characteristics of an innovation-hostile organization.

Welcome to Me Too Ltd., a company run by an authoritative leader with an oversized ego who does not tolerate any dissenting opinions to his dictatorial management style. This conservative company leader cautiously avoids taking any risks and strives to preserve the status quo. Consequently, stability is also clearly favored over change by all subordinated senior and middle managers and by the company as a whole.

Me Too Ltd. has a hierarchical structure with many management layers. Most decisions are concentrated at the highest levels of this steep organizational pyramid, which makes the decision-making process very slow and cumbersome. Power and authority in this hierarchy are based on seniority rather than on skills and abilities. Me Too Ltd. has stable divisions (departments based around functions) that are run as closed silos by bossy senior managers. Within these silos, every employee is expected to follow the rigid job definitions set by senior or upper middle management. Thus, most workers or employees on the lower hierarchy levels perceive their jobs as routine work and boring.

The managers of Me Too Ltd. motivate their rather indifferent subordinates using a "carrot and stick" approach. This is their sole motivation strategy. Implicit in this extrinsic motivation is the assumption that employees do not want to work. As the carrot, Me Too Ltd. uses financial incentives such as performance bonuses and promotions to reward positive adherence to their orders. For employees whose behavior deviates from the company's expectations, the stick brings a range of financial penalties, and demotions. When necessary, non-compliant people are fired. Somewhat predictably, some employees leave of their own volition. The staff turnover rate (one of the more reliable ways to gauge company culture) is high – and increasing. Me Too Ltd.'s risk-averse culture clearly discourages new initiatives necessary to succeed in today's fast-changing business climate. Managers show zero tolerance for failure and tend to punish mistakes rigorously, often making an example of the employee concerned. All employees are alerted: One mistake and you'll get a warning, two mistakes and you're out! Unsurprisingly, in such an environment, no employee dares show initiative, suggest novel ideas, or try out anything that deviates from the norm.

Me Too Ltd.'s culture clearly favors collectivism, sameness, and conformity among its employees. The uniformity and commonness of the workforce are ensured by hiring people with similar backgrounds. This is further stressed by the requirement for employees to wear a uniform at work. Any expression of individuality receives short shrift. A new employee beginning to work for Me Too Ltd. is expected to shut up and fit in. The work atmosphere is very serious. Management frowns upon laughing and smiling and interprets such aberrations as a sign that people are slacking. Senior management has set up an effective control regime and formalized work control systems (such as work time logging systems). A key role of middle managers is to use these frameworks to monitor employees and their behavior at work.

In this organization, vertical communication predominates. Often, the top-down information flow stops at a certain middle management level. The employees jokingly call this the waterline. Office politics is a fact of life. A lot of politicking takes place at the different management levels of Me Too Ltd.'s steep organizational hierarchy. Many managers play tactical games to gain power over their peers and to garner influence with their superiors. Information is an important weapon in these political power games, and the information flow within Me Too Ltd. is controlled and tactically managed. Information is shared to a very limited extent across the organization and then only on an infrequent "need-to-know" basis.

At the bottom of the hierarchy, workers and employees are often starved of important information, such as the firm's interim performance or important strategic moves. Because of the pervasive atmosphere of fear and intimidation in the closed communication culture, individuals tend to keep information to themselves rather than share it openly with each other.

Politics and restricted information flows indicate that Me Too Ltd.'s senior management team subscribes to a competitive, closed-system business paradigm.

At Me Too Ltd., networking and collaboration are alien concepts – not only intra-organizationally within the firm's different divisions, functions, or work units but also inter-organizationally in relation to other companies (such as suppliers, distributors, or even industry peers). Virtual forms of networking and collaboration are not yet on the radar screen of senior managers.

In Me Too Ltd., management rarely articulates or enacts support for creative ideas and innovation. As staffing is very tight at Me Too Ltd., all employees and middle managers are constantly busy keeping up with their monotonous routine work. For most employees within the company's lower ranks there is simply not enough time to think about creative improvements or innovative projects. If someone nevertheless comes up with a great idea for a new product and wants to bring it to life, she will find little practical support from middle management and no monetary resources to develop a prototype. Last but not least, it goes without saying that Me Too Ltd. regards training in general and creativity training in particular as an unnecessary expense: a waste of time and money. After all, what is the value of providing training to employees if senior management follows the maxim of "That's the way we've always done things here at Me Too Ltd.!"

Do you know – or maybe even work for – a company that resembles Me Too Ltd. in surprisingly many ways? Then, I have some good news for you: in the rapidly changing, increasingly competitive global business world of the new millennium, organizational dinosaurs like Me Too Ltd. are destined to become extinct based on the fundamental principle of Charles Darwin's theory of evolution: *"Favorable variations have a tendency to be preserved, unfavorable to be destroyed."*

6.2. INNOVATIVE VS. IN-NO-VATIVE COMPANIES: WHO'S WHO?

Take a moment to think about the following questions: What companies do you consider to be highly innovative? What factors have made these firms become innovation leaders? Would you want to work for such a company? Why (not)?

What innovative companies do you know?

When we train or consult organizations at my innovation company Thinkergy on how to build more innovation-friendly companies, we ask these questions as a warm-up exercise, While the smaller creative ventures and local innovation heroes vary in different countries, some well-known firms appear in the delegates' list of innovative companies, with Apple, Google, and Microsoft often featured first.

Interestingly, most businesspeople also intuitively have a good understanding of organizational and cultural factors that differentiate innovative companies from normal organizations. And while a few delegates dare to admit they rather would not want to work for an innovative company (either because their cognitive style favors efficiency and adaptation over creativity and innovation, or because they dislike working in a firm that constantly wants to push the boundaries forward), a vast majority of workshop delegates would sign on at an innovative firm given half a chance.

What in-NO-vative companies do you know?

If time permits, we also ask workshop delegates the exact opposite set of questions: *"What companies do you consider NOT to be innovative? What factors prevent these firms from becoming innovation leaders? Would you want to work for such a company? Why (not)?"*

Interestingly, the energy levels rise when the delegates list examples of in-NO-vative *"Me Too"*-companies — and of the cultural factors that stand in their way. Laughter, cheers, and a bit of disgust mixed with *"Schadenfreude"* fills the room, indicating that the delegates had their fair share of negative customer experiences with the blacklisted firms and their poor products and services. Having worked in such an in-NO-vative company before, some delegates are even intimately familiar with what's wrong with these companies.

What can we learn from this exercise?

Most businesspeople and customers intuitively grasp what innovative companies do right — and what in-NO-vative companies do wrong. They are able to pinpoint many of the striking differences in "the way we do things around here" in innovative versus in-NO-vative companies. So, if not only highly paid consultants but laypeople can distinguish poor from best practice and identify what wrongs we need to right, why isn't every company innovative?

Changing an established organizational culture is very hard. It typically takes at least 2-3 years of focused effort to make a successful transition to a more innovative culture, and those inside the organization who benefited from the old culture may resist change or even sabotage it. We will discuss more about this below in section 6.4, *"The Creative Transformation Marathon."*

What companies lead global innovation rankings?

A few well-known business magazines and global

consulting firms regularly release lists that rank the world's most innovative companies. The different rankings vary in the methodology and metrics used to rank innovators, thus producing variations in the firms listed as innovation leaders, but also having some names appear in every ranking.

Boston Consulting Group (BCG)'s annual list of the world's top innovative companies is my favorite ranking. Because it has been done consistently every year since 2006, it allows us to see shifts and trends in the populace of innovation leaders over time. BCG has steadily evolved its ranking methodology, adding over time objective financial metrics (such as total shareholder premium, revenue, and margin growth) and cross-industry ranking to its initial approach to having executives subjectively rank the most innovative companies inside their industry.

In its most recent 2023 ranking, BCG's ten top innovators read (in rank order): Apple, Tesla, Amazon, Alphabet, Microsoft, Moderna, Samsung, Huawei, BYD, and Siemens. Interestingly, with the exception of featuring third in 2019, Apple has topped the ranking every year since 2006.

In recent years, other business magazines such as Forbes and Fast Company released their own innovation rankings:

- Forbes ranks a firm's innovativeness based on sales growth and the *"innovation premium"* (defined as the difference between their market capitalization and the net present value of cash flows from existing businesses (based on a proprietary algorithm from Credit Suisse HOLT)) they achieved. Forbes only considers firms with seven years of public financial data and USD 10 billion in market cap. Moreover, Forbes only focuses on industries investing in innovation, excluding non-R&D-intensive industries such as banking and financial services or energy and mining.

- In contrast, Fast Company ranks innovation leaders overall and in many different business segments based on the impacts of recent innovative contributions that they've made. Thereby, Fast Company blends subjective editorial judgment with objective artificial intelligence that mines and topographically maps out millions of innovation-related news articles, blog posts, company profiles, and patents across more than 40 sectors to identify trends and the companies that drive them. Due to the different ranking approach of Fast Company, many smaller creative agencies and tech firms (that don't size up to the BCG or Forbes lists) achieve top ranks alongside the usual suspects.

Lessons and trends from the global innovation rankings

When we compare the movements within the BCG ranking over the last 17 years, and also factor in the names of other global innovator lists using different ranking methodologies (Forbes, Fast Company), we can discern a few general rules of thumb as well as emerging trends related to the world's top innovative companies since 2006:

1. Sustainable innovation leaders seem to live by one of Steve Jobs' mottos: *"Innovation distinguishes between a leader and a follower."* Thirteen companies have managed to stay on the BCG list between 2006 and 2023, earning them the title of *"continuous innovators"*: 3M, Amazon, Apple, Alphabet (Google), BMW, Daimler (Mercedes-Benz), Dell, General Electric, IBM, Microsoft, Nike, Procter

& Gamble, and Samsung. Their consistent presence in the BCG list indicates that these companies have cultivated innovation-friendly cultures that are unswayed by top managers and management fads coming and going.

2. In fast-moving industries, particularly those using digital technology, today's innovation leaders may lose their relevance and drop out of the rankings quickly if they miss out on emerging technologies (think of digital device market leaders such as Blackberry, Motorola, and Nokia in the 2000s).

3. Innovation seems to be gaining more traction in Asia. In the past, innovation leaders mainly originated in the US, Europe, or Japan. Recent rankings indicate that dynamic innovation increasingly takes place in Asian Emerging Markets (most importantly, China and India, but also in smaller countries like Indonesia, Malaysia, and Thailand).

4. Innovation shifts from industrial to digital, clean, and human-centered in line with the advent rise of the Sixth Wave: In 2006, many industrial companies such as BP, Toyota, GE, BMW, and Honda ranked prominently among the top 50 innovation leaders. In the recent rankings, new companies pioneering solutions in the Sixth Wave tech spaces feature high on the league tables. Prominent names include *"digital innovators"* (e.g., Nvidia, Amazon, Alphabet, Meta, etc.), *"clean innovators"* (such as Tesla, BYD, and SpaceX), and *"human-centered innovators"* (such as Moderna, BioNTech, and Siemens).

5. Innovation leadership doesn't equate anymore with being big. In the same strand, while innovative Multinational Corporations (MNCs) used to dominate rankings in the past, newer rankings are a blend of MNCs, new up-and-coming Emerging Market Corporations, as well as scale-up ventures in the emerging new tech spaces of the Sixth Wave. This shift supports John Naisbitt's view that we already talked about earlier in Chapter 1: *"We're shifting from a managerial to an entrepreneurial society."*

Conclusion: *"Continued innovation is the best means of defeating competition,"* noted the famous innovator Thomas Edison. What was true more than a hundred years ago is even more true today. Every company leading innovation in its industry today has to continue innovating with a focus on making meaning and on making the world a better place. Otherwise, it will sooner rather than later lose its relevance and be replaced by a new class of innovative companies.

> "Innovation has nothing to do with how many R&D dollars you have. When Apple came up with the Mac, IBM was spending at least 100 times more on R & D. It's not about money. It's about the people you have, how you're led, and how much you get it."
> —STEVE JOBS

THE WORLD'S TOP INNOVATIVE COMPANIES

2006 → 2016 → 2023

BCG's World's Top 50 Innovators in 2006

#	Company	#	Company
1	Apple	26	Porsche
2	Google	27	Genentech
3	3M	28	Cisco Systems
4	Toyota	29	Nike
5	Microsoft	30	Motorola
6	General Electric	31	Daimler
7	Procter & Gamble	32	Infosys
8	Nokia	33	Ryanair
9	Starbucks	34	Pixar
10	IBM	35	SonyEricsson
11	Virgin	36	Whole Foods
12	Samsung	37	Capitol One
13	Sony	38	Tesco
14	Dell	39	Danone
15	IDEO	40	BP
16	BMW	41	PepsiCo
17	Intel	42	Hewlett-Packard
18	eBay	43	Disney
19	IKEA	44	JetBlue
20	Wal-Mart	45	W.L. Gore
21	Amazon	46	Skype
22	Target	47	FedEx
23	Honda	48	Bang & Olufson
24	Blackberry	49	Renault
25	Southwest Airlines	50	L'Oreal

BCG's World's Top 50 Innovators in 2016

#	Company	#	Company
1	Apple	26	Pfizer
2	Google	27	General Motors
3	Tesla	28	JPMorgan Chase
4	Microsoft	29	Johnson & Johnson
5	Amazon	30	AXA
6	Netflix	31	Nike
7	Samsung	32	Expedia
8	Toyota	33	Allianz
9	Facebook	34	SpaceX
10	IBM	35	Xiaomi
11	Bayer	36	Walt Disney Co
12	Southwest Airlines	37	Hilton
13	Hewlett-Packard	38	Renault
14	BMW	39	NTT Docomo
15	General Electric	40	Intel
16	Daimler	41	Marriott Int'l
17	Uber	42	3M
18	Dupont	43	Dell
19	Dow Chemical	44	Orange
20	BASF	45	Siemens
21	Airbnb	46	Huawei
22	Under Armour	47	Bristol-Myers Squibb
23	Gilead Sciences	48	Honda
24	Regeneron	49	BT Group
25	Cisco Systems	50	Procter & Gamble

BCG's World's Top 50 Innovators in 2023

#	Company	#	Company
1	Apple	26	Proctor & Gamble
2	Tesla	27	Nestlé
3	Amazon	28	General Electric
4	Alphabet	29	Xiaomi Technology
5	Microsoft	30	Honeywell Int'l
6	Moderna	31	Sony
7	Samsung	32	Sinopec
8	Huawei	33	Hitachi
9	BYD	34	McDonalds
10	Siemens	35	Merck & Co Inc
11	Pfizer	36	ByteDance
12	Johnson & Johnson	37	Bosch
13	SpaceX	38	Dell
14	Nvidia	39	Glencore
15	ExxonMobile	40	Stripe
16	Meta	41	Saudi Aramco
17	Nike	42	Coca-Cola
18	IBM	43	Mercedes-Benz
19	3M	44	Alibaba
20	Tata Group	45	Walmart
21	Roche	46	PetroChina
22	Oracle	47	NTT Data
23	BioNTech	48	Lenovo
24	Shell	49	BMW
25	Schneider Electric	50	Unilever

Sources: BCG Global Innovation Survey, 2006, 2016, and 2023 (https://www.bcg.com/publications/2023/advantages-through-innovation-in-uncertain-times]; https://www.fastcompany.com/most-innovative-companies/2017; https://www.forbes.com/innovative-companies/list

6.3. BORING MEETINGS? PLAY IN-NO-VATION BINGO!

Does your business's culture encourage innovation? Or do you work for an in-NO-vative company with a culture that discourages new ideas, initiatives, and change?

"Life must be lived as play," said Plato. Especially in difficult times, you should heed that advice and have some fun in your business. One great way is to play In-NO-vation Bingo, an adaptation of the classic Buzzword Bingo. In-NO-vation Bingo makes long, mind-numbing gatherings more fun and at the same time helps you see how innovation-hostile your meetings are. Here's how to play:

1. Make your Innovation Bingo card

Divide a sheet of paper in thirds, both vertically and horizontally, to make a 3x3 grid.

2. Load up the card

Choose nine of the innovation-hostile sentences below, using some random method (we look at the second hand on a watch to get a random number), and write one in each of the nine squares in the grid.

Once the nine squares on your card all have innovation-hostile statements in them, you're ready to play.

3. In your meeting, listen to win

During your meeting, listen to what's said. Whenever you hear someone say something that's in one of the boxes on your card (or something that means the same), then put an "X" in that box. When you have three "X"s in a row — horizontal, vertical, or diagonal — yell *"Bingo!"* You've just won! Sadly, it means that your company is losing

Yes, but...	I don't like it.	Are you kidding me?
That's against the guidelines.	We don't have enough ... (to do this).	It's impossible.
Let's not rush things.	I like the idea, but ...	People will laugh at us.

LOADED IN-NO-VATION BINGO CARDS

We tried it before, and it doesn't work.	It's not realistic.	Don't rock the boat.
I am very concerned that ...	This is ridiculous.	It won't work!
Let's talk about it later.	That's not the way we do things around here.	You clearly don't understand the field.

out on innovation. (Note: To avoid the tongue-lashing that would likely result from calling out *"Bingo,"* you may resort to looking at each other and silently mouthing the word *"Bingo"* instead.

4. Learn from Innovation Bingo

Meetings clearly express an organization's culture. Innovation Bingo highlights the language used in meetings to illustrate if your corporate culture is innovation-hostile. Innovation thrives in an environment that is open to it. If your co-workers sound like politicians and the Innovation Bingo game is over quickly, your culture discourages innovation, growth, and change.

IN-NO-VATIVE STATEMENTS TO LOAD THE INNOVATION CARD:

(1) Yes, but… (2) We tried it before, and it doesn't work. (3) I am very concerned that… (4) That's against the rules. (5) We don't have enough resources to do this. (6) It wasn't invented here. (7) I am afraid that… (7) We'll have to think carefully about this. (8) People will laugh at us. (9) Let's form a committee to look into it. (10) That's not our problem.

(11) I like the idea, but… (12) It won't work! (13) I'm very worried that… (14) What's the ROI for this idea? (15) Let's not rush things. (16) I don't like it. (17) Have you thought through the implications? (18) This is laughable. (19) You clearly don't understand the field. (20) Write it down, and we'll look at it later.

(21) Don't rock the boat. (22) We've always done it this way. (23) That's too risky. (24) It will cost too much. (25) It's a good idea but we're too invested in another idea. (26) Sounds interesting, but… (27) No one will buy it. (28) No comment. (29) That's not the way we do things around here. (30) That's really stupid.

(31) If it ain't broke, don't fix it. (32) That's fine in theory, but it doesn't work like that. (33) We don't have time for this. (34) Let's commission a study. (35) Good idea, but it's impractical. (36) It's too much work. (37) This idea could reduce sales of an existing product. (38) It might not work. (39) Let's talk about it later. (40) Let's not talk about it.

(41) Be serious. (42) No one else does it. (43) It's unfeasible. (44) We can't make it happen. (45) It's impossible. (46) Let me think about it. (47) It's too radical. (48) Are you crazy? (49) We can't do it. (50) Let's keep it for later.

(51) This is ridiculous. (52) Hmm. (53) Are you kidding me? (54) In your dreams! (55) We're too busy. (56) Let's see a cost-benefit analysis first. (57) No one will understand this. (58) It's not realistic. (59) Write a memo. (60) It's never been done before.

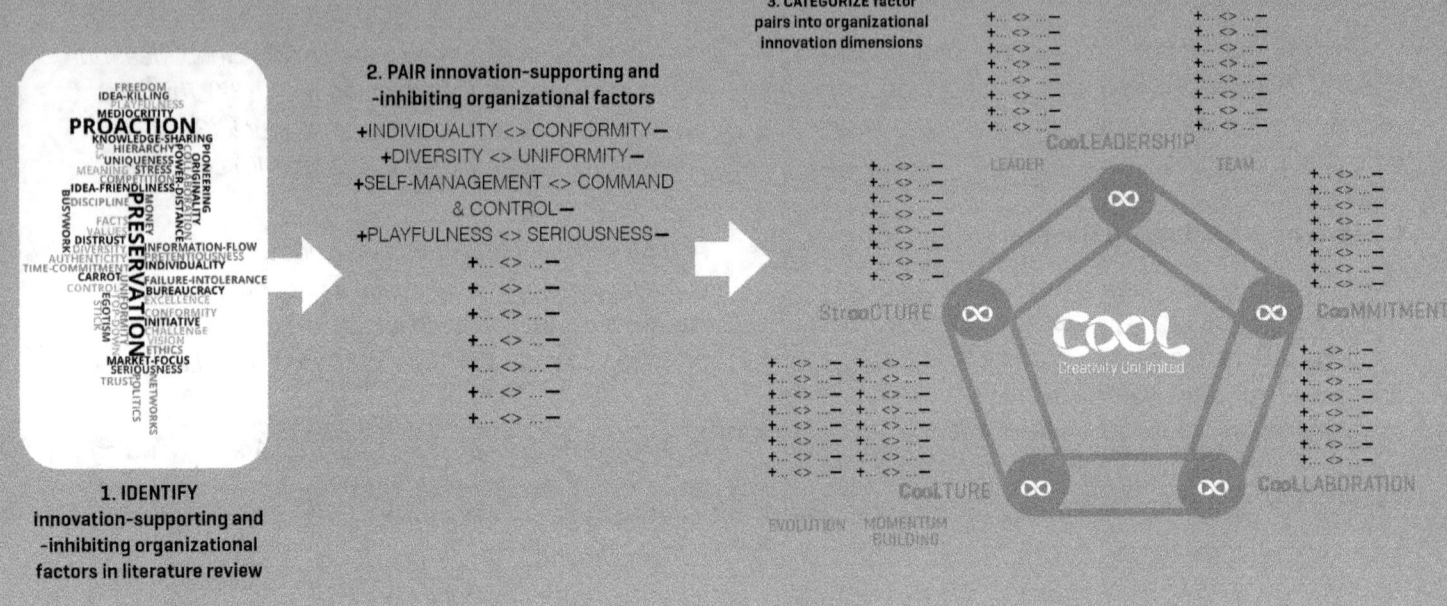

6.4. FINDING THE FACTORS THAT MATTER FOR ORGANIZATIONAL INNOVATION

In the era of the innovation economy, many corporations say they are eager to become more innovation-friendly organizations. But transforming an in-NO-vative into an innovative organization is easier said than done. You don't only have a few cosmetic fixes or small renovations to make but need to undergo a major organizational redesign that impinges upon many organizational factors.

But what factors really matter for innovation? And how to find out how a company is doing with regard to each of these factors? In the following, allow me to share with you how I approached the challenge: *"How to effectively help companies to become more innovative?"*

Step 1: Unveil factors affecting organizational innovation by reviewing the related literature

The literature on organizational change and innovation is full of academic papers and business books suggesting a myriad of factors that hinder or support organizations to become more innovative. So, I started by collecting as many organizational factors pro and con innovation as possible.

For example, a command-and-control management style, collectivism and conformity pressure, or internal focus and bureaucracy are all said to inhibit corporate innovation, while a work environment characterized by diversity, playfulness, and self-management promotes creativity and innovation.

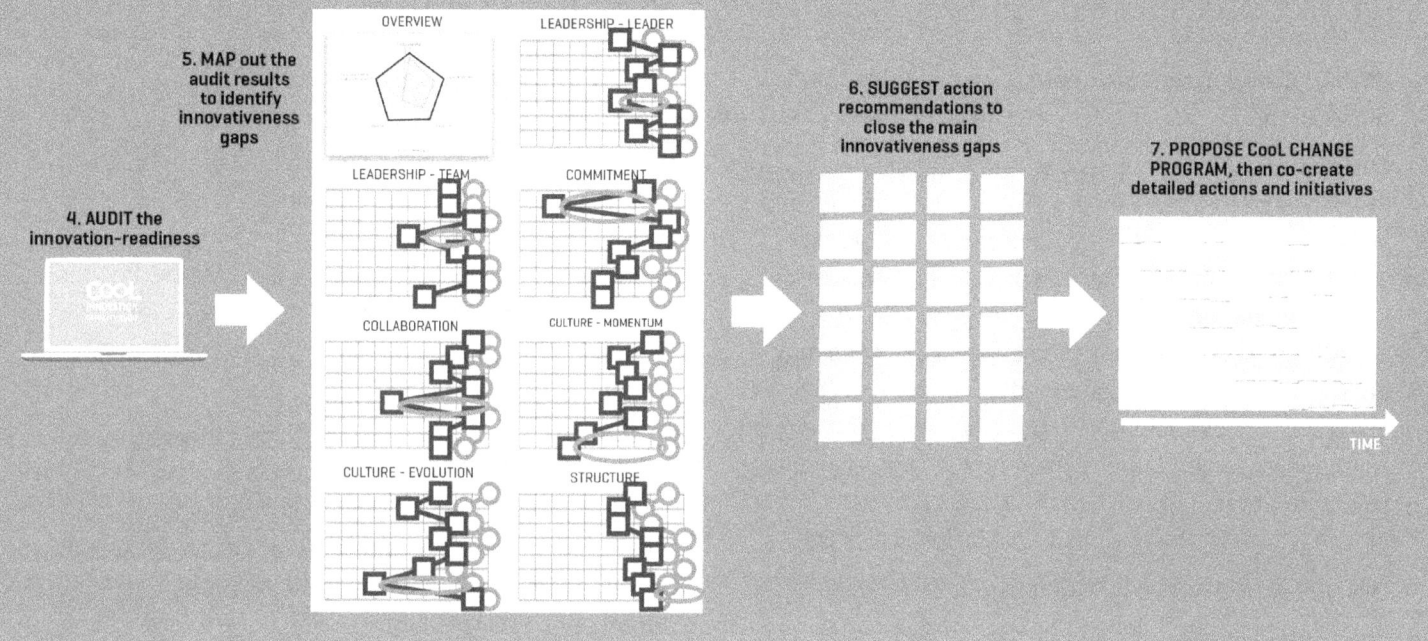

Step 2: Innovation-supporting and inhibiting factors can be paired

When I reviewed studies on organizational innovation more than a decade ago, I also noticed that many of the factors supporting or inhibiting organizational innovations connect to each other and build antagonistic pairs. In other words, every positive factor that supports an organization to become more innovation-friendly can be connected to an opposite innovation-hostile factor. Here are three examples:

1. Companies that motivate their employees intrinsically through interesting, challenging projects tend to produce more innovation than those who largely rely on extrinsic motivational factors only (we will discuss this in a separate section below).

2. Many innovative companies allow their staff to dedicate a certain amount of their work time to innovative projects, while most normal organizations don't allow their staff to set aside separate time slots for innovation.

3. Top innovators often have action-oriented leaders who walk their innovation talk by actively being involved in cutting-edge innovation efforts (e.g. think of Steve Jobs' leading the teams that developed the iPhone and iPad, see Walt Disney at a drawing board in the middle of the studio, or picture Elon Musk contributing ideas to solve wicked engineering challenges at SpaceX or Tesla). In contrast, CEOs of normal companies tend to only talk the innovation talk without really walking their talk by actively involving themselves in top-notch innovation projects.

Finally, I ended up with 56 antagonistic factor pairs that seem to play a role in organizational innovation. But 56 is a high number of variable pairs to manage. So what's next?

Step 3: Categorize factor pairs into organizational dimension

The management literature discusses certain dimensions that influence organizational behavior and change, such as the culture or structure of an organization. Most of the 56-factor pairs that support or inhibit organizational innovation lean towards one clear organizational dimension. (However, in some cases, academics may argue whether a particular variable pair is more of a cultural or structural factor; I admit they may have a point with their view, and that it is irrelevant for practitioners who care about making their organization more innovative rather than winning an academic debate).

Ultimately, I settled on five dimensions to categorize the different factor pairs: leadership, commitment, collaboration & communication, culture, and structure & systems.

Two of these five dimensions, leadership and culture, have allotted a higher number of variable pairs, indicating they are more complex and nuanced. To keep the factors relating to these two dimensions more manageable, I broke them down into two subsets each: the top leader and the leadership team, and culture momentum building and culture evolution.

So, now that we have 56 variable pairs catering to five dimensions of organizational innovation, what are we going to do with them? We use them to identify an organization's present readiness and future potential for innovation through an innovation audit.

Step 4: Audit the innovation readiness of an organization

Our innovation audit uses bipolar rating scales to measure both a company's current state and its desired future state for each of the 56-factor pairs along the 5 five dimensions of CooLness.

Ideally, an audit exercise involves all business units or business functions of an organization and cuts through 2-3 organizational levels (e.g., top management, middle management, workforce) to draw a well-rounded picture of the organization's current state of innovative affairs and its ambition and readiness for innovative change in future.

After the data collection, we analyze the survey responses quantitatively using statistical software. To interpret and deepen the quantitative audit results qualitatively, we also conduct a series of interviews with selected members of the organizations representing different units and hierarchy levels.

Step 5: Map out the audit results to analyze innovation gaps

In the next step, we visualize the audit results in a series of charts. Thereby, the mean scores for both the current state and desired future state for each of the 56-factor pairs are mapped out in line charts linked to the five dimensions. We usually do this for the organization in toto and for different business units and hierarchy levels to identify best and worst practices as well as bring out biases of top managers (who tend to see the present state of the organizational factors more rosy than their subordinates).

Here is an example of a common innovation readiness gap in many organizations: Failing with a new innovation project often has negative consequences for the people involved, even though many managers encourage their subordinates to take initiative in general.

The ensuing pattern and gap analysis of the

organizational innovation audit charts allow us to identify what "gap areas" need the most attention. Moreover, it also helps us to form an opinion if a company stands a realistic chance to successfully transform into an innovation-friendly organization — or rather, is a difficult or even hopeless case where it would take the organization massive changes (such as replacement of the top management team) to evolve from in-NO-vation to innovation.

Step 6: Develop action plans to close identified gaps

Next, we propose an initial action plan for top management to consider that outlines possible action recommendations to close each of the identified innovation gaps. This is the starting point to then add more ideas on action initiatives that come from the relevant managers and staff involved in a particular gap to close.

Step 6: Map out the innovation project change timeline and action initiatives

Finally, we propose an innovation change transformation project to top management that outlines the phases and related key transformational actions to top management. If the leadership team is committed to moving forward, we use this draft plan and action map as a starting point to co-create with the senior leaders the details of the transformation journey from an in-NO-vative to an innovative organization.

At my innovation company Thinkergy, we call this journey making a CooL change — in line with our innovation culture transformation method CooL—Creativity UnLimited. (The name suggests that we want to help companies find a suitable pathway to transform an in-NO-vative, *"Me Too"*-copycat culture into a cool, innovation-focused organization with unlimited creativity (*"CooL"* - Creativity UnLimited).

CooL versus other organizational innovation methods

Just as many roads lead to Rome, so can many other organizational innovation and change methods assist companies who are serious about transforming into an innovation-friendly culture. Numerous consultancy companies and academics have proposed their own approaches to guide companies through organizational change. So, survey the market for a method that resonates with you and your company. Thereby, it will be helpful for you to understand the commonalities and differences between organizational innovation methods as follows:

- Organizational innovation methods typically suggest a set of innovation-supporting organizational factors. Often, these are clustered into a smaller set of dimensions. Most methods also use an audit tool to measure the current state of innovativeness in a firm for the given set of organizational variables. Finally, based on the audit results, all methods suggest action recommendations on how to transform the organization towards becoming more innovation-friendly.

- Different organizational innovation methods vary in scope and details from each other. For example, they differ in the number of variables they consider, in the way they link these factors to a varying number of related dimension, and in the nature of the action recommendations they make to transform into an innovation-friendly organization (e.g., adopting best practices of top innovators, or idiosyncratically creating one's own innovation practices).

Conclusion: Before you embark on your organizational innovation transformation journey, allow me a word of warning: Evolving from a copycat into a cool, innovative company is not a quick fix. It takes focused, concerted, and continuous efforts of the leadership team and key parts of the organization for a period of at least 2-3 years. We metaphorically explain this arduous journey in the next section titled *"The innovation transformation marathon."* We will also explain two of the fifty-six-factor pairs in two separate articles and give examples of how a company may address them if an innovation readiness audit identifies a major gap for each of these factor pairs.

> "There is this idea that you put two people, who cannot stand each other, into a room, hoping that all this negative energy leads to a creative result. I disagree. Co-operation, confidence and fun - that is the way."
> —JOHN LASSETER

6.5. ARE YOU READY TO COMMIT TIME TO INNOVATION?

"If you want creative workers, give them enough time to play," suggested the English comedian John Cleese. One key factor distinguishing the vital few innovative companies in every industry from their many in-NO-vative peers is how much time the organization commits to innovation. Let's understand how time impacts creativity and innovation and what companies that want to become more innovative can do to shift the odds in their favor.

An imagination experiment: The Roman galley

Imagine for a moment being an unfree rower on a Roman galley. Day in and day out, your miserable job is to pull the oars alongside the other rowers to the rhythm of a drum beaten by one of the overseers.

As time passes, the number of rowers on your galley goes down in several rounds as the captain decides there is not enough food to keep and feed the entire crew. Moreover, the drummer has also steadily sped up the drum beat — first barely noticeable. You and the other remaining rowers feel increasingly worn out, and some rowers disappear from their oars because they burned out.

Then, to your great surprise, your captain appears one day and announces: "While pulling the oars, I want you to also come up with ideas on how to improve our galley in radical ways." How would you feel? How creative are the ideas from you and the other rowers likely to be? And even if you came up with an outstanding idea to improve the prospects of your galley, when would you find time to implement it?

From the galley to the corporate office floor

Fortunately, none of us has to work our fingers to the bone on a Roman galley anymore. But working in an established in-NO-vative corporation resembles in many ways the scenario in our little imagination experiment:

- While we've mostly moved beyond the hard physical work of pulling oars, the monotonous and drudging nature of many modern work activities (attending to a daily flood of emails, sitting in —often unnecessarily long— meetings, responding to inquiries of external and internal customers, plodding through countless small to-do items, among others) mentally and psychologically drains the energy reservoirs of modern knowledge workers and managers alike.

- Nowadays, business is not only taking place in an ever-changing and increasingly complex, risky, and surprising environment, but it has also been speeding up (as discussed earlier in section 1.1). This means that expected response times and cycle times (such as the new product development cycle time or time-to-market related to innovation) have shortened, too, leading to more haste to keep up with the increasing pace.

- At the same time, many companies underwent several *"rightsizing"* exercises, which is a euphemistic way to describe massive job cuts seen in many established industries in the past 2 to 3 decades.

- What does this mean for the average employee or manager? They have to handle more—and more complex—work at an ever-faster pace (no wonder the number of burnouts has increased in recent years). On top of all that, after we've moved into the innovation economy, they're now also expected to contribute game-changing ideas and additional work efforts to corporate innovation initiatives.

Can corporations work an ever smaller workforce harder and faster while at the same time boosting their innovativeness? In other words, can fewer managers and knowledge workers produce more and better ideas and game-changing innovations in less time? No way. Arguably, they may push out a few incremental innovations and maybe even be able to pull off some evolutionary innovations that are low-hanging fruits. However, corporations keen to produce novel, original, and meaningful evolutionary innovations and game-changing revolutionary innovations need to commit time. Outstanding creativity and game-changing innovation take time. Here's why.

Innovation begins with creativity — and creativity requires time

Chapter 2 presented the innovation formula: Creativity + Action = Innovation. You also learned that innovation always begins with creativity — with novel, original and meaningful ideas. Research studies indicate that creativity is unlikely to occur in a company where overcrowded work schedules make busy employees feel like they are on a treadmill.

In a famous study on the connection between creativity and time pressure, Harvard professor Teresa Amabile discovered some stunning results:

- The more time-pressured people feel on a given day, the less likely they are to think creatively.

- This result holds true not only on that day but also on the two subsequently following days (a phenomenon that Amabile called *"time pressure hangover"* (in comparison to the hangover after a long night out).

- Moreover, the experts who judged the creative output of the group under time pressure and of the control group with sufficient time noticed that the drop in creativity was worst when time pressure was highest.

- Furthermore, the time-pressured people were under the impression that their unoriginal outputs were highly creative contributions. In other words: The participants under time pressure in the study were not able to objectively judge the creative quality of their work, which in business may lead to the selection of unoriginal business ideas for real-life implementation.

If you want your employees to be creative as the starting point of innovation, send them on a mission instead of forcing them to run like frantic mice on a treadmill — and commit sufficient time budgets that allow them to come up with novel, original and meaningful ideas.

Innovation results from acting on creative ideas — and action requires time

Creativity is the pivotal starting point of innovation, but it is not an end in itself; we need to act on a creative idea to arrive at innovation — and taking initiative on a novel, original and meaningful idea requires a substantial time commitment, too.

Nowadays, a creative idea is typically activated by an activation project team. Thereby, the team often comprises members from multiple disciplines (such as engineers, programmers, designers, and marketers, among other domain specialists) that either belong to internal business units or come from external supply partners and who collaborate on the project full-time or part-time for weeks, months or even a couple of years. Add up the total work hours of everyone involved, and you quickly end up with a substantial time requirement. As such, taking action on a standout idea to transform it into an evolutionary or revolutionary innovation requires companies to set aside a substantial time (and related financial) budget.

INNOVATION AUDIT RESULTS: COMMITMENT

Negative		Positive
INNOVATION TALK (NO LEADERSHIP SUPPORT)		WALK THE INNOVATION TALK (LEADERSHIP SUPPORT)
PERMANENT STRESS AND LACK OF TIME		TIME COMMITMENT TO INNOVATION INITIATIVES
LIMITED, SELECTIVE HUMAN CAPITAL DEVELOPMENT		ACTIVE, EXTENSIVE HUMAN CAPITAL DEVELOPMENT
NO INVESTMENT CREATIVITY & INNOVATION WORKSHOPS		INVESTMENT IN CREATIVITY & INNOVATION WORKSHOPS
NO USE OF SYSTEMATIC INNOVATION PROCESS METHODS		USE OF SYSTEMATIC INNOVATION PROCESS METHODS
NO RESOURCES FOR IDEA DEVELOPMENT		BUDGETS & RESOURCES FOR IDEA DEVELOPMENT
NO SYSTEMATIC INNOVATION MANAGEMENT		INNOVATION MANAGEMENT SYSTEM IN PLACE
NO MEASUREMENT OF INNOVATION PERFORMANCE		INNOVATION PERFORMANCE MEASUREMENT

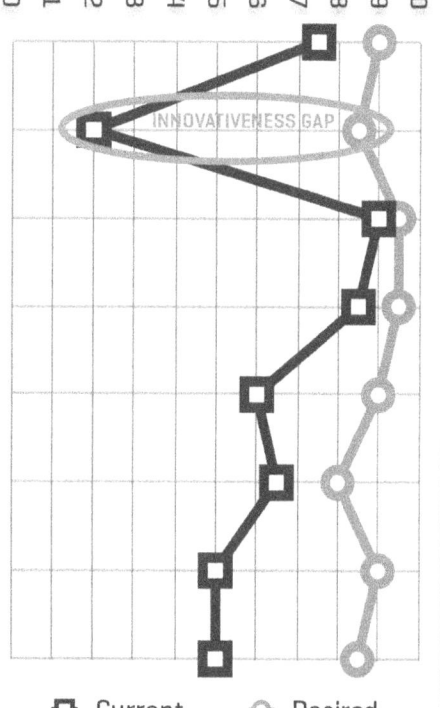

INNOVATIVENESS GAP

☐ Current   ○ Desired

PERMANENT STRESS AND LACK OF TIME

TIME COMMITMENT TO INNOVATION INITIATIVES

How to commit more time to innovation initiatives?

POSSIBLE ACTION IDEAS TO CLOSE THE IDENTIFIED INNOVATIVENESS GAP FOR THE FACTOR "TIME COMMITMENT"

ACTION 1: Adopt 3M's 15% rule or —even better— Google's 20% rule, thus allowing staff to work on their own pet projects ca. 1 day a week

ACTION 2: Create a mechanism for staff to signal to managers that today is "innovation day," so they cannot disturb with ad hoc tasks

ACTION 3: Raise your overall headcount to have a 15-20% buffer (to cover the extra time needed for innovation)

ACTION 4: Allow employees to flexibly decide on their work times and breaks (within a core range where all should be in for joint project work)

ACTION 5: Have staff share every Friday what progress they've made on their pet project, and what they plan to do next to advance it they've learned

ACTION 6: Create a time account where staff can built-up work time that they later can use en bloc to work on innovation at home

ACTION 7: Have an official "innovation work day" every month where staff works individually or jointly on their innovation project

ACTION 8: Commit time for regular innovation project team challenges once a semester or year that are chosen anew by each team

So what? Commit time to creativity and innovation

Companies that are serious about moving from in-NO-vation to innovation can't work their employees like rowers on a galley (or like hamsters running on a treadmill). If executives want to promote corporate creativity and produce tangible innovation results, they need to commit extra time to creativity and innovation. How? Here are three tips for your consideration:

1. **Allow for slack when setting headcount numbers.** When reviewing the staffing of a business unit or team, make sure that the headcount is not too tight. Plan to avoid the "work like being on the treadmill" trap when the daily schedules of your people are completely filled up with routine work or crisis management. Give your employees some space and time to come up with creative results. Psychologist Mihaly Csikszentmihalyi, a leading researcher on creative genius and individual creativity, expressed the time dilemma as follows: *"The important thing to remember is that creative energy, like any other form of psychic energy, only works over time. It takes a certain minimum amount of time to write a sonnet or to invent a new machine. People vary in the speed they work - Mozart wrote concerti much faster than Beethoven did - but even Mozart could not escape the tyranny of time. Therefore, every hour saved from drudgery and routine is an hour added to creativity."*

2. **Adopt the 15% (or 20%) rule.** One cornerstone in 3M's innovation culture is a tradition known as the *"15 percent rule"*, which encourages 3M researchers to spend up to 15% of their work time on projects of their own initiative. Google's engineers can spend even up to 20% of their work time to follow through on pet projects outside their main job. According to Google's former CEO Eric Schmidt, this approach is *"a systematic way of making sure a middle manager does not eliminate that innovation."* Likewise, be willing to give employees time to follow through on projects of their own interest - based on the understanding that they are innovation-focused or customer-related.

3. **Busyness ≠ Productivity ≠ Creativity.** Remember that productivity is fueled by results and not by the amount of hours spent behind a computer screen in the office. Many Asian organizations have devolved company cultures that require rigid adherence to fixed office hours and also glorify those serious, hard-working employees who put in the longest hours. However, the number of hours spent in the office does not necessarily equate with work productivity. Furthermore, spending too much time in the office seems to be a counter-productive strategy for producing novel ideas and creative responses to the multifold business challenges caused by fast-changing market environments. Call a meeting of your team and find out when and where they get their best ideas using the beginning question above. Then encourage your employees to spend some time each day on their individual *"fun activities"* that spur their creativity. Finally, make a credible statement that you will assess the performance of an employee based on the ends and not on the means. I count the hour for my daily run as work time as I get lots of great ideas while running.

4. Set time aside to lead, ideate and innovate. As a leader, don't forget to live what you pray. *"Learn to pause - or nothing worthwhile will catch up to you,"* recommends the poet Doug King. Find some time every day to work *on* instead of *in* the business. And *"indulge yourself"* in your favorite idea-boosting activities — and soon you will notice that you generate more and more meaningful ideas for your business and that your vision gets sharper.

6.6. WANT TO SUCCEED FASTER? PLAN TO FAIL EARLIER

What do Michael Jordan, Woody Allen, Thomas Edison and Ingmar Kamprad have in common? Being great risk-takers and self-declared failures, all of them would stand a good chances of losing their jobs in the average modern corporation.

A number of surveys conducted over the past years with corporate leaders and senior managers indicate that failure is seen as negative in most companies and might have negative career implications. For example, in a 2007 study, McKinsey found that only 23 percent of companies view failure as a welcome learning opportunity, while failure of a project has more or less negative consequences in more than three out of four firms — and might even sink your career prospects in one of ten companies.

It's no wonder that most business people are afraid of making a mistake, losing a deal, or trying anything risky. Failure reflects negatively on the loser and may lead to serious negative consequences.

In Asia, where I've mostly done business during the past two and a half decades, the fear of losing face, both on the individual and organizational level, further reduces the willingness to take risks and possibly fail. *"Better safe than sorry"* describes the resulting climate.

Now realize that risk and chance, as well as failure and success, are necessary complements, are two sides of the same coin. For example, if you want to achieve a higher yield on an investment, you need to choose an asset category with an implicit higher risk, and vice versa.

In order to help you understand the symbiotic relationship between failure and success, let's hear it from our *"losers' parade"* featured above:

- Michael Jordan became the most successful NBA player because he planned to fail: *"I've missed more than 9,000 shots in my career. I've lost almost 300 games. Twenty-six times I've been trusted to take the game-winning shot and missed. I've failed over and over in my life and that is why I have succeeded."*

- Another North American sports legend, NHL top scorer Wayne Gretzky, similarly planned to fail: *"You miss 100% of the shots you never take,"* he once said.

- In the performing arts, Woody Allen is regarded as one of the leading film directors because he planned to fail: *"If you are not failing every now and again, it's a sign you're not trying anything innovative."*

- In business, Ikea founder Ingmar Kamprad summarized the paralyzing effects of a risk-averse culture and the necessity of allowing his employees to fail: *"Bureaucracy complicates and paralyzes. Exaggerated planning can be fatal. Only while sleeping one makes no mistakes. The fear of making mistakes is the root to bureaucracy and the enemy of all evolution."*

- When admiring the beautiful, aesthetically designed and hyper-functional household appliances of the Dyson brand today, few consumers know that company founder James Dyson confronted the fear of failure and the threat of bankruptcy for nearly two decades in his persistent efforts to reinvent a hugely improved vacuum cleaner. He summed up his experiences as follows: *"There's a terrible moment when failure is staring you in the face. And actually, if you persevere a bit longer you'll start to climb out of it."*

One of the cornerstones of the corporate culture of the long-term innovation leader 3M is the so-called McKnight Principle (named after 3M's longtime chairman William McKnight):

> "Mistakes will be made (by giving people the freedom and encouragement to act autonomously), but the mistakes he or she makes are not as serious in the long run as the mistakes management will make if it is dictatorial and undertakes to tell those under its authority exactly how they must do their job. Management that is destructively critical when mistakes are made kills initiative — and it is essential that we have many people with initiative if we are to continue to grow."

IBM's long-term chairman Thomas J. Watson also emphasized the importance of failure to succeed in business and innovation:

> "Would you like me to give you a formula for success? It's quite simple, really: Double your rate of failure. You are thinking of failure as the enemy of success. But it isn't at all. You can be discouraged by failure or you can learn from it, so go ahead and make mistakes. Make all you can. Because remember that's where you will find success."

Clearly, both William McKnight and Thomas Watson understood that superior business growth based on innovation flows from a *"plan-to-fail"* attitude coupled with action orientation. Why does planning to fail seem to be such a great recipe for success in innovation and other areas?

"I have not failed.
I have just found 10,000 ways that won't work.
Many of life's failures are people who did not realize how close they were to success when they gave up.
I am not discouraged, because every wrong attempt discarded is another step forward."
— THOMAS EDISON

"I failed my way to success."
— THOMAS EDISON

INNOVATION AUDIT RESULTS: CULTURE MOMENTUM BUILDING

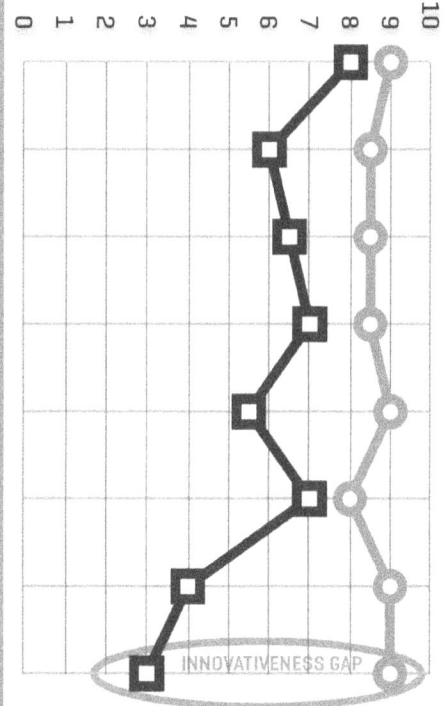

Negative	Positive
DISTRUST	WALK THE INNOVATION TALK (LEADERSHIP SUPPORT)
COLLECTIVISM & CONFORMITY	INDIVIDUALITY
COMMAND & TIGHT CONTROL	FREEDOM & SELF-MANAGEMENT
SERIOUSNESS & NEGATIVITY	PLAYFULNESS & POSITIVITY
ROUTINE & EXTRINSIC MOTIVATION	CHALLENGE & INTRINSIC MOTIVATION
INTERNAL FOCUS & BUREAUCRACY	EXTERNAL FOCUS ON CUSTOMERS & MARKET
IDEA-HOSTILE CLIMATE (JUDGMENT & IDEA KILLING)	IDEA-FRIENDLY CLIMATE (IDEA SHARING & NURTURING)
FAILURE INTOLERANCE	INITIATIVE & FAILURE TOLERANCE (PROTOTYPING CULTURE)

INNOVATIVENESS GAP

FAILURE INTOLERANCE

How to move towards a failure tolerant culture of taking initiative?

INITIATIVE & FAILURE TOLERANCE (PROTOTYPING CULTURE)

POSSIBLE ACTION IDEAS TO CLOSE THE IDENTIFIED INNOVATIVENESS GAP FOR THE FACTOR "FAILURE TOLERANCE"

ACTION 1: Always praise employees for taking initiative — regardless on whether the action resulted in a failure or success

ACTION 2: Hold Post Mortem-exercises at the end of each project to learn from failures — and unexpected successes

ACTION 3: Have a "Best Failure of the Month" Award; harvest the learnings and commend the person for taking initiative

ACTION 4: Discourage or stop long e-mail exchanges that solely serve the purpose to "cover one's a@@"

ACTION 5: Have top executives openly talk about failures that they've made — and the related lessons they've learned

ACTION 6: Establish rapid prototyping as a standard practice to try out promising new ideas

ACTION 7: Have executives and managers act as role models for rapid prototyping - or have them give constructive feedback

ACTION 8: Count the failures that employees or teams involved in innovation make, & give out an annual award for "most trials / failures"

Evolution functions on the basis of trial and error and the principle of negative feedback. Being a part of nature, we humans do so, too.

Whenever you fail or make a mistake or error, just dispassionately observe the result as a piece of negative feedback indicating that your current approach is not working and that it is time to try a new one. So detach yourself from a bad outcome and simply ask: What can I learn from this? How can I vary my approach? Then try again, and again, until you find the right approach. So, follow the advice of Virgin's founder Richard Branson: *"Don't be embarrassed by your failures, learn from them and start again."*

Similarly, the popular innovation technique of rapid prototyping also uses the same principles. David Kelley, one of the founders of the innovation company IDEO, explains that: *"Prototyping lets you fail earlier to succeed sooner."* Rapid prototyping means that you build a series of increasingly realistic prototypes and iterate based on user feedback. Thereby, you're not so much interested in what people like about a prototype. When you show a prototype to users, the magical question to ask is: *"Tell me what's wrong with it."*

Interestingly, many people love to give critical feedback, and if a comment about what's wrong with your prototype is sensible (or in other words, if you failed earlier), you right this wrong in your next prototype. As David Kelley noted, the more and earlier you fail, the sooner you will arrive at a final version that makes meaning and that users really appreciate.

Trial and error and the principle of negative feedback were also at the heart of Thomas Edison's innovation strategy. *"I have not failed. I have just found 10,000 ways that won't work. Many of life's failures are people who did not realize how close they were to success when they gave up. I am not discouraged, because every wrong attempt discarded is another step forward,"* commented Edison on his more than 10,000 experimental trials (and prototypes) before finding the right design for a scalable light bulb. Adopt the same mental robustness and persistence of the great inventor toward failure.

Like the legendary inventor, modern innovators use experimentation and rapid prototyping to find out what customers like. For example, Facebook's founder Mark Zuckerberg confided that: *"One of the things I'm most proud of that is really key to our success is this testing framework … At any given point in time, there isn't just one version of Facebook running. There are probably 10,000."*

Similarly, Amazon.com founder Jeff Bezos explained: "Our success at Amazon is a function of how many experiments we do per year, per month, per week, per day."

Finally, Steve Jobs also emphasized: *"The greatest artists like Dylon, Picasso and Newton risked failure. And if we want to be great, we need to risk it too."* And he went on to explain: *"Failure doesn't mean you will never achieve, it just means it takes a bit longer."*

Conclusion: As a corporate leader aiming to promote innovation inside your company, initiate a cultural shift towards a higher risk tolerance and encourage employees to take initiative. This also means that business leaders need to personally walk their failure talk by leading in harmony with three messages:

1. Always remember that we grow and learn by trial and error, not by trial and rightness.
2. Thus, plan to fail — and ask others to do so too.
3. Then fail and persistently try until you succeed.

6.7. THE CREATIVE TRANSFORMATION MARATHON

Imagine being a sluggish, overweight couch potato. One day you think, *"I want to run a marathon."* Is that realistic? We all know of examples of people who have done this — but we know there are many more who tried and failed or who never got beyond the thought.

Transforming a lethargic, innovation-hostile corporation with a *"me too"* mindset into an agile creative company (*"Creativity Unlimited"*) is like turning that couch potato into a successful marathon runner. Just as couch potatoes can't get out of the chair and immediately complete a marathon, innovation-hostile companies cannot become agile and creative overnight. In both cases, it takes careful planning and sustained commitment to succeed.

Change requires a major impetus

Why would a couch potato suddenly decide to run a marathon? It might be concern over poor health, a desire to lose weight, gaining control over a bad habit like smoking or drinking, or a mid-life crisis.

Likewise, when sluggish corporations decide to become creative organizations, it's usually a reaction to a crisis: a decline in revenue, profit margin, market share, or customer satisfaction; a new competitive threat like innovative Big Tech and Fintech companies present to banks; or market deregulation and globalization which create new opportunities for both the company and potential competitors.

Are you ready to change?

How should a couch potato start on the path to becoming a marathoner? Of course, go to the doctor and get a check-up. You may feel ready to start right away, but that might be dangerous for you. The only way to know for sure is to ask the doctor.

The first thing the *"Me too"* company should do is have an innovation expert audit it for innovation readiness. Such an audit begins with assessing where you are and where you want to be. Then the innovation expert will identify deficiencies that need to be corrected. The audit results allow you to gauge the odds of succeeding at the desired creative transformation and how much time it's likely to take.

Change starts at the top

Following their check-up, novice runners may ask themselves if they are ready and able to undergo the effort and hardships needed to finish a marathon. Success starts with a strong, determined mind, as well as a compelling enough reason to overcome weaknesses and setbacks and continue on to the finish line.

Companies with slow, bureaucratic, innovation-hostile cultures need to start by honestly confronting the findings of the innovation readiness audit. Next, the leadership team needs to decide that they are willing to lead the required changes. They need to ask themselves: *"Are we really willing to lead this innovation transformation? Are we willing to commit our own time and efforts to this? Are some of us ready to transform ourselves into a creative leader so we can credibly lead by personal example?"*

Commit time and money to your goal

Once the couch potato has resolved to run the marathon, they need to invest in some equipment — shoes, clothes, pulse monitor, etc. — and make time available to train. Success becomes even more likely with the services of a professional coach.

In the same way, commitment is the acid test of a corporate leadership team's seriousness about transforming their organization. Commitment means putting money behind the change. Even more importantly, it means that the leaders must devote their own time to start and lead the creative change. Finally, it means using the services of an innovation professional who, like a running coach, plans the organizational changes, with actions to be taken and milestones to meet, and measures the progress with a set of innovation-related performance indicators.

Find others to help achieve your goals

Once marathon runners-to-be have started using their new equipment, they feel the immediate pain — and slow gain — of becoming a runner. It's easier to get through the initial pain by joining a running club. Being with other active runners gives a novice moral support to help get through the inevitable lows of fatigue, soreness, and minor injuries.

Corporate innovation is a sport of individual efforts made as part of a team. It thrives when people collaborate and communicate with one other. Members of the leadership team can start changing the organization by publicly declaring the what, why, and how of the transformation. This will help identify supporters within the organization who are eager to contribute and collaborate and then use them to start small, successful innovation projects to provide encouragement for the long marathon of transforming into an innovation-friendly organization.

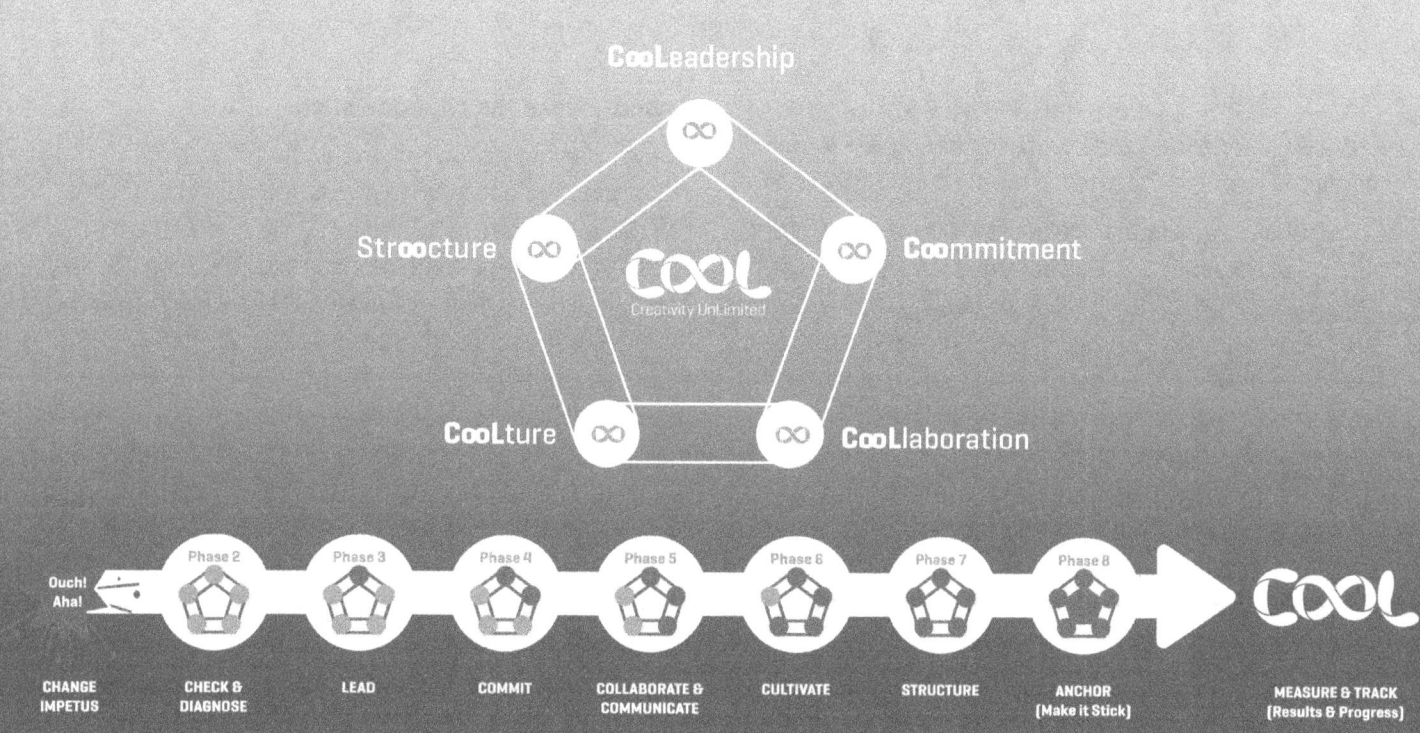

Cultivate 1: Build momentum for a lasting change

After years on the couch, novice runners must slowly ease into regular exercise. If they're very unfit, they may need to begin by walking, then alternate between running and walking, before they can run longer distances without stopping. In this first phase, the goal is to put the inert body back into motion and to make a habit of exercising and running regularly. Every small improvement and minor achievement contributes to this aim and helps build the momentum necessary to continue on to the ultimate goal.

Likewise, a lethargic company that has committed to becoming innovative needs to start by building cultural momentum for organizational creativity and innovation before permanently changing *"the ways things are done around here."* Using the gap analysis from the innovation readiness audit, the company should focus on initiatives that change the organizational climate to make it more creativity-friendly, for example by encouraging individuality or by asking people to suggest ideas and take initiative.

Cultivate 2: Change for good

Once a novice runner has become an apprentice, they can move on to more advanced ways of running. With the help of a coach, our marathon runner-in-the-making can learn to run more efficiently (by doing coordination exercises) and faster (by running intervals or using *fartlek*, a technique for adding variety to longer runs).

They should also increase their weekly total distance and start competing in shorter races to prepare for a full marathon.

Corporations in cultural transition need to take cultural change more seriously. This can be done by fighting politics and internal competition or dealing with a reactive cultural climate. An external innovation consultant can help accomplish this by devising ways to counter and resolve the identified issues in a targeted way. For example, one way to counter a widespread culture of mediocrity is to enter competitions with the goal of winning an international innovation award.

Structure: Re-organize to match your new identity

Once the couch potato has become a regular runner, they need to reorganize their lives to fit their new-found passion. They might change their schedules to allow for regular training sessions, combine their holidays with training camps, or change their diet to improve their performance.

Similarly, the evolving creativity organization needs to adapt its organizational structure, processes and systems to make them fit the new focus on creativity and innovation. For example, to improve external market orientation, customer intimacy, decision speed and multi-directional collaboration, they might flatten the organizational structure and experiment with network models, change the HR systems to creativity-focused policies, or implement innovative systems to support the new direction. This is also the time to confront systemic obstacles standing in the way of organizational creativity and to bid farewell to those who still oppose creative change.

"Never underestimate the magnitude of the power of the forces that reinforce the status quo."
—JOHN P. KOTTER

Anchor: Make the changes stick

Finally, it's time for the runners to start their first marathon. By now, they have learned how to run regularly, economically, and speedily — and the final hurdle is finishing the 42.195 km race. The moment they cross the finish line, they have succeeded in transforming themselves from couch potatoes into marathoners. But as proud as they are, and should be, they need to set new goals, lest they fall back onto their couch — plan the next race, set a faster time target for the next marathon, or plan a vacation around a marathon. These things will help anchor their new identity and make it permanent.

In the same way, the newly creative organization should focus on competing creatively and shifting from cost leadership to differentiation. They might start innovation projects that enable the firm to launch differentiating, meaningful new products or introduce even more innovation initiatives to anchor the new culture in the firm for good.

Conclusion: It is possible. Just as a lazy, out-of-shape couch potato can remake themselves as a successful marathon runner, a bureaucratic corporate behemoth can become an agile, creative, innovation-friendly company. But in both cases, accomplishing this goal takes time, money and hard work. And it starts with the strong, determined minds that are necessary to lead a change and to succeed.

In the next chapter, we will introduce the concept of creative leadership development as the connecting dot to the supportive leadership mindsets to drive a CooL creative change with creative leadership support. But before that, I will discuss in the final section of the present chapter how a set of well-defined innovation measures can support organizations in their creative transformation marathon.

6.8. WHAT GETS MEASURED GETS INNOVATED

How does your company measure your innovation efforts? Do you have a compendium of innovation-related Key Performance Indicators (KPIs) in place to systematically track your innovation progress?

Conventional wisdom in management circles knows: *"What gets measured gets done."* So how can you approach this topic for your firm?

First, understand that there is no *"one size fits all"* approach to innovation and how to measure it; you have to devise your own innovation KPI system that fits your business focus and company.

Secondly, go beyond the standard measures and consider unusual measures that wouldn't necessarily come out of a controller's hard-wired brain. Finally, systematically track INPUT, PROCESS, and OUTPUT-related measures to gain the full picture of your innovation efforts.

1. Input-related Innovation KPI:

At the front end of your innovation measurement system, track how many resources you commit to innovation.

- A popular finance-related practice is to measure the Total R&D cost spent (or related indicators such as R&D cost over sales or Outsourced R&D cost ratio). Here, remember to link your expenditures to what comes out in the end—that's why you need to measure your innovation input, process, and output, look at your complete innovation KPI system, and then gain true intelligence of your innovation activities.

- People-oriented measures track the *Number of people committed to innovation* (absolute or relative as percentage of total staff). One word of caution: What matters as much as –or even more than– the number of people committed to innovation is the right selection of players for your innovation team (considering aspects like the appropriate mix of personality types, areas of expertise and business functions).

- Another common input indicator is the *Number of ideas suggested* by employees over a certain period of time. Don't solely rely on this number if your aim is to produce breakthrough innovation, as most of these suggestions tend to produce ideas for incremental improvements rather than the next iPhone.

- An example of an unusual KPI for your HR team is to follow the *Number of different expertise areas* prevalent in the total workforce to measure the important cultural innovation dimension of diversity.

2. Process-related Innovation KPIs:

Process-related innovation KPIs are rather sparsely covered in the literature. Here are some suggestions on what you should monitor:

- Set and monitor quotas for critical deliverables at the different stages of the innovation process method that you use. If we guide corporate clients through an innovation project with Thinkergy using our X-IDEA innovation method, we first set a quota of 25+ *Novel insights gained* in the initial Xploration phase. Then we specify the *Number of ideas* that move from one subsequent project stage to the next: e.g., a team of ten needs to produce 1,000 raw ideas in 4 hours of Ideation; roughly 150-200 of these are discovered in the subsequent Development stage, where they are developed into 30+ realistic idea concepts before moving into the Evaluation stage; and finally 3-5 top ideas are pitched and prepared for real-life implementation in the Activation stage.

- A common time-related approach is to gauge the cycle times of their innovation process, both for certain parts of the process or for its entire duration (e.g., *Time to market*).

- Particularly once moving towards the final evaluation and activation stages, many firms also count the *Number of new promising innovation projects* and the *Total or Average expenditure per individual innovation project*.

- Renowned innovation leaders recommend or practice some unusual measures in their firm. So, observe the *Average number of laughs per employee per day*, determine the *% time that a manager talks in a meeting* (the lower the better according to IDEO founder David Kelley), or invite employee experimentation at work by introducing a new KPI *% of employee work-time used for individual pet projects* (20% at Google for all employees and 15% for R&D staff at 3M).

3. Output-related Innovation KPIs:

Not surprisingly, most innovation-KPIs suggested in the literature focus on the output side.

- The two measures *% Revenues from new products (services) over total revenues* and *% Revenue growth from new products (services) over total revenues growth* lead the armada of output-oriented innovation-KPI. Beware of two pitfalls here: each ratio goes up when overall sales go down (trap 1), and managers can easily manipulate the result by counting line extensions as new products (trap 2).

- Other popular indicators on the output side are *Number of new products (services) launched*, *% New products over overall products* (beware again of trap 2), *Innovation ROI*, *Cannibalization of existing product sales by new product sales*, *Total revenue growth*, and *Operating margin growth*.

- Some companies also assess the *Overall number of patents filed* and the *Number of new patents filed in a certain period*. Here don't forget that patents only lead to tangible innovation if they are used in cash-generating ways.

- Finally, an example of an unusual KPI to evaluate your firm's innovation output is to count the *Number of media coverage for your products (services)*.

> What's measured improves.
> —PETER F. DRUCKER

CooL MEASURES
INNOVATION KPI SYSTEM

 **INPUT**

 **THROUGHPUT**

 **OUTPUT**

Finance-related measures
- Total R&D cost spent
- R&D cost over sales
- Outsourced R&D cost ratio

People-oriented measures
- No. of people committed to innovation
- % of staff committed to innovation over total staff
- Number of ideas suggested by employees over a time period

Diversity-oriented measures
- No. of different expertise areas prevalent in the total workforce
- No. of countries represented in workforce

X-IDEA Stage Quotas
- X: # of insights, # of initial Ideas
- I: # of Raw Ideas
- D: # of Idea Concepts
- E: # of Prototypes, # of Top Ideas
- A: # of Sponsored/Approved Top Ideas,
- # of Top Idea Activation Projects

Cycle Times
- Time to market

Other Throughput KPI:
- No. of prototypes produced
- % of employee work-time used for individual pet projects
- Average number of laughs per employee per day
- % time that a manager talks in a meeting

- % Revenues from new products (services) over total revenues and
- % Revenue growth from new products (services) over total revenues growth
- Number of new products (services) launched,
- % New products over overall products
- Innovation ROI
- Cannibalization of existing product sales by new product sales
- Total revenue growth
- Operating profit margin growth
- Overall number of patents filed
- No. of new patents filed in a period
- No. of media coverage for your products (services)

- Beware of common measurement traps & pitfalls
- Understand internal dynamics
- Interpret measures in context to overall financial KPI
- Link I-P-O measures if possible

> "A business has to be involving, it has to be fun, and it has to exercise your creative instincts."
> – RICHARD BRANSON

CHAPTER 6 — EXECUTIVE SUMMARY: INNOVATION CULTURE

- ❖ Me Too Ltd. is a fictitious account of what it's like working in a company with a copycat mentality. Many people have worked for such an organization at some point in their professional careers and know what it feels like to be stuck in an in-NO-vative company.

- ❖ What if you're stuck working in an in-NO-vative company? You can still have some fun by playing "innovation bingo" in meetings dominated by politics and idea-killing sentences.

- ❖ Innovative companies differ from in-NO-vative companies in certain organizational factors that foster or inhibit creativity and innovation. These factors can be categorized into five base dimensions (leadership, commitment, collaboration, culture, and structure.

- ❖ Companies that want to go on the transformational journey to change from a copycat culture into a cool creative culture first need to audit what factors hold them back before developing an effective action plan to close the identified innovativeness gaps. We discuss the process using the example of two organizational factor pairs:

  - ✳ In-NO-vative copycat companies tend to impose heavy workloads and frantic schedules on a tight workforce. In contrast, innovative companies commit sufficient free time pockets that enable their employees to come up with outstanding creativity and evolutionary or even game-changing revolutionary innovations.

  - ✳ A creative culture encourages people to take initiative and learn quickly from failures rather than viewing failure as negative or damaging to one's career.

- ❖ Transforming an in-NO-vative copycat company (Me Too Ltd.) into an innovative company (Creativity UnLimited) is like stepping up to run a marathon. This metaphor helps explain the challenging transformation of gradually building an agile, creative organization.

- ❖ Innovation metrics allow companies to measure and track their progress in their efforts to build an innovation-friendly culture.

CHAPTER 7

CREATIVE LEADERS
SMALL PICTURE (IV)

How to reconnect to your creativity. How to develop genuine creative leaders for the innovation economy.

1. The Rise of Creative Leadership
2. Creative Leadership: Hot or Not?
3. Why Creative Leadership Matters Now
4. Creative Leaders: Who? What? Why?
5. Incubation: A Walk on the Mysterious Side of Creativity
6. How to Creatively and Effectively Develop Creative Leaders
7. Introducing the Design Features of the Genius Journey Method
8. Rediscover Your Creative Self
* *Executive Summary*

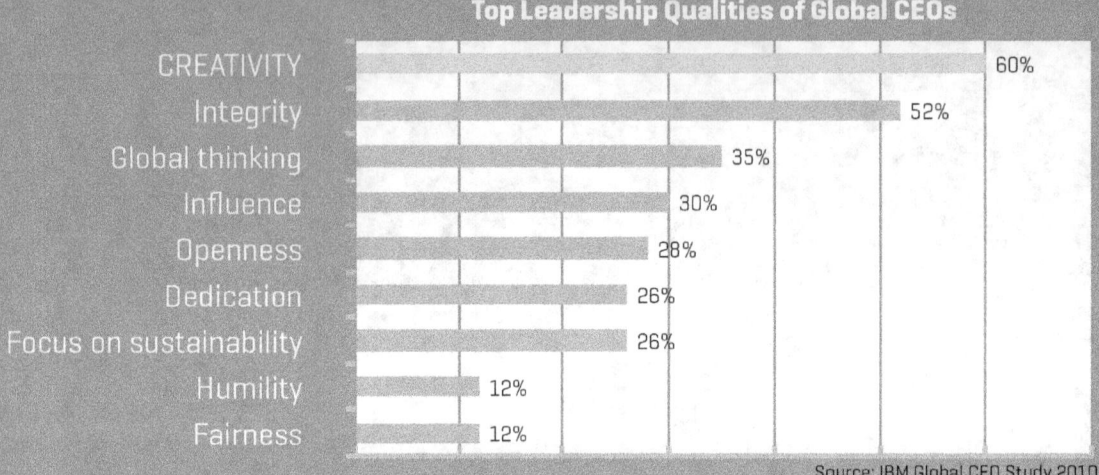

7.1. THE RISE OF CREATIVE LEADERSHIP

The call for creative leadership

In 2010, IBM's Global Chief Executive Officers Study surveyed 1,541 CEOs in 44 countries. When asked to identify the most important leadership qualities to capitalize on complexity, *"creativity"* was the most frequently mentioned, chosen by 60% of those interviewed. In Asia-Pacific, that number was 70%.

The authors of the study stated: *"In an uncertain and volatile world, CEOs realize that creativity trumps other leadership characteristics. Creative leaders are comfortable with ambiguity and experiment to create new business models. They invite disruptive innovation, encourage others to drop outdated approaches and take balanced risks. They are open-minded and inventive in expanding their management and communications styles, in order to engage with a new generation of employees, partners and customers."*

The response to the call

In 2011, IBM conducted a follow-up study with more than 700 Chief Human Resource Officers (CHROs) from 61 countries to investigate how the Human Resources function responds to the CEOs' assertion that the development of future creative leaders would have the greatest effect on their organizations' future success. Not surprisingly, the majority of the interviewed CHROs highlighted the need for their organizations to identify, develop and empower creative leaders. One British. HR director is cited as saying, *"We have strong managers, not leaders — and we need strong creative leaders to achieve our strategic objectives."*

However, while HR officers and their teams were well aware of this need for developing creative leaders, only one in three organizations claimed to be successful in meeting it — an astoundingly low number given the stated importance of creative leadership development.

One explanation for this surprising gap between realizing the need to develop creative leaders and the failure to set up a creative leadership development program lies in the nature of the beast: An effective creative leadership development program needs to be creative! In other words, it needs to differ dramatically from existing leadership development programs.

The authors of the IBM CHRO Study 2011 emphasized this important point: *"To instill the dexterity and flexibility necessary to seize elusive opportunity, companies must move beyond traditional leadership development methods and find ways to inject within their leadership candidates not only the empirical skills necessary for effective management, but also the cognitive skills to drive creative solutions. The learning initiatives that enable this objective must be at least as creative as the leaders they seek to foster."*

As part of this movement, and as a response to this wider, unsatisfied need for a truly creative and effective creative leadership development method, I created Genius Journey, a truly novel, creative method for developing creative leaders that is featured in this book. With my innovation company Thinkergy, we offer Genius Journey training courses, and I also teach the subject matter as a university course in *"Creative Leadership"* to graduate students in management. Before we introduce the Genius Journey method below, however, let's first take the time to clarify what creative leadership is by defining some relevant terms.

What is creative leadership?

Finding a clear answer to this question is a key difficulty that CRHOs and their teams have to overcome in their efforts to develop creative leadership candidates. When you review the academic literature, you come across hundreds of definitions for both the terms leadership and creativity, all of which are right in one way or another. However, due to the novelty of the concept, you will find comparatively few attempts to define the term creative leadership. Yet how can you develop creative leaders if you don't know what it actually means?

Against this background, I've developed my own definition of the concept, starting off with definitions of the singular concepts of leadership and creativity.

Apart from many other equally correct definitions, we may define leadership as *"the action of leading a group of people or an organization; or the state or position of being a leader"*.

In Chapter 2, you learned that for an idea, a person, or a product to be deemed creative, it needs to be novel (fresh, new, avant-garde, unprecedented), meaningful (valuable, worthwhile, useful, relevant), and unique (original, one-of-a-kind, individual).

When we put all the essential pieces together, we can define the term *"Creative Leadership"* as *"the action of leading a group of people or an organization towards novel, unique and meaningful outcomes; or the state or position of being an* authentically *creative leader in an organization."*

Notice the emphasis on the word *'authentic.'* In order to credibly lead a creative organization, you must be genuinely creative yourself, be able to creatively walk your creative talk, and lead by creative example—i.e., exemplify the cognitive mindsets and creative actions that you want your followers to adopt and adapt.

In a 2007 study by McKinsey titled *How companies approach innovation,* most of the 722 executives in the survey agreed on the two most important factors to improve innovation performance: Making innovation a core part of the leadership agenda; and modeling behavior that encourages innovation, such as taking risks. It seems like more and more business leaders have become aware that they need to creatively lead the innovation efforts of their companies from the top and from the front. However, developing into an authentically creative leader takes time and effort; ultimately, it requires you to change your mindset, expand your mind, and realize your personal genius potential.

7.2. CREATIVE LEADERSHIP: HOT OR NOT?

What is creative leadership? Introducing the concept

Who do you consider to be a leader? Many people are justly called leaders. They lead and inspire others as business leaders (CEOs or entrepreneurs), thought leaders, scientific leaders, artistic leaders, political leaders or social leaders, among others. Clearly, people such as Walt Disney, Richard Buckminster Fuller, Albert Einstein, Pablo Picasso, Nelson Mandela and Mahatma Gandhi are all examples of leaders who shaped the 20th century with their ideas and deeds — and all of them exemplify the essence of what it constitutes to be a creative leader, too.

Other important leaders also shaped the 20th century with their ideas and deeds — think of people such as Adolf Hitler, Joseph Stalin, Mao Zedong or Pol Pot. However, these leaders are held responsible for the mass liquidation of millions of innocent human beings and represent the antithesis of a creative leader.

So what is creative leadership all about in concrete, practical terms?

Creative leadership is ... hot and not

To bring the rather academic definition of creative leadership to life, let's contrast the thesis (hot) and antithesis (not) of the defining elements of creative leaders in practical terms. While reading on each pair of antagonistic factors, ask yourself: Are the leaders you know and follow hot (= creative leaders) or not (= uncreative leaders)? And, even more importantly, ask yourself: Are you hot or not?

HOT — originality: Creative leaders create original ideas, products, and solutions. As one-of-a-kind individuals, they insist on their own originality and on creating unique value propositions.

NOT — copycat: Creative leaders do NOT have a copycat mentality. It is NOT OK for them to imitate, copy and steal the ideas of others to quickly get ahead of them.

HOT — novelty: Creative leaders focus on creating and promoting novelty, such as new products, novel solutions, unprecedented concepts, fresh services, and avant-garde campaigns, just to name a few.

NOT — anachronism: Creative leaders do NOT hold on to old ideas. They do NOT stand for the preservation of an outdated status quo.

HOT — making meaning: Creative leaders focus, first and foremost, on making meaning, on creating new value

propositions that make the world a better place and improve the quality of people's lives.

NOT — solely making money: Creative leaders do NOT start by focusing on what makes them money. While later on, they enjoy making money from their meaningful creations, their passion is always about making meaning, NOT money.

HOT — equality: Creative leaders create value for many, not just a small minority.

NOT — elitism: Creative leaders do NOT only do things that create value for themselves or those few who are close to them or affiliated with them.

HOT — worthy common cause: Creative leaders are good and do good. They pursue a worthy common cause that goes beyond themselves, such as widely promoting the benefits of a meaningful new technology, righting something that is terribly wrong, or preventing the end of something good.

NOT — personal cause: Creative leaders do NOT only follow a personal cause that goes at the expense of wider parts of society or the environment.

HOT — value compensation: After creating unique, meaningful, novel products and solutions, creative leaders charge an adequate value for their goods. They do this not because they are greedy, but to compensate for their substantial development costs and efforts, enabling them to continue bringing out more meaningful innovations and operating at the forefront of change.

NOT — value discounting: Creative leaders do NOT believe in doing things on the cheap. They usually do NOT give discounts on their products to boost sales like many other companies do (which compete on products that are similar to everybody else's products).

HOT — long-term orientation: Creative leaders consider the long-term consequences of their actions on all of their stakeholders, society at large, the environment and even the well-being of future generations.

NOT — short-term gains: Creative leaders do NOT want to realize a short-term advantage if the action triggers negative implications in the long run.

HOT — ethics: Creative leaders are ethical. They keep their word and honor their promises. They do what is right in the right way. If they err and make a wrong move on their path, they admit it and pay the price for their wrongdoing.

NOT — unethical behavior: Creative leaders do NOT engage in unethical practices; they are NOT corrupt and can NOT be corrupted by others.

HOT — cooperation and co-opetition: Creative leaders embrace a cooperative paradigm of *"we win, you win, everyone wins."* They cooperate with others whenever possible and co-opete with their peers. They compete on product, but cooperate in other areas that advance an industry or the common good.

NOT — reckless competition: Creative leaders do NOT want to win at all costs and do NOT believe in a purely zero-sum competitive paradigm (*"I win, you lose"*).

HOT — individuality: Creative leaders respect the individuality of others. They encourage their followers and others to do their own thinking — and even to challenge the leader to advance the common cause.

NOT — conformity: Creative leaders do NOT surround themselves with mindless henchmen who blindly follow their leaders' commands and uncritically conform to orders and the prevailing groupthink.

HOT — meritocracy: Creative leaders mentor and promote people in their organization based on their merits and contributions to the greater good and the common cause.

NOT — dutiful mediocrity: Creative leaders do NOT promote mediocre people purely based on their unwavering loyalty to the leader and their blind compliance with orders.

HOT — leaving a legacy: Last but not least, creative leaders leave a lasting legacy when they go. They live on in the minds and hearts of future generations thanks to their creations, words of wisdom, unselfishly motivated social deeds, charitable giving, and productive lives of worth and example.

NOT — leaving a mess: Creative leaders do NOT only focus on themselves and their close kin at the expense of others, thus enabling them to live on when those who still know them in person have gone as well.

Conclusion: We live at the dawn of the age of creative leadership. If you're like me and believe in all that is hot and disdain all that is not, then join the movement and start working for and following only truly hot creative leaders. Or, even better, become a hot creative leader yourself.

"Innovation distinguishes between a leader and a follower."
– STEVE JOBS

7.3. WHY CREATIVE LEADERSHIP MATTERS *NOW*

Mankind is at a critical crossroads, and we need to evolve to a new level of thinking. We need to switch the dominant paradigm that we use to run this world from a competitive, ego-driven world of scarcity to a cooperative, self-driven world of abundance. We need to move to higher levels of consciousness to creatively and ethically address the fundamental challenges that we face as a species now and in future. What are some of these challenges?

The sustainability challenge

At the moment, we consume 1.6 times the resources that our planet can naturally redistribute at the cost of future generations and other species. Experts predict that by 2030, humanity needs a second Earth to satisfy our greed for more resources — and by 2050, even a third planet won't suffice if nothing changes.

How can mankind change its greed for ever more resources? How can people feel good about wanting less? How can we start consuming and sharing the available resources fairly and sustainably? How can we create win-win-win-win solutions where I win, you win, everyone wins, the environment wins, and future generations win?

The Global Warming Challenge

How to respond to the challenges imposed by climate change that affect our lives and businesses?

How to respond to the rising occurrence of increasingly extreme weather phenomena, such as super-hurricanes and typhoons, floods and droughts, among others?

How to respond to the predictions of many scientists that large landmasses and even entire countries might be lost to the rise in ocean sea levels?

The Financial System Challenge

What if the global financial system collapsed? Well, it nearly did in 2008. As not much has changed since, it is likely to do so in the future.

So how to respond to the challenge of the global financial system that has become so vast, fast and complex that it cannot be controlled anymore by regulators and supervisory institutions? Where no one really can accurately understand, model and contain the latent risks given the vast number of interdependent variables? How to deal with the rising debt mountain that many governments, companies, and private households continue to accumulate although they're unlikely to be able to service and fully repay it? How to stop or contain the aftermath of a likely collapse of the global financial system and the world economy?

The Labor Challenge

How to distribute and compensate work fairly and mindfully in a world where more and more jobs are automated? Where many people lose their work to artificial intelligence and robots while a few others are forced to work longer hours and be available and on call 24/7? Where young job seekers struggle to find meaningful, well-paid work while older employees either are prematurely made redundant or are asked to work more years before being able to retire comfortably?

The Aging Societies Challenge

How to respond to the challenges of aging societies? Where in many countries, close to 40% of the population will be older than 65 years 20-30 years from now? Where elderly people who don't want to —but often will be— living in poverty and want to be —but often won't be— well cared for by the rest of the society?

The Singularity Challenge

What if mankind was not at the top of the evolutionary pyramid? What if artificial intelligence (AI) and superintelligent robots overtook humans as the most advanced species?

Futurists predict that this may well happen. Some AI experts think that technological singularity — the point at which artificial smarts can match, and then overtake, human intelligence — might even happen within the next two decades.

"The danger of the past was that men became slaves. The danger of the future is that man may become robots," noted Erich Fromm. And if you see how many people have become zombified and go through their daily lives enslaved by the virtual worlds of their mobile devices, we may even be on a self-destructive path to becoming both slaves and robots in one.

***

"We shall require a substantially new manner of thinking if mankind is to survive," said Albert Einstein. I agree. We need new ways of thinking — creative thinking, entrepreneurial thinking, meaningful thinking. We need to think like creative leaders and cultivate the mindsets of genius. We need to look at all these problems and challenges as huge opportunities to create

new meaningful solutions and new meaningful value propositions. We need to predominantly focus on making massive meaning, not money (although it is inevitable that those who make great meaning also make great money).

I believe that in order for mankind to rise to meet all of the aforementioned challenges, we need a new creative Renaissance, a new creative age, an *"Innonaissance."* We need to develop a critical number of authentic creative leaders who inspire the organizations they start or work for to produce meaningful ideas and radical innovations that resolve the massive challenges we face in intelligent, meaningful, and ethical ways.

I believe that we need to completely rethink the way we do things: the way we do business, the way we organize and distribute work, the way we utilize, recycle and regrow, reproduce and regenerate resources, the way we consume and share resources, the way we finance our lives, businesses and countries, the way we use and interact with technology, the way we deal and interact with each other.

We need to focus on making more meaning for all stakeholders involved in these fundamental challenges, which includes our planet and the future generations that have to live in the well-preserved or messed-up and plundered world that we will leave for them. We need to live, learn, think, act, work, create and lead as creative leaders and geniuses do. We need to realize the inner genius that, as Albert Einstein noted, is in all of us. We need find ways to enable you to rediscover your inner genius and become an authentic creative leader.

Over 40 years ago, the forward-thinking universal genius Richard Buckminster-Fuller stated, *"Mankind is in its final exam as to whether or not we survive as a species."*

I agree. That's why I created a creative leadership development method called Genius Journey, which I will introduce to you in the following sections of this chapter. If you like the concept and methodology, then feel invited to travel this journey and to do your part to ensure that we will pass the final exam together.

"Whether it is to be Utopia or Oblivion will be a touch-and-go relay race right up to the final moment. Humanity is in 'final exam' as to whether or not it qualifies for continuance in Universe," cautioned Richard Buckminster Fuller once again, and added: *"Nature is trying very hard to make us succeed, but nature does not depend on us. We are not the only experiment."*

So why don't you join me in dreaming of creating a better, more ethical and more meaningful world? Why don't you finally realize yourself and your full genius potential? Why don't you become an authentic creative leader who produces meaningful creations, outputs and results and inspires others to live a good, creative life, too? Join me now in becoming a creative force of good. And together, let's create solutions that ensure that we pass our final exam.

> "Really, the only thing that makes sense is to strive for greater collective enlightenment."
> —ELON MUSK

7.4. CREATIVE LEADERS: WHO? WHAT? WHY?

Take a few minutes to think about the following questions: What genius creators and creative business leaders do you know or admire? What mindsets and action routines do these individuals exhibit that make them stand out from the crowd? What can you learn from them?

Who do you consider creative leaders?

When we train delegates at Thinkergy on how to become more creative as an individual and evolve into a creative leader, we ask these questions as a warm-up exercise. Apart from some less well-known domestic or regional creative leaders, a similar selection of creative leaders and geniuses appears around the world. Albert Einstein and Steve Jobs almost always end up high on the list. Other business leaders that regularly show up are Walt Disney, Richard Branson, Elon Musk, Bill Gates, Henry Ford, David Ogilvy, Jack Ma, and James Dyson.

But creative leaders are not only business leaders. We can also find them in science, the arts, and in sports:

- Other universal or scientific geniuses include Leonardo da Vinci, Johann Wolfgang von Goethe, Aristotle, Isaac Newton, Richard Feynman, Charles Darwin, Richard Buckminster Fuller, and Benjamin Franklin.

- Spiritual leaders and geniuses Jesus of Nazareth, Gautama Buddha, Lao Tze, among many others.

- Creative leaders, top achievers and artistic geniuses abound in the creative arts in the widest sense. Examples may include the painters Pablo Picasso and Salvatore Dali; the writers Mark Twain, George Bernard Shaw, and Ralph Waldo Emerson; the musical geniuses and creative leaders Wolfgang Amadeus Mozart, Ludwig van Beethoven, and John

Lennon; or the movie directors Alfred Hitchcock, George Lucas, and Steven Spielberg..

- Finally, the list of top achievers and kinesthetic geniuses in sports surely includes Bruce Lee and Mohammad Ali.

Are your favorite geniuses and creative leaders on my list? In any case, identifying outstanding creative top achievers is a pivotal first step in understanding the concept of genius or creative leaders. The next step is to define these concepts, and then investigate what mindsets and action routines make these creative top achievers so special — and if they share a set of uncommon mindsets.

Defining the concept of genius and creative leaders Albert Einstein said: *"There is a genius in all of us."* I believe that Einstein was right: *"There IS a genius in all of us."* We were all little geniuses in our early lives before our education and socialization systems disconnected almost all of us from our personal genius. But what does *"genius"* really mean?

The noun *"genius"* originates from the Latin verb *gignere* (gigno, gignere, genui, genitus), which can be translated as *"give birth to, bring forth, bear; beget; be born."* The original meaning of genius was "attendant spirit present from one's birth, innate ability or inclination." One modern definition is *"Exceptional intellectual or creative power or other natural ability."* Elsewhere, the term is defined as *"an exceptionally intelligent person or one with exceptional skill in one area of activity."*

Here let me ask you another question: Could there be one thing, anything, that you might be better at doing than anyone else? Might you have a special talent, an innate ability or inclination that's really *"your thing"* — something extraordinary that you're naturally able to do exceptionally well? This could be something intellectual or creative in nature, but it could also be some other skill or activity that you naturally excel at. If you answer affirmatively, you acknowledge that indeed, there is a genius hidden in you.

Understanding the mindsets and action routines of geniuses and creative leaders

What are the commonalities in the ways of thinking and doing things among all those creative leaders? To learn more about the mindsets of genius leaders, I read biographies and semi-biographical books on creative top achievers such as da Vinci, Edison, Jobs, Disney, Branson, Musk, and others. I also studied academic psychological accounts on the traits of geniuses or creative top achievers.

Finally, I compared these findings with my personal experiences gained during my personal creative journey from a corporate banker to a leading business creativity and innovation expert — and linked them to the mental conditions that were prevalent before, during and after I experienced Eureka moments of breakthrough creativity. I am the only person I know who experienced a Eureka moment twice in their life — it's like hitting the jackpot in the lottery twice, and it made me curious about what I did and what I was thinking that allowed me to experience the kiss of genius. (Well, I wouldn't have minded hitting the lottery jackpot twice, but that wasn't part of my journey to make me become who I have become).

From my reading, introspection and self-experimentation, I gained three insights related to geniuses and creative leaders that I am going to share with you now:

- First insight: Geniuses produce extraordinary ideas and results because they think, work, and behave differently than ordinary people. We can also say that they deliver abnormal results because they are not normal; they are *abnormal*.

- Second insight: Most geniuses share a similar set of *abnormal* action routines and mindsets that vary noticeably from those of normal people.

- Third insight: Normal people can reconnect to their genius if they adopt and practice these *abnormal* creative success mindsets of geniuses.

But how can we effectively enable people to acquire the abnormal success mindsets of genius? How can we help people reconnect to their inner genius? How can we effectively develop authentic creative leaders for the innovation economy? I answered all these questions by developing a comprehensive creative leadership development method. It's called Genius Journey, and I will introduce it to you in the following sections.

What is Genius Journey? And how does it work in a nutshell?

Genius Journey is a highly effective, experiential and enjoyable creative leadership development method that I created for the innovation company Thinkergy, which offers training and coaching programs in the Genius Journey method. I have also taught the method in a Creative Leadership course at graduate study programs at two Asian universities.

Genius Journey is a truly creative and experiential creative leadership development program, as it uses a journey metaphor to support the acquisition of creative mindsets and action routines. How does this work in a nutshell?

- Genius Journey takes you on a journey where you visit 10 destinations.

- At each of the ten destination stops, you learn about one mindset that stops you, limits you, keeps you small, keeps you thinking inside this tiny little box, and keeps you producing ordinary ideas and normal results.

- And at each stop of the journey, you will also discover the corresponding mindset that sets you free, unboxes your thinking, expands your consciousness, empowers you to become outstandingly creative and successful, and reconnects you with your inner genius.

- Finally, each stop features a set of exercises that help you to achieve the desired mindset changes.

Conclusion: Einstein was right: *"There is a genius in all of us,"* in you and in me. What is my genius all about? I am a genius at devising systematic and highly effective yet fun-to-use innovation methods that help organizations become more innovative and individuals become more creative. Genius Journey is one of the four innovation methods that I created for Thinkergy (alongside X-IDEA, TIPS, and CooL-Creativity UnLimited, which we touched upon in the previous three chapters).

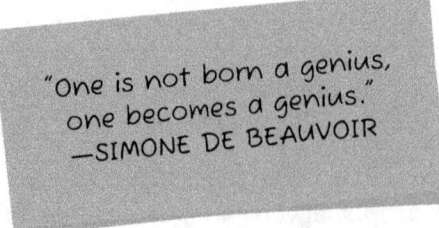

"One is not born a genius, one becomes a genius."
—SIMONE DE BEAUVOIR

7.5. INCUBATION: A WALK ON THE MYSTERIOUS SIDE OF CREATIVITY

One of the many paradoxical aspects of creativity is that in order to gain breakthrough results, you either need hundreds of ideas or just one. The former describes the normal situation in which you assemble a collection of brains to take part in an ideation and subsequent idea concept development session (as outlined in Chapter 4). The latter leads us to the mysterious process of incubation.

Incubation is a cognitive process wherein you consciously work on your challenge for an often-prolonged period of time, and then completely set it aside. In that way, you give your unconscious mind time to recombine thoughts and stimuli and to deliver the solution all of a sudden. Many geniuses have described this process as key to their breakthrough idea:

- The Greek mathematician Archimedes had pondered on a tough problem posed to him by the king of Syracuse (How to find out if the new laurel crown of the king is completely made from gold?). When he decided to take a bath to relax from hard thinking, he conceived the solution to his challenge (objects of different densities displace different volumes of water).
- Sir Isaac Newton worked for years on the problem of gravitation. He conceived the breakthrough idea behind his law of gravitation while resting under an apple tree and observing an apple falling down.
- Friedrich August Kekulé conceived his breakthrough insights into the ring structure of benzene when dreaming of a snake biting on its tail.
- Albert Einstein described the process of incubation that led to his special theory of relativity as follows: *"Hard? It took me ten years to get from my first questions about light to my theory of relativity. I went through all sorts of nervous conflicts. And after all that, it came to me suddenly. It was a beautiful day, my friend Besso and I were out walking. I was doing most of the talking, I told him that I had been struggling with a question and needed his help. But as I spoke, the answer came to me. I stopped in mid-sentence and ran home. The next morning I went to him again. 'Thank you,' I said, 'I have completely solved the problem.'"*

Have you noticed that most interestingly, all those breakthrough moments occurred when the thinkers were taking some time off from working on their problem and were engaged in relaxing activities? This is an important point. Remember that incubation requires three things to work: Firstly, extensive mental preparation in an initial phase of deep immersion with you problem. Secondly, the courage to completely let go of your problem. And last but not least —in order to gain the necessary courage— faith and belief that the right solution will come to you in time.

Do you face a tough and important creative challenge? Consider resolving it subconsciously by activating the creative process of incubation as follows:

1. Formulate your challenge as an action question starting with the words *"How to?"* (Deeply explore your challenge over a prolonged period of time. Thereby recall Thomas Jefferson's advice: *"The more I do, the luckier I get."* Collect possible ideas and solutions to your problem or challenge, and keep on adding more *"dots"* as you continue to dig wider and deeper.

2. Once you feel that you have come close to the solution, stop your mental effort. Completely let go of the problem and do something else. Maintain an open mind and a spirit of inquiry, and pay attention to any stimuli in your environment. Acknowledge that you don't know if you are going to get the right solution or not. Have the courage to surrender and let go. Have faith that the right idea will appear.

3. After you have completely forgotten about your challenge — if you're lucky and have faith—, the breakthrough solution might appear *"out of the blue."* This sudden moment of creative insight, when your unconscious mind delivers you the right solution, is also known as illumination. It feels as if you are hit by a flash of intensely bright energy light. You get extremely fired up and energized as you immediately know, *"That's it!"* Archimedes got so excited by his discovery that he even forgot to dress, taking naked to the streets shouting *"Eureka!"* (*"I have found it!"*).

4. Finally, take action on your breakthrough idea. Formulate it and visualize or prototype it so that it's easy for others to follow your thoughts on verifying the breakthrough solution.

The English psychologist Graham Wallas conceptualized the four steps of preparation, incubation, illumination, and verification as one of the first creative process models. He drew upon the letter exchanges of two scientists, the German physicist Hermann von Helmholtz and the French mathematician Henri Poincaré, who both introduced and reported on the cognitive preconditions that allowed them to experience Eureka moments of breakthrough creativity.

Conclusion: Incubation does not only work for geniuses — I have experienced its magical powers myself twice in my life. The first time, I was under immense pressure to solve a tough measurement problem in my doctoral thesis within a week. I had already worked on my thesis for two years and had intensely thought about how to solve this particular problem, but to no avail. Fortunately, I was courageous enough to completely let go in spite of the deadline — and conceived the breakthrough solution on my third day of relaxation while running alone in the forest.

My second kiss of genius happened over Chinese New Year 2003. After one year of intense exploration of what I should really do with my life instead of working as a well-performing but dispassionate banker in Hong Kong, I was reading beside a swimming pool when out of nowhere, an energetic flash of insight struck me: I suddenly gained total clarity of who I am and what I should do with my life. That moment was the birth of Thinkergy and Dr. D, and it happened in Bangkok at the advent of the Year of the Black Sheep. Since then, I have been on my mission to create and empower creative leaders.

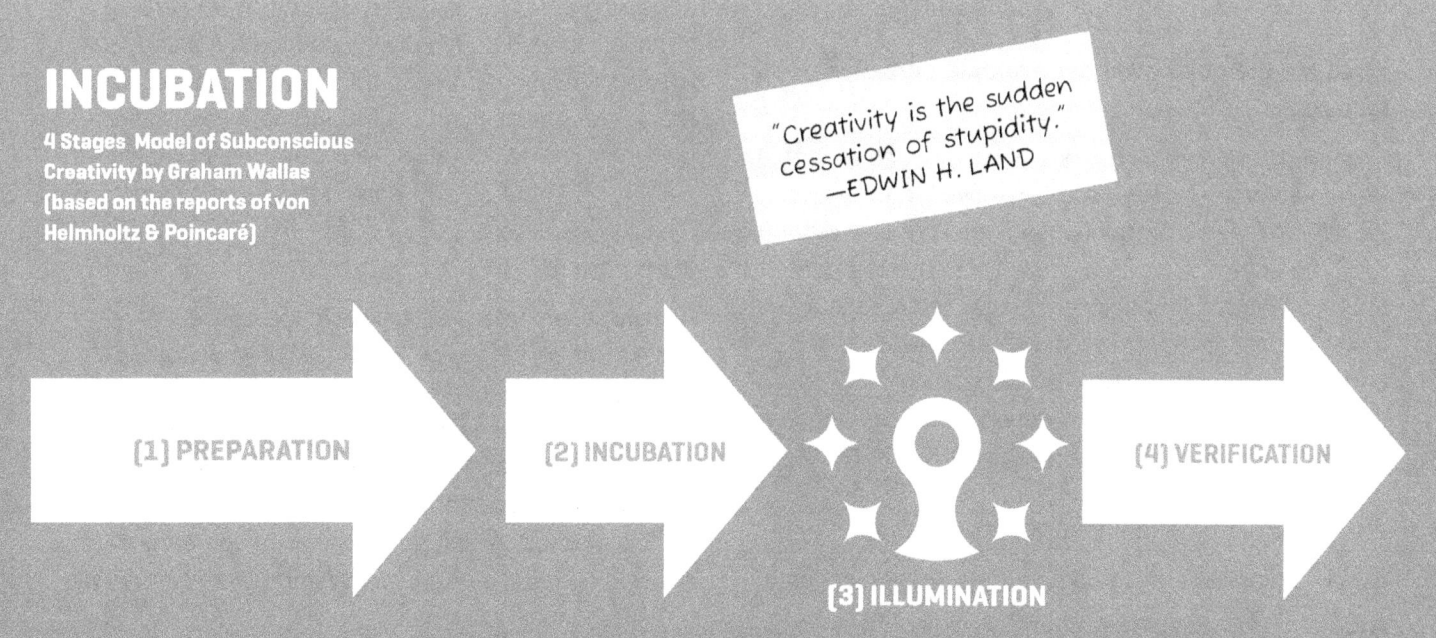

INCUBATION
4 Stages Model of Subconscious Creativity by Graham Wallas (based on the reports of von Helmholtz & Poincaré)

"Creativity is the sudden cessation of stupidity."
—EDWIN H. LAND

[1] PREPARATION → [2] INCUBATION → [3] ILLUMINATION → [4] VERIFICATION

7.6. HOW TO CREATIVELY AND EFFECTIVELY DEVELOP CREATIVE LEADERS?

Section 7.1 echoed a call of the CEOs of the world's top companies for a more creative leadership style to better cope with the rising complexity and dynamism in business. However, we also learned that most top human resources executives of the same companies acknowledged in a follow-up study their difficulty in effectively developing creative leaders.

One key reason for this is that creative leadership development programs cannot follow traditional formulae but instead must employ truly CREATIVE (or, in other words, novel, original, and meaningful) training formats. So, how can we move beyond traditional leadership development methods to both effectively and creatively transform performance-oriented top managers into genuine creative leaders for the innovation economy? And what objectives does such a method need to achieve?

What are the objectives of developing creative leaders?

Creative leadership development should ideally enable leaders to be creatively productive every day, and to easily and reliably produce meaningful creative outputs when needed; this ability is essential to being a genuine creative leader or successful creative entrepreneur. Moreover, creative leaders should be able, by their capability and skills as well as their personalities, to credibly lead creative teams working on important innovation projects from the front.

A trip back in time to my creative beginnings

Nearly a decade ago, I had pondered these questions using slightly different language: *"How to creatively teach businesspeople on how to effectively redevelop their inner creativity and rediscover their true creative selves?"*

For me, it was clear that a truly effective individual creativity training program must go beyond simply teaching creativity tools or solving simple creative puzzles; it also had to address the underlying mindsets and action routines of genius that empower creativity on higher levels and can lead to moments of breakthrough creativity,; and to make learners experience the power of these mindsets, it had to involve a mix of special creative delivery formats and activities that ideally related to an overriding theme or a metaphor.

What got me started to ponder these questions?

Well, I am the only person I have met so far who has had the great privilege of experiencing two Eureka moments in my life. When it happened the first time, I was immensely happy and relieved that I received the breakthrough solution for a tough operationalization problem (how to effectively and objectively measure a certain construct in my theoretical model) in my doctoral thesis three days before I would have been kicked out of the program.

Roughly five years later, I experienced my second Eureka, which set me on my path to become an international expert in business creativity and applied innovation. This time, however, I got immensely curious to understand why I was so lucky to experience this awe-inspiring moment of breakthrough creativity twice in my life. So, I asked myself questions such as: *"How did it happen? What did I do to start the process and support*

1st EUREKA 1997

2nd EUREKA 2002

* How did it happen?
* What was my mindset like right before and while it happened?
* What did I start doing to activate and support the process?
* What did I stop doing to free my thinking?

1. INTROSPECT mental conditions before and during the Eureka experiences

2. IDENTIFY creativity-supporting START- and -inhibiting STOP-mindset factors through introspection

WHAT I STARTED TO THINK AND DO	WHAT I STOPPED TO THINK AND DO
★ COURAGEOUSLY BELIEVED SOLUTION WILL COME, AT THE RIGHT TIME	– WORRY ABOUT FAILING AND MY FUTURE
★ ALTERNATING FOCUSED WORK WITH RELAXATION	– STOPPED READING EXPERT LITERATURE
★ BEING POSITIVE AND DOING PLAY ACTIVITIES I ENJOY	– STOPPED WORKING ON THE CASE
★ COLLECTING FRESH DOTS OUTSIDE THE TUNNEL OF MY EXPERT DOMAIN	– STOPPED WORKING NONSTOP
★ PRACTICE FLOW-INDUCING ACTIVITIES	– STOPPED CUTTING DOWN ON RELAXING, ENJOYABLE ACTIVITIES

LITERATURE REVIEW:
- PSYCHOLOGICAL STUDIES
- (AUTO-) BIOGRAPHIES AND VIDEOS & INTERVIEWS
- SEMI-BIOGRAPHICAL GENIUS TRAINING BOOKS
- INDIVIDUAL CREATIVITY TRAINING BOOKS
- OTHERS

3. STUDY literature on genius and creative leaders

4. CONFIRM creativity-supporting and -inhibiting mindset factors in literature

PAIR START VS. STOP FACTORS
+BELIEF <> FEAR–
+SELF <> EGO–
+OPENNESS <> JUDGMENT–
+POSITIVITY <> NEGATIVITY–
+... <> ...–
+... <> ...–
+... <> ...–
+... <> ...–

UNVEIL SEQUENCE & HIERARCHY

5. PAIR creativity-supporting START- and -inhibiting STOP-mindset factors, and unveil hidden sequence of hierarchy of factor acquisition

6. CREATE JOURNEY-metaphor as overriding theme to allow for creative and effective creative leadership development

GENIUS JOURNEY
by thinkergy

6. CONCEPTUALIZE, test and finalize **GENIUS JOURNEY** method

it? What did I stop doing and did differently compared to before? What was my mindset like right before and while it happened?"*

At that point in time, I was still an absolute beginner in the domain of creativity, so I had not learned yet about the creative process model of subconscious creativity featured in the previous section. However, I could sense that there seemed to be some underlying principles going on that supported and set in motion the process that enabled me to get lucky. I noticed that before my two Eureka experiences, I had started to think in certain ways and to do some unusual things that had opened up the channel for subconscious breakthrough creativity to freely flow; at the same time, I had also stopped certain common thinking and action patterns that seemed to have blocked my creativity beforehand.

Learning more about the mindsets of geniuses

To contrast the findings of the introspection of my mindset before and during my Eureka experiences with that of famous creative top achievers, I started to dig into the relevant literature on genius and creative leaders:

- Psychological research on individual creativity and genius allowed me to learn more about the personality traits and creativity-inducing mindsets that outstanding creative leaders and geniuses tend to exhibit vis-à-vis the less creative majority of people.
- Biographical accounts and autobiographies of creative leaders and geniuses such as Leonardo da Vinci, Albert Einstein, Thomas Edison, Walt Disney, Steve Jobs, Charles Kettering, Elon Musk, and Richard Branson. This enabled me to *"get into the head"* of creative top achievers and to validate the creativity-inducing factors identified by psychological research with the real-life mindsets and action behaviors that positively differentiate creative leaders from ordinary people and enable them to produce extraordinary ideas, creations, and results.
- Semi-biographical business books combine the study of the lives of selected famous creative leaders with a creativity-enhancing learning program that emphasizes positive, creativity-enhancing mindsets, and typically also offers a set of corresponding exercises to actualize and practice the suggested creativity-supporting factors. For example, Michael Gelb presented a number of creativity-oriented learning programs based on da Vinci, Edison and a collection of ten other creative leaders. One interesting variation from this category is the work of Robert Dilts who investigated and expressed the cognitive strategies of creative leaders like Mozart, Einstein, Disney, Freud, da Vinci and Tesla using the methodological instruments of Neurolinguistic Programming (NLP).
- Finally, other authors such as Michael Ray and Rochelle Myers or Julia Cameron shared successful practical course programs to enhance individual creativity and develop creative leaders with a wider audience. In their books, they identify creativity-supporting and -limiting factors, and also suggest a set of exercises to cultivate a more creative mindset.

My literature review confirmed three points:

1. Most creative leaders share a common set of positive, creativity-empowering action routines and mindsets that correspond to the ways I thought and did things before my personal creative breakthrough experiences.

2. Indeed, there also seem to be corresponding negative mindsets and actions that limit creativity; to get into creative flow and open the channels for breakthrough creativity to flow freely, one needs to stop engaging in these negative thought and action patterns.

3. Similarly, to my review of the literature on organizational creativity, the identified positive, creativity-empowering factors can be linked to negative, creativity-limiting factor pairs. Judgment and closed-mindedness (negative) vs. curiosity and openness (positive) is one example of such factor pairs.

4. My personal Eureka experiences allowed me to add an additional element that goes beyond the creativity-inducing factors that researchers had already previously identified: I noticed that the creativity-empowering factors don't stand next to each other in parallel, but rather seem to follow a sequence that unfolds in a certain hierarchy of mindsets and actions. In other words, some foundational mindsets and action routines need to be acquired first to successfully master more advanced mindsets later. For example, before candidates can really develop an open, curious, positive, and playful beginner's mind, they first need to learn to overcome their fears and keep their egos in check.

So, there was only one missing peace: An overriding creative theme or metaphor that allows for developing creative leaders in a truly *creative* way.

A creative metaphor: Developing into a creative leader is like going on a journey to reconnect to your inner genius

Have you recently gone on a journey? Where did you go? And when you returned home, were you the same person with the same mindset as before your trip?

Journeys are transformative because they make us become a bigger, wiser, more knowledgeable, and experienced person. When we travel, we encounter new countries, cultures, and people. We visit new places and experience other histories, traditions, rituals, and ways of doing things. We appreciate new ways to live life and look at its various aspects. We experience unfamiliar situations and little adventures. All these accumulated experiences make us become bigger people with an expanded, enhanced level of consciousness.

In short, a journey makes a perfect metaphor for a method of developing genius and creative leadership. It is a truly creative format for teaching creative leadership know-how and skills that is at the same time educational and experiential, technical and spiritual, introspective and action-oriented, individual and social. The journey metaphor also allows for training creative leadership candidates in truly creative ways — a journey into the wonderful, magical, and mysterious world of creativity.

Finally, I had all the components on hand to create both an effective *and* truly creative method to develop creative leaders. I called the method Genius Journey.

What is Genius Journey? And why does it work?

Genius Journey is a creative leadership method that I designed to cater to a wider unsatisfied need that we noticed in the leadership development market: The need to create authentic creative leaders.

The Genius Journey method sends creative leader candidates on a experiential journey to acquire the creative success mindsets and action routines of top

creative leaders and to transform into an authentic creative leader for the innovation economy.

Who is Genius Journey for?

I created the Genius Journey method to enable C-level executives, creative entrepreneurs, and talented upper and middle managers to evolve into creative leaders. The method can also help professionals in the creative industries and the arts up their creative game and unblock temporary creative blocks. The Genius Journey method can also unblock the thinking of scientists and researchers who work on the frontier of new breakthrough research projects and are stuck in the tunnel of their deep expertise. Last but not least, it can help you rediscover your true creative self.

So, if you're a member of this target audience, you can learn how to gradually evolve into an authentic creative leader by joining one of our Genius Journey training courses or longer development programs offered by Thinkergy. Moreover, in the coming years, I intend to also feature the Genius Journey method in a series of two to three separate books to a wider audience.

So, can every leader become a creative leader?

In general, yes. However, some people will find this creative transformation more difficult than others. Let me explain.

At Thinkergy, before we accept someone into our creative leadership development program, we prefer to first test their mindset and cognitive preferences using TIPS. The results from the cognitive test help us identify those who are unlikely to benefit from such training because they tend to have psycho-static minds that favor the preservation of the status quo and more traditional approaches and naturally focus more on helping organizations realize efficiencies and economies of scale.

For all psycho-dynamic or -neutral profile types, who are well-suited to develop into a creative leader, knowing the TIPS profile can hint to likely mindset and skills gaps that those candidates yet need to acquire in order to successfully evolve into a creative leader.

In the final two sections of this chapter, I will first explain the different design elements that make this method creative before giving you a gist of the factors that stop or start your individual creativity.

> "Thousands of geniuses live and die undiscovered — either by themselves or by others."
> —MARK TWAIN

7.7. INTRODUCING THE DESIGN FEATURES OF THE GENIUS JOURNEY METHOD

Genius Journey is an action-oriented creative leadership development method that enables candidates to sustainably redevelop their personal creativeness. It equips candidates with supportive creative mindsets and action routines of genius thinkers and creative business leaders to enhance their personal creativeness and gradually develop them into authentic creative leaders to lead their organizational units (team, division, start-up venture, company, and corporation, among others) in the Innovation Economy.

The Genius Journey method employs a methodology and pedagogy that is both *effective* (achieving lasting mindset changes) and *creative* (employing truly creative elements and pedagogical tools needed to develop creative leaders). What special methodological and pedagogical features does Genius Journey use?

Genius Journey: Closing identified delivery gaps through an integrative design

Genius Journey has been purposely designed to provide a truly creative format for creative leadership development. It retains useful common features of programs to enhance individual creativity and develop creative leaders but closes the identified delivery gaps and common blind spots of other approaches. The Genius Journey method integrates the following design features into one elegant system architecture:

1. Creative journey format: Genius Journey complies with the sine qua non that a course in creative leadership needs to be run in an original, truly creative format by constructing the whole method around a journey metaphor: *"Developing candidates into authentically creative leaders is like sending them on a journey to reconnect to their inner genius."*

Accordingly, the Genius Journey program is split up into three conceptual parts:

- The check-in, where candidates prepare for the creative leadership program.

- The journey, where the candidates learn creative leadership mindsets and skills. In the upcoming Genius Journey book series, I intend to split the journey into three parts to make the knowledge and skills acquisition more manageable and easy: the journey to your creative self, the journey to your creativity, and the journey to your genius.

- The check-out, where the candidates consolidate all their learnings and are introduced to strategies that help them to sustain the learned mindsets and action routines after going back to their everyday work and life.

The pedagogical employment of a journey metaphor to illustrate personal limitations and growth enablers draws on Joseph Campbell's seminal work of comparative mythology, which describes the classic model of the hero's journey to achieve personal transformation and mastery.

2. Creativity-limiting and supporting factors: The Genius Journey method distinguishes ten antagonistic pairs of factors that support or limit creativity. Stop Factors inform the candidates about mindsets and action routines that limit their creativity, while Start Factors

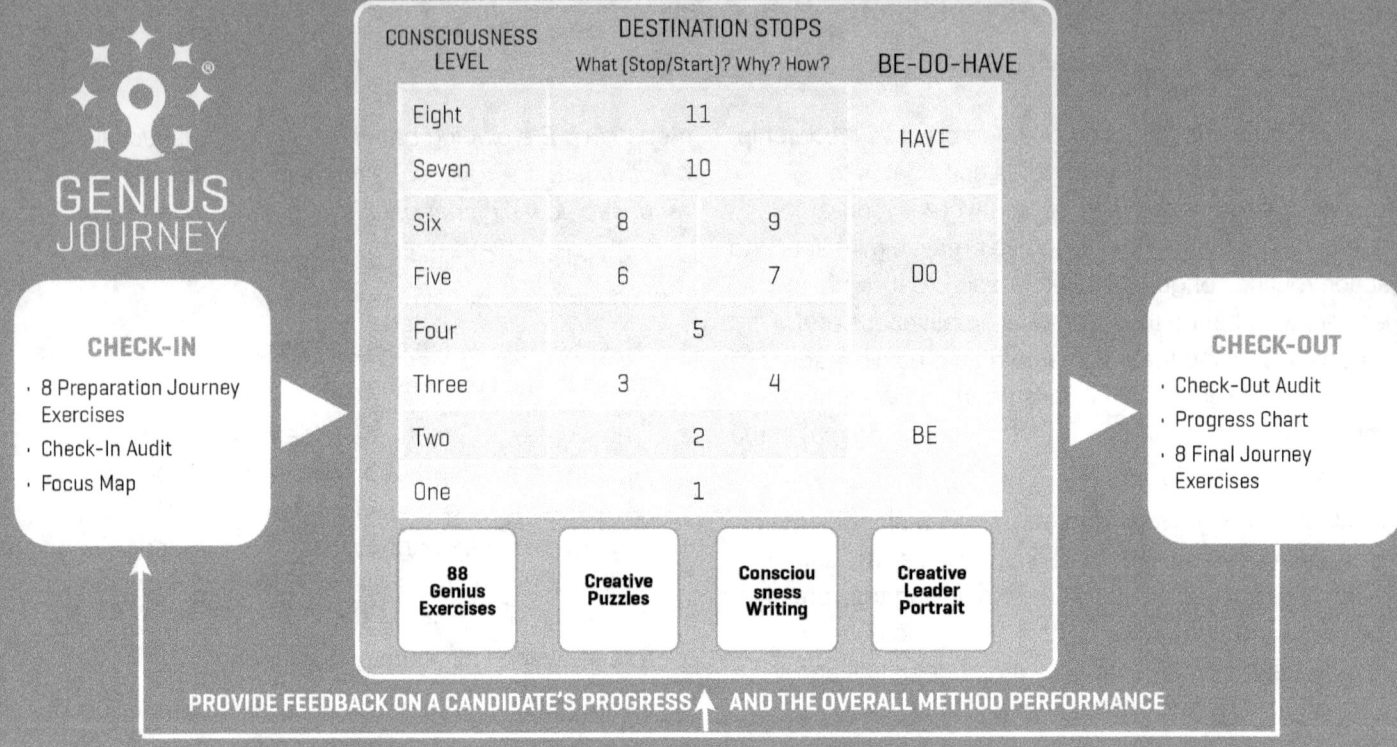

suggest corresponding positive mindsets and activities that are conducive to creative thinking. Thereby, the creative leader candidates learn about the factors that limit or empower their creativeness in a consistent What-Why-How approach:

- First, they learn what they need to **stop** being or doing, and instead what they need to **start** being and doing.
- Next, they are informed why this is important to evolve into authentic leaders.
- Finally, they learn how exactly they can achieve the desired positive creative mindset and behavioral changes (this is linked to a supporting exercise pack discussed below).

3. Sequence of acquisition of creativity-supporting factors: The creative journey format guarantees measured knowledge and skills acquisition, thus achieving a step-by-step personal transformation over time. The candidates encounter 10 destination stops on their Genius Journey, whereby they also physically move to different locations that support the acquisition of a particular creative mindset. At each destination stop, the candidates first learn about one limiting mindset that stops their creativity, and about one corresponding empowering mindset they need to adopt instead.

The progressive journey leads the candidates to a final 11th destination, which is the ultimate goal of learning how the creative leader candidates can increase their odds of experiencing a Eureka moment of breakthrough creativity. As such, Genius Journey leads towards the creative process of subconscious peak creativity (as described earlier in section 7.5), thereby also integrating Mihalyi Csikszentmihalyi's creativity-inducing concept of flow.

4. Hierarchy of creativity-supporting and -limiting factors: Unlike other methodological approaches to developing one's individual creativity, the Genius Journey method presents the creativity-supporting and -limiting factors in a hierarchical order, thus maintaining that foundational factors need to be developed first before higher-order values can be successfully and sustainably cultivated. Therefore, the Genius Journey method introduces the concepts of eight levels of consciousness that are linked to the 11 destination stops of the journey as well as to the Be-Do-Have philosophical concept of Zen Buddhism: First, be who you really are (core identity); then, do what you want and need to do (activities); finally, have peak creativity and creative outputs (results).

5. Comprehensive exercise pack: Genius Journey comes with a comprehensive exercise pack of 88 *"Genius Exercises"* and 16 *"Journey Exercises"*:

- At each of the 11 destinations of the Genius Journey, the candidates are exposed to 8 Genius Exercises that guide them towards how to overcome their limitations and start cultivating the corresponding creativity-empowering mindset and action routines. Some exercises are more cognitive or introspective in nature, others more action-oriented and physical; the mix of exercises cater to a wide range of personal and cognitive styles, and different candidates gain important personal insights and discoveries through different exercises.

- At check-in, 8 Journey Exercises prepare the candidates for the program, while the concluding 8 Journey Exercises guide the candidates towards strategies for integrating and applying all learnings into their daily work and lives.

6. Supporting additional creative exercises: Genius Journey adopted a number of useful supportive practices from other programs to hone the creative leader candidates' creative thinking abilities, such as:

- The practice of maintaining a notebook;

- Stream-of-consciousness writing exercises (as an adaptation of Julia Cameron's suggested practice to counter creative blockages by writing daily *"morning pages"*);

- Practicing solving creative puzzles. Thereby, I also developed a range of open-ended creative puzzles (with a theoretically infinite range of solutions that amplify creativity) to supplement a range of well-known standard puzzles (such as the well-known 'Nine Dots'-puzzle) that have only a finite number of solutions.

- Moreover, the Genius Journey method suggests creative leader candidates study the life of an admired creative leader of their own choice and compare the findings with the creative mindsets and action routines suggested by the Genius Journey method; after performing these biographical studies in parallel while going through the program, the creative leader candidates then consolidate all learnings and inspirations in a portrait of their chosen creative leader.

7. Audit tool to identify major limitations and track progress: Genius Journey also uses an assessment tool at the check-in and checkout to identify initial mindset gaps and to track progress.

- First, candidates are asked to assess their current and desired state for the various creativity-supporting Start and creativity-limiting Stop Factors on bipolar scales.

- The results are then consolidated in a personal *"Genius Journey Map"* that visualizes mindset gaps and highlights those areas that a candidate should focus on most while going through the program.

- At check-out, the same test is repeated to track personal progress and improvements by the end of the program. If senior executives go through a Genus Journey coaching program, 360-degree assessments from subordinates, peers, and superiors may also be sought to externally validate a candidate's self-perception.

Genius Journey: An effective and creative framework to develop authentic creative leaders

Genius Journey is a new method in the emerging domain of creative leadership development that expands and improves on the narrow pool of earlier methodological approaches to enhance individual creativity and develop creative leaders. Genius Journey has been designed to close identified delivery gaps of other programs and integrate a wider range of relevant methodological design features into one elegant, effective and creative architecture. It achieves these improvements with the help of an elegant system architecture that has been purposely designed into the method.

Key aspects that distinguish Genius Journey from other comparable methods are summed up as follows:

1. Genius Journey is an integrative method that unifies special design features (i.e., creativity-limiting and -enabling factors; a creative delivery format; sequence and hierarchy of factors; creativity-enhancing exercises and activities; an audit toolset; and the inclusion of the concepts of flow and subconscious peak creativity, among others).

2. Genius Journey employs a journey metaphor as both a creative and effective delivery format to develop authentic creative leaders and guide the overall method design. The different stages of the journey offer an intuitive, non-obstructive way to introduce the features of sequence and hierarchy of creativity- limiting and -enabling factors (i.e., mindsets and action routines that largely determine what the candidates think and do). Thereby, the Genius Journey model maintains that creative leader candidates need to master foundational creative mindsets before they are able to successfully acquire and sustain more advanced mindsets and action routines, thus gradually expanding the candidates' creative competencies and consciousness levels.

3. The Genius Journey model leads towards the ultimate objective of gaining access to subconscious states of peak creativity (Eureka moments) that are the source of most notable creative breakthroughs, thus including the process model of breakthrough creativity into the method. This important feature both inspired and guided the development of Genius Journey, as unlike most other contributors in the domain, the inventor of the method was fortunate to personally experience two Eureka moments at critical stages of his professional life, and subsequently began working on developing a structured framework that makes it more likely for others to also gain

access to this subconscious states of peak creativity.

4. Genius Journey develops creative leaders by taking the candidates through the question sequence *"What? Why? How?"* As such, at each destination stop of the journey, the creative leader candidates first learn what limiting mindset or behavior they need to stamp out, and what empowering mindset or action routine they need to adopt instead; then, the method explains in detail why these changes are important to cultivate a creative mind and evolve into an authentic creative leader; and finally, the candidates find out how exactly they can achieve this mindset change. To support the *"How"*-transformation process, the method offers a comprehensive Genius Journey exercise pack (with over a hundred exercises) to the candidates that is supported by other creative exercises and activities (such as creative puzzles, stream-of-consciousness writing exercises, maintaining a notebook, studying the life of one admired creative leader) as well as an audit toolset (to identify mind- set gaps at the start of the program and later on track the creative mindset improvements).

The resulting new creative leadership development method Genius Journey has been successfully used in training courses and coaching projects that the innovation company Thinkergy conducted with multicultural audiences and individual business executives. It was also tested and fine-tuned over several terms in a graduate management course in Creative Leadership. Finally, several research studies confirmed the transformational effectiveness of the program in developing creative leaders.

Genius Journey will be featured more extensively in a series of two to three upcoming business books. The books contain the details of the methodology following the What-Why-How approach (*"What is it that you need to STOP thinking and doing? What do you need to START instead? Why is this mindset change critically important to connect to your personal creativity? How exactly can you do it?"*). However, in the final section of Chapter 7, I want to give you an idea of what factors stop your creative flow or get it started.

> *"We don't receive wisdom; we must discover it for ourselves after a journey that no one can take for us or spare us."*
> —MARCEL PROUST

7.8. REDISCOVER YOUR CREATIVE SELF

Do you consider yourself highly creative? You should answer with a roaring *"Yes!"* We were all born creative and exhibited high levels of creativity as young children.

Unfortunately, most people lose their innate creativity while growing up. Parents, school teachers, our friends and peers in adolescence, and society at large silence our deep curiosity and quash our inner creativity. In recent years, however, there has been a call in the business world for more creativity to better capitalize on our fast-changing business environment.

So how can you rediscover your creative self and become a creative leader? Travel the Genius Journey with its ten stops. At each destination stop, learn what mindsets and action routines STOP you and limit your creativity — and what corresponding empowering thoughts and actions get your creativity STARTED and can reconnect you with your genius.

1. STOP your worries, doubts and fears. START being a courageous, action-oriented believer

"Courage is the first of the human qualities, because it is the one that guarantees all others," noted Aristotle. Innovation always means a change from the status quo, and human beings don't like to change. You can expect massive resistance to any innovation you might introduce one day. So start your journey to reconnect with your creative self by developing courage as demanded by Aristotle.

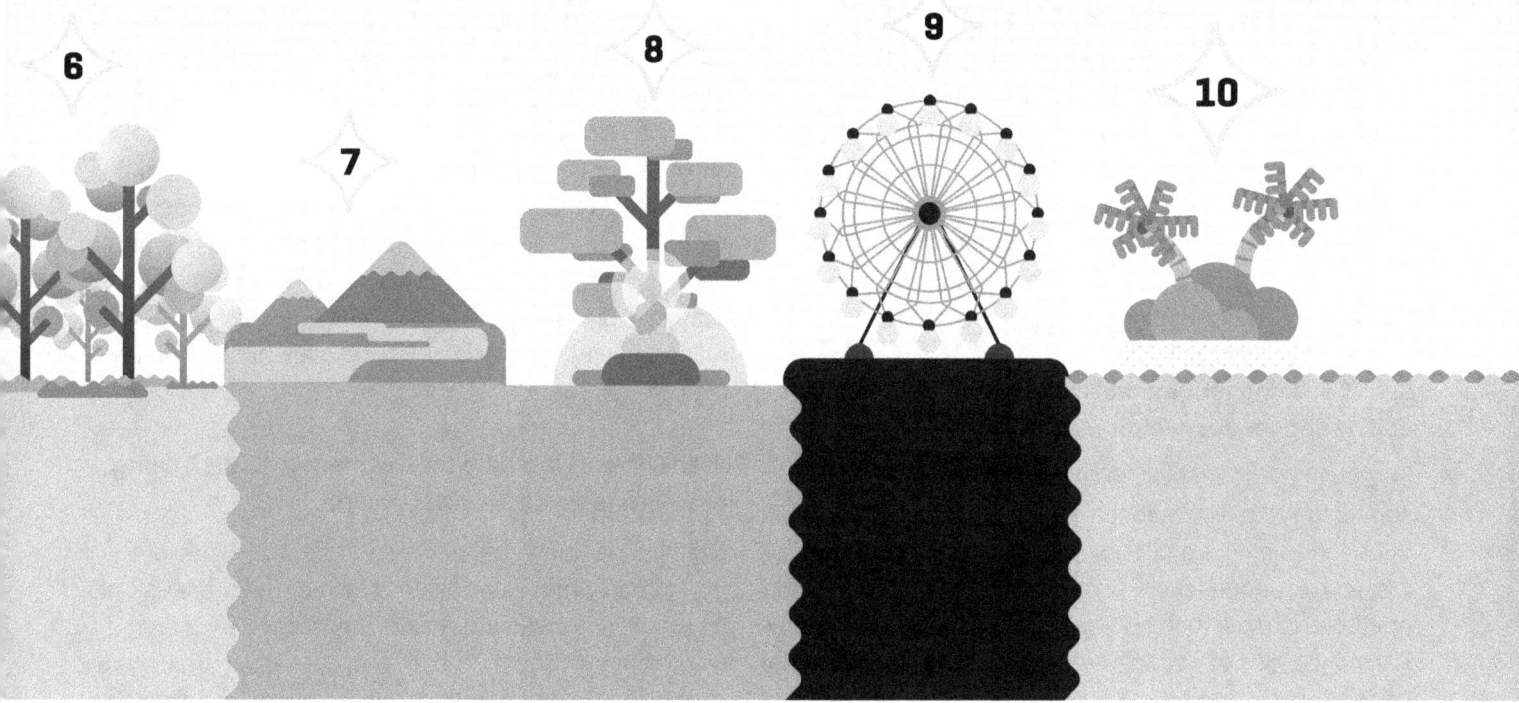

Regularly fight your doubts, worries and fears, and consider following the advice of Ralph Waldo Emerson: *"Always do what you fear."* Remember that the sound of fear and the sound of courage are one and the same: your loudly beating heart. The difference is taking action despite your fear.

Belief is your biggest ally to courageously move forward. As Lord Buddha said: *"He is able who thinks he is able."* The source of your belief may be a particular religion or other form of spirituality. Or you may simply believe in yourself and that you can realize your dreams as Muhammad Ali's did: *"It's lack of faith that makes people afraid of meeting challenges, and I believed in myself."*

Apple's CEO Steve Jobs expressed the necessity to believe in your path as follows: *"Again, you can't connect the dots looking forward; you can only connect them looking backwards. So you have to trust that the dots will somehow connect in your future. You have to trust in something — your gut, destiny, life, karma, whatever. This approach has never let me down, and it has made all the difference in my life."* So believe with your heart before you move on, because as Henry Ford commented: *"If you think you can do a thing or you think you can't do a thing, you're right."*

2. STOP your ego. START being yourself.

Is there anyone in the world who looks, thinks, and acts exactly like you? Surely you will disagree here. So would you agree with me that you were created as an original? Nod your head. You are original. We all are created as originals and not as a copy of another person. Hence, we had better follow the advice of Ralph Waldo Emerson:

"Insist upon yourself. Be original." So, stop being a copycat by imitating others and playing a role that other people want you to play. Stop wearing that ridiculous mask behind which you hide your true Self. Your biggest enemy is your own ego. Your ego is also the highest hurdle to overcome on your way to becoming a highly creative individual. We all have to endure the inner fight between our ego and self. Start taking control of your true *Self* by stopping taking yourself too seriously.

3. STOP being judgmental and closed-minded. Start cultivating an open, curious beginner's mind.

Do you know some people who constantly find something to criticize about other people or other ideas? Such judgments are often an expression of fixation, closed-mindedness and intolerance of different ways or opinions. In most cases, they are the outer expression of the insecurities of judgmental people, who innately suffer under the nagging voice of their strong inner critics.

In contrast, notice how open young children are toward new knowledge, different perspectives and interesting ideas. They are immensely curious. They constantly ask questions to satisfy their voracious curiosity. Do the same and re-adopt the curious beginner's mind that you had as a young child. Cultivate a life-long passion for learning. Become open to entertaining new concepts, new knowledge, new skills, new technology and —most importantly— new people regardless of their background.

4. STOP being a negative, serious pessimist. START being a positive, playful optimist.

Please take an empty glass and fill it half with water. Now describe what you see. Some people say the glass is half empty. We call them pessimists who focus on the problem in everything. In contrast, optimists say the glass is half full. They see the opportunity that is hidden within each problem. In life, what you see is what you get, and it's always what you get. Leonardo da Vinci knew about the importance of positive thinking and recommended: *"Avoid grievous moods and keep your mind cheerful."* So, follow da Vinci's advice and watch your attitude: always stay positive and be persistent with your plans and projects. Please recall that Thomas Edison needed more than 10,000 trials before finding the right design for the light bulb.

5. STOP working only for the money. START being passionate and love what you do.

Creative people usually love what they do. They are not primarily motivated by money but work because of the challenges and enjoyment it provides. Research studies have confirmed over and over again that intrinsic motivation breeds creativity, while extrinsic motivational factors such as financial rewards are rather counter-productive to spur truly original ideas.

Do you love what you do? If your answer is yes, congratulations. For those of you who said no, you have not yet aligned your work with your passion. What things do you find exciting? What do you want to learn more about all the time? What do you love doing?

Find the answers to these questions and try to integrate things that you are passionate about into your work step-by-step. Steve Jobs, the co-founder of Apple and one of the most remarkable comeback stories in business, commented on the darkest hours of his career when he was fired from Apple in 1985: *"I'm convinced that the only thing that kept me going was that I loved what I did. You have got to find what you love."*

6. STOP being trapped in the expert tunnel. START learning and living like a T-Shaped Person.

"All experts are blind. Expertise means you become blind to everything else. You know more and more about less and less, and then one day you arrive at the ultimate goal of knowing all about nothing," noted the Indian guru Osho.

Over the past two centuries, we have developed into an expert culture that favors specialists over generalists. Don't get me wrong: You need to have great depth and expertise in at least one domain. But being an expert in one area is not good enough if you want to become a creative leader. You need to complement your expertise with a breadth of knowledge in many other areas. This allows you to connect the dots between something in your general knowledge, skills and experience repertoire and a problem that you try to solve in your expert domain.

Leonardo da Vinci stated: *"Everything is connected to everything else."* He knew that breakthrough ideas are often found in the intersection between different concepts, ideas or knowledge disciplines. Consequently, da Vinci was not only an artist. He was also an inventor, a military engineer, and a scientist. Let da Vinci's famous sketch of the Vitruvian Man be a role model of what you should become: a *"T-shaped person"* with deep expertise in at least one area of specialization and with broad general knowledge and skills in many other areas.

7. STOP thinking with only half your brain. START becoming an integrated whole-mind thinker.

School and university education strongly emphasize cognitive processes that build up the left side of our brains, which take care of rationalization, analysis, logic, planning and calculation. In contrast, our education systems do little to foster right-brain thinking activities,

GENIUS
- Exceptional intellectual or creative power or other natural ability
- An exceptionally intelligent person or one with exceptional skill in one area of activity

"There is a genius in all of us"
— ALBERT EINSTEIN

such as generating original ideas, engaging our fantasy and imagination or listening to our intuition. What is the result of our unbalanced mono-brain education? Most business people are superb logical analysts and rather poor creative thinkers.

Do you know the principle of Yin and Yang? This important philosophical concept of the Chinese culture symbolizes the balance in all of creation: Sun and moon, male and female, day and night, summer and winter and, of course, left-brain thinking and right-brain thinking. Make an effort to regain the vital Yin-Yang balance in your mind. Become a whole-mind thinker by training your creative thinking abilities to complement your well-honed analytical thinking skills. How?

Take creativity training with an experienced creativity coach to quickly make up for what you missed in school. Regularly try creative puzzles and mind-teasers that you can find on websites and in some books and magazines. In addition, exercise your right brain by experimenting with creativity techniques to get ideas for a tough business nut that you have to crack.

8. STOP being inflexible, habitual and inert. START moving, changing and flexing yourself.

Imagine a tall, mighty oak tree that tops all surrounding trees in a forest. Now also envision a tiny bush of bamboo. Which of the two is stronger? The correct answer depends on whether we face a stable or unstable environment. On a sunny day, the solid oak tree is surely stronger than the tiny bamboo. However, in the eye of a heavy thunderstorm, the oak tree might break, while the flexible bamboo bends with the wind.

Business in the new millennium is rather unstable and turbulent, too. A once mighty business can quickly break apart under the pressures of an increasingly competitive, fast-changing business environment if leaders and managers insist on their established points of view and rigidly hold on to old habits. So, make an effort to fight your habits. Become more flexible and proactively approach change. Develop a tolerance for ambiguity, uncertainty and paradoxes. Remember the oak tree and the bamboo: the more flexible you are, the more power you have in times of change.

Finally, keep on moving forward, as standstill will make you fall behind quickly in times of rapid, exponential change.

9. STOP being mentally preoccupied with the past and future and engaging in mindless action. START living and working mindfully now.

Leonardo da Vinci also knew about the importance of perceiving the environment with all five senses. *"The five senses are the ministers of the soul. Yet, the average human looks without seeing, listens without hearing, moves without physical awareness, inhales without awareness of odor or fragrance, and talks without thinking,"* he observed.

Geniuses such as da Vinci, Mozart, or Einstein fostered living in a stimulus-rich environment. As a consequence, many of them were synesthetes. They could take in an impression with one sense and connect the stimulus to an impression relating to another sense (e.g., *"this sound tastes like lemon"*). Synesthesia is built on the principle of combining different sensory impressions and stimuli. And noticing and combining different stimuli may similarly lead you to a novel idea. So, consider adopting this genius strategy.

Cultivate present-moment awareness and sharpen your five senses: visual (seeing), auditory (hearing), kinesthetic (feeling or touching), olfactory (smelling) and gustatory (tasting). A fun way to start is to have a wine-tasting evening with your friends or business partners. But make sure that you and your guests truly savor the wine with all your five senses. One final word: Don't forget to sharpen your sixth sense, too: a well-developed intuition is priceless when it comes to making difficult decisions.

10. STOP being busy all the time. START harmonizing focused doing and relaxed being.

When do you typically get your best ideas? When you're busy working your ass off at work? Or rather when you undergo relaxing activities, such as doing sports, having fun with friends, taking a shower, among many others? All around the world, people confirm with their answers that we get our best ideas when we are relaxed.

When you relax, you *ARE*. Taking a break and undergoing relaxing activities allows you to refresh your mind, gain a new or more detached perspective on the issue at hand, and look at your work and your current work challenge at hand with a fresh mind when you return from your break to continue working on it. As Leonardo da Vinci put it: *"It is well that you should often leave off work and take a little relaxation because when you come back to it you are a better judge."*

Moreover, and even more importantly, like all other people, you tend to get your best ideas not when you consciously work and think, but when you take a break and let go. If you learn to bring focused, passionate Doing and relaxed Being into a balanced, harmonious rhythm, you more often and more easily *"get into the zone"*, the highly enjoyable state of optimal experience or "being in flow" where time ceases to exist and you effortlessly and easily perform at your best in the present moment. And when you get into the state of flow, it's possible that you experience a moment of breakthrough creativity at the peak of the Genius Journey, the 11th and final secret stop.

START letting go to get into flow and get a breakthrough

Breakthrough ideas typically come as sudden flashes of insight after a thinker has worked hard on a tough, important challenge for a longer period of time (days, weeks, months, and even years) and then takes time out to relax and let go of the issue at hand. Once you give your mind a break from constant doing and from conscious thinking about the challenge, you allow your subconscious mind to incubate on the problem and *"breed out the right solution."* Once you *"get illuminated"* and receive a breakthrough idea from a subconscious source, you have total certainty that *"this is it"*, and you just need to take time to flesh out and verify the idea. As such, the process of incubation has four stages: Preparation, Incubation, Illumination, and Verification.

Archimedes had his famous *"Eureka!"* moment while taking time off work to take a bath. Follow his example: Work hard, but at the same time, make sure that you regularly stop doing and give yourself some time to relax and BE and completely let go of your challenge. But letting go may require huge courage. That is why you have to start the Genius Journey to discover your genius with destination stop number one: Stop your doubts, worries, and fears. Start to be a courageous, action-oriented, and persistent believer.

> "The people who are crazy enough to think they can change the world are the ones who do."
> —STEVE JOBS

CHAPTER 7 — EXECUTIVE SUMMARY: CREATIVE LEADERSHIP

Creative leadership is on the rise to lead organizations to success in the innovation economy and to creatively maneuver the highly dynamic business environment of the 21st century driven by speed, exponential changes, complexity, risks and surprises.

- Creative leaders make meaning and follow a positive agenda that serves the greater good as a constitutional part of their definition. Their values and actions distinguish them from traditional or authoritarian leaders.

- Creative leadership aims to elevate leaders in business and other fields to higher levels of consciousness and creativity that are needed to resolve the huge challenges of humanity.

- While creative leadership is an emerging new domain in business, creative leaders have existed for centuries in business as in the sciences, arts, and social and political causes.

- Breakthrough ideas almost always flow from subconscious or superconscious sources. The process of incubation allows creative leaders to tap into these sub- and superconscious realms and experience Eureka moments of peak creativity. Humanity needs more of these extraordinary breakthrough ideas to collectively resolve the huge challenges that threaten our prosperity and survival.

- While top business leaders express a need and desire to develop creative leaders, there is a disconnect in effective creative leadership methods that are creative in their course design, methodology, and pedagogy. While most traditional leadership approaches fall short of creativity, programs to enhance individual creativity go in the right direction but lack critical components that encourage breakthrough creativity.

- Genius Journey is a new creative leadership development method I developed to close the gap in both effective and creative leadership programs. The method uses a journey metaphor to guide candidates towards transformational mindset shifts to become authentic creative leaders for the innovation economy.

- Creative leadership candidates who travel the Genius Journey visit ten destinations where they learn what limiting mindsets stop them and what empowering mindsets allow them to reconnect to their inner creativity to reach their full creative potential.

"When nature has work to be done, she creates a genius to do it."
— RALPH WALDO EMERSON

BE ORIGINAL

Photo by Alex Knight on Unsplash

CHAPTER 8

WHAT ELSE? AN INNOVATION OUTLOOK
GRAND PICTURE (II)

What else might drive innovation in future? And what role are you going to play in the innovation game?

1. Is the Pendulum Swinging Back?
2. Why So Afraid of the Future? Human Up!
3. How the Generational Shift Will Impact Business and Innovation
4. These Creative Laws Govern Innovation
5. Innovative Spaces: From Cubeville to Idea City
6. Innovation: Are You Just Talking the Talk or Walking Your Talk?
7. What's Your Innovation Mastery Level?
8. Success Ingredients of Top Achievers in Innovation and Beyond
* Executive Summary

8.1. IS THE PENDULUM SWINGING BACK?

In Chapter 1, we learned that humanity has moved into the innovation economy, where the key competitive advantage of individuals, companies and countries alike is creation — the ability to use existing and newly emerging theories, know-how and technologies to create novel, original and meaningful value. In the coming 2-3 decades, creativity and innovation rule are said to be the key drivers of business success and economic prosperity.

That is, provided the pendulum that drives or impairs the free flow of goods, people, ideas and capital isn't swinging back.

The pendulum: Swinging back and forth between two extreme poles

In Chapter 1, I detailed the timing, direction, and impact of change. We learned that change typically unfolds in one of four directional movements: linear change, cyclical change (or the wave), the spiral, and finally, the pendulum.

The pendulum describes a directional movement where forces of change swing back and forth between two extreme poles in fairly regular time intervals. In many countries, political change follows the movement of a pendulum. For example, in the USA, political power regularly swings back and forth between two parties promoting more liberal (Democrats) and conservative (Republicans) policies, with occupying the presidency and control of both Congressional chambers representing the extreme pinnacle of power. But how about economic change?

Economic change seems to follow a pendulum movement, too. Here, the (international) movements of ideas, goods, people and capital are the decisive factor swinging the pendulum back and forth between the poles of *"free flow and international/global trade"* and *"protectionist barriers and nationalistic/domestic trade."*

Describing the economic change pendulum over time

How did the pendulum swing back and forth between these poles of free trade and globalization on the one side and protectionism and deglobalization on the other side in the past two centuries?

The period 1850-1914 saw a high phase of modern globalization, with international trade playing a major role in the economic activities of the leading European countries. The era marked an apex in intellectual activities, witnessing many groundbreaking scientific discoveries (such as Einstein's theory of relativity in 1905), which inspired new ventures in burgeoning industries like chemistry and electricity.

This period of economic, intellectual and technological progress and prosperity ended with the outbreak of World War I, a major discontinuity that made the pendulum swing back: The period between 1914 and 1949 was a time of deglobalization. Nationalistic parties and autocratic leaders took power in many countries and protected their local economies by regulating and limiting the free movement of goods, people, ideas, and capital. Protectionism and the cold-hearted pursuit of national interests by most countries led to the Great Depression and culminated in World War II.

After the deglobalized period of two World Wars had destroyed millions of people and nations, the pendulum swung back again: The period 1950 to 2008 saw a fresh phase of globalization driven by the goods and foreign direct investments of thousands of multinational companies, supported by a series of multilateral trade agreements (the GATT rounds) that reduced tariffs and non-tariff trade barriers, by the creation of free-trade agreements (such as the EU, NAFTA, ASEAN, among others), and technological innovations (such as computerization and the Internet) and transportation advances (such as container ships) that reduced costs and time intervals of international trade. This latest phase of globalization produced a new flood of prosperity and technological progress and also doubled the number of countries that embraced the concepts of human rights and democracy in its last two decades.

The financial crisis of 2008 was a major discontinuity that, some experts argue, has made the pendulum swing back and has started a new phase of deglobalization. In the past years, many countries saw again the rise of reactionary leaders who won elections based on protectionist populist policies or took power by military force. Politicians are talking about *"building walls," "My country first," "Cleaning up the problem of drugs or illegal immigrants,"* and *"Fining companies who export jobs and capital"* get voted into power in many countries. Regulators try to control and limit the free flow of power, people, capital and ideas to protect the local economy and domestic political interests. So, is the pendulum swinging back? And will this lead to a new outbreak in trade wars —or even shooting wars— that will limit prosperity and competition?

What are the consequences of inhibiting or promoting free (international) movements of goods, people and ideas?

Protectionist and nationalistic policies temporarily secure the interests of the old establishment and secure jobs in old industries through tariffs, non-tariff trade barriers, and unfavorable investment regulations or immigration policies. They temporarily prolong the life of corporate

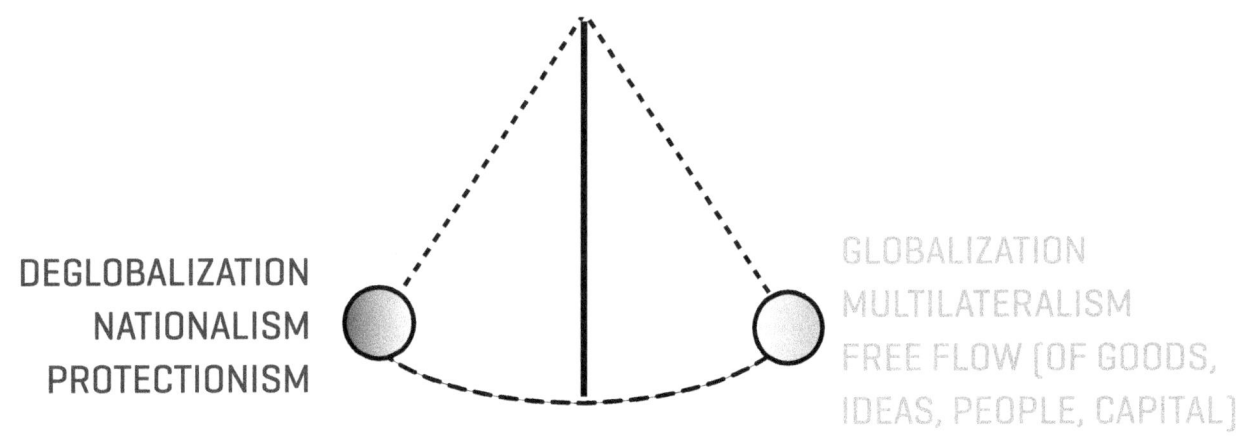

DEGLOBALIZATION
NATIONALISM
PROTECTIONISM

GLOBALIZATION
MULTILATERALISM
FREE FLOW (OF GOODS,
IDEAS, PEOPLE, CAPITAL)

Timeline

- **US Independence & Revolutionary Wars (1775-1783)**
- **1789-1815 French Revolution & Napoleon Wars**
- **European Revolutions (1848)**
- **WWI (1914-1918)**

Decades: 1750s | 1760s | 1770s | 1780s | 1790s | 1800s | 1810s | 1820s | 1830s | 1840s | 1850s | 1860s | 1870s | 1880s | 1890s | 1900s | 1910s

THE GRAND REVOLUTIONS →
← **RESTORATION**
1ST WAVE OF GLOBALIZATION →
← **INTERWAR**

POLITICS & ECONOMICS:
- Age of Enlightenment · First democratic governments in the US and France · "Liberté, égalité, fraternité" ·
- Vienna Congress (1815) · Biedermeier period ·
- 1st wave of globalization driven by nation states · International trade (colonization & Imperialism) · Scientific progress ·

INDUSTRIES & TECHNOLOGIES:
- Telegraph Electricity · Internal combustion engine ·
- Steam · Railway · Steel · Telegraph · Electricity ·

---

dinosaurs and some old jobs, but at a high cost: They cut off local markets and consumers from access to superior goods, cutting-edge technologies, revolutionary ideas, foreign direct and capital investments, and the brightest global talents. But eventually, the pendulum will swing back again, the market will open again, and the local corporate dinosaurs will face the fate of creative destruction.

In contrast, policies promoting the free international flow of goods, people, ideas and capital lead to waves of new technological innovations, ventures, investments and prosperity. They create new jobs in new leading industries that will drive economies and create prosperity for the next decades. They attract some of the smartest minds who think the boldest ideas and have the energy and talents to make them happen. Innovation and economic growth flourish in times and environments where ideas, goods, people, and capital flow freely.

But does economic development really follow a pendulum movement?

Instead of swinging like a pendulum, the economic movement of "globalization vs. deglobalization" and "economic freedom vs. protectionism" that impact innovation may also follow a more optimistic pattern: the spiral. Thereby, while moving back and forth, we also make regular upward leaps as we learn from past mistakes, and also produce new waves of innovations and technologies that create more prosperity and progress for ever more people. So, we may temporarily

Timeline

WWII (1939-1945) · **End of Bretton Woods currency accord & oil crisis (1971-1973)** · **Financial Crisis (2008-)**

1920s | 1930s | 1940s | 1950s | 1960s | 1970s | 1980s | 1990s | 2000s | 2010s | 2020s | 2030s | 2040s | 2050s

- **1ST GLOBALIZATION**
- **INTERWAR PERIOD**
- **2ND WAVE OF GLOBALIZATION**

Great Depression · Rise of communism & fascism · Collapse of international trade — and many democracies

2nd wave of globalization (driven by Multinational Corporations) · Multilateral trade agreements (GATT) · Free-trade agreements (EU, ASEAN, NAFTA) - International agreements on FX rates

Chemistry · Internal combustion engine ·

Aviation · Petroleum · Electronics ·

Digital Networks · Software · New media

---

move back in the coming years, but let's be hopeful that in the long run, humanity will continue to move up on the global prosperity spiral.

How is the "tug of war" of opposing economic directions going to turn out?

Well, it's too early to say. On the one hand, political forces promoting protectionism and nationalism have gained momentum or even power in many countries in the aftermath of the financial crisis of 2008. It seems we've begun moving backward on the pendulum (or spiral) towards more deglobalization, protectionism, and preservation. At the same time, innovation will continue to drive economic prosperity in the coming decades, with digitization only further amplifying this meta-trend. This offers major opportunities for those countries and creative cities that decide to boldly go forward and create free environments that attract international capital and the brightest scientific and creative minds to become an innovation hotbed driving the Sixth Wave of technology innovation (ca. 2020-2045).

> "When the winds of change blow, some people build walls and others build windmills."
> —CHINESE PROVERB

8.2. WHY SO AFRAID OF THE FUTURE? HUMAN UP!

In recent months, I have encountered many businesspeople who somehow seemed afraid: afraid of making a mistake at work; afraid of failing with a project they've been assigned to lead; afraid of not having all the details of how an event will unfold; afraid of making decisions; afraid of standing up for their beliefs, values and convictions; afraid of harming their career; afraid of potentially losing their job. Many of the worried faces belonged to smart and seasoned business professionals who had every reason to walk and stand tall. I started to wonder: Why are they so afraid?

What's behind the emotional state of being afraid?

Doubts, worries, and fears. As we discussed in the last chapter, learning to overcome doubts, worries, and fears is the pivotal first step to entering the realm of unlimited creativity in my creative leadership method, Genius Journey.

Fear is a natural response to prevent us from physical harm. But the doubts, worries, and fears of modern businesspeople rarely concern physical survival but are based on emotional and psychological dread that takes place only in our minds. Common examples of such socially conditioned and learned fears are the fear of losing control, of social rejection ("losing face"), or of having to confront the unknown. Often, these fears don't constitute a real threat now but relate to an event imagined to possibly take place in the future.

What's wrong with being afraid?

Doubts, worries and fears stop you from producing results, from growing as a person or as a business, and from reaching your full potential. They keep you small, stagnant, and limited. In order to start the journey to rediscover your genius and true potential, you need to stop your doubts, worries, and fears, and start being a courageous, action-oriented and persistent believer.

Some of you may want to argue: It's easy to talk down to me from your point of view. Just imagine walking in my shoes: I have a family to feed. I have bills and debts to pay. I have a job to lose. I may not have enough money to retire when I am old. Can't you see why I am so afraid?

Well, I was once walking in shoes very similar to yours — heavy, bulky and ill-fitting shoes. When I realized who I really am and what I should really do with my life, I courageously walked away from a high-paying job in corporate banking. I've continued my journey on the less-trodden path — boldly and barefoot. I have never looked back.

My new journey into the unknown was adventurous and risky, arduous and at times rocky, but also highly rewarding and wondrous. In 2005, I started the innovation company Thinkergy and embarked on a mission to create innovators. In the last decade, I didn't make as much money as I would have in my old career, but it didn't really matter (and it was always enough to pay the bills and live simply but comfortably). In the coming decade, I believe I am going to make a lot more money in my new career, but that really doesn't matter either.

What matters is that, in primal human style, I have courageously moved forward with those who chose to join me on our Thinkergy journey, and we creatively deal with all the opportunities and challenges that we encounter.

How can you stop being so afraid?

Human up! Commit to becoming a true human being again. Have you ever wondered how primal humans rose to the pinnacle of the evolutionary pyramid? Because of our long teeth and sharp claws? Because of our giant size and heavy weight? Because we move faster or outmuscle all others?

Humans have become the dominant species because we think smartly and act courageously. We flexibly and creatively deal with dangers and challenges. We try things and fail, then try again until we succeed. We eagerly and curiously learn and grow. We creatively invented tools to hunt, defend ourselves, and make our lives easier. We care and feel for others. We cooperate and jointly develop effective tactics and strategies to hunt prey and overcome predators and competitors.

Humanity's journey started in the African savannah with a small group of primal humans who had the curiosity and tremendous courage to explore and venture into the unknown. They wandered lands and continents. They crossed mountain ranges and oceans. They flexibly and creatively dealt with new challenges of life in a foreign, often hostile environment. In his theory of evolution, Charles Darwin observed, *"It is not the strongest of the species that survives, nor the most intelligent, but the one most responsive to change."* That's us! That's you!

We're all descendants of these brave, action-oriented, curious, flexible creative primal humans who, against all odds, conquered the world. So why are you so afraid of not being able to live up to the future? How did we allow society and our institutions to condition us and turn so many of us into fearful, docile sheep — to neglect our essential nature of being bold, confident and creative?

What can you do to bounce back?

Human up! Stop all those doubts, worries and fears in your mind. Shape up and stand up confident and tall. Go primal and reconnect to your essential core as a courageous, flexible, creative, and caring human.

We need to *"human up"* quickly to ensure our species stays on top of the pyramid in light of the onset of artificial intelligence (AI), robots, and smart interconnected machines. What will keep us on top is not our ability to carefully deliberate, calculate, analyze, and scrutinize. It's our courageous human core, our ability to flexibly adapt, create, cooperate, care, and love.

In order to remain the dominant species, we had better learn how to rein in all those doubts, worries, and fears and reconnect to our essential core of being courageous, action-oriented, and creative humans. But how exactly can we *"human up"*? Here are ten tips.

1. Let go of the illusion of total control of your destiny. *"If you want to make God laugh, tell him about your plans,"* said Woody Allen. We're living in a highly dynamic world with too many variables beyond our control. So, while I endorse making plans, I recommend executing them in a flexible way to respond to changes and surprises.

2. Believe all will work out well in the end. Have you ever experienced a negative incident that, in hindsight, turned out to be a blessing in disguise? Start seeing setbacks and temporary failures as what they really are: feedback to stir you forward toward personal happiness and success. Don't be afraid. Honestly confront the facts of your present reality, do what's needed to survive now and increase the odds of future success, and believe that in the end, everything will turn out well. Consider living by the following mantra: *"Everything that happens to me is the best possible thing that can happen to me."*

3. Realize most doubts, worries and fears aren't real. They are just disempowering, limiting thoughts going on in your head. As Mark Twain put it, *"I have been through some terrible things in my life, some of which actually happened."*

So, instead of entertaining fearful thoughts about a distant future, focus on what you need to do now. Practice mindfulness to gain more awareness of your inner dialogue, let anxious thoughts pass without attaching energy to them, and pay attention to the present moment.

4. Just do it. *"Always do what you fear"*, recommends the American essayist Ralph Waldo Emerson. So, human up. Proactively facing a fear is the fastest way to overcome it, and to turn the unknown into a new experience. So, why not human up and finally ask your boss for the raise you both know you deserve?

5. Be bold but don't be stupid. The Greek philosopher Aristotle considered courage *"the mean between fear and recklessness"*. For example, if you're afraid of snakes, consider visiting a snake farm to encounter and learn about their ways, and maybe touch a non-poisonous one — but don't be reckless and walk in front of a cobra. In business, courageously take action on new projects, but don't engage in activities that may bring you into serious trouble, such as doing things that are illegal, highly speculative or unethical.

6. Shape up. Getting and staying fit will not only make your body stronger, leaner and more flexible; thanks to the body-mind connection, it will also have the same effects on your mind. Physical exercise positively changes the neurochemical balance in your brain to make you more confident, courageous and happy. As the ancient Romans already knew, *"Mens sana in corpore sano"* (A sound mind in a sound body).

7. Open up. Anxiety is a sign of a closed, judgmental mind. It's the opposite of the curious, open and flexible mindset of primal humans who explored the world and learned how to seize its opportunities. So, open your mind to new trends, ideas, viewpoints and ways of doing things to keep from falling behind in a fast-changing world. As the American social philosopher Eric Hoffer said: *"In a time of drastic change it is the learners who inherit the future. The learned usually find themselves equipped to live in a world that no longer exists."*

8. Relax, recharge and sleep. Sleep is crucial to optimum physical and cognitive performance. Consider taking a power nap once you notice your energy levels are down, and plan for enough downtime in your day to recharge and relax. Most importantly, ensure you get 7-8 hours of reenergizing sleep every night.

9. Reconnect to the hunter in you. Nowadays, too many businesspeople have become *"farmers"*: they passively sit back, hoping to perpetually reap the rewards of the seeds sown long ago, and to squeeze the last drops of milk out of ragged cash cows. Recall that primal humans were hunters. It's in our essential primal nature to move and actively hunt for —and bring down— prey that often is much bigger than us. Become a hunter again, too: life is full of new opportunities once you venture out.

10. Move on when too much is wrong. When you work in an environment that regularly fills your mind with doubtful, worrisome and fearful thoughts, it's a sign that something is seriously wrong. Whether you feel afraid of a venomous colleague or drained by constant political maneuvering, acknowledge persistent feelings of anxiety, stress and unhappiness for what they really are: a signal to make a change.

Leave that poisonous, energy-sapping or stagnant environment behind for a new hunting ground. Join another firm, find or join a start-up, or dedicate your talents to a meaningful non-profit organization. Life is too short to waste on a cause that doesn't feel right for you. So, if it's time for you to move on, human up!

> *"Most people, unleashed, are innovators. We're this great species of tool-using animals who likes to make our world better."*
> —JEFF BEZOS

8.3. HOW THE GENERATIONAL SHIFT WILL IMPACT BUSINESS AND INNOVATION

A major generational shift is taking place in the workplace in this decade. So, let's understand more about the concept of social generations, how the socialization of different generational cohorts impacts the way they think, work, decide, communicate, manage and lead, and how they tend to respond to change and innovation.

Background: Training a group of global nomads

In April 2017, I had the pleasure of training a fascinating group of highly successful businesspeople in our creative leadership method Genius Journey. Led by an impressive young Briton, the training group entirely consisted of an accumulation of global nomads who flew in from all around the world to Phuket, Thailand, for a joint gig and team holiday. Together, the group operates an online platform for business coaches used to organize an annual international online conference and to disseminate quality content for a global coaching community.

All Millennials in their late 20s or early 30s, these fourteen delegates came from eight diverse nationalities (UK, US, Australia, New Zealand, Austria, Croatia, Romania and India); with one exception, none of them actually lived in their home country. Moreover, while the group had a hub connecting all spokes, both were "moving targets": the hub had only recently shifted from Costa Rica to Croatia, and most of the individuals (spokes) were regularly traveling to different countries. Nevertheless, they all collaborated together successfully across different time zones using the internet and modern communication solutions.

Why do I tell you this story? Being myself a member of Generation X, training this group of international global nomads and witnessing them working in the evening after our training with other colleagues who couldn't make the offsite made me realize the huge differences in work styles, work-life aspirations and educational backgrounds of Millennials (also known as Generation Y) compared to those generations who still tend to run or influence most businesses today.

For the first time, I fully understood the importance of appreciating the style differences between social generations, and I began investigating and pondering how the impending generational shift in the workplace will affect business and innovation.

Introducing the concepts of social generations

In social science, the concept of social generations describes cohorts of people born within a specific time period (ranging between 15 to 30 years) who jointly experience significant historical landmark events and witness the emergence of certain iconic technologies and trendy cultural phenomena during their formative years and while coming of age.

Because the shared experiences within a single generation differ from those of previous or later cohorts, generations tend to vary from each other in their values, aspirations and motivations, the ways they work, communicate, make decisions, interact with certain technologies, etc.

	Ca. 1925-1946 **TRADITIONALISTS**	Ca. 1946-1964 **BABY BOOMERS**	Ca. 1965-1980 **GENERATION X**	Ca. 1981-1995 **MILLENNIALS**	Ca. 1995-2010 **POST-MILLENNIALS**
Also known as	Silent Generation	"Boomers"	"MTV Generation"	Generation Y	Generation Z, Gen 2020
Social Markers / Landmark Events	Great Depression (30s) Fascism / Communism World War II (39-45)	Cold War and Cuba Crisis Vietnam War (65-73) Moon landing (69) Civil/women's rights (60s)	AIDS, nuclear arms race (80s), Challenger & Chernobyl disasters(86), Berlin Wall (89)	New Millennium Dot Com Boom (& Bust, 90s) 9/11 (01)	9/11, Afghanistan/Iraq war (00s), Asian tsunami (04), Global financial crisis 08), Wiki Leaks & Arab spring
Iconic Technologies (* = Go-to product*)	Radio, Motor vehicles, Aircraft	Transistor radio, TV*, Audio cassette	VCR, Walkman, Personal Computers* (IBM PC, Macintosh)	Internet, Mobile phones*, Email, SMS, DVD, Playstation, Xbox, iPod	iPad/Tablets*, Apps Google, Facebook, Twitter, Wii, PS3, Android
Cultural phenomena (music, movies, TV))	Jazz, Swing (Glen Miller, Frank Sinatra) Gone with the Wind, Advent of TV	Rock 'n Roll (Elvis, Beatles, Rolling Stones), Disco Easy Rider, The Graduate, Color TV	MTV pop culture (Madonna, New Wave, Nirvana), House E.T., Star Wars	Rap, Hip Hop (Eminem, Puff Daddy, Britney Spears, Jennifer Lopez) Titanic, Reality TV, Pay TV	Justin Bieber, Rihanna, Taylor Swift Avatar, 3D movies, Smart TV

Introducing the present generations and their sociological background

Let's gain an overview of the different generational cohorts and the landmark events, technologies and cultural phenomena that shaped them (here note that the time spans between different generations are indicative only and vary in the literature, and the terminology follows the most common one developed in the USA):

- The **Lost Generation** (1883-1900) describes the cohort who grew up in the culturally and scientifically rich period of the late imperialistic era and fought in World War I, a traumatic experience that led to their name coined by Gertrude Stein and popularized by Earnest Hemingway. At the point of writing, there is one remaining survivor of this generation.

- The **G.I. Generation** (1901-1924) includes those who lived through WWI in their younger years. Because they had to master the Great Depression and fight in World War II, they are also called the *"Greatest Generation"* in the USA.

- The **Traditionalists** (1925-1945) include most of those who were born or growing up during the Great Depression and World War II and who fought the Korean War and, in some cases, during the Vietnam War. Also called the Silent Generation (or *"Silents"* because they were socialized at a time of conformity to authority), they grew up with Jazz and Swing (Glen Miller, Frank Sinatra), flocked to *"Gone with the Wind"* in the cinema and saw the advent of TV.

- The **Baby Boomers** (1946-1964) got their name from the baby boom following World War II. They are a large demographic cohort, and due to the long time span, they are sometimes split into early boomers (1946-1955) and late boomers (1956-1964). They grew up during the early Cold War era with the Cuban Missile Crisis and the Vietnam War and witnessed the moon landing and the civil and women's rights movements that challenged the established order. Important cultural phenomena shaping the Boomers were Rock 'n' Roll (Elvis, Beatles, Rolling Stones, Woodstock) and the Boomtown Disco period, the movies *"Easy Rider"* and *"The Graduate,"* and the arrival of Color TV.

- I am a member of **Generation X** (Gen X, 1965-1980), the *"baby bust"* generation characterized by a drop in birth rates following the invention of the birth control pill. We experienced a series of negative landmark events and social markers, such as the AIDS crisis, a renewed nuclear arms race in the late Cold War era, the Challenger explosion and the Chornobyl nuclear disaster, but also the sensational fall of the Berlin Wall and lifting of the iron curtain in Eastern Europe. Sometimes called the *"MTV generation,"* we enjoyed watching pop videos (Madonna, Michael Jackson) and listening to new wave and house music. Movies such as E.T., Star Wars or Alien made an impact on us, too, and the Walkman, VCR and in particular Personal Computers (IBM PC, Macintosh) were iconic technologies for us.

- The **Millennials** (Generation Y, 1981-1994) grew up during the Dot-com boom, enjoyed the turn of the Millennium and suffered from the 9/11 terror attacks. Being mostly the offspring of the demographically large baby boomers, they are also a huge cohort that has meanwhile surpassed the number of Baby Boomers in the US. Millennials witnessed in their youth a series of major technological shifts such as the advent of the Internet, mobile phones, email, SMS, and the DVD. Cultural phenomena that shaped Millennials were hip hop (Eminem, Puff Daddy) and singers like Britney Spears or Jennifer Lopez, the movie *"Titanic,"* the emergence of Reality TV and Pay TV, and fancy new gaming playing consoles (PlayStation, Xbox).

- The **Post-Millennials** (1995-2010) witnessed the wars in Afghanistan and Iraq, the Asian tsunami and the global financial crisis of 2008 as landmark events. Also known as Generation Z or Gen 2020, they grew up with the iPad (and other tablets), social media (Facebook, Google, Twitter, Snapchat) and mobile apps. Culturally, Post-Millennials often have a thing with musical interpreters such as Justin Bieber, Rihanna, or Taylor Swift, and were greatly influenced by the movie *"Avatar"* and other 3D movies.

Introducing the work styles of different generations

Let's better understand the different mindsets, aspirations, and work styles of those generations that still form an active part of the workforce. Of course, every generation consists of many different individual types, so the following descriptions represent more of a dominating tendency for each social cohort. Nevertheless, the portrayed differences reflect the specific social markers and technologies as well as the educational upbringing of different generations.

- Having to live through the Great Depression and World War II in their early lives, **Traditionalists** learned the hard way. Being educated in a more formal, instructive, disciplined, and military-style education system, "Silents" show great respect and deference for authority. They follow established rules and policies and feel uncomfortable with conflict, change and new technologies. Most Silents dutifully and loyally worked hard in one career for one employer throughout their working life.

- The **Baby Boomers** grew up in the economic boom after WWII. They were educated in a structured, data-focused and evidence-based style. Boomers are career-focused workaholics who are driven by titles and financial rewards and show respect for power. While being early IT adopters, they feel unsure about new technological advances and take time to embrace change.

- **Generation Xers** like me grew up in the sober social and economic climate of the 80s. After witnessing the first waves of corporate rightsizing exercise early on in our work careers, many Gen Xers developed a pragmatic to pessimistic outlook on traditional corporate careers and evolved into self-reliant, independent free agents. They are pragmatic and resourceful, creative and entrepreneurial, self-managing and adaptable, cynical and skeptical of authority. They value work-life balance and personal freedom. Gen Xers are digital immigrants who grew up with PCs and the Internet and feel comfortable keeping up with newly emerging technologies.

- **Millennials** were mostly raised by baby boomer *"helicopter parents on steroids"* and a more nurturing, *"touchy-feely"* education system that was more participative, emotional and story-based. No wonder that many Gen Yers approach work collaboratively and are very socially engaged. They are said to be idealistic, dedicated and goal-oriented, and want to do meaningful work. Millennials are digital natives who are "native speakers" of the digital language of computers, the Internet, videos, video games and social media that they all learned to master in their adolescence.

- **Post-Millennials** are technology natives who've widely used the Internet from a young age. These *"technoholics"* often entirely depend on IT for doing things, with a limited grasp of offline or non-digital alternatives. Many Gen Zers start entering the workforce, often in new apprenticeships or part-time jobs. As permanent, long-term jobs will become fewer and fewer, many Post-Millennials will likely become flexible career multi-taskers who move seamlessly between established organizations and smaller *"pop-up"* ventures in rather short-term, transactional project roles, all the while longing for more security and stability.

Upcoming generational shifts in the labor market

By 2030, organizations will face massive human resources challenges due to generational shifts in the labor market:

- After the first wave of Baby Boomers (1946-1955) began already retiring en masse in the second half of the 2010s and early 2020s, the second wave of Boomers (1956-1964) who have been a driving force in established organizations in recent years will also leave in the second half of the 2020s.

- Gen Xers will gradually rise to power in established businesses threatened by the fast-changing, highly dynamic modern market environment. They will also continue to lead the business side of start-ups together with more digital-affine Gen Y leaders.

OVERVIEW OF WORK ASPIRATIONS, BEHAVIORS AND STYLES OF DIFFERENT SOCIAL GENERATIONS AT WORK

Born	Ca. 1925-1946	Ca. 1946-1964	Ca. 1965-1980	Ca. 1981-1995	Ca. 1995-2009
GENERATIONS	**TRADITIONALISTS**	**BABY BOOMERS**	**GENERATION X**	**MILLENNIALS**	**POST-MILLENNIALS**
General qualities and work ethic	Straightforward, thorough, dutiful, hard-working, respect authority, adherence to rules and policy, reluctant to change, uncomfortable with conflict	Workaholic, driven to succeed, team player, social and service-oriented, desire-to-please, but questions authority	Independent and self-reliant, creative and entrepreneurial, adaptable (telecommuting ok), openly speaks opinions	Dedicated and goal-oriented, looking for meaning, desire to "do it all," multi-taskers, highly involved and tenacious	To be determined
Motivational trigger	Recognition & acknowledgement	Titles and financial rewards	Work-life balance, self-reliant, entrepreneurial,	Making meaning, dedicated and goal-oriented	Playing life, longing for more security and stability
Etiquette	Formal	Professional	Casual	Relaxed	To be determined
Career views	Relational: Loyal service for life-long employment	Organizational; careers defined by employers	Portfolio: loyal to profession, not employer	Digital: works "with companies" not "for" them	Opportunistic: Work on gigs that excite me and pay me
Job changing	Unwise	Sets me back	Necessary	Part of my daily routine	What's a job? I have gigs
Average tenure	35-50 years	15 years	5 years	18-24 months	To be determined
Ideal leaders	Authoritarian Commanders; ultimate respect for authority	Commanding thinkers; respect for power	Co-ordinating doers; collaboration is key	Empowering collaborators; freedom is key	Inspiring Co-Creators
Own leadership	Command and control	Get out of the way	Coach	Partner	RSS Protagonist
Decision-making	Seeks approval	Team informed	Team included	Team-based	Sonar / individualistic
Problem-solving	Hierarchical	Horizontal	Independent	Collaborative	Global tribe / independent
Feedback	No news is good news	Once per year	Weekly / Daily	On Demand	Continuous, social sonar
Education: Learning Format & Environment	Formal and instructive Military style Didactic & disciplined	Relaxed & structured Classroom style Quiet atmosphere	Spontaneous & interactive Round-table style, relaxed	Multi-sensory & visual Cafe-style, music & multi-modal	Student-centric & kinesthetic, Lounge room style, multi-stimulus
Training focus	Traditional, the hard way, on-the-job, top-down	Technical, data, evidence, "Too much and I'll quit"	Practical, applications, case studies, required to keep me	Emotional, participative, stories, continuous, expected	Multimodal, interactive, eLearning, playing life
Technology use	Uncomfortable	Unsure	Unable to work without it	Unfathomable if not provided	Lifelong use
Communication (style, frequency)	Formal letter, Face-to-face Linear, in digestible amounts Top down	Face-to-face preferred, phone or email OK Semiformal, as needed, guarded	Email and Text Irreverent, whenever needed Hub and spoke	Text & Social Media (online and mobile); asynchronous, real-time, collaborative	Handheld devices, FaceTime Electro-social, highly connected
Influencers	Authority, Officials	Evidential experts	Pragmatic practitioners	Experiential peers	User-generated forums
Sales & Marketing Branding (& influencers)	Print & radio Persuasive Brand emergence (telling)	Mass / traditional media Above-the-line Brand-loyal (authorities)	Direct / targeted media Below-the-line Brand switches (experts)	Viral / electronic media Through friends No brand loyalty (friends)	Interactive campaigns Positive brand association Brand evangelism (trends)
Financial values	Long-term saving Cash, no credit	Long-term needs Cash & Credit	Medium-term goals Credit savvy, life-stage debt	Short-term wants Credit dependent Life-style debt	Impulsive purchases E-Stores Life-long debt

Source: Adapted from: Lancaster, L. C. & Stillman, D. (2003). When Generations Collide. New York, HarperBusiness (and a potpourri of other Internet resources).

- In 2016, Millennials overtook the baby boomers as the biggest group in the labor market. In the coming years, they will gain strong influence as Bruce Tulgan notes: *"We should not expect the new Millennial workforce to eventually 'grow up and settle down' and start thinking and behaving more like those of previous generations. Rather, the 'grown-ups' will find themselves thinking and behaving more and more like the Millennials."*
- The chairs left behind by the retiring Baby Boomers will be filled by Gen Zers starting their work life (although not the ones in the corner offices).

Implications of generational shifts on innovation:

How will these generational shifts impact innovation? No one knows for sure. However, by factoring in the educational upbringing, general work qualities, and attitudes towards technology and change, I foresee at the risk of being wrong the following nine innovation impacts of generational shifts:

1. Expect innovation to flourish when the pragmatic, creative, and entrepreneurial Gen Xers innovate alongside the collaborative, idealistic Gen Yers supported by the fresh ideas of the flexible, multicultural, and balanced Gen Zers. Coupled with the shift from a managerial to an entrepreneurial society, I even foresee an Innonaissance (an innovation-driven Renaissance).

2. Innovation focus will shift to meaningful emphasis from making money first "regardless of what it takes" (Boomers) to focusing on "making meaning first, then we will make money anyway" (idealistic Millennials coupled with pragmatic Gen Xers).

3. After the gradual disappearance of the remaining Baby Boomers in the next decade, everyone remaining in the workforce will be a digital citizen: either an immigrant (Gen X), native (Gen Y), or digital everything (Gen Z). Expect almost all innovations to have digital elements by 2030.

4. Powered by the advent of the Sixth Wave of technological change, new digital, clean and human-centered lead technologies and related industries will emerge and will propel economic growth for the next two decades.

5. When contrasting the different educational upbringing of the generations, and linking it to the four bases of TIPS (theories, ideas, people, systems), I noticed that the Traditionalists were educated in a disciplined military style (Systems base), Baby Boomers in an evidence- and data-focused style (Theories), Gen Xers in a pragmatic, applications and solutions-oriented style (Ideas), and finally Millennials in a collaborative, story-oriented and kinesthetic style (People).

Interestingly, I also spotted a pattern in how the influence of the different TIPS bases impacted the innovation focus of different eras: mass-market, systemic and operational (1946-70, run by the G.I. Generation supported by Traditionalists); systemic, data-based and quantitative (1970-95, run by Traditionalists and the Baby Boomers); and data-based, conceptual and entrepreneurial (1995-2020, driven by Baby Boomers seconded by Gen Xers). Looking ahead to the next 25 years, I predict the character of many innovations to be more entrepreneurial, social, qualitative, and life-affirming (echoing the Sixth Wave's focus on digital, clean, and human tech).

6. Advanced creativity training courses and innovation project workshops will continue to predominantly take place in real-life formats. This is because of the educational upbringing (Cafe-style, social and collaborative) and preferred training focus (emotional, participative, stories, continuous, expected) of the now largest generation at work (Millennials), coupled with the training preferences of Gen Xers (spontaneous, interactive, round-table style, relaxed with a practical, applications-oriented focus), who will increasingly sign the checks to pay for innovation education.

7. Regarding the process side of innovation in the future, I also foresee the emergence of virtual and mixed reality solutions that allow innovation team members based in various creative cities to collaborate in real-time on an innovation project in a virtual reality space under the guidance of an innovation process expert.

8. With the gradual departure of the Baby Boomers from the C-suite of big corporations, I forecast the renovation and creative cultural transformation of many established corporations led by the more pragmatic, entrepreneurial and creative Gen X leaders.

9. Innovation will continue moving from the closed towards a more open paradigm as collaborative Millennials and technology-addicted Post-Millennials gradually gain more influence in the labor market—provided open innovation is organized in a win-win-win way.

Conclusion: Generational shifts and developments —hopefully— never stop, and the next generation has already emerged: Generation Alpha (2011 to mid-2020s — my daughter Zoë is part of Gen Alpha).

Do you now have a better grasp of both the generational differences in socialization, education, and work behavior (work aspirations, attitudes, and styles) and the scope of the generational shifts in the labor market unfolding in the next decade? Once the remaining hordes of Baby Boomers have gone into their well-deserved retirement, many ways of how we do business and innovate will change. Hopefully, my predictions and rationales are useful to realign your business and innovation set-up.

> There is a mysterious cycle in human events. To some generations much is given. Of other generations much is expected. This generation of Americans has a rendezvous with destiny.
> —FRANKLIN D. ROOSEVELT

8.4. THESE CREATIVE LAWS GOVERN INNOVATION

Have you ever thought about creative laws that govern an innovation process? In the context of a particular domain, a law is a statement of fact, deduced from observation, that a particular natural or scientific phenomenon always occurs if certain conditions are present. It may also be a generalization based on a fact or event perceived to be recurrent. Allow me to share with you a series of creative laws that other innovation experts and I have noticed during our years of work in the innovation domain.

1. *"Every advance in human life beings with an idea In the mind of a single person,"* notes the Canadian-American motivational speaker and author Brian Tracy. Creative outputs such as ideas or new products are deemed creative if they are novel (new, avant-garde, unprecedented, or fresh), original (individual, unique, surprising, uncommon or one of a kind) and meaningful (significant, valuable, useful, relevant, appropriate and worthwhile). The first three creative laws relate to this output-oriented definition of creativity:

- **The creative law of novelty:**
  "The more novel an idea is, the more creative it is deemed."
- **The creative law of meaning:**
  "The more meaningful and valuable an idea is, the more creative it is."
- **The creative law of originality:**
  "The more original and surprising an idea is, the more creative it is."
  - A corollary to the law of originality is the **creative law of individuality:**
    "The more someone insists upon one's individuality, the more original one's ideas."

2. Cognitive measures indicate the degree of creativity of the creative outputs of an individual or an innovation team. The following creative laws relate to the outputs of a creative thinking session:

- **The creative law of fluency:**
  "The more fluent your creative thinking, the more ideas you produce, the higher the likelihood of having at least one truly creative idea within your pool of ideas."
- **The creative law of flexibility:**
  "The greater the variety of different idea categories, the greater your idea flexibility, and the better you are as a creative thinker."
- **The creative law of elaboration:**
  "The more elaborated an idea is (or in other words: the more words it has), the more likely people will look at it and use it further."
- **The creative law of real ideas:**
  "An idea is only useful if it's written down as a real, full idea, as any idea elements not committed to paper will vanish from the mind. In linguistic terms, a real idea is a sentence with a verb (i.e., 'Do something')."

3. Innovation facilitators often use creativity tools to stimulate an innovation group's creative thinking in the idea generation phase. Here, we can observe ...

- **The creative law of creativity tools:**
  "The broader the range of creativity tools a facilitator uses the higher the chance that some tools resonate and trigger truly outstanding ideas."

4. Creativity techniques use triggers (such as an association, mental images, or a scheme) as a stimulus to propel your thinking to a new starting point, from where it is easier to come up with fresh, uncommon ideas. In their book *Sticky Wisdom*, Matt Kingdon and his colleagues from the innovation company *?What If!* emphasize the importance of quality stimuli for quality creativity in ...

- **The creative law of stimulus:**
  "The quality and uniqueness of a stimulus input have a direct impact on the quality and uniqueness of the idea outputs."

5. Even the most potent creativity tools and most unique stimuli may fail to reveal their magic when a person *"has not collected enough dots to connect,"* or in other words, lacks a broad knowledge, skills, and experience repertoire. Hence ....

- **The creative law of knowledge:**
  "The broader your knowledge, skills and experience repertoire, the more dots you have to connect, the easier it is to use a stimulus as a launch pad for highly novel and original ideas."

- A corollary to this law is the **creative law of diversity:**

  "The more diverse the knowledge, skills and experiences within an innovation team, the more diverse dots it has to connect, the more original their ideas."

6. While specialized knowledge is a necessary prerequisite to mastering a domain, it may trap your creativity in the *"expert tunnel"* if it is not complemented by broad general knowledge.

Likewise, working at an intellectual hotspot of a domain (such as a top-notch university or a global business hub) may make it more difficult to break away from mainstream thinking and come up with truly novel, original ideas. These observations are reflected in the following:

- **The creative law of expertise:**

  "The deeper your specialized domain knowledge, and the narrower your general knowledge, the higher the danger you get trapped in the expert tunnel, and the lower the likelihood that you come up with truly novel and surprising solutions."

- **The creative law of the periphery:**

  "Outsiders working at the periphery, or even outside, of a domain are more likely to come up with truly outstandingly creative ideas than people working in the domain epicenter."

7. After you've generated a wide range of ideas, look for those that intrigue you. Then, design them into outstanding concepts through elaboration (i.e., detailing your idea out), combination (i.e., connecting related ideas with each other into a more valuable concept), and transmutation (i.e., taming a wild idea). Here, three more creative laws come into play:

- **The creative law of the vital few:**

  "80% of the value of an ideation session is contained in only 20% of all ideas. Discover those vital few ideas that carry within the seed of a truly great idea."

- **The creative law of the intersection:**

  "Extraordinary ideas can often be found in the intersection between seemingly unrelated ideas, concepts or disciplines. Design more novel, original and meaningful idea concepts by combining interesting ideas with each other."

- **The creative law of X steps removed:**

  "Outstanding ideas are often 'X steps removed' from the original idea. Take X steps away from the initial idea (either in sequence or in parallel) to uncover a novel, original and meaningful concept."

At Thinkergy, we have accounted for these creative laws in the design of our systematic innovation method X-IDEA. When we guide an innovation team through an innovation project, we ensure that all workshop participants successfully play on these creative laws, too.

> *"If the rules of creativity are the norm for a company, creative people will be the norm."*
> —JIM GILMORE

8.5. INNOVATIVE SPACES: FROM CUBEVILLE TO IDEA CITY

Where do you get good ideas? When you ask people around the world this question, one place almost certainly will NOT feature prominently, if at all: in the office. Why? While a non-creative culture is often to blame (as discussed in Chapter 6), another reason is that most office spaces are not specifically designed to encourage creative work.

So, how can we design modern offices for the innovation economy that encourage creativity and collaborative innovative work? Here are 10 tips for creative office design, partially inspired by visiting exemplary creative office spaces (creative agencies as well as Stanford University's D School) and considering my own experiences of working in the creative field.

Tip 1. First impressions matter.

On his first visit to the Silicon Valley-based industrial design company IDEO, management guru Tom Peters said: *"The moment I stepped into the office I knew that this is a creative place."*

So, think carefully when designing the entrance of your creative office to send a signal to your employees, customers and other visitors that this is where innovation occurs. For example, at the D School, you enter the office space via the pantry. Many creative agencies that I visited similarly feature either a bar, a flashy creative artifact, or a game element (such as table football or a pinball machine) in their entrance area to signify *"We're different."*

Tip 2. Expansive, bright thinking needs expansive, bright offices.

Make sure your creative office never physically constricts your creators; small spaces will produce small ideas.

Have many big windows and good lighting, because light is important in stimulating creative ideas. As the US writer Aaron Rose said: *"In the right light, at the right time, everything is extraordinary."*

Moreover, for a creative office space, choose a room with high ceilings if at all possible. One way to define the word *"ceiling"* is *"upper limit."* So, rooms with low ceilings limit your thinking and are good for focusing on details (such as reviewing contract clauses or financial statements). In contrast, creativity flourishes in rooms with high ceilings (which is also known as the *"cathedral effect"*) and tends to encourage your employees to think and dream big.

Tip 3. Keep it rough.

Ideation and innovation are messy and chaotic. Don't spend money on expensive carpeting and wallpaper. Instead, go for a room design where the inevitable spillage of paint or glue is no disaster. Focus on the creative work process, not on the room or the things in it. The space is for thinking about ideas, and worrying about things like nice furniture is time and energy wasted.

Tip 4. The room must fit the idea, or the idea will be deformed to fit the room.

Traditional offices are designed to separate people from each other by putting them in boxes. Managers reside in their private offices, while common employees are crammed into small cubicles. No wonder thinking is constrained and *"inside the box"* — *"Cube-villes"* actively discourage innovation.

A creative office eliminates fixed boxes to invite collaboration and unrestricted communication between employees and managers. We discuss this separately in the boxed text on the next page.

Tip 5. Make it easy to write on.

Have as many whiteboards as possible to allow employees to write down and sketch out ideas and map out information. Notice that windows and glass surfaces in the office make for a good whiteboard or sticky note space, too. Nowadays, special new dry-erase paints (such as IdeaPaint™) allow you to easily turn any wall, door or even table surface in your office into a whiteboard.

Tip 6. Put your office on wheels.

At the D-School, all furniture is on wheels. Movable tables, sofas, and whiteboards coupled with stackable chairs and small stools allows for quick reconfiguration of the office space for different tasks such as ideation sessions, prototyping, and final project presentations. Movable transparent (and ideally also writeable) separation walls make a single room either private or a large open space to cater to the differing needs of different tasks.

Tip 7. Invest in supportive technology, not expensive furniture.

The D School project was started after SAP founder Hasso Plattner gave a private donation of US$30 million. Despite the extravagant funding, all furniture in the D-School came from budget furniture store Ikea. In a creative office, the going gets rough from time to time, and damage is to be expected. Your furniture should be durable, but inexpensive enough that it's easy to replace.

> "But innovation comes from people meeting up in hallways or calling each other at 10:30 at night with a new idea, or because they realized something that shoots holes in how we've been thinking about a probem."
> — STEVE JOBS

Your technology, on the other hand, must be state-of-the-art. When I visited the D School in 2007, I noticed plenty of workstations equipped with the latest iMacs, high-end printers, flat-screen TVs, LED projectors, video equipment and cutting-edge software - all linked together by a wireless network.

Tip 8. Creativity requires rest and play.

A creative office needs spaces where employees can recharge. Put a day bed in a darkened corner with a curtain so employees can take a nap when they need to. Provide a relaxation corner with a TV, music, video games, books and magazines.

Your most creative days were probably in kindergarten, so provide your employees with some opportunities for play in your creative office, too. Trust that this will ignite creative sparks for your business challenges, in line with Plato's advice: *"Life must be lived as play."*

Tip 9. Don't skimp on raw materials.

A creative office needs sufficient working materials: Post-it notes, flip chart paper, scissors, glue, masking tape, cardboard, foam, cloth, modeling clay, and so on. Store the different materials in transparent boxes on wheeled shelves. And make sure they don't run out; each minute your people spend looking for a marker is a minute they're not creating. Worse yet, they may lose the thread of a great idea.

Tip 10. Ensure large empty walls and table surfaces to map out and display creative artifacts and prototypes.

When we worked on the X-IDEA innovation method and toolbox, our Thinkergy project office had a wall where all hundred plus tools we were working on were displayed

"Like most creative people, I don't fit well into boxes."
- LAURELL K. HAMILTON

on the wall together with a status light system. At any stage in the project, the team saw how much we had already achieved (and still had left to do) for the project in total and each tool in particular.

We also regularly used the surface of a large empty table in the office to lay out and map out process flows and build prototypes of the toolbox and other deliverables. So, apart from having a desk for all your workers, have a number of collaborative big tables in the office as joint creative workstations that allow for laying things out and moving them around on the table.

Conclusion: Well-designed creative office spaces can enhance creativity and collaboration. But note three important points related to creative office design.

1. Designing a creative office doesn't necessarily require a firm to spend big bucks; it's rather a creative exercise in how to best accommodate as many of the 10 tips as possible within the constraints of your given budget (available for creative office redesign) and space (spatial specs of your office).

2. Even the most expensive and spacious creative office doesn't necessarily make an organization more creative. It's the combination of your creative processes, people, culture and leadership that will do so.

3. Don't just simply copy what others have been doing who designed a creative office space before. Do your own thinking to bring to life the specifics of your company, your industry, and your history.

Open vs closed offices? Keep the best of both worlds

In the information age, most office spaces of knowledge workers followed one of three models:

- One traditional office model promoted a layout with many small offices, where employees were working either alone or with a few colleagues without much interaction with colleagues from other units and teams.

- The other extreme was the open-space office model. In *"Cubeville"* (a name coined by Dilbert creator Scott Adams), dozens of employees work alongside each other squeezed into small cubicles placed in an open office space. They are supervised by managers sitting in private corner offices overseeing the whole floor.

- A third model is a hybrid of the two extremes. It blends private offices for the higher ranks with the open space arrangement for the normal charges.

Neither model supports creativity and innovation. Why? The first model discourages chance encounters and conversations between colleagues who hide almost all day behind closed doors in their offices, thus limiting the chance of having a stimulating, creativity-inspiring conversation with other colleagues. The second model doesn't give employees enough privacy for undisturbed, concentrated conceptual work. Finally, the third model creates hierarchy and distance between the privileged few with their own office and the many others forced to work in open spaces.

So, what's the solution? Combine both open and closed office space arrangements and remove the hierarchy: Give every employee a desk in the open office, where they start and close their day. Also give them the right to "book" one of the private offices for 0.5-1 day, when they need to engage in a creative, conceptual work project. The need for such closed office spaces depends on your industry and how many *"Brain"*-workers you have in your team (referring to the TIPS work style mentioned in Chapter 5). As a result, this approach links private office space to a concrete creative project requirement, not to hierarchy. At the same time, it keeps the collaborative benefits of open offices.

IMAGINING A SPACE FOR INNOVATION: THE THINKERGY INNOVATION PLAYGROUND

Most organizations prepare their people to innovate by training them in windowless, sterile meeting rooms that stifle creativity and innovation. How can people think out of the box when they're forced into such a box?

The Thinkergy Innovation Playground is the ultimate non-box, a space formed from organic shapes to encourage inspiration and insight. It's the perfect space for creating new products, training new innovators, and holding conferences that require open and alert minds.

The Playground's five primary spaces are designed to foster the kinds of thinking associated with the five stages of innovation: Xploration, Ideation, Development, Evaluation, and Action (X-IDEA, Thinkergy's innovation method).

Facilities at the Playground also include a cafeteria and outdoor activity areas.

The Thinkergy Innovation Playground will be run by the creative breakthrough company Thinkergy. As the perfect complement to our innovation methods — X-IDEA, TIPS, CooL, and Genius Journey — the Playground will be a great place for creating ideas that make you say *"Wow"* and for turning talents into innovators and creative leaders.

Do you have a bold, big vision of a creative city that needs an effectively designed and professionally run innovation space? Then contact me on the Thinkergy website, and perhaps we can jointly realize your city's playground vision.

The 5 main zones of the Thinkergy Innovation Playground are arranged to follow the sequential flow of Thinkergy's X-IDEA Innovation Method:

X — The first stage of X-IDEA, Xploration, is inspired by space exploration. The Xplorer's Home Base encourages a deeper understanding of a team's real innovation challenge.

I — Onto the second stage of X-IDEA: Ideation. The Idea Playground makes it easy to get as wild and imaginative as children do, generating hundreds or even thousands of raw ideas.

D — For the third stage, Development, there's the Genius Lounge. In the relaxed atmosphere of a lounge, meaningful idea concepts are developed while enjoying nice music and a drink.

E — Then there's the Juror's Chamber. This fourth innovation zone is a neutral space for objectively evaluating idea concepts and rapidly prototyping the most promising ones.

A — Last but not least, take Action and succeed in The Arena of Dreams. In this auditorium space, top idea concepts are pitched to a juror panel for support and funding to make them real. This zone is also used for regular events and conferences related to innovation and forward-thinking.

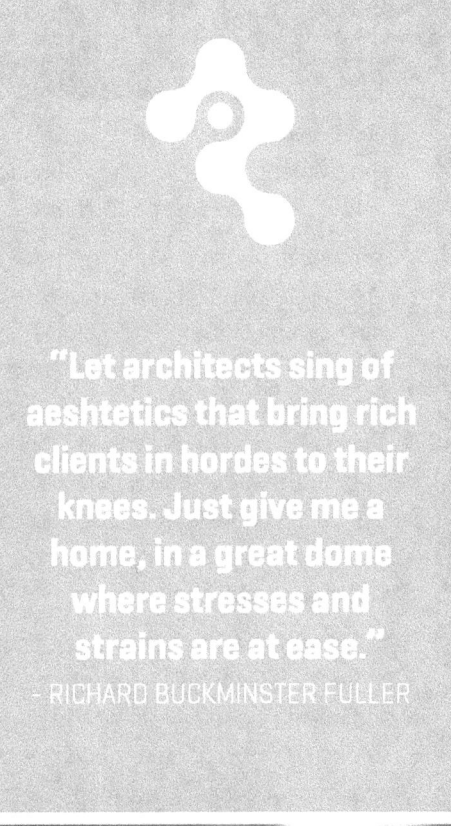

"Let architects sing of aeshtetics that bring rich clients in hordes to their knees. Just give me a home, in a great dome where stresses and strains are at ease."
— RICHARD BUCKMINSTER FULLER

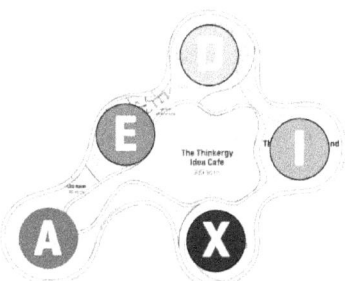

8.6. INNOVATION: ARE YOU JUST TALKING THE TALK OR WALKING YOUR TALK?

These days, it's almost impossible to read the business news without finding articles referring to the world of innovation in one way or another.

Companies announce that they are going to grow faster than their competitors because they are going to innovate better products. Self-proclaimed *"innovation experts"* who in the past sold marketing, benchmarking, and Six Sigma as the *"one and only way to heaven"* and who have only recently jumped on the moving innovation train now start to bombard audiences with shallow articles and low-value talks full of innovation buzzwords, from *"out-of-the-box"* over *"disruptive"* and *"cutting-edge"* to *"breakthrough"* and *"innovate or die"* as unavoidable crescendo.

Public sector agencies organize conferences and events where they —rightfully— celebrate the concept of the Innovation Economy without effectively adopting the success lessons of other countries and translating these into meaningful policies. Yes, there's a lot of talk about creativity and innovation. But how about the doing side of innovation?

In a global innovation survey conducted by the firm Information Architected Inc. in 2009, 17 out of 20 managers agreed that innovation management is absolutely critical to their firm's business success. However, 51% of the companies participating in the survey did not have any formalized innovation management practice.

Asked what is the biggest impediment to managing innovation, half of the participating managers cited a lack of a systematic innovation process, followed by a lack of innovation resources, leadership and adequate funding. Interestingly, seven out of ten respondents state that the challenging economic conditions following the global economic downturn in 2008 raised the need for actively managing innovation, but only 24% of firms had done anything specifically to manage innovation in the two preceding years.

So how about your company? Do you still only talk about how important innovation is for your business — and how much you are going to innovate soon? Or do you already walk your talk and do what it takes to produce tangible innovation results?

To find out how your company is doing, have your executive team openly and honestly discuss the set of questions on the next pages. These questions help you track the degree of your innovation efforts and get started walking your innovation talk in earnest. Thereby, I group the questions following the logic of our innovation frames presented in this book: First, probe the questions relating to the environment and the big picture of innovation. Then, discuss how you're doing for each of the four small picture frames (process, people, culture, leadership). Finally, investigate the final outlook questions.

Conclusion: In 2007, IBM, one of the global innovation leaders, released a number of hilarious advertisement spots that contrasted the corporate hype on innovation with the corporate reality (to view the videos, go to YouTube and type 'IBM' and 'innovation' into the search field). In the ironical spots, you see business people doing the innovation talk; managers creating special rooms where they intend their employees to innovate sometime in the future; firms hiring bozos as *"innovation trainers"* or *"innovation experts"* who master all the industry jargon and buzzwords but are completely clueless on how to really do innovation; and so on. All spots culminate in a funny ending that highlights the ridiculousness of the firm's *"innovation efforts"* and IBM's main message: *"Stop talking. Start doing."*

I have nothing more to add.

Chapter 1: The Environment:

- To what extent is our business affected by the five drivers of the extreme future?
    - Speed: What aspects of our business have accelerated over the past years? What do we need to speed up to keep up with the faster pace? What aspects should we counter-intuitively slow down to create meaningful differentiation in frantic times?
    - Change: What has changed in our industry or strategic business unit (SBU) over the past 3 years? What changes do we predict for the coming 3-5 years?
    - Complexity: What aspects of our business have become more complex over the past years? How may we counter complexity by simplifying certain things?
    - Risk: What new risks have emerged in our business over the past years? What risks have increased in impact or volatility?
    - Surprise: What —positive and negative— surprises have we experienced in our business over the past 1-3 years? What have we learned from these surprises? How may we better prepare to capitalize on future surprises?
- To what extent does our business (and related industry) already reflect the spirit of the innovation economy? What level of economic evolution does our present set-up reflect (primal — agricultural — industrial — informational — innovation-driven)?
- To what extent is our business threatened by the shift into an entrepreneurial society? How may we benefit from the trend by reframing the threat as an opportunity? How can we make our business more entrepreneurial?
- How do we rate the velocity, direction and impact of changes affecting our industry?
    - Change velocity: How fast do things change in our category or industry? To what extent has the tempo increased in recent years?
    - Change direction: What paths of change (linear, cyclical, pendulum, spiral) can we identify for different change phenomena affecting our business (e.g., political, economic, societal, technological)?
    - Change impact: What is the impact of changes affecting our category / industry / business? (incremental - evolutionary - revolutionary)? Why?
- In which cyclical season (spring - summer - autumn - winter) are: Our key products? Our company? The economies of our key markets? What does this mean for us?
- How can we make our business ride the Sixth Wave of technology innovation (ca. 2020-2045)?
- To what extent is our business threatened by the *"change or die"* phenomenon? What positive frame (*"change to live better"*) can create a lasting attraction for innovation? How can we create support groups to give emotional reassurance during a transformation period?
- What are the vital few core human values and core human activities that our business focuses on that stay the same, regardless of changes in how we satisfy them?

- To what extent will demographic changes (population growth or decline, aging society) affect our business in different countries in the next 2-3 decades? How can we reposition our value propositions or geographical set-up to benefit from these trends?

Chapters 2 and 3: Core Principles and Rules of the Game:

- How have we defined innovation so far? How have we defined creativity so far? How are we going to redefine the concepts going forward?

- To what extent do our products make meaning (e.g., make the world a better place, improve the quality of people's lives, right a wrong, prevent the end of something good)? How can we ensure we make even more meaning going forward?

- What innovation types have we focused on in the past? What innovation types should we (additionally) focus on in the future? How can we better utilize the full spectrum of modern innovation types?

- Which of the rules of the innovation types game do we already follow? What other rules can we use in future to create more meaning, leverage and differentiation?

- How many innovations have we successfully activated during the past 3 years? How many do we want to activate in the next 3 years?

- Looking at the portfolio of innovation initiatives that we successfully activated in the past 3 years, what is the percentage for each of the following impact categories: Cost-saving initiatives (*"piggy banks"*) — Incremental improvements — Evolutionary Innovations — Revolutionary innovations? What should the proportional split for these impact categories look like for our innovation initiatives in the next 3 years?

- How much are we spending on innovation per year (as % of our total revenues)? What's the break-up into different categories (such as traditional R&D, HR Development/ Training, Consulting, Innovation and Ideation Projects, Top Idea Development Budgets, Innovation Management Systems, etc.)? How effective is our current innovation spending? What would be more effective ways to boost our return on innovation spending?

- To what extent do we actively protect and manage our Intellectual Property (IP)?

- To what extent may the open innovation model be useful for our innovation efforts? If we embrace open innovation, how can we make it a win-win-win for everybody involved? And how can we avoid that ideas and upcoming innovations are prematurely leaked to the market (or shared with competitors)?

- To what extent are our innovation efforts constrained by the dilemma of innovation management (i.e. goal conflict between achieving both high organizational efficiency and high organizational creativity)? What organizational model are we currently using that may explain our dilemma? How we change our structure to move towards higher organizational creativity? How may a functional or cognitive approach help us to more effectively resolve the dilemma and strengthen our innovation efforts?

Chapter 4: Innovative Process

- How many innovation projects have we completed in the past 3 years? How many people were involved? How much time did we invest in each project?

- How many projects should we do in the next 3 years? How many of those should lead to evolutionary or even revolutionary innovations? What does this mean for our budgeting (time, people, finances) of these planned new innovation initiatives?

- What innovation process method are we currently using? How effective is it? How do we know it is effective — and that we are not just patting ourselves on our own backs?

- How do we generate new ideas? What creativity tools other than *"brainstorming"* are we using for Ideation? How many ideas do we usually produce in the creative phase? How many of these ideas are intriguing (i.e. either really interesting or wild)? Do we employ a process method with two separate creative phases that allow us to move beyond the obvious conventional ideas?

- How do we typically interact with each other and communicate ideas and outputs in an innovation project? To what extent do we play on the full spectrum of innovation communication styles (solo/pool/team brainwriting, buddystorming, bodystorming, brainstorming, round-robin brainstorming, think-pair-share) to enhance the quantity and quality of our outputs in the creative process phases?

- To what extent do we involve external parties (such as our customers, distributors, vendors, suppliers or creativity coaches/innovation companies) in our innovation projects or at least our idea generation efforts?

- Do we have an innovation pipeline? How many ideas are in it? How often do we review it? What is the degree of integration of meaningful ideas in it with existing products and solutions?

- How can we ensure that we provide our innovation partners and creative agencies with complete innovation project briefs (specifying all 5W2H questions—what, why, who, when, where, how, and how much) that allow them to develop focused project proposals that save all parties time and coordination costs?

Chapter 5: Innovative People

- What cognitive profiling method or personality test are we currently using? How effective is this method in helping us identify the creative types in our workforce? Can it tell us how everyone may contribute to our innovation efforts in harmony with their preferred cognitive styles and natural talent?

- To what extent do we consider cognitive profiling results while composing teams to participate in an innovation project?

- Do we know who are the vital few change drivers in our organization who have a natural talent for a) coming up with meaningful ideas, b) validating the top concepts, and c) effectively pitching the benefits of an idea to the market?

- Do we know who in our organization is naturally suited to effectively lead or drive a particular phase in our company lifecycle?

- Do we know how different people in our organization will respond to creative organizational change? And who has the natural potential to be developed into creative leaders (and who has a greater inclination to manage performance and internal efficiencies)?

- Who is in charge of innovation in our organization? At what management level have we positioned this responsibility? Do we separate an innovation manager (managing innovation from the back) and creative leader(s) (driving innovation initiatives at the front) using different cognitive profiles and talents?

Chapter 6: Innovative Culture

- What are our Top 5-10 organizational barriers to innovation? Why these factors and not others? How might we overcome these barriers?

- Have we ever done a professional external audit of the present innovation capacity and future potential of our organization? If yes, did we come out as more of an in-NO-vative or innovative company? If no, why not? When would now be the best time to get started?

- What motivates people to join innovation initiatives? What are the factors that limit employee motivation to innovate? How do we currently reward innovation? What might be a better way to reward innovation?

- What is our default response to people failing with an (innovation) project? Do we tend to blame and penalize failure, and praise people who take initiative regardless of the outcome? How often do our people take initiative on a meaningful idea that they have? What can we do to move towards a more failure-tolerant and action-oriented culture?

- Who are corporate innovation leaders from our own or other industries that we admire? Why? What success factors may we adopt or adapt to become more innovative?

- How much time do we commit for our people to work on innovation initiatives? Do they have a certain percentage of their contractual work time to allocate to their own innovative pet projects (such as they do at 3M and Google)? Or are our people kept busy with their day-to-day business affairs and are more like running on a treadmill?

- To what extent are we willing to transform our organization from in-NO-vation to innovation? And willing to commit to lead the change effort of ca. 3 years?

- How do we measure our innovation activities? Do we have measures that capture our innovation input, innovation process and innovation output? How effective is each of these measures to realize our strategic objectives and innovation goals?

Chapter 7: Creative Leadership

- Do we agree that creativity is a key leadership skill to successfully lead our firm in the innovation economy? Why (not)?

- Which of the *"hot"* characteristics of creative leadership do we already represent? Which other qualities should we aim to also acquire going forward?

- With our business focus, expertise, and passion, which of humanity's big challenges (sustainability, global warming, labor, aging societies, financial system stability, singularity) may we be able to help resolve?

- What creative leaders do we admire? Why? What creative success mindsets may we adopt or adapt for our own leadership style?

- Has any of us already experienced a true Eureka moment of breakthrough creativity? What big challenges are we passionate about resolving using the incubation process?

- What experiences do we have with creative

- leadership development programs (books, training courses, study programs)? How effective were these programs in making individual leaders more creative? How creative was the delivery style and format of these programs?
- How creative is each of us? What are individual mindsets and action routines that impair or support our creativity?

Chapter 8: The Outlook

- Do we agree that the pendulum seems to be swinging back towards a more nationalistic and protectionist environment? What does it mean for our business? And how long do we think it will take until the momentum reverses again towards more globalization and free movement of goods, ideas, people, and capital?
- Are we afraid of the future and its challenges? How can we *"human up"* to make our company honor and rise up to the legacy of our brave, creative and collaborative human roots and development history?
- To what extent do different attitudes and styles of the various generations (Baby Boomers, Gen X, Gen Y, and Gen Z) working in our company affect our business and innovation performance? How can we effectively play on these generational differences to make everyone contribute to our innovation efforts and business success?
- How may we use the emergence of creative cities to amplify our innovation efforts and long-term business success?
- To what extent do our office space arrangements support our people to be creative and innovative? How many of the creative office design tips do we practice? How may we quickly and effectively move towards a more creativity-friendly office design?
- What is the *"innovation mastery level"* of the different members of our executive team? How may we move some members up to a higher level? And where on the mastery levels would we position our company? Why?
- How many of the success ingredients of top achievers does our company exhibit? How can we play on the strengths and talents of the leadership team to move us towards peak performance?

> *"My greatest strength as a consultant is to be ignorant and ask a few questions."*
> —PETER DRUCKER

8.7. WHAT'S YOUR INNOVATION MASTERY LEVEL?

People like to know how they rank — think of handicaps in golf, colored belts in karate, and degrees in education. When Apple's Steve Jobs passed away in 2011, it made me think about levels of mastery in innovation, distinguished by different levels of knowledge, experience and achievement.

The Innovation Mastery Pyramid is a classification system for innovators. As you move up the pyramid, your breadth and depth of knowledge, experience and achievement in innovation increases, while your number of peers decreases.

Bozos

The basement of the innovation mastery pyramid comprises those who do not value creativity and innovation despite the evident benefits. We use Steve Jobs' term for non-performers to label those who dismiss innovation — because of unawareness, inability, or stubborn ignorance — as innovation *"bozos."*

Dreamers

Innovation dreamers are a step above the bozos. Innovation is commonly defined as ideas plus action or implementation. Dreamers create ideas but fail to do anything about them, whether out of laziness or complacency, fear of ridicule, or being too busy.

Novices

Next are people who are new to the field of innovation and have an active interest in learning more. These innovation novices read books and articles on creativity and innovation, attend conferences and talks, and attend creativity or innovation training courses. Although their natural creativity may be lower than that of dreamers, their active learning puts them a step above.

Apprentices

As novices start applying their innovation knowledge in their daily work, they become innovation apprentices. An apprentice might use a thinking tool in a meeting, apply a creativity technique to generate ideas, or use a systematic innovation method while working on a project.

Practitioners

Innovation practitioners are those who perform real-life innovation projects, often leading a team to turn an idea into reality. This experience gives innovation practitioners deeper insights into what it takes to produce tangible innovation results.

Guides

Innovation process experts who have gained expertise in guiding other innovators become innovation guides. Their broad knowledge and deep understanding of the innovation process allow them to guide others in innovation, although they have not yet produced an innovation by themselves.

Champions

An innovation champion has, at least once, successfully turned a meaningful idea into something tangible in the world. This could be a new product or service that has been delivered to users, a new solution that is in use, or something new that customers have experienced.

Heroes

Innovation heroes have spent a long time working in innovation and have a track record of meaningful innovation. This elite group includes such people as James Dyson, Charles F. Kettering, Edwin H. Land, and Art Fry.

Legends

At the top of the innovation pyramid are those few innovators who have achieved multiple radical innovations in different areas that created great value, often leading to the creation of entirely new industries.

For example, Thomas Edison earned 1,093 patents and invented the incandescent light bulb and the gramophone. His inventions enabled the creation of companies such as General Electric.

Similarly, Steve Jobs of Apple not only drove the creation of groundbreaking new products such as the Macintosh, the iPod, the iPhone and the iPad, but also new business models such as the iTunes Music Store. The enormous value created by legends, coupled with the scope of change, distinguishes them from innovation heroes.

Conclusion

Having developed a suite of four integrated innovation methods (X-IDEA, TIPS, CooL, and Genius Journey) for Thinkergy, I see myself as an innovation champion. In the years to come, our creative development team at Thinkergy and I intend to activate other innovations in our pipeline, so that someday, perhaps, I will move up to a higher level on the Innovation Mastery Pyramid.

How about you? Where are you on the Innovation Mastery Pyramid? Where would you like to be? And how will you get there? In the innovation economy, one thing is likely to hold true: the further up the pyramid you are, the better you'll be.

Race for IDEAS

thinkergy
know how to wow

INNOVATION MASTERY LEVELS

- ★
- LEGENDS
- HEROES
- CHAMPIONS
- GUIDES
- PRACTITIONERS
- APPRENTICES
- NOVICES
- DREAMERS
- BOZOS

"Only one who devotes himself to a cause with his whole strength and soul can be a true master. For this reason mastery demands all of a person."
—ALBERT EINSTEIN

- INNOVATOR HALL OF FAME (COMPLETED INNOVATION)
- INNOVATION IN PROGRESS
- INNOVATION IN TRAINING
- NO ACTION ON INNOVATION

8.8. SUCCESS INGREDIENTS OF TOP ACHIEVERS IN INNOVATION AND BEYOND

"Experience without theory is blind, but theory without experience is mere intellectual play," the German philosopher Immanuel Kant once said. Do you have both theoretical knowledge and practical experience in what you do? And can these two success ingredients alone lead you to outstanding professional success?

In the following, let me share with you the key success ingredients of a first-rate professional with the help of a Venn diagram. It illustrates the three bases of professional success, the three intersecting mid-levels of success, and the success peak where all bases intersect).

Base Ingredients of Professional Success

Base 1. Knowledge (*"I know"*):

"The natural desire of good men is knowledge," said Leonardo da Vinci. The first base of professional success, knowledge, can be defined as facts, information and skills acquired by a person. Typically, if you start as a novice in a professional domain, you first build up foundational knowledge and skills that allow you to become a practitioner in your chosen field.

Base 2. Experience (*"I do"*):

"There are many truths of which the full meaning cannot be realized until personal experience has brought it home," noted the English philosopher John Stuart Mill. Experience is the second base on which professional success is grounded. You acquire practical experience over time while working in a particular profession.

Mid-Level A (Intersection 1x2): Competence and expertise (*"I know how to do this well"*)

"To know and not to do is not yet to know," goes a Zen saying. Apply your knowledge, in reality, to move to a higher professional level and become competent in what you do. Competence is the ability to do something successfully or efficiently.

If you master the discipline to diligently continue learning and applying, you build up more professional expertise (i.e., expert skill or knowledge in a particular field). But apart from discipline, you need a third success base.

Base 3. Talent (*"I am a natural at it"*):

The third —and arguably most important— base you need to succeed big is talent, which is a natural aptitude or skill for your chosen pursuit. When something is EEE (easy, effortless, and enjoyable) for you that is DDD (difficult, drudging, and de-energizing) for most others, you have a talent for this pursuit. Developing the latent qualities that constitute your natural gift may lead you to future professional success.

Mid-Level B (Intersection 1x3): Scholarship (*"I am a natural and know all about it"*)

When you have a natural aptitude for a domain and study it hard, you become a learned scholar. Scholarship is academic study and achievement on a high level, and it is driven by curiosity: The more curious you are to learn all about *"your"* natural domain, the more and harder you will study, the more you will learn and understand on a theoretical level.

But scholarship alone won't put you at the very top of your professional domain either: as long as you don't practice what you preach, you still lack the practical experience to reach the peak. Accomplished career academics tend to play —and stay— on this level.

Mid-Level C (Intersection 2x3): Self-Actualization (*"I am a natural and can do it"*)

Self-actualization means the realization of one's talents and potential. Some people notice early on that they have a knack for something — and then, driven by passion and enthusiasm for their gift, they just start doing it without having been formally educated in the domain. For example, many natural entrepreneurs start a venture without having undergone a formal theoretical education in entrepreneurship.

The Peak (Intersection 1x2x3): Success, harmony, and ingenuity (*"I am a natural in it, know all about it, and know how to do it"*):

If you combine all of these elements of professional success, you eventually will reach the peak and become one of the acclaimed top leaders in your professional domain.

At this point, who you are, what you know, and what you do are in perfect harmony. You can regularly experience the peak state of flow at work, which drives you forward as a reward in itself but also supports moments of peak creativity.

Albert Einstein provides a good example. For years, he had been at the scholarship level (1x3); he had a talent for physics (base 3) and knew all about it in theory as an accomplished academic (base 2). However, he was only able to resolve the creative puzzle leading to his relativity theory after closing base 3.

Einstein acquired practical experience while working as a clerk in the patent office in Bern, where he gained fresh practical stimuli from reading technical patent applications and doing imagination experiments on his theories. All these stimuli ultimately connected to his groundbreaking relativity theory in a Eureka moment of peak creativity while hiking with his friend in the Swiss Alps.

Here is a second example: Thomas Edison started as a self-actualized inventor and entrepreneur: Early on, he had noticed his respective talent for inventing things (base 3) and, without having a formal engineering or scientific education, began doing it and monetizing his inventions (base 2).

After succeeding with his first inventions (a voting machine and the telegraph), however, Edison realized that he needed to further his theoretical knowledge (base 1) to become a top innovator. Hence, in his New Jersey innovation factory, he set up his own library with ten thousand books and regularly spent time reading in it to close his educational gap from his early life. Working on all three bases and all accomplishment levels allowed Edison to file over one thousand patent applications in his life and to come up with and monetize many more ground-breaking inventions (such as the incandescent light bulb and the gramophone, among many others).

Do you want to become a creative leader in your chosen domain, too? Our creative leadership method, Genius Journey, involves configuring your mindset to raise your antennas for moments of peak creativity.

But what if you're not sure about your natural talent yet? Our innovation people profiling method TIPS can help you to gain more talent awareness on your *"natural thing"* and to locate domains and ecosystems that resonate with your preferred cognitive style.

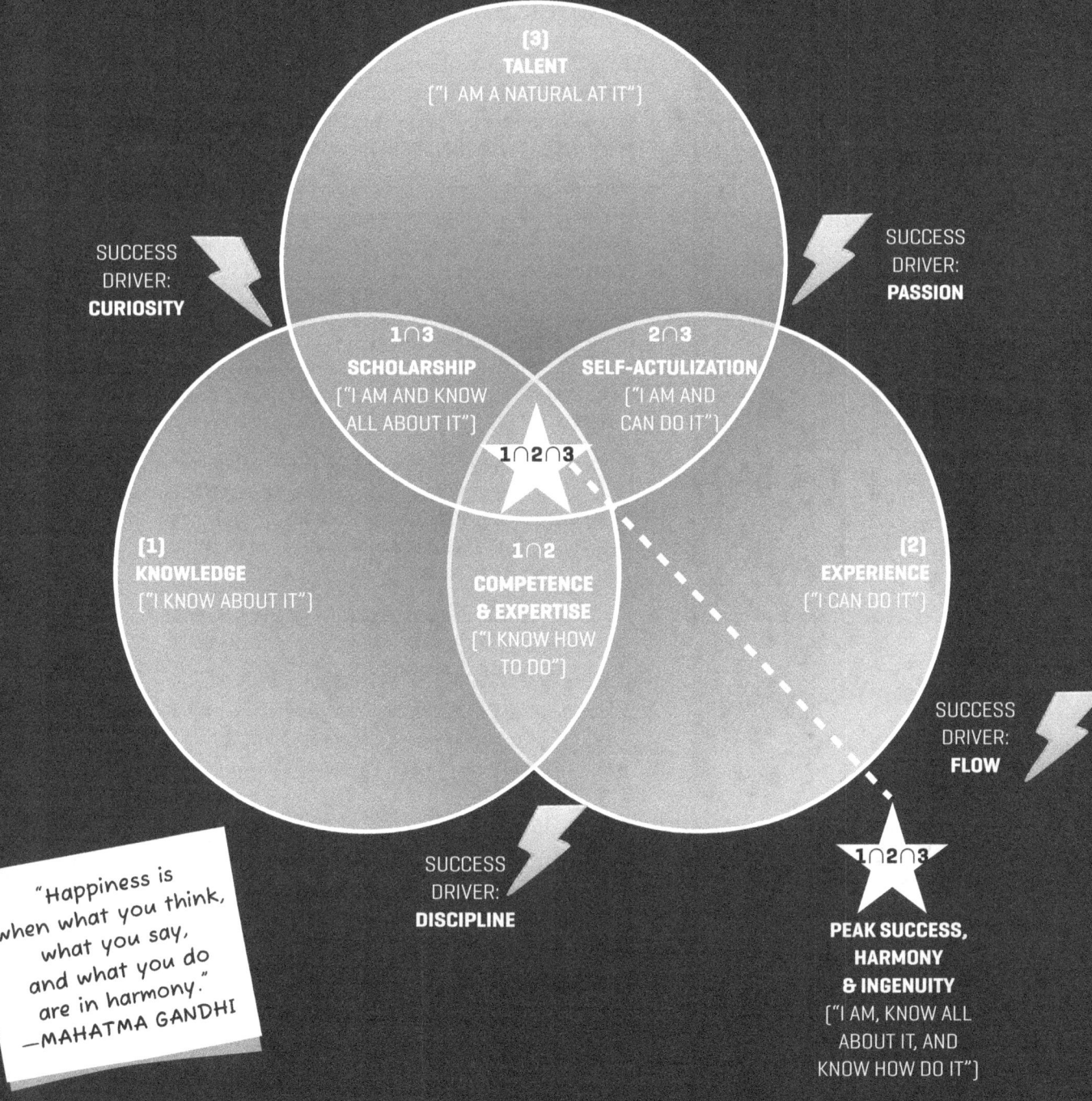

> "We are called to be architects of the future, not in victims."
> — RICHARD BUCKMINISTER FULLER

CHAPTER 8 — EXECUTIVE SUMMARY: WHAT ELSE? AN INNOVATION OUTLOOK

- ❖ Innovative change vs. preservation of the past are two poles on a continuum of social and political movement. In the aftermath of the financial crisis, the pendulum might have started to swing back towards a more closed, preserving, and nationalistic world.

- ❖ While the pendulum seems to be swinging back and humanity faces massive challenges that threaten our prosperity and even survival, not everything is doom and gloom. So far, humanity has always been able to out-innovate itself from major challenges. So, let's human up and start a new Innonaissance.

- ❖ With most Baby Boomers retiring by 2030, the next generations of innovators (Gen X and Gen Y plus the now-entering Gen Gen Z) will likely make innovation become more digital, open, global, meaningful, and life-affirming.

- ❖ While new innovation process methods (such as Design Thinking or X-IDEA) come and go every few years, a set of underlying creative laws governs all these methods and drives their efficacy and creativity. These laws often relate to the quality and quantity of outputs that innovation teams produce during an innovation project.

- ❖ Creative office spaces follow certain design principles and functional criteria that offer both space for individual conceptual work and playful collaboration and co-creation.

- ❖ Many organizations talk the innovation talk, but few walk it in earnest. Do you? Find out by answering a set of questions to help you check to what extent your firm has done its homework for each innovation frame presented in this book.

- ❖ Honestly determine your (and the other members of your team's) innovation mastery level. Then, put in the time and effort needed to move to the next level, knowing that taking shortcuts and prematurely jumping up to higher levels may likely be your downfall when unexpected things happen down the road (and they will in innovation).

- ❖ Evaluate which of the three ingredients of outstanding personal success you still miss: knowledge, talent, and/or passion. Then, make a plan to gradually acquire the missing know-how to close your gaps and move towards becoming a top achiever in innovation, business, and life.

SUPPLEMENT: HOW TO WRITE A GOOD CREATIVE BRIEF

If you want to get creative professionals talking, ask them about the quality of the creative briefs they receive from their clients — when they receive one at all. The briefs they get are often misleading, self-contradictory, and worse than useless. Without a good brief, these people cannot do their best work for you. How can you write a good brief that will inspire them?

What is a creative brief?

A creative brief is written by a client to communicate the requirements of an upcoming project, and to request feedback and, normally, a project proposal. The brief describes what the client wants to accomplish with the project, and outlines important project parameters, such as desired outcomes, the wants and needs of key stakeholders, time and budget allotments, etc.

Why are creative briefs needed?

Imagine an architect whose client says only, *"I want you to build a house for us next year,"* or an investment broker who receives a call with instructions *"to buy that technology stock,"* or a surgeon who is told to operate on a patient, but not told which operation to perform. How well do you think each of those projects will turn out? Creative professionals often receive briefs as sketchy as those, which lead to similarly dismal results. Unless a creative brief clearly states an organization's objectives and expectations for a project, that project is unlikely to succeed.

Unfortunately, when clients approach companies in the creative industries, the information they provide is often only verbal, vague and limited. Those in creative agencies or innovation companies then have to try to pry other information they need out of their clients. This wastes time, and can lead to contradictory information.

Have you ever played Chinese Whispers as a child? Then, you understand another problem related to unwritten briefs. Often, project information goes verbally from executives to managers to those who deal directly with the creative agency, and the information received by the person at the end of the communication chain is typically different from what was intended originally. The result? Bad briefs, bad proposals, and a long, frustrating project that produces poor results.

How to write a good creative brief?

The requirements for a good creative brief vary, depending on the type of project and the sort of agency being asked to create a proposal. A brief that asks an industrial design firm to create packaging for a new product will be quite different from one asking an architecture firm to design a new corporate headquarters, which will again differ from one sent to an innovation company that is supposed to facilitate a more complex innovation project. But in any case, a creative brief needs to address all of the 5W2H questions — what, why, who, when, where, how, and how much. Here's a structure I suggest:

1. **Project introduction:** In the first part of the brief, you say what you want the project to accomplish, and how the creative agency can help. For example, you may want to develop a new product and are asking an innovation company to facilitate an ideation project to create product ideas.

2. **Company:** This states who you are. It should include your name, your products, your company size, your values, your current market, and your basic methods of operation, such as product development, production, or distribution. For some projects, you may also include things such as your brand strategy, positioning, media plan, etc.

3. **Customers:** Next, provide information about the project's target audience, including demographics, purchasing power, perceived wants and needs, etc.

4. **Competition:** Review your competitors and analyze their strengths and weaknesses.

5. **Project parameters:** Describe the creative challenge the project is meant to address, specify the project objectives, and list the expected outcomes to be produced by the project. It's a good idea to state how the project's success will be measured. Be certain to define the scope of the project so the creative agency can get an idea of the resources needed.

6. **Project schedule:** List the phases of the project and specify any important dates, key milestones, and deadlines. When appropriate, also specify where project activities will take place.

7. **Project resources:** Last but hardly least, state the project budget, and what resources, human and otherwise, your organization will commit to the project.

Why talk numbers?

Telling a creative agency or innovation company your project budget may seem like a poor tactic, but you should do it anyway. Why? Knowing this information allows an agency to check the reasonableness of the project. Does the budget fit the scope of the project? Can the agency accomplish the objectives of the project? Is the agency able to make a profit — and yes, you want them to make a profit. How to make this a success for both the client and the creative agency — as well as for those end users who are targeted by the project?

Conclusion: Taking the time to write a good creative brief allows your partners in the creative industries to give you better feedback, provide you with a better project proposal, and drive the project to a successful conclusion.

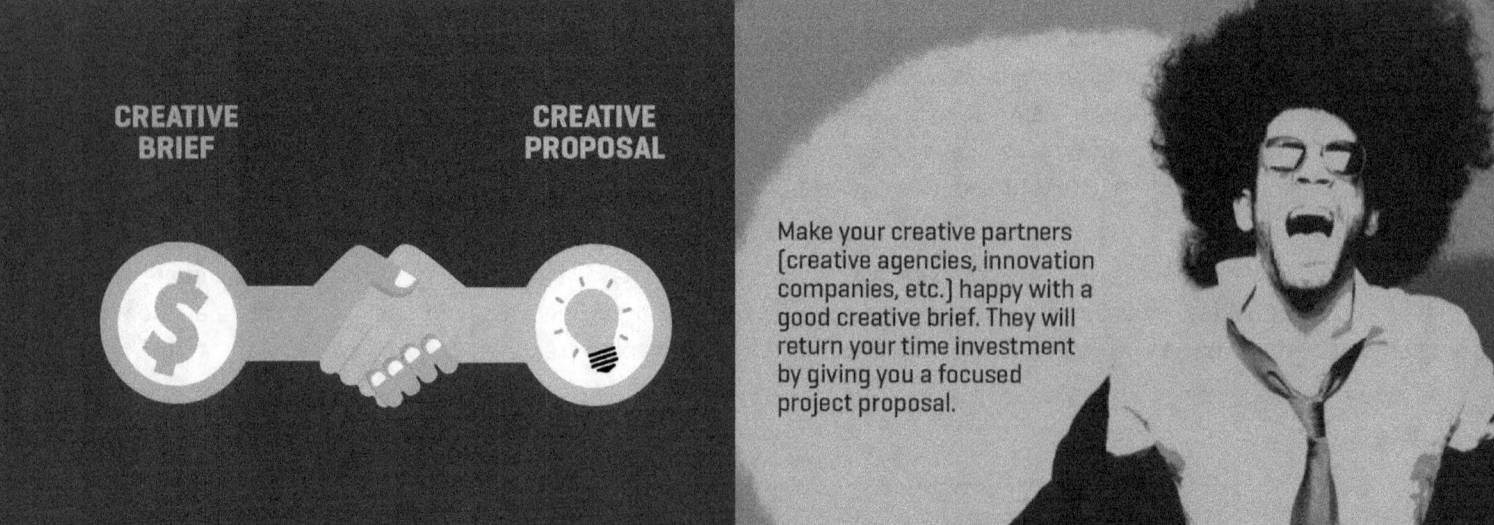

Make your creative partners (creative agencies, innovation companies, etc.) happy with a good creative brief. They will return your time investment by giving you a focused project proposal.

REFERENCES & RESOURCES

Amabile, T. M. (1997). Motivating Creativity in Organizations: On Doing What You Love And Loving What You Do. California Management Review, 40, 39-58.

Amabile, T. M. (1998). How to Kill Creativity. Harvard Business Review, 76, 76-87.

Amabile, T. M., Hadley, C. N. & Kramer, S. J. (2002). Creativity Under the Gun. Harvard Business Review, 52-61.

Bessant, J. & Tidd, J. (2015). Innovation and Entrepreneurship, 3rd Ed., Chichester, Wiley.

Best, K. (2006). Design Management. Managing Design Strategy, Process and Implementation, Lausanne, AVA Publishing.

Black, R. A. (1995). Broken Crayons. Athens, GA, Cre8ing Places Press.

Black, R. A. (2016) M.I.N.D Design: What is your thinking style. http://www.cre8ng.com/minddesign.shtml

Boston Consulting Group (2006). Innovation 2006. Boston.

Boston Consulting Group (2006). Measuring Innovation 2006. Boston, MA.

Boston Consulting Group (2008). Measuring Innovation 2008. Squandered Opportunities. Boston, MA.

Boston Consulting Group (2009). Innovation 2009. Making Hard Decisions in the Downturn. Boston, MA.

Boston Consulting Group (2017). The World's Most Innovative Companies [Online]. Available: https://www.bcgperspectives.com/content/interactive/innovation_growth_most_innovative_companies_interactive_guide/ [Accessed].

Bragg, A. & Bragg, M. (2005). Developing New Business Ideas, Harlow, Prentice Hall.

Branson, R. (1998) Losing my Virginity. The Autobiography, London, Virgin Books.

Branson, R. (2006) Screw it, let's do it. Lessons in life, London, Virgin Books.

Branson, R. (2011) Screw Business as Usual, London, Virgin Books.

British Design Council (2007). The Value of Design. Factfinder report. London.

Brown, T. (2008). Design Thinking. Harvard Business Review, 86, 84-92.

Brown, T. (2009) Change by Design, New York, HarperCollins.

Canton, J. (2007). The Extreme Future. The Top Trends That Will Reshape the World in the Next 20 Years. New York, Plume - Penguin Group.

Cameron, J. (1992) The Artist's Way. A spiritual path to higher creativity, New York, Penguin Putnam.

Campbell, J. (1949) The Hero with a Thousand Faces, New York, Pantheon Books.

Chesbrough, H. W. (2003). A Better Way to Innovate. Harvard Business Review, 83, 12-13.

Chesbrough, H. W. 2006. Open Innovation, Boston, MA, Harvard Business School Press.

Clegg, B. & Birch, P. 2002. Crash Course in Creativity, London, Kogan Page.

Collins, M. A. & Amabile, T. M. (1999) Motivation and Creativity IN Sternberg, R. J. (Ed.) Hand- book of Creativity New York, Cambridge University Press.

Christensen, C. (1997). The Innovator's Dilemma, Boston, MA, Harvard Business School Press.

Csikszentmihalyi, M. (1990). Flow: The Psychology of Optimal Experience. New York, Harper Perennial.

Csikszentmihalyi, M. (1996). Creativity. Flow and the Psychology of Discovery and Invention. New York, Harper Perennial.

Csikszentmihalyi, M. (1997). Finding Flow: The Psychology of Engagement with Everyday Life New York, Basic Books.

Deutschman, A. (2005). Change or Die. Fast Company.

De Bono, E. (1990). Lateral Thinking, London, Penguin.

De Bono, E. (1992) Serious Creativity, London, Harper Collins.

De Bono, E. (2000). Six Thinking Hats, London, Penguin.

Diehl, M. & Stroebe, W. (1987). Productivity Loss in Brainstorming Groups: Towards the Solution of a Riddle. Journal of Personality and Social Psychology, 53, 497-509.

Diehl, M. & Stroebe, W. (1991). Productivity Loss in Idea-Generating Groups: Tracking down the Blocking Effect. Journal of Personality and Social Psychology, 61, 392-403.

Diller, S., Shedroff, N. & Rhea, D. 2006. Making Meaning. How Successful Businesses Deliver Meaningful Customer Experiences, Berkley, CA, New Riders.

Dilts, R. (1994). Strategies of Genius Volume I: Aristotle, Sherlock Holmes, Disney, Mozart. Capitola, CA, Meta Publications.

Dilts, R. (1994). Strategies of Genius Volume II: Albert Einstein. Capitola, CA, Meta Publications.

Dilts, R. (1994). Strategies of Genius Volume III: Freud, da Vinci, Nikola Tesla. Capitola, CA, Meta Publications.

Dyer, F. L. & Martin, T. C. (1910) Edison, His Life and Inventions, Harper & Brothers.

Fast Company. (2017). The World's 50 Most Innovative Companies 2017 [Online]. Available: https://www.fastcompany.com/most-innovative-companies/2017 [Accessed].

Feist, G. J. (1999). The Influence of Personality on Artistic and Scientific Creativity. Handbook of Creativity R. J. Sternberg. New York, Cambridge University Press: 273-296.

Florida, R. (2005) Managing those Creative Types, Gallup Management Journal, August 11, 2005

Forbes (2017). The World's Most Innovative Companies (2017 Ranking) [Online]. Available: https://www.forbes.com/innovative-companies/list/

Gabler, N. (2006) Walt Disney. The Triumph of the American Imagination, New York, Vintage Books.

Graham, D. & Bachman, T. T. (2004) Ideation. The Birth and Death of Ideas, Hoboken, NJ, John Wiley & Sons.

Graham, P. (2009). Maker's schedule, managers schedule. Published in July 2009 on: http://www.paulgraham.com/makersschedule.html

Gelb, M. J. (1998) How to Think like Leonardo da Vinci, New York, Dell Publishing.

Gelb, M. J. (2003) Discover Your Genius. How to Think Like History's Ten Most Revolutionary Minds, New York, HarperCollins Publishers.

Gelb, M. J. (2004) Da Vinci Decoded, New York, Delta.

Gelb, M. J. & Miller Caldicott, S. (2007) Innovate like Edison, New York, Penguin.

Gladwell, M. (2000). The Tipping Point: How Little Things Can Make a Big Difference, New York City, Little Brown.

Goldenberg, J. & Mazursky, D. 2002. Creativity in product innovation, Cambridge, Cambridge University Press.

Hamilton, R. (2006). Your Life, Your Legacy. Singapore, Achievers International.

Hedge, J. (2013) The Essential DISC Training Workbook: Companion to the DISC Profile Assessment (Vol. 1), Redding, CA, DISC-U.org.

Henry, D. 2006. Creativity Pays. Here's How Much. Business Week.

Herrmann, N. (1981) The Creative Brain, Training and Development Journal, 35, 10, 10-16.

Herrmann, N. (1989) The Creative Brain, Lake Lure, NC, Brain Books.

Herrmann, N. (1996) The Whole Brain Business Book, New York, McGraw-Hill.

Herrmann, N.(1991) The Creative Brain. The Journal of Creative Behavior, 25, 4, 275-295.

Houghton, J. D. & Diliello, T. C. (2010) Leadership development: the key to unlocking individual creativity in organizations. Leadership & Organization Development Journal, Vol. 31 230-245.

Howe, N. & Strauss, W. (1991). Generations. The History of America's Future, 1584 to 2069, New York, William Morrow & Company.

Howkins, J. (2001). The Creative Economy. How People Make Money from Ideas. London, Penguin.

Huston, L. & Sakkab, N. (2006). Connect and Develop. Inside Proctor & Gamble's New Model for Innovation. Harvard Business Review, 85, 58-66.

IBM (2010) Capitalizing on Complexity. The Global CEO Study 2010.

IBM (2011) Working beyond Borders. The Global Chief Human Resource Officer Study 2011.

Isaacson, W. (2007) Albert Einstein: His Life and Universe, London, Simon & Schuster.

Isaacson, W. (2011) Steve Jobs: A Biography, New York, Simon & Schuster.

Inayatullah, S. (2002) Understanding P. R. Sarkar: The Indian Episteme, Macrohistory and Transformative Knowledge, Leiden, NL, Brill Academic Publishers.

Jensen, R. (1999) The Dream Society: How the Coming Shift from Information to Imagination Will Transform Your Business, New York, McGraw-Hill.

Jobs, S. (2005) You've got to find what you love. Text of the Stanford Graduation Commencement address on June 12, 2005.

Jung, C. G. (1921) Psychologische Typen, Zurich, CH, Rascher.

Jung, C. G. (1971) Psychological Types, Princeton, NJ. Princeton University Press.

Kahney, L. (2008) Inside Steve's Brain, New York, Portfolio.

Kawasaki, G. (2004). The Art of the Start, New York, Penguin.

Keeley, L. (2013). Ten Types of Innovation. The Discipline of Building Breakthroughs, New York, Wiley.

Kelley, T. & Littman, J. 2002. The Art of Innovation, London, Harper Collins Business.

Kelley, T. and J. Littman (2005). The Ten Faces of Innovation. New York, Random House.

Keirsey, D. & Bates, M. (1984). Please Understand Me: Character & Temperament Types, Del Mar, CA, Prometheus Nemesis Book Company.

Keirsey, D. (1998) Please Understand Me II: Temperament, Character, Intelligence, Del Mar, CA, Prometheus Nemesis Book Company.

Kirton, M. J. (1976) Adaptors and innovators: A description and measure. Journal of Applied Psychology, 61 (5), 622-629.

Kirton, M. J. (2003) Adaption-Innovation: In the Context of Diversity and Change, New York, Routledge.

Koestler, A. (1989, 1964]. The Act of Creation, London, Penguin.

Kotter, J. P. (1996). Leading Change, Boston, MA, Harvard Business Review Press.

Lancaster, L. C. & Stillman, D. 2003. When Generations Collide. Who They Are. Why They Clash. How to Solve the Generational Puzzle at Work, New York, HarperBusiness.

Lafferty, J. C. (1980) Life styles inventory self-development guide, Chicago, IL, Human Synergetics.

Mauzy, J. & Harriman, R. (2003) Creativity, Inc., Boston, MA, Harvard Business School Press.

Marston, W. M. (1928) Emotions of Normal People. London, Kegan Paul, Trench, Trubner & Co. Ltd..

McGregor, J. (2006). The World's Most Innovative Companies. Business Week. April 24, 2006.

McKinsey (2007). How companies approach innovation: A McKinsey Global Survey.

Medina, J. (2008). Brain Rules. 12 Principles for Surviving and Thriving at Work, Home, and School. Seattle, WA, Pear Press.

Michalko, M. (1991) Thinkertoys, Berkley, CA, Ten Speed Press.

Michalko, M. (2001). Cracking Creativity, Berkley, CA, Ten Speed Press.

Miller, W. C. (1999) Flash Of Brilliance: Inspiring Creativity Where You Work, New York, Perseus Books.

Moore, G. A. (1991). Crossing the Chasm, New York, Harper Business Essentials.

Mukerjea, D. (2003). Building Brainpower. Singapore, Horizon Books.

Mukerjea, D. (2004). Unleashing Genius. Singapore, Horizon Books.

Murakami, T. (2000) Encouraging the Emergent Evolution of New Industries. Nomura Research Institute.

Myers, I. (1980) Gifts Differing: Understanding Personality Type. Mountain View, CA, Davies-Black Publishing.

Myers, I. (1990) Introduction to Type: A Description of the Theory and Applications of the Myers-Briggs Type Indicator. Gainesville, FL,Center for Applications of Psychological Type Inc.

Naisbitt, J. (2006). Mind Set! Reset Your Thinking and See the Future. New York, HaperCollins Publishers.

Nickerson, R. S. (1999). Enhancing Creativity Handbook of Creativity R. J. Sternberg. New York, Cambridge University Press: 392-430.

Nussbaum, B. (2005) Get Creative! How to Build Innovative Companies. Business Week.

Osborn, A. F. (1953) Applied Imagination, New York, Scribner's.

Osterwalder, A., Pigneur, Y., Smith, A. & ET.AL. (2010). Business Model Generation, Self published.

Parnes, S. J. (1967) Creative Behavior Guidebook, New York, Charles Scribner.

Peters, T. (2003). Re-Imagine! Business Excellence in a Disruptive Age. London, Dorling Kinserley.

Pink, D. H. (2005). A Whole New Mind. New York, Riverhead Books.

Rae, J. 2014. Design Can Drive Exceptional Returns for Shareholders. Available: https://hbr.org/2014/04/design-can-drive-exceptional-returns-for-shareholders.

Ratney, J. J. and Hagerman, E.(2008). Spark. The Revolutionary New Science of Exercise and the Brain. New York, Little, Brown and Company.

Ray, M. & Myers, R. (1986) Creativity in Business, New York, Broadway Books.

Reis, D. (2007). It all begins with great ideas. Thinkergy Blog and Bangkok Post, April 12, 2007.

Reis, D. (2007). Going beyond 'Me Too Ltd'. Me Too Ltd. to Creativity Un-Limited. Thinkergy Blog and Bangkok Post, April 26, 2007.

Reis, D. (2007). Brainstorming: The Good, the Bad and the Ugly. Thinkergy Blog and Bangkok Post, June 7, 2007.

Reis, D. (2007). Solving the dilemma of innovation management. Thinkergy Blog and Bangkok Post, June 21, 2007.

Reis, D. (2007). Me Too Limited: Would you want to work here? Thinkergy Blog and Bangkok Post, August 2, 2007.

Reis, D. (2007). Climb up the Value Pyramid to Higher Profitability. Thinkergy Blog and Bangkok Post, August 30, 2007.

Reis, D. (2007). The innovation world. Thinkergy Blog and Bangkok Post, September 13, 2007.

Reis, D. (2007). Rediscover your creative self (Part 1). Thinkergy Blog and Bangkok Post, September 27, 2007.

Reis, D. (2007). Rediscover your creative self (Part 2). Thinkergy Blog and Bangkok Post, October 11, 2007.

Reis, D. (2007). From Cubeville to Idea City. Thinkergy Blog and Bangkok Post, November 8, 2007.

Reis, D. (2008). Creative leadership: Be, Do and you will Have. Thinkergy Blog and Bangkok Post, January 17, 2008.

Reis, D. (2008). What gets measured gets innovated. Thinkergy Blog and Bangkok Post, January 31, 2008.

Reis, D. (2008). The science and art of innovation. Thinkergy Blog and Bangkok Post, March 13, 2008.

Reis, D. (2008). The art of innovation. Thinkergy Blog and Bangkok Post, March 27, 2008.

Reis, D. (2008). Want to succeed? Plan to fail. Thinkergy Blog and Bangkok Post, May 8, 2008.

Reis, D. (2008). Motivation: What drives your employees to work? Thinkergy Blog and Bangkok Post, May 23, 2008.

Reis, D. (2008). Appreciating the paradoxes of the innovation world. Thinkergy Blog and Bangkok Post, June 19, 2008.

Reis, D. (2008). Idea Killers: Avoid innovation traps. Thinkergy Blog and Bangkok Post, July 23, 2008.

Reis, D. (2008). Mastering the Drivers of the Extreme Future. Thinkergy Blog and Bangkok Post, July 31, 2008.

Reis, D. (2008). Diversity - Less of the same is more for innovation. Thinkergy Blog and Bangkok Post, October 9, 2008.

Reis, D. (2009). Innovation is about making meaning. Thinkergy Blog and Bangkok Post, April 23, 2009.

Reis, D. (2009). Incubation: A walk on the mysterious side of creativity. Thinkergy Blog and Bangkok Post, June 4, 2009.

Reis, D. (2009). Understanding triggers to unlock creativity techniques. Thinkergy Blog and Bangkok Post, July 2, 2009.

Reis, D. (2009). Ten ideas about ideas (Part 1). Thinkergy Blog and Bangkok Post, August 27, 2009.

Reis, D. (2009). Ten ideas about ideas (Part 2). Thinkergy Blog and Bangkok Post, September 10, 2009.

Reis, D. (2009). Innovation: Are you talking the walk or walking the talk? Thinkergy Blog and Bangkok Post, November 19, 2009.

Reis, D. (2010). Defying complexity with creative leadership. Thinkergy Blog and Bangkok Post, September 16, 2010.

Reis, D. (2011). Understanding who really makes innovation happen. Thinkergy Blog and Bangkok Post, March 3, 2011.

Reis, D. (2011). Invite the World to a Party. Thinkergy Blog and Bangkok Post, March 17, 2011.

Reis, D. (2011). Appreciating entrepreneurs. Thinkergy Blog and Bangkok Post, August 4, 2011.

Reis, D. (2011). The more things change, the more they stay the same. Thinkergy Blog and Bangkok Post, September 1, 2011.

Reis, D. (2011). Boring meetings? Play Innovation Bingo! Thinkergy Blog and Bangkok Post, November 24, 2011.

Reis, D. (2011). What's your innovation mastery level? Thinkergy Blog and Bangkok Post, December 9, 2011.

Reis, D. (2012). Better brainstorming in Asia. Thinkergy Blog and Bangkok Post, March 29, 2012.

Reis, D. (2012). The creator-manager dilemma. Thinkergy Blog and Bangkok Post, July 19, 2012.

Reis, D. (2012). The brainiac-brawniac scheduling conflict. Thinkergy Blog and Bangkok Post, August 2, 2012.

Reis, D. (2012). The rise of creative leadership. Bangkok Post, October 11, 2012.

Reis, D. (2012). Developing creative leaders. Bangkok Post, October 25, 2012.

Reis, D. (2013). Creativity is… (Part 1). Thinkergy Blog and Bangkok Post, June 20, 2013.

Reis, D. (2013). Creativity is… (Part 2). Thinkergy Blog and Bangkok Post, July 4, 2013.

Reis, D. (2013). What kind of innovator does your business need? Thinkergy Blog and Bangkok Post, August 15, 2013.

Reis, D. (2013). Is genius hidden in you? Thinkergy Blog and Bangkok Post, October 10, 2013.

Reis, D. (2013). Getting to Eureka. Thinkergy Blog and Bangkok Post, October 24, 2013.

Reis, D. (2013). How do you prefer to think, work, interact and live? (Part 1). Thinkergy Blog and Bangkok Post, December 5, 2013.

Reis, D. (2013). How do you prefer to think, work, interact and live? (Part 2). Thinkergy Blog and Bangkok Post, December 19, 2013.

Reis, D. (2014). Creative leadership: Are you hot or not? Thinkergy Blog and Bangkok Post, January 16, 2014.

Reis, D. (2014). Why creative leadership is needed now (Part 1). Thinkergy Blog and Bangkok Post, February 13, 2014.

Reis, D. (2014). Why creative leadership is needed now (Part 2). Thinkergy Blog and Bangkok Post, February 27, 2014.

Reis, D. (2014). Are you committed to innovation? (Part 1). Thinkergy Blog and Bangkok Post, March 13, 2014.

Reis, D. (2014). Are you committed to innovation? (Part 2). Thinkergy Blog and Bangkok Post, March 27, 2014.

Reis, D. (2014). The new innovation economy.. Thinkergy Blog and Bangkok Post, May 8, 2014.

Reis, D. (2014). Building a functional bridge over the efficiency-creativity divide. Thinkergy Blog and Bangkok Post, May 22, 2014.

Reis, D. (2014). What is your innovation style? Thinkergy Blog and Bangkok Post, October 9, 2014.

Reis, D. (2014). How to write a good creative brief. Thinkergy Blog and Bangkok Post, December 4, 2014.

Reis, D. (2014) X-IDEA: The Structured Magic of Systematic Innovation. ISPIM Asia-Pacific Innovation Forum 2014. Singapore.

Reis, D. (2015). Do you suffer from innovation fatigue? Thinkergy Blog and Bangkok Post, January 8, 2015.

Reis, D. (2015). What's your style that lets you succeed? Thinkergy Blog and Bangkok Post, May 28, 2015.

Reis, D. (2015) Genius Journey: Developing Genuine Creative Leaders for the Innovation Economy. XXVI ISPIM Innovation Conference. Budapest, Hungary.

Reis, D. (2015). The creative transformation marathon (Part 1). Thinkergy Blog and Bangkok Post, June 11, 2015.

Reis, D. (2015). The creative transformation marathon (Part 2). Thinkergy Blog and Bangkok Post, June 25, 2015.

Reis, D. (2015). The innovation manager of the future. Thinkergy Blog and Bangkok Post, July 9, 2015.

Reis, D. (2015). Open innovation: The good, the bad, and the ugly. Thinkergy Blog and Bangkok Post, July 23, 2015.

Reis, D. (2015). Tracking the dimensions of change over time. Thinkergy Blog and Bangkok Post, December 10, 2015.

Reis, D. (2016). Dos and Don'ts for a successful innovation project. Thinkergy Blog and Bangkok Post, January 21, 2016.

Reis, D. (2016). Resolving the real-life challenges of innovators. Thinkergy Blog and Bangkok Post, February 18, 2016.

Reis, D. (2016). Success ingredients of top achievers. Thinkergy Blog and Bangkok Post, March 17, 2016.

Reis, D. (2016) TIPS: Getting the people-side of innovation right. 2016 ISPIM Innovation Forum, Boston, USA, 13-16 March 2016.

Reis, D. (2016). Stripping innovation down to its essential core. Thinkergy Blog and Bangkok Post, April 14, 2016.

Reis, D. (2016). These creative laws govern innovation. Thinkergy Blog and Bangkok Post, April 28, 2016.

Reis, D. (2016). Why using one creative process stage leads to dull ideas. Thinkergy Blog and Bangkok Post, May 26, 2016.

Reis, D. (2016) Ideation vs. Development in X-IDEA: How to move beyond conventional ideas in an innovation project? XXVII ISPIM Innovation Conference 2016, Porto, Portugal, 19-22 June 2016.

Reis, D. (2016) Teaching Business Creativity to Young Professionals: Course Design, Pedagogy, and Methodologies. Proceedings of the International Conference "Creative Industries in Asia: Innovating with Constraints." 1-2 July 2016.

Reis, D. (2016). Manage people better by relating to their personal styles. Thinkergy Blog and Bangkok Post, July 7, 2016.

Reis, D. (2016). Leaders and Innovation Managers: Same same but different. Thinkergy Blog and Bangkok Post, August 4, 2016.

Reis, D. (2016). Understanding the cycles of change with TIPS (Part 1). Thinkergy Blog and Bangkok Post, September 29, 2016.

Reis, D. (2016). Understanding the cycles of change with TIPS (Part 2). Thinkergy Blog and Bangkok Post, October 13, 2016.

Reis, D. (2016). Escaping the GIGO principle of innovation. Thinkergy Blog and Bangkok Post, November 24, 2016.

Reis, D. (2016). Creative cultural change is like striving to live a healthier life. Thinkergy Blog and Bangkok Post, December 8, 2016.

Reis, D. (2017). Why so afraid? Time to "human up" (Part 1). Thinkergy Blog and Bangkok Post, January 19, 2017.

Reis, D. (2017). Why so afraid? Time to "human up" (Part 2). Thinkergy Blog and Bangkok Post, February 16, 2017.

Reis, D. (2017). How to put the right people into the right job. Thinkergy Blog and Bangkok Post, April 13, 2017.

Reis, D. (2017) Picturing "The Executive's Guide to Innovation." Thinkergy Blog and Bangkok Post, May 11, 2017.

Reis, D. (2017) The ten rules of the innovation types game (Part 1). Thinkergy Blog and Bangkok Post, June 8, 2017.

Reis, D. (2017) The ten rules of the innovation types game (Part 1). Thinkergy Blog and Bangkok Post, June 8, 2017.

Reis, D. (2017) The ten rules of the innovation types game (Part 2). Thinkergy Blog and Bangkok Post, June 22, 2017.

Reis, D. (2017) Understanding the inner workings of innovation methods. Thinkergy Blog and Bangkok Post, July 6, 2017.

Reis, D. (2017) How cyclicality drives business and innovation. Thinkergy Blog and Bangkok Post, July 20, 2017.

Reis, D. (2017) How innovation affects financial performance. Thinkergy Blog and Bangkok Post, August 17, 2017.

Reis, D. (2017) Why and how to protect your intellectual property Thinkergy Blog and Bangkok Post, August 31, 2017.

Reis, D. (2017) The world hates Innovation. Here is why. Thinkergy Blog and Bangkok Post, September 28, 2017.

Reis, D. (2017) Is the pendulum swinging back? Thinkergy Blog and Bangkok Post, October 12, 2017.

Reis, D. (2017) Innovative companies vs. in-NO-vative companies: Who's who? Thinkergy Blog and Bangkok Post, October 26, 2017.

Reis, D. (2017) It's not only what tools you use, but how you use them. Thinkergy Blog and Bangkok Post, November 9, 2017.

Reis, D. (2017). How generational shifts will impact business and innovation (Part 1). Thinkergy Blog and Bangkok Post, November 23, 2017.

Reis, D. (2017). How generational shifts will impact business and innovation (Part 2). Thinkergy Blog and Bangkok Post, December 7, 2017.

Reis, D. (2018). How to scrutinize cognitive profiling methods (Part 1). Thinkergy Blog, August 16, 2018.

Reis, D. (2018). How to scrutinize cognitive profiling methods (Part 2). Thinkergy Blog, August 30, 2018.

Ridderstråle, J. & Nordström, K. (2000). Funky Business. Harlow, Prentice Hall FT.

Rogers, E. M. 1962. Diffusion of Innovations, New York, Free Press of Glencoe.

Sarkar, P. R. (1967) Human Society Vol. 2, Anandanagar, India, Ananda Marga Press.

Schnetzler, N. (2004). Die Ideenmaschine, Weinheim, Wiley.

Schumpeter, J. A. (1975, 1942) Capitalism, Socialism and Democracy, New York, Harper.

Stum, J. (2009). Kirton's Adaption-Innovation Theory: Managing Cognitive Styles in Times of Diversity and Change. Emerging Leadership Journeys, 2 (1), 66-78.

Sternberg, R. J., Ed. (1999). Handbook of Creativity New York, Cambridge University Press.

Sternberg, R. J. & Lubart, T. I. (1999) The Concept of Creativity: Prospects and Paradigms. IN Sternberg, R. J. (Ed.) Handbook of Creativity New York, Cambridge University Press.

Sutton, R. I. (2002). Weird Ideas That Work, New York, The Free Press.

Thinkergy I2012). The Thinkergy Innovation Playground. Available: http://thinkergy.com/innovation-playground/

Tidd, J. & Bessant, J. 2013. Managing Innovation: Integrating Technological, Market and Organizational Change, 5th Ed., Chichester, Wiley. Trott, P. (2002). Innovation Management and New Product Development, Harlow, England, Pearson Education.

Tulgan, B. (2016). The Great Generational Shift: The Emerging Post-Boomer Workforce. Available: http://rainmakerthinking.com/assets/uploads/2016/06/Gen-Shift-White-Paper-2016_June.2016.pdf.

VanGundy, A. B. (2005). 101 Activities for Teaching Creativity and Problem Solving, San Francisco, Pfeiffer.

VanGundy, A. B. (2007). Getting to Innovation. How Asking the Right Questions Generates the Great Ideas Your Company Needs, New York, Amacom.

van Wulfen, G. (2011). Creating Innovative Products and Services. The FORTH Innovation Method, Farnham, Gower.

Vernon, R., & Wells, L. T. (1966) International trade and international investment in the product life cycle. Quarterly Journal of Economics, 81 (2), 190-207.

Vernon, R. (1979) The product cycle hypothesis in a new international environment. Oxford bulletin of economics and statistics, 41 (4), 255-267.

Verganti, R. (2009). Design-Driven Innovation. Changing the Rules of Comptetition by Radically Innovating What Things Mean, Boston, MA, Harvard Business Press.

Von Oech, R. (1986). A Kick in the Seat of the Pants, New York, HarperCollins Publishers.

Von Oech, R. (1998). A Whack on the Side of the Head, New York, Warner Books.

Von Stamm, B. (2003). Managing Innovation, Design and Creativity. Chichester, West Sussex, John Wiley & Sons.

Von Stamm, B. (2003) The Innovation Wave. Meeting the Corporate Challenge, Chichester, West Sussex, John Wiley & Sons.

Wallas, G. (1926) The Art of Thought, New York, Wiley.

Weiner, E. & Brown, A. (2006). Future Think. How to Think Clearly in a Time of Change, Upper Saddle River, NJ, Prentice Hall.

Williams, W. M. & Tang, L. T. (1999) Organizational Creativity IN Sternberg, R. J. (Ed.) Handbook of Creativity New York, Cambridge University Press.

WIPO (2004). What is Intellectual Property? Geneva: WIPO Publication No. 450(E).

PROFESSIONAL INNOVATION SERVICES SUPPLIERS

Please find below (listed in alphabetical order) a summary of innovation services providers that I respect as quality innovation collaborators, or that have been prominent players in their application area for a longer time. We also list the solution that I have developed for Thinkergy in each application area.

INNOVATION PROCESS METHODS

Design Thinking (IDEO Method):
   https://www.ideou.com/pages/design-thinking

FORTH Method by Gijs van Wulfen:
   http://www.forth-innovation.com

The Idea Machine by Brainstore AG: http://www.brainstore.com

Systematic Inventive Thinking by SIT: http://www.sitsite.com

What If Innovation: http://www.whatifinnovation.com

X-IDEA Innovation Method by Dr. Detlef Reis / Thinkergy:
   http://thinkergy.com/x-idea/

INNOVATION CULTURE AUDITS AND TRANSFORMATION METHODS

CooL - Creativity UnLimited by Dr. Detlef Reis / Thinkergy:
   http://thinkergy.com/cool/

There are lots of innovation capacity or capability audits offered by academic institutes and consulting companies, google for suppliers near you.

CREATIVE LEADERSHIP DEVELOPMENT METHODS

Genius Journey by Dr. Detlef Reis / Thinkergy:
   http://thinkergy.com/genius-journey/

"Think like da Vinci" and "Innovate like Edison" by Michael Gelb: https://michaelgelb.com

PEOPLE PROFILING METHODS FOR BUSINESS AND/OR INNOVATION

Basadur Profile by Dr. Min Basadur:
   https://www.basadurprofile.com/default.aspx

Herrmann's Brain Dominance Instrument by Dr. Ned Herrmabn:
   http://www.herrmannsolutions.com

Insights Discovery by Andi and Andy Lothian:
   https://www.insights.com

FourSight Thinking Profile:
   https://foursightonline.com

Myers-Briggs Type Indicator (MBTI):
   http://www.myersbriggs.org/my-mbti-personality-type/mbti-basics/home.htm?bhcp=1

Kirton Adoption-Innovation Inventory by Dr. Michael Kirton:
   https://kaicentre.com/?v=5b79c40fa7c2

MIND Design by Robert Alan Black, Ph.D.:
   http://www.cre8ng.com/minddesign.shtml

TIPS Innovation People Profiling Method by Dr. Detlef Reis / Thinkergy: http://thinkergy.com/tips/

Wealth Dynamics by Roger Hamilton:
   http://www.wealthdynamics.com

About the Author:
DR. DETLEF REIS

Dr. Detlef Reis (aka "Dr. D") is the Founder and Chief Creator of the creative breakthrough company Thinkergy (www.thinkergy.com). Founded in Hong Kong and now with bases in Hong Kong, Bangkok, and San Diego, Thinkergy energizes creative leaders and their teams (across all seasons of the company lifecycle) with breakthrough know-how to make them triumphantly drive the Sixth Wave of Technology Innovation.

For two decades, Dr. D and Thinkergy have successfully delivered over a hundred innovation training and project workshops to leading multinational corporations, large local corporations, small—and medium-sized enterprises, startups and scaleups, creative agencies, government organizations, and non-governmental and Intergovernmental organizations in Asia, Europe, North America, the Middle East, and Africa.

The author is the creator of Thinkergy's four proprietary innovation methods: X-IDEA, Genius Journey, TIPS, and CooL – Creativity Unlimited.

Dr. D is also an Adjunct Associate Professor at the triple-accredited School of Business, Hong Kong Baptist University (HKBU). Since 2007, he has taught a course in Business Creativity in HKBU's Master in Business Management Program (ranked in the world's top 100 by the Financial Times). Moreover, he has been a faculty member at leading business schools in Thailand (College of Management, Mahidol University, 2004-2016; Institute for Knowledge & Innovation South-East Asia, Bangkok University, since 2016).

In his early business career, the author worked for Deutsche Bank for more than 16 years, which allowed him to fund his (Ph.D.) studies in Germany. He feels grateful for being given the opportunity to work for Deutsche Bank in Vietnam, the Philippines, and Hong Kong, where he held the position of Vice President in the Global Banking Division before he left the bank to found Thinkergy.

The author is a regular blogger and has published over 425 articles since 2007 (most also featured in the Bangkok Post's business column 'Creativity Un-Ltd.'). He is also a sought-after keynote speaker on creative leadership, creativity, and innovation at conferences and corporate events.

Dr. D graduated with a doctorate in international management from Saarland University in Saarbrücken, Germany, and published his dissertation in a book in German.

Unleashing WOW!

The Creative Leader's Guide to Breakthrough Innovation

Free Bonus Gifts

Thank you for embarking on the "Unleashing WOW!" journey.

This is just the beginning of your extraordinary path to innovation.

Join our United Creative Minds of Thinkergy community and unlock a treasure trove of bonus materials designed to amplify your creativity and innovation.

Ready for your next breakthrough? Your creative journey is just a click away! Go to WildeSpark.com/UnleashingWow and unlock your free resources today.

Unleashing WOW! Action Pack - Over 30 worksheets and guides to help you bring the concepts in this book to life.

Plus - Gain access to a wealth of videos, ideation techniques, ebooks, and much more.

www.ingramcontent.com/pod-product-compliance
Lightning Source LLC
LaVergne TN
LVHW061932070526
838199LV00060B/3825